The Golden Hearts

Jerry D Cook

This book is a work of fiction. Names, characters, places, and incidents are the product of the author's imagination or are used fictitiously. Any resemblance to actual events, locales, corporate or government entities, facilities, or persons, living or dead, is coincidental.

Cover art by the author

Publisher: *Lightsource*

ISBN-13: 978-09997180-1-8

Library of Congress Control Number: 2019900304

To my Sweetheart Leslie

Table of Contents

Departure

The *Gouden Leeuwin*, a returning merchant ship, sits at anchor in the Port of Amsterdam at the dawning of its second day queued up for moorage. In a tiny cabin belowdeck, Nicklas Voorhaven awakens to the sound of a deep baritone, heard through the bulkhead, requesting permission to come aboard. "Aye, Sir," answers a sailor from above. Once again Nicklas is wishing, as he has wished this entire voyage that his cabin had a porthole so he could see who is making this early morning visit.

He hears a second voice, and without being able to see the speaker he can only imagine, from the peevishly scolding tone, a petty tyrant, "Aye, and we need to assess your inventory before we can allow you moorings," this second voice must belong to a VOC clerk, "Be quick with that ladder," sounding again like a demanding yapper, and if indeed this is the clerk that will be reviewing paperwork Nicklas is relieved that he has his all in order.

The pinnace that has brought these visitors out from the dock can be heard thumping repeatedly against the bulkhead, accompanied by the unraveling clatter of the ladder's rungs, and the bumping of the oars being stowed. If Nicklas' cabin had a porthole, and if he were to look out, he would see that the first up the ladder is liveried in the uniform of a VOC lieutenant who returns the salutes of the sailors on deck, then turns to assist the two men he is escorting. These men are lawyers, and both make quite a struggle of climbing the rope ladder; banging the bulkhead with the toes of their boots, and busting their knuckles on the ladder's rungs. When they finally stand upon the deck, Lieutenant Gerardus Hamet, clearly unhappy with this morning's chore, tells the nearest Ensign, in the baritone heard earlier, "These, ahem, *gentlemen,* seek council with your Captain."

The uniformed sailor salutes, "Aye Sir," then turns and leads them toward the quarterdeck.

Next up the ladder is the ornery little clerk, followed by his aide, who is an oversized fellow looking out of place amongst the crowd of sailors that have gathered. And lastly is the oarsman, having left his boat tied to the ladder, hoping to find the galley and a warm cup of coffee.

Still wishing that he could see what was going on above, Nicklas, in his nightshirt and loose hair, pulls on his trousers and takes off barefooted for the cabin of his employer. He knows that he should be getting properly dressed and be present in his cabin when the Company clerk visits, but he wants Trinjntje to be aware of the yappy registrar's early arrival, believing that her cargo of plants and trees will be assessed with close scrutiny. He rushes to her cabin on the next deck up where, unlike his dark closet below, there are windows allowing sunshine in for her botanical cargo. He reaches the top of the ladder and is confounded by the sight of two of the ship's petty officers closing a lock through a freshly installed hasp on the door of her cabin.

"You've locked her in?" Nicklas queries dumbfoundedly.

"Quartermaster's orders," states the older of the bosuns, "Under ship's arrest."

"And what are the charges?"

"Ah," with a wide grin, "it seems our *Mejuffrouw* Olmsfeld has been dipping into the ship's fresh water supply for the purpose of irrigating her precious cargo of plants and trees and mosses and molds and green growy things," says the younger bosun.

Nicklas, gathering by the way both of these sailors are grinning and winking conspiratorially at him, determines that Trinjntje isn't really in trouble. He hears footsteps behind him and the voice of the *Gouden Leeuwin's* Captain addressing him, "Nicklas Voorhaven," prompting him to turn and salute, even though he is not a sailor under this man's command. Captain Cornelius Janszoon tells him, "It is strongly advised that you have your papers in order," then after eyeing him up and down, "And that you be attired with a bit more propriety for your meeting with the representative of the VOC port commission." Then with a bit more urgency, "Quickly now!" The Captain turns his attention to his two young officers, "I am trusting that you are certain that my niece is in her cabin." As they both salute and nod, the Captain, glancing back at Nicklas who hasn't yet moved, orders him again, "Best be on your way!"

Nicklas takes off, moving as swiftly he can, sliding down the ladder in two bounds. He reaches the main deck and spins around directly into the purposefully moving cluster of official visitors. Here is a ship's Ensign escorting a VOC officer accompanied by two other gentlemen dressed in black. Nicklas guesses, by their attire, that these others must be representatives of either the law, or the clergy. Another clue of their line of business is the way they hold their noses up in virtuous smugness. Nicklas must make way for this passing group by flattening himself up against the bulkhead. Looking up the steps at the clenched jaw of the captain he is certain that he should keep moving, but curiosity immobilizes him.

"Cap'n Sir," the Ensign salutes, then announces, "Lieutenant Gerardus Hamet requesting your council, Sir."

"Captain Janszoon," Hamet delivers a formal salute, "These men," indicating the two lawyers, "come from the bailiff's office bearing papers of extradition for one of your passengers."

Captain Cornelius Janszoon, ordinarily an even-tempered man, is playing a different role today. He speaks first to the sailor that has escorted these others, "Ensign, it is certain that you have more pressing duties." With a salute he dismisses the man, who is pleased to go. Then turning his attention next to the VOC officer, "Lieutenant Hamet, I am surprised that you would assume to have the power to bring these pettifoggers, or anyone not in the employ of our mother company, aboard this ship before we have even docked!"

Hamet wants to reply to this reprimand, but the Captain's icy glare freezes the words before he dare speak, and so, recognizing his own dismissal, salutes the Captain and backs himself down the ladder. Once upon the main deck he addresses the two lawyers as he slips past them, "You will have to introduce yourselves," disapprovingly, "Sirs."

A strained silence ensues as Captain Janszoon scrutinizes these shysters standing on the deck below him. In a pre-dawn visit from a nephew he has been warned to expect such a visit. The boy had rowed out in the darkness with a note advising of the possibility that a situation like this may occur. He is wondering whether he has prepared properly for whatever circumstances are about to unfold. The first of the two legalists to speak, without introducing himself, is the tall one with the long forehead, long beak of a nose, long pointy chin, and an exaggerated Adams apple protruding from a long neck. "We have here," opening a leather binder to show this sailor captain the sheaf of papers within, "orders from the highest authority for the arrest of a person believed to be aboard this ship, the *Gouden Leeuwin*." The man is attired passably enough to be a practitioner of the law, although the hem of his coat is a bit frayed, his shirt wrinkled, and his shoes scuffed. The Captain holds his silence, letting his visitors do the talking.

The tall fellow's shorter rounder partner makes to step up the ladder, but when the captain's dark gaze falls upon him, the foot he has raised drops back upon the deck. With a gratingly high voice he tells the Captain, "We represent a consortium of concerned citizens." As his partner before him, he opens his own leather binder displaying another stack of scribbled papers, "We have orders signed by the leading authorities of your United Republic." He looks to his partner, then back up to the Captain, proclaiming, "Our instructions are to bring your passenger, *Mevrouw* Trinjntje Olmsfeld, into custody." Pausing to allow the importance of his directive to sink in, and upon receiving no reply, continues in earnest, "We expect, nay, we demand full cooperation from all aboard this ship."

There ensues a long heavy silence until Captain Janszoon speaks slowly, yet harshly, to these men, "You, who practice the law of the land must remember that the law of the sea provides a ship's Captain ultimate power over anything occurring aboard his ship." Then with an almost imperceptible bit of menace, "One does not ***demand*** of a Captain whilst aboard his ship." Janszoon makes a show of breathing in for calm before continuing with a lighter tone, "One may ask. One may plead. Or perhaps one will beg his case as if before his Lord, but ***never***," his voice rising and his expression darkening, "does one assume to be in possession of higher authority!" He has delivered this speech a few times over his many years as a Captain: putting diplomats, bureaucrats, and even royalty in their places.

The two *Aggravates*, with no diminishing of smugness, glance toward each other, both rolling their eyes, wordlessly agreeing that they are dealing with a bumpkin. The taller of the two, places a foot on the first step of the ladder leading up to the deck whereupon the Captain is standing, but Janszoon halts him, "Do not presume that you are qualified to rise up from the deck where you currently stand."

With a haughty shake of his head the man begins speaking slowly; cleverly articulating each syllable, as if talking to a dunce. "Your. Employer. *Vereenigde Oost-Indische Compagnie.* The VOC. The Dutch East India Company; howsoever you might refer to them, may not hold sway as you believe. Much has changed since you were last in this port." He brakes his speech momentarily with a look to his associate, each smiling smugly, then proceeds, explaining to this dullard, "Should you continue with your current tactic of non-compliance you may find yourself ***in the midst of a crisis***."

"In the midst of a crisis ..." Janszoon echoes flatly, "Hmmmm, sounds somewhat threatening coming from mere *minions* such as the two of you." Now a smile edges up the corners of the good Captain's mouth. He stands taller, and all his men that have gathered round stand taller also, awaiting what is coming next. "Be that as it may," speaking loud enough for all to hear, "it does seem to me that the two of you have spoken threatening words. Threatening words spoken aboard ship toward the Captain demonstrates what we sailors refer to as Mutiny." Suddenly, these sailors have moved in, closing in on the two, and not appearing at all friendly. Captain Janszoon continues, "If you choose to remain on board this ship you shall hereby be tried by Ship's Tribunal on charges of Mutiny." He pauses to let what he has said sink in. The charge of mutiny is usually followed by the sentence of death. Then the captain finishes, "Or, should you choose not to remain on board, you will be allowed back to shore where you can tell your masters that the passenger you seek is already being held prisoner." The two lawyers exchange surprised expressions at this news. Before they think to ask what the charges are, Janszoon tells them, "*Mevrouw* Trinjntje Olmsfeld is being held on board this ship, subject to the law of the sea, and therefore unavailable to *your* laws." With a nod of his head he dismisses them all, turning on his heel and marching back to his duties. Sailors forcibly take hold of the two stymied lawyers, shuffling them unceremoniously back to the ladder they had climbed earlier.

Lieutenant Hamet, waiting there amongst a crowd of sailors, taunts the two black-coated legal experts, "Going home empty-handed?" While the two are hastily descending he turns to an Ensign and advises, "Probably ought to have one of your men down there with them. Would not want 'em stealing our boat while we wait on the clerk to finish his business."

♡♡♡

Nicklas, after watching the interchange between the captain and the lawyers, is on the run. Once below deck as he comes upon his own doorway he is met with a different set of circumstances; two sailors, whose duty is to escort the VOC dockmaster's clerk, stop him from entering his own cabin. A skeletal little man inside stands up quickly as if caught in a suspicious act, then yaps at the sailors, "Who is this man?" It is the same peevish voice heard earlier coming through the bulkhead from the boat that had brought all these visitors aboard. While eyeing Nicklas' tousled hair, loose shirt, and bare feet he tells them, "Don't let him near," holding up his arm as if to fend off an attack from a madman.

Nicklas, quickly tucking in his shirt and smoothing back his hair, settles himself and then speaks evenly, "My name is Nicklas Voorhaven, and this is my cabin, and those are my bags and parcels. May I have your name please?"

This disdainful regulator does not offer his name. So Nicklas continues, "I would be pleased to show you my inventory manifests if you will allow me access to the drawers of my desk."

Now the regulator looks again to the sailors inquisitorially, "Why are you not restraining this vagabond? Can either of you Ensigns verify that what this man says is true?" Both sailors nod affirmatively.

Nicklas is wondering if he really looks so dangerous. Then, offhandedly to the sailors, he says quietly, "Perhaps the nature of this man's office has made him the object of many a smuggler's ire." They share concurring grins at that remark. "Perhaps he thinks that everyone is a smuggler, and not to be trusted."

Then the man's assistant steps out from within the confines of the cabin presenting himself in the tiny doorway. It is clear, by his size and his stature, why he has been chosen for this duty; even though he is dressed as a gentleman, he carries himself more like a mercenary thug. He is big: very big.

"Sir, er ... Sirs?" Nicklas attempts to smooth things out, "It is most unfortunate that you caught me out of my cabin," thinking that these regulators must be used to hearing lies, he decides to make up a little one of his own. He begins by striking a theatrical pose with one arm raised while placing his other over his chest, "Crossing the deck just now, coming back from the loo," everybody can relate to that, "I was held up by the presence of a crowd surrounding a couple of unknown guests." Doing his best to be entertaining, and hoping for a smile he begins a sweep of his raised arm and starts whirling his other hand, "alas, I was unable to proceed until our Captain had finished with his business, and the crowd disassembled," now he brings the back of one hand to his forehead, "fearing that I would be mistaken for shirking my responsibilities, I momentarily lost myself to despair," now sweeping both arms forward, "but then became very thankfull again upon remembering that I have prepared all my paperwork in advance, and that I have it all completed and placed, bundled and tied, just there in the top drawer of my cabin's desk." Bowing deep with arms extended and fingers pointing, in the same theatrical manner, toward the small desk that every passenger cabin holds.

This Company Counter, remaining protected behind the huge man stooped in the doorway, is looking toward Nicklas with derision. At last he tells him, "I am Port Authority Regulator's Assistant Greely DeVoss, and this is my deputy." Then slapping the arm of the big man, waves him toward the aforementioned desk drawer, "Let us see if this man tells the truth." There is barely enough space within the cabin for the two men to maneuver as they exchange places.

Part of the private cargo that Nicklas is bringing back with him consists of spring-loaded toy animals. One of those startling spring-loaded toys is set as a booby trap to pop out of his drawer as it is being drawn open. Nicklas chuckles, "Er, Sir, may I warn you --"

"Something funny *Meneer* Voorhaven?"

"Yes. Best be careful opening that drawer." But his warning comes too late. The big oaf has opened the drawer and the toy snake has sprung out. The thug has banged his head resoundingly against the beams above and spilled the drawer's contents.

"Clumsy oaf," yips clerk DeVoss as he picks up a neatly tied bundle of papers that has rolled to his feet.

Nicklas swings an arm full circle and on the downward swoop bows to the dock clerk, "The primary objective Sir, for my voyage, has been that of purveying botanical specimens, in the employ of Trinjntje Olmsfeld, daughter of Christophorus Olmsfeld," hoping that it will help to drop the name of an important man, "A director of the VOC. My secondary enterprise, as per my contract with Director

Olmsfeld, has been filling the hold space allowed to me with cargo of my own choosing. It is a diverse cargo, and I would be so disappointed, after all my attention to detail," Raising the back of his hand to his forehead once again, "If I were to discover that I have made a mistake in my paperwork." Now with his eyes wide, hands at his heart and the sweetest possible expression he is able to contrive, "Why, I would be happy to buy you a drink," throwing out the opportunity for a bribe if necessary, "once I am finally off this ship, and I will be more able to express my appreciation of your forgiving my tardy presence here today." He finishes with a full bow, nose extended to knee.

Ignoring the theatrics, Clerk DeVoss unties the string holding the prepared roll of papers. Inventories are compared to manifests, a signature signed, initialed, and dated, then tossed loosely on the desk. With an offhanded wave of dismissal Port Authority Regulator's Assistant Greely DeVoss moves out of the doorway and on to the cabin of his next victim. Before taking a step to follow, his oversized assistant lays a heavy paw on Nicklas' shoulder and whispers menacingly, "Meet us upstairs of the Polder Inn before the bells ring ten, and mind yourself to be early as there's usually a line of dummies like you." Smirking now, he turns and lugs after his master. The two sailors assigned as their escort follow reluctantly.

Nicklas breathes a sigh of relief, satisfied that he has met the requirements of the magistrate's clerk: that is, until upon entering his tiny compartment he discovers one of his satchels open on the floor where it has been dropped. Looking inside he realizes right away that something is missing. The ornate reliquary, the receptacle that usually holds the necklace that the Djiboutian Prince had thrust upon Trinjntje in his bid to wed her, is empty; the necklace gone. Now he understands why he is supposed to meet with the crooked company agents later. "They will want more than a gratuity: they will be demanding a ransom." He considers chasing down the thieves, but re-considers, postponing the inevitable until later. "Trinjntje did not want the necklace, did not even care what became of it; that is why I am carrying it for her! I should report this to someone." But the entire crew is busy with the docking, and so he decides to bide his time and waits, along with the other passengers, to disembark.

♡♡♡

Trinjntje Olmsfeld welcomes the sun's rays that are streaming through the windows of her ship-borne garden. Her cabin is actually a suite of three upper-deck cabins arranged as a sea going plant nursery. This miniature jungle is the cargo that she is bringing back with her as a capital venture bestowed upon her by her father. She is light-heartedly watering her plants from a barrel of ship's rainwater, which the Captain has allowed for her use now that they are in their home port. Because she has had to ration her own supply of fresh water some of her smaller seedlings really need a drink. "Twould be a pity to lose any of these plants this close to home after traveling so far." There is a knock at her door, "A moment please," she calls, "I am finishing up." Setting down her watering can, she calls out musically as she steps to the door, "Hellooo." Upon turning the handle she discovers it will not open. She rattles the door in its casing.

From the other side of the door she hears her uncle, "Good Morning Trin." Again she rattles the door, this time putting a little more effort toward getting it to open. "Trinjntje!" Spoken sharply to get her attention, then softening his tone when she has stopped jouncing the door, "Trin, I have ordered a lock upon your door for the protection of your privacy."

"The protection of my privacy?" She is disappointed to hear this: for it is the so-called *'protection of her privacy'* that has put her on this voyage in the first place.

"It seems that there is still a dispirited group that remains intent upon taking you into custody." The very reason her father had sent her away, hoping that when she returned the charges against her would be forgotten. "Somehow they have contrived to get two of their *prōvocātōrs* aboard this ship, even before we are docked." These zealots, even though the Spaniards and their inquest have been ousted from this new Republic of the Netherlands, remain intent upon finding evil where there is none. "I have made it appear that you are being held in custody under charges presented against you according to my power to uphold the law of the sea. I ask that you acquiesce behind this locked door until this afternoon."

"Ohhh kay. I mean, certainly Uncle Cor, whatsoever you deem necessary." Hiding again. "Will you be able to have someone bring me hot coffee, oh, and some of the sweet buns that have sugar sprinkled on top? Please." She will sit tight for now counting on everything working out.

"Have you enough food otherwise to bide you over until later this afternoon."

"Yes," just as Janszoon has figured, "But, oh, can I still have the coffee and buns?"

"I will send someone straight-away with your coffee and sugar-buns." Any one of the galley crew will jump at the opportunity to serve this dear woman. "Trin?" Again calling his sister's daughter by her childhood name, "I must remind you that this has been my last voyage as Captain." Janszoon has determined to retire from the services he has rendered these past thirty years. "There will be a ceremony on deck later this afternoon, after which there will be a newly assigned Captain for the *Gouden Leeuwin*." He knows that she is listening, even though she gives no response. "I will collect you shortly before the hour of three, and we shall attend this ceremony. Your father will be with the officials making the presentation and I am certain that your mother will be here also. I have sent a request to him that we all depart this ship together when the ceremony is finished."

"I will be ready Uncle Cor." She calls him by the nickname her mother uses.

"Til then."

"K." She has her trunks packed and formal attire laid out on top, deciding that for now she might as well remain in her silken loungewear. She is anxious to know what her father's plan for her will be. If he intends to send her on another of these voyages collecting greenery for all his friends' gardens then he will have to think again. It will make no difference how fine a gentleman this new Captain may be. She speaks her displeasure out loud to all her plants, "I will run away before going back to sea!" Not aware how long she stands lost in this funk, she is surprised when she hears another knock at her cabin's door, "Yes?"

There is the clink of a key in the lock, the release of the hasp, and then the door opens and an ensign enters with a broad smile announcing, "Hot coffee and sugar-buns *Mevrouw*, " while allowing a galley boy to enter bringing a covered tray and setting it on her table. As soon as the boy's hands are free he snatches the cap off his head, bows to Trinjntje, and backs out the door. The smiling ensign tips his cocked hat gallantly to her, then he is out the door also. She hears the lock placed through the hasp again and sighs.

♡♡♡

Returning aboard the pinnace that serves as ship-to-shore tender, Lieutenant Gerardus Hamet is contemplating the outcome of this morning's misbegotten legal task, allotted him as per the position he holds as an officer for the VOC here in Amsterdam. He is sitting upon the farthest fore-ward bench, intentionally maintaining distance from the other passengers returning with him. Mulling over this morning's vulgar episode he smiles at how Cornelius Janszoon, from a family of ships Captains that goes back generations, has handled the entire situation perfectly. Hamet is especially pleased to have been dismissed by the Captain from the proceedings. Likewise, he is very pleased that these two advocates are returning with less than they had boasted they would be bringing back with them; considerably less. He regards these two lawyers to be of the lowliest rank of legalists, and he resents that in their arrogance they see fit to twist the laws to their own purpose, according to their personal agendas.

Adding to Hamet's general mood of distaste and disgust is the presence of today's duty clerk, Greely DeVoss, who is an untrustworthy sort. Even worse that he is allowed an assistant that is no better than a hoodlum to protect him from many rightly deserved drubbings. This conniving clerk has only recently returned from an extended posting at the farthest away of all VOC stations, Batavia, in the Jayakartan archipelago. He wonders what kind of caper Greely had pulled off to finally be allowed back home. He and his overgrown oaf seem overtly smug. They are confiding secretively, first murmuring, and then snickering. Gerardus continues speculating and reckons that Clerk DeVoss will get himself into trouble again, and then get shipped out again, or thrown in prison; the scoundrel! Glancing back he decides that all these folks, except for the oarsman, ought to be locked up, and the key thrown away.

♡♡♡

Nicklas, waiting to disembark, stands at the gunwale looking down at the various crews of dock workers. There is a crew moving full cargo nets suspended from the swinging boom of the dock's large crane. There is another crew dragging a gangplank across the wharf, and another stacking crates high on a wagon, and now a crew is returning from a warehouse with an empty wagon to be filled again. Nicklas enjoys watching the busy crowd of dock hands and clerks. He wishes he would see that scoundrel of a clerk, DeVoss! He has known many clerks, and some with disagreeable manners, but never has he met one as impudent as this little creep. Nicklas has served as a clerk, he knows what it's like. Before this voyage he had clerked in the offices of the VOC here in Amsterdam.

Waiting for the opening of the gangway, with sailors stacking cargo all around him on the deck, has Nicklas thinking back on the circumstances that led up to him being on this voyage. It is all because of the tulip craze. Tulipmania has amassed fortunes for many gardeners, and has spawned an overall interest, across the land, in leisure gardening. It has become trendy to have walled gardens, and a sign of success to have a grandly designed garden. It is fashionable to have a garden with all manner of exotic plantlife. Botanists have been hired by the VOC to bring back these exotic specimens from the Isles of the East Indies, and the jungles of the African and Asian continents. There had previously been a low percentage of success, leading the Board of Directors to seek out Director Olmsfeld's daughter Trinjntje, a tutored woman, and a self-educated botanist. Anticipating the success of her first expedition led to the outfitting of a ship specifically with the intention of bringing back copious amounts of the amazing bulbs, citrus plants, coffee trees, flowering shrubs, herbs, and all sorts of precious seeds.

When the announcement for a botanist's assistant had been posted on the board in the offices where he clerked others had scoffed, but Nicklas chose to apply for the position. After the interview process, which included a meeting with Director Olmsfeld and his daughter Trinjntje, he accepted the job. The offer included room in the ship's hold for him to bring back a generous tonnage of personal cargo, along with a forward payment of half the promised salary. He has used that advance for purchasing merchandise that now fills the cargo space allotted him. Now here he stands, almost two years later, waiting for who knows what bureaucratic details need to happen before the gangway will be opened.

While he and the rest of the small crowd of passengers wait, the offloading of cargo which does not require an open gangway is already underway. As the dock crane swings its heavy ball and hook close to where he is standing he is nudged respectfully out of the way. "Excuse me Nicklas. Sir," says a sailor as he jumps up on the top of a pile of crates wrapped in a cargo net. Reaching up the man grabs the swinging hook and then inserts it through two loops of the net. Ready now, he gives the signal to the crew operating the crane that this net is ready to be lifted up and over the gunwale to the dock. He looks down to Nicklas standing on the deck below him, "Who knows when they'll open that gangway and allow you to pass." He scans the rest of the crowded deck, checking to see who may be watching, then back to Nicklas. He smiles while tilting his head and lifting his chin gesturing a challenge for Nicklas to ride along with him on this cargo net. The slack is nearly gone out of the heavy rope, giving Nicklas little opportunity for indecision, and so he impulsively climbs the squares of the net as it lifts off the deck, hanging on while it swings over the gunwale and is then lowered into a waiting cart, whereupon he releases his grip and drops to his feet. From above him the sailor congratulates him, "Well done Sir!" Then after loosening the hook from the net steps into it to be lifted back aboard for the next load, casually tipping a salute. The cart pulls away and in the moment before the next cart moves forward Nicklas passes through the gap and begins walking through town.

♡♡♡

A young man, a dock hand by the looks of him, while eating his breakfast has been watching through the windows of the port café as a ship-to-shore tender full of official looking men returns to the wharf. The first two men out of the boat, one tall and lanky, the other short and round, both dressed all in black, hasten off with their heads down. A port officer follows, but clearly does not want to walk with the two before him, nor with the last two out of the boat. The smaller of this last two stands head to head with his brutish companion, talking earnestly for a moment before they move off together behind the others. The little man's coat pockets bulge, possibly illegally confiscated goods procured under the pretense as contraband. "Hm. A thief in the position of monitoring the thieves." Due to this young man's current cynicism, this seems typical of the VOC regulatory commission's bureaucracy.

The fellow leaves enough coins to cover his meal and then moves out thinking that it will be a delightful privilege to lighten the pockets of such a squeaker. So into the crowd he moves, appearing to be intent upon where he is going, yet focusing on his quarry. Then as he is readying to make his snatch a crowd of boys jostles in to beat him at his game. He is clever though, and uses the distraction. While the boys lift what is in the pocket on the right side of the man's coat he picks for himself what is in the left side pocket.

Greely DeVoss, after the jostling, and realizing what has occurred, shoves his bodyguard, "Be after those brats and bring me back whatever it is they have stolen!" Still patting his pockets he realizes, with alarming dismay, that both pockets have been emptied. Spinning around he scours the crowd, but is unable to determine if any of the receding backs are in cahoots with the party of schemers that have lifted his treasures. “Curses!” he cries, “a decent man’s property ain’t safe around here no more!”

The bodyguard, an out of work mercenary having just arrived in Amsterdam from Berlin, and being new to the Dutch way of speaking, is not certain that he understands what has just occurred. He responds to the little man’s squawking and takes off as fast as he can after the crowd of youngsters, only to be instantly thwarted as they split up and run in all directions. He chooses to follow the boy that looks to be oldest, and so possibly their leader. He chases the youngster down a narrow alley, over a fence, through a vegetable garden, over another fence, and into a hog pen where his feet sink nearly up to his knees in slop. He watches the brat bounding across the hogs’ backs, and then up to the top of the fence. When the big goon attempts to move, he pulls a foot loose from out of a boot that is stuck in the muck and losing his balance flails backward, landing completely mired in the slop. The hogs all watch disinterestedly, while the grinning boy on the fence calls out, “I’ll wait around while you get out of the mud, then you can chase me some more if you like.” He laughs away at the big man’s predicament.

♡♡♡

Trinjntje, sipping from a cup of coffee while munching on a warm sweet-bun, walks along the path that runs between the pots holding the trees and shrubs that she is bringing back with her. Even during high seas these large porcelain pots have stayed in place because of the slats Nicklas has nailed to the deck-boards to hold them in their places. Here at harbor where there are no waves incessantly tilting her space up and down, she is still walking these pathways of her arboretum carefully. She consciously shifts her weight while focusing on the motion of her body; akin to dancing, consciously feeling sinew and bone as she moves gracefully along these narrow aisles that she knows by heart. When she makes her way around to her little table she sets down her cup and considers having more coffee, but a look into the tin pot tells her there are only grounds left. She has eaten all the buns. The harbor bell has just rung eleven times. She has a long while before the ceremony, so she sets off again through the weaving pathways of this ship's hold garden that is her home, only this time she turns sideways and cartwheels herself gracefully. She deliberately stops in a handstand with her toes reaching close to the underside of the deck above. Again she becomes aware that here in the still water of the harbor, it is not necessary for her to compensate for a moving deck. She holds the handstand while focusing on the pulse of her heart, feeling it in her ears and in her neck. She likes the familiar sensation of being upside-down. Dropping her legs outward, then bending her torso sideways, she brings one foot to the deck, and then tilts herself fully upright. She continues to focus on breathing gently and silently through her nose. She focuses on the clarity of her thoughts. This is what she has practiced these many long months at sea.

She has never expressed to anybody that plants share an awareness similar to our own. She has discovered that it is best to keep her opinions regarding these kinds of things to herself. She understands that plants function according to the movement around them; the birds and the bugs, the wind and the rain, and the path of the sun across the sky. So she has developed routines of keeping movement ever present for her plants to behold so they will feel that they are still in a natural setting. She keeps the windows open whenever possible and often sings to invite the wind in to caress the leaves. She likes to dip her hands in the water bucket and fling rain from her fingertips. Knowing how important her mood is to her plants, her first priority each day is to be happy. Her primary intention always is to be happy.

Most days she plays her little harp or bangs on her drum, but she has them packed in a trunk. She still has her little flute, so she walks the maze of pathways between the potted plants while alternately clapping her hands, then playing away on her flute, and then singing. She rocks back and forth on her feet focusing on the feeling of her long hair sweeping across her shoulders. She hears the harbor bell ring twice, "Oh, how quickly time passes when I keep busy." She at last changes from her silk pajamas and puts on her dress, pins up her hair, finishes with shoes and hat, and then sits, with gloves at hand, to await whomsoever it will be that will collect her for her uncle's ceremony.

♡♡♡

In his own cabin Captain Cornelius Janszoon is busy packing his belongings into his chest. He lines the bottom with his books. He wraps his personal sandglasses inside his extra shirts. He folds his assortment of quadrants; Mariner's, Gunner's, and Astronomer's within his cold-weather coat. His astrolabe and nocturnal get rolled up inside his spare trousers. He tucks his collection of compasses in between the folds of other assorted garments. He lays his Cross Staff in diagonally, leaving barely enough room for his collection of charts, maps, and journals. Lastly he places his grandfather's framed Compass Rose on top, but before setting the lid down and buckling the straps he must change for the ceremony.

He removes his jacket and spreads it lengthwise across the top of everything else inside the trunk, then folds the sleeves in over the top. He empties his vest pockets, unbuttons all those buttons, and lays it flat on top of the coat. His shirt and trousers likewise are spread out flat on top of everything else; and then all the layers are folded over in half, and in the space of the empty other half he places his old weathered cocked hat. Now he closes the rounded top, and buckles the straps of the big old trunk that has carried all he owns for these many years.

Turning to his closet he opens the door and pulls a shirt from its hanger, a shirt that has yet to be worn. He holds it up admiring its brilliant whiteness, then slips it over his head. Next he slides his legs through the trousers that match the splendid coat still on its hanger in the closet. He then fits into his magnificent cream colored silk vest, buttons up all the buttons while admiring the matching colored silk braid that runs down the front. Next he sits down again on the bunk to pull on his boots. He then picks up what he had removed from the pockets of the previously worn vest and deposits it all into the big side pockets of this new vest. Finally he lifts the coat off its hanger and stretches his arms through the sleeves and is taken aback at the luxuriance of the turned back lapels and cuffs of the same creamy silk to match the vest. He twists his torso and feels the freedom of movement that comes with a properly fitted garment. As he smooths his hand down a sleeve he glories in how he loves this shade of blue that is brighter than the traditional deep blue he has always worn before. From his closet's top shelf he withdraws his new cocked hat. It is the same bright blue to match his coat and trousers. He caresses the silken braid that is stitched all around the three-cornered brim before placing it on his head.

There is a knock at his cabin door. "Enter."

"Captain Sir," holding out a key, "I brought the key that you asked for."

"Thank You," he takes the key, "and you will be gathering my trunk?"

"We will Sir," indicating toward the other sailor standing behind him, "and soon as we get your chest on the main deck we will return for your niece's trunk."

"Well done." Janszoon steps through the doorway allowing the two sailors access to his chest, "Pardon me," standing as tall and dignified as he can, "I am to be making an appearance before a crowd. Reassure me please, that I have everything tucked in and buttoned properly."

"Oh Sir. You have done well." Now the man bends forward at the hip, "I bow to your resplendency!"

"You look the regal gentleman Sir," adds the other sailor while saluting sharply.

♡♡♡

The pickpocket, Dirk, hearing the commotion being raised by the pipsqueak that has just been robbed, restrains himself from looking back, not wishing to allow for any incriminating considerations to be prompted. He continues on his way along the wharf, bypassing a couple easy lifts, until he comes to an ale-house with an empty bench. He is served a tankard of foamy brew and declines the offer for a meal. After scanning the other patrons and determining that nobody is paying him any attention, he decides to take a look at what he has pilfered. Withdrawing the velvet bag from his inner pocket and keeping it hidden below the table he loosens the drawstring and peeks inside at what appears at first to be a golden chain, but then, "Oh My God!" There are some unusually large jewels, and so much gold! Catching his breath, he hastily pulls the bag's drawstring tight and hides it away back inside his secret pocket. He scans the crowded room again wondering if there is anyone present who has NOT beheld the shining glory that must have flashed bright enough for everybody in the room to notice.

Nobody affords him special attention. Nobody is eyeing him warily. Nobody is jumping closer to get a better look.

Nobody with a vested interest has rushed breathlessly across the room to claim their lost bit of what appears to be Crown Jewels set within Hearts fashioned of Gold. He tells himself that he must not actually be holding on to such an item as this. He needs to catch his breath. The excitement of petty thievery has now escalated to grand larceny of an unparalleled measure. Once again he is wishing that he had stayed home working as a miller with his father and brother.

"Aieii Dirk, y'look as'f y've seen a ghost!" A member of the dock crew he had, until a couple of days ago, been working with, takes a seat at his table. "Are ya sick? Is that why we've not been seein' ya?"

"Umm," Not sure of this fellow's name, he guesses, "Beuregard? Hey, it's good to see you."

"Bo. Call me Bo," the big galoot tells him as he jams his sausage biscuit into his mouth and bites off what would be three bites for most people, and then whilst chomping away asks, "Didja hear? The Director Olmsfeld's daughter, the crazy one, has returned from the Far East on this mornin's tide. It's said she turned down the marriage offer of a prince who is a Lord of all East Afreeka." Here he takes a break from prattling gossip to push the remaining hunk of his sandwich into his maw, then continues jabbering as he grinds away, "And that she's brought back with her a bona fide jungle of trees, and plants, and flowers and all sorts of growy things."

Dirk, having barely heard a word this big sloppy guy has spoken, stands and says, "It's good to see you again, but I've got to be on my way." Rising up from the bench to leave he turns back thinking to tell his co-worker not to mention seeing him to anyone, but decides to say nothing and is nearly running as he leaves behind the blubbering fool's queries. He cannot remember his nerves ever being wracked as they are now. He tells himself that he has to get somewhere that he will be able to calm down and think clearly. He needs a chance to apprize this piece of merchandise. He decides it will be best to return to his room.

Upon reaching his building on the third channel he races up two flights of stairs and then lowers and climbs the ladder to his top story chamber. After pulling the curtains across the gable windows he decides it is finally safe to take another look at what is in the velvet silk-lined bag. He loosens the drawstring and withdraws a necklace that he spreads out on the table. He is spellbound by its magnificence. It is a necklace of Golden Hearts held together by an intricate array of golden filigree. There is a first row of five Golden Hearts; each set with a sizable ruby in the center. Then a second row of three Golden Hearts set with emeralds. Then another row of two more golden hearts set with diamonds of a size only told of in fables. A final golden heart forming the point of the array is set with a splendidly stunning opaque blue stone such as nothing this young fellow knew existed. So entranced is he by this most astounding adornment that he loses track of the passing time. In the back of his mind he wonders how such a magnificent item has ended up in a dock clerk's pocket. He has no idea what to do with this. He decides then and there to leave Amsterdam. He figures that he can be in Utrecht or Antwerpen within a few days. He needs to be away from here. There is something uncanny about this necklace. "Is this thing glowing?" There seems to be a radiant aura, but he tells himself, "This is but my imagination roused by the grandeur of this thing."

♡♡♡

Nicklas walks along the wharf, enjoying the feeling of certainty to his steps here on solid ground, but it is not only the sense of being away from the swaying of the ship, it is also the excitement of looking forward to what lies ahead for him. During this long voyage, while the ship was at sea his duties as botanical assistant were minimal, because Trinjntje took care of the plants. But whenever they were in port he was busy getting all the new plants and trees that Trinjntje had picked out onto the ship. Also, while in port, he was searching for his own items to fill the area allotted for him in the ship's hold, and then getting those goods loaded aboard ship. Anytime in port was a very busy time for him. And now, here he is ready to step into the office where he had been employed, hmmmm, was it only two years ago? It seems an eternity. Once inside the VOC office he introduces himself to a clerk who offers him a seat. He turns toward a lobby crowded with people who, like him, are holding packets of papers that require processing, and he wonders how long he will be waiting, and if he should come back later, there is so much he wants to do. He is not seated long before a door opens and all eyes turn in anticipation of their number finally being up, but the clerk calls "Nicklas Voorhaven," bidding him to follow through the doorway without having to sit and wait nearly as long as all the others here before him. He is led to an office holding a desk large enough to signify this being an important man's office, and is told by the clerk who has escorted him, "Since word of the *Gouden Leeuwin's* arrival this morning we have been expecting you. Can I get you a coffee?" It seems that he is being given preferential treatment.

As he is being served his cup of coffee an older gentleman comes in. Nicklas faintly remembers this man from his time clerking here. This senior clerk seats himself at his desk while welcoming Nicklas home and declaring, "I would have jumped at the chance to do what you have done, but I have my wife and my children, you know, my family."

Nicklas nods while handing over his papers for review, "Family, yes, that is one of the many things I have on my list to do. I will have to travel to Antwerpen to visit my family."

"Ah, yes, I often hear this 'so much to do' sentiment from returning travelers." Then it is all business. His choices are explained to him by this man who has repeated these choices often enough that his words flow too fast for actual comprehension to occur, "You can sign here ..." going on and on indeterminately, then shuffling papers, and rearranging the piles before starting in again, "Or, you can sign here ..." The man is required to make this full speech in order to meet the strict specifications of the Company's best practices. When he has finished Nicklas chooses to sign the second offer, based upon what he has gleaned from other merchants. As he signs these pages of script he remembers back on the drudgery of penning copies such as these in duplicate and triplicate, day after day. After an entire stack of papers have been signed and Nicklas has received an envelope with his copies. He receives a draft for the remaining portion of the salary due to him for services rendered as botanist's assistant.

The smiling administrator stands and shakes hands with Nicklas, then asks, "Will you be taking more voyages of this nature?"

"Right now I'm not thinking of taking voyages of any nature," holding up one finger, "but it has been an inspiring adventure, and I have learned many valuable skills," now waving the folded draft to emphasize his next point, "and I have earned a good wage."

"La, and you will likely earn a fortune for your cargo, most do. You are a lucky man."

"Indeed I am," As Nicklas is standing he notices the worn leather of his boots, "There is something else to add to my list of things to do now that I am back."

"Something else?"

"Yes," laughing, "I need some new boots."

"You will be able to afford an entire new wardrobe. Good day to you Nicklas my friend."

After leaving VOC headquarters, Nicklas makes a stop at the bank where he signs another sheaf of paperwork, setting up an account, before leaving with a fat wallet and full coin purse. His next stop is the bath house, emerging a while later washed and shaven. Then on to a tailor's shop where, being a standard sized fellow, he is able to fit into a suit of ready-sewn clothes from off the racks. The bootmaker next door has a pair that fit and are of a style he has always admired: tall boots of sturdy black leather, trimmed with belts through silver buckles at the top.

At last he makes it to one of his old favorite public houses. He is served a pint of their fine brew, and he is reminded how great the beer is here. As his dinner is being served, he remembers that he has been instructed where to meet the crooked clerk DeVoss, so he asks the man who runs the place as his full plate is set before him, "Can you provide me directions, please, to the Polder Inn."

The man's expression becomes stern as he clamps his hand on Nicklas' shoulder and moves closer so others cannot hear, "Oh young Master, you will not want to be going there." He veers his eyes around the room warily, then whispers, "The Polder Inn is known to be a layabout for smugglers and thieves." Then bending even closer, telling him in a fatherly tone, "No decent gentleman will have business to attend at the Polder Inn."

Somewhat taken aback, Nicklas answers, "Oh, I thank you Sir, and will instead make my way directly to my rooms after I have finished this fine repast." Relieved to not have to attend to this business after all, he tips his head to his host, "You have done me a great service my friend."

The older man slaps Nicklas heartily on the shoulder, "Tell me now of your voyage my good man."

♡♡♡

Janszoon takes the ladder down in a bound with his hands sliding along the rails, then he crosses this lower deck, and once on the other side grabs another ladder's rails and hoists himself to the next deck, moving gracefully and efficiently as any sailor. At Trinjntje's cabin he uses the provided key to remove the padlock, and then knocks. Almost immediately the inner latch can be heard being drawn back, and next the door opens, and Trinjntje's eyes, upon the sight of her uncle dressed in such splendor, expand in their own luster, "Oh, Uncle Cornelius," she curtsies, dropping deeply, as if for royalty, "Sir," and as she straightens tells him teasingly, "la, the iridescent hue of your coat brings out a sheen of blue in your hair." She steps back taking a fuller look, "Splendid!"

Beholding her, dressed in her own finery, he plays along by taking her hand in his own and presenting a respectful kiss upon her long fingers. Then holding her hand within both of his responds, "My Dear," while taking her other hand and holding both admiringly, "One is hard pressed to believe that these hands be a gardener's, so smooth and finely manicured are they."

"Oh Uncle," tossing her head, laughing easily, "You are quite accomplished with your gentlemanly charm."

Looking past her, deeper into the interior of her spacious suite, at all the plant life therein, he asks, "Permission to enter and walk the paths of your ships garden one last time."

"Please," she waves him in, "by all means."

He steps past her into the wide area of the entire aft portion of this deck, lit by the sunlight streaming through cantilevered window panes. He has visited this garden often, even believes now that every ship should have a garden like this. He gazes upon all variety of plant life; healthy prospering greenery: trunks, vines, and branches; buds, blossoms, and blooms; berries, nuts, and fruits. The enclosed atmosphere of outdoors; exuding a thick warm odor of dirt, moss, mushrooms, beetles, worms, and slugs. He turns back to her, "I have told you before, but allow me to tell you again that this area you have here has inspired me," Now raising his arms into tree branches, "I am pleased that you and all this were a part of my last voyage!"

She tips her head acknowledging his compliment, and then gently asks, "Will you never sail again?" He smiles, but says nothing. "Need we be on our way lest ye be late for your own ceremony?"

"Right you are!" He extends an arm directing her to lead.

Arriving upon the main deck he leaves her with the growing crowd of sailors and guests while attending to his Captain's duties a final time on the quarterdeck. She watches above her at the sailors in the rigging and imagines, as she is wont to do, how wonderful twould be to climb the lines and to walk the yards that hold the sails aloft. She gazes out at all the other ships in the harbor noticing all the sailors in the riggings moving with such grace and ease while calling out playfully to each other. She pensively considers the lack of comraderie in her life.

A commotion on the wharf draws her attention and she shifts her gaze to the gathered crowd there. A regal coach arrives accompanied by a troop of mounted soldiers. Before the coach is fully stopped a footman jumps from the back and rushes to open the door and tip down the step before reaching up offering a hand to the lady now departing from within, Trinjntje's mother, Doortje, who turns her attention toward the crowd while opening a brightly colored parasol. Next to step down is Trinjntje's father, Christophorus, dressed in traditional business attire. They are joined by two more men; one wearing an Admiral's coat with gold at the collars, lapels, and cuffs; the other, attired in dark blue Captain's coat, Janszoon's replacement. The Admiral leads the others up the gangway onto the *Gouden Leeuwin.* Captain Janszoon has made his way to the main deck to greet these important guests. The ceremony is short. The Admiral, wearing a chest full of badges, introduces the new Captain, also displaying an array of medals. He then presents a commemorative medallion to Captain Janszoon, who promptly places it in his pocket, choosing not to wear medals as adornment. There are salutes all around. Hands shaken. Then the ceremony is over. Cornelius extends his elbow for his sister, Trinjntje's mother. Christophorus steps quickly across the deck with his elbow extended likewise for his daughter. She takes his arm and proceeds along with him, following after her mother and uncle down the gangway and into the waiting coach.

As Captain Janszoon, Trinjntje and her parents make their way to the coach the noise of the milling crowd crescendos. The presence of this crowd reminds Trinjntje of her family's celebrity status. Her father has become one of the nation's richest men. Her mother is a celebrated descendent of royalty. And then, there is herself, known for her tutored education, for her scientific knowledge of botany, and scandalously, for her unmarried status. Some honor her, while others fear her. In this crowd that has gathered today both sides are represented. Many toss flowers, even full bouquets as they pass while cheering optimistically. Other men and women stand in solemn flocks singing of trials and tribulations.

The carriage does not travel far before stopping at VOC headquarters where Christophorus and Cornelius are to be let out. Doortje informs her daughter, "Your uncle has to sign all the paperwork finalizing his departure from the Company. Cornelius says that it is imperative that it be done today, for his plans are already set in motion for him to leave early tomorrow for his new estate." Then to her brother, "La, you have planned this for so long Cor, I can understand your excitement to be on your way."

"You must come visit once I am settled in," he tells his sister, then to Trinjntje, "I am looking forward to your assistance in my gardens."

Christophorus then tells his wife and daughter, "This business will not take long. I will see you at dinner. I want to hear all about your voyage Trin."

As their carriage begins moving again Trinjntje asks her mother, "Why is there a troop of soldiers escorting us Ma?"

"Well, Trinjntje," she gazes out her window a moment, then turning back, "You know, in every society, even a modern society as ours, there are separating factions of thought. Here, where there are so many freedoms, people are allowed to express their differing opinions, and as there is more expression there becomes greater division between the differing factions."

"Mother, please. What does this have to do with the troop of soldiers escorting our carriage through the streets of Amsterdam?"

"Okay, I am getting to that dear." She is not enjoying this conversation, "Talk of your return has become somewhat of a rallying point between the opposing groups; dividing the puritanical factions and the progressive factions."

"My arrival a rallying point? How is that so?"

"Oh Trin, you have never given much attention to this sort of thing, but you had already been a rallying point, even before leaving on your voyage. Your father had so hoped that with two years passage what you are seen as would be forgotten."

"What I am seen as has always been different from who I am."

"Yes, we know that, but the progressives see you as a symbol of independence and freedom while the puritans fear you as the symbol of intemperance and selfishness."

"Fear me?"

"Oh," sounding frustrated, "fear twists everything, until nobody understands, or even thinks to understand. I tell myself that it is not really you that they fear."

Upon reaching the gates of the Olmsfeld estate a few of the crowd gathered there need to be forcibly held back to allow the carriage to pass through. Under the portico at the front entry the coach stops, and the two step out. At the base of the steps leading up to the doorway Trinjntje pauses, looking back at the gate and the crowd gathered there, she knows that she cannot stay here to witness this every day. Her mother takes her elbow drawing her up the steps and through the door into the grand entryway. Once inside she holds her arms wide for a hug. "I missed you so. Now that you are home let us forget about what is going on out there."

"I am all for that," Trinjntje agrees, as men come through the atrium and up the stairs with her trunks, "for now I will see my things get put away where I want them."

"All right Dear, I will have some tea made."

When Trinjntje comes back downstairs her ma calls from the outdoor patio where a tray of tea and biscuits await. "Oh Ma, I will not be able to sit still long enough to enjoy my tea. Could we instead walk the garden paths?" And so they stroll under the trellis with its tangled Wisteria, past the blooming rhododendrons, and out beneath the blossoming dogwood, and into the rose garden where the petals of new buds are beginning to unfold.

"You've missed the blooming of the daffodils and tulips." Doortje comments as they stand before the spent foliage. "Come into the nursery and see what has been saved for you." The greenhouse, situated against a tall stone wall intended to hold in the warmth, had been built as a sanctuary for Trinjntje once her parents had deemed it inadvisable for her to roam the city. Inside is a mechanical wonder of splashing fountains, made possible by the turning of the little windmill upon the garden's wall. There are gentle breezes flowing through the opened window panes: panes that can be adjusted by manipulating the clever handles that turn the gears to open or close.

Growing up, and even as an adult, Trinjntje was as likely to be found here as with any of her tutors. Her love of growing things had overridden any other desires. Now, they each cover their dresses with garden aprons and busy themselves with the chores of caring for all that grows here. While chattering away, they carry flats of newly grown petunias, geraniums, and snap-dragons for transplanting into the warm dirt outside. The robins that return to this garden each spring loiter close to the freshly-turned earth hoping to snatch worms. The chick-a-dees, whistling their backward call, line up on the branches overhead. A charm of finches flit to and fro off the fence and trellis. The din of a multitude of honeybees, bumblebees, and wasps creates an underlying tone of busyness.

As they are putting away the trowels and hanging their aprons Trinjntje tells Doortje, "I'm off to the stable. I will not be long." And down the drive she goes, remembering the wonderful horse that had carried her around the city, and away into the surrounding areas, for so many years. The grooms are all there to greet her as she walks into the barn. These are the men that taught her to ride a horse. These men who, even after it had been deemed inadvisable for her to ride out and about, had cooperated in her subterfuge of dressing as a stable boy taking the lady's horse out for exercise. She takes a moment to visit, telling them of riding nimble horses in Africa, camels in Persia, and elephants in Asia.

They all know how she loves to ride, "Regrettably Trinjntje, your father has not seen fit to keep any light riding stock. All we have here are the heavy horses."

"Tis a shame, for I have been anxious to ride again."

"Perhaps your father will allow you a horse."

"Perhaps."

When she comes back inside her father is home, and dinner is served.

During the meal she tells an abbreviated account of her travels, "The first hundred days were total boredom, and the next hundred days we sailed into ports that held nothing of interest, and finally we reached the jungles and collected plants and trees and seeds to bring home. I was lucky to have Nicklas to assist with all the heavy lifting."

"So, you got along with the man?" Her father asks.

"Oh yes. Nicklas was the perfect choice; he is cheerful, hardworking, and good company."

They are looking at her in a funny way. Doortje asks, "Are you in love?"

"I do love him," Trinjntje smiles, "we have become close friends." She laughs at the surprise she sees, then tells them, "La, Nicklas is at least ten years younger than I; he is not interested in anyone my age." Then teasing some more, "Or anyone as frightening and selfish as you say some think me to be."

"What have you been telling her?" Chris asks Doortje.

"What indeed. She asked why there was a troop of Company soldiers escorting our carriage."

"And how long have there been people at your gate singing these doleful hymns?" Trinjntje asks.

"That crowd has only arrived this day. They will be gone tomorrow."

"Will they?" Doortje asks, "Tell her Chris."

"There is nothing to worry about," He says. "As for the soldiers," he shrugs, "I thought they would add a nice touch to the arrival home of our long gone daughter."

"Not a precautionary measure against what Ma tells me are opposing factions?"

"Do not worry Trin, as long as you are here everything will be fine."

As these words are spoken the walls seem to close in on Trinjntje, "Are you saying that I will have to stay within the confines of this property?"

"I only hope that the fear of others does not instill fear in you. It is our greatest wish that you be happy."

After dinner in the parlor Christophorus tells Trinjntje, "The success of your voyage will add substantially to your bank balance," and to the VOC coffers she thinks to herself, "and the freight that your assistant has brought back is remarkable in variety, so his own bank account will be likewise rewarded substantially." She cares naught for her own wealth, but she is happy for Nicklas.

"It has been so long without hearing your music," Doortje says, "will you play something for us please?"

"Oh, I would like that. I only had my little harp with me." She seats herself at her mother's elegant full-size harp, then after a little warm up begins playing some of her favorites. The longer she plays the clearer her mind becomes until, from a distance, she hears the bells toll eleven. "Oh," she starts to say she has lost track of the time, but notices both her parents are asleep. She tiptoes out and up the steps to her room.

Closing the door behind her she beholds everything as it has always been. Opening her closet she finds her same old clothes ready to wear again. She opens a bottom drawer, withdraws the stable-boy outfit that she used to wear to disguise herself when she went riding. Sadly, she no longer has a horse to ride. She thinks back on the crowd that had gathered the day she sailed out on her botanic voyage, and how that crowd has grown to the rabble that has welcomed her home today. She holds no desire to be a celebrated personage. She does not know how, or care, to answer all the imposing questions asked of her. Being lauded at social events, or vying for the most available bachelor are not endeavors that inspire her affection. During her long voyage she had felt confined and had so looked forward to the freedom of being home, but now it feels as if a perimeter is closing in around her. It occurs to her that she may have to do something daring in order to experience the freedom she longs for.

She examines herself in the mirror, at how long her hair has grown while away, and laughs thinking that it would be a quick giveaway were she to attempt her stable-boy disguise, and besides, she reminds herself again that she will not be riding. She determines that she will be better off wearing her walk-about disguise. As a girl she had loved roaming the city, and she loved even more roaming beyond the outskirts of the city. As she matured, it became unseemly for a woman of her stature to be seen roving about the city alone, and so rather than quit her wandering she had taken up disguising herself as a man, always pleased that she fit in wherever she wished to roam. Opening a drawer of the table next to the mirror, she withdraws her scissors, and then after spreading a sheet over the floor to catch the clippings, she trims her hair shorter, leaving it long enough that she is still able to gather it all with a ribbon, long enough to touch her shoulders which is an acceptable length for a woman, or a man.

Next, she wraps a linen scarf to flatten her breasts, then pulls on a clinging knit shirt that is unmistakably women's finery, but it does not show after being covered by a man's shirt, a man's vest, and a man's overcoat. It is not the suit of a gentleman, nor is it the suit of a working man: it is the suit of a vagabond. She pulls on soft sturdy trousers, knit stockings, and well-worn leather boots designed for walking. The tails of her coat cover her distinctly womanly derriere, and a long woolen cloak is drawn over her shoulders to cover it all, including the belt that holds a sheathed knife at her waist. She places upon her head a French style hat, *le beret*, because sometimes playing the foreigner has proven distraction enough to be left alone. She places the strap of her still packed travel bag over her shoulder, a red leather carryall of an appropriate style suitable to a woman or a man. She is ready to go. She will travel light.

Leaving Éire

Mara awakens from dreaming and has to reorient herself again to the view of her empty home from her mat on the floor. The bed, table, and her great loom sit beneath sailcloth tarps down on the quay. All other household items are packed inside wooden crates that are stacked inside the dock storehouse. Everything that they are taking with them is ready to be loaded awaiting Robert's return. Winter is mostly past here at the northernmost tip of Ireland, yet she remains lying in the comfortable warmth of her quilt. She is reluctant to rise because she has so much to do this day. Based upon how many days Robert is usually away on similar voyages, he will probably be arriving home today. So she tosses aside the warm comfort she has been relishing and dresses herself. Then after stirring up the coals and adding a couple turves to her fire she hangs a kettle to warm over the flames while she is out taking care of her animals. Her sweet fuzzy cat follows along behind her out the door and across the yard under a sky filled with the lavenders and pinks of sunrise.

"Good Morning my Dears," she greets them all as she slides open the barn's door on its squeaking iron rollers. She tosses hay into the mangers for the horses. She no longer has the sheep to feed for they are gone, sold off in preparation for this move. The chickens have been pared down to just these few hens already in their travel coop, ready for their journey to a new home. Robert has told her to expect this voyage they have planned to last a fortnight. She is bringing these chickens and her nanny goat to travel with them so they will have fresh eggs and milk. She places the bucket beneath her nanny and hums a cheery melody, matching the rhythm of the splashing, as she squeezes the milk from the happy little goat's tiny teats. While she is milking she hears someone out in the yard and wonders who would be here so early. Whoever it is must not be aware that there is no longer any merchandise being traded here. All has been sold and their storehouse stands empty.

Whoever it is tries at the house's door, "Auntie?" Then comes across to the barn, "Auntie?"

"Over here," she calls out to whomsoever it may be, while wondering which of all the younger family members has not already sailed off to America.

"Good Morning Auntie."

She looks up from her milking. The young fellow standing there is vaguely familiar from the yearly family gatherings, "Is it Michael?" Trying to remember the name of one of her niece's offspring.

"Mike."

"I am almost finished here, then I'll be with you." She wonders what has brought him this far so early in the day. The young fellow is flushed and breathing heavily. "Have you been running?"

"Aye," he answers softly, "Ma wanted you to have the news."

Finished, she pats the little goat's rump, then picks up the pail of milk, "Follow me into the house. I'll give you something to eat."

"Oh, I cannot be long for I must be on my way. I have been charged with getting the news to all the family households in these outlying counties."

"If you cannot stay for breakfast, well then at least let me provide something that you can eat along your way."

Knowing that Aunties will never allow a youngster such as him to say no, he dutifully follows her. In the house she sets down the bucket, lays a cloth over the top, and then begins slicing bread, ham, and cheese for sandwiches, "Now, what is this news that is so important?"

"Several ships full of Cromwellians have arrived, and are traveling this way escorted by troops of redcoats that are showing no mercy." This is unwelcome news. "We of Éire are losing our homes and our lands. Ma and Pa have been forced out. I have been sent north to tell ye all that there is no hope, and that ye must flee."

"How long til they are here?"

"I am barely ahead of them. They will be on your road by this afternoon, or by tonight. I am doing my best to stay ahead of them"

"Uncle Robert and I have already made plans for this and will be sailing out with our belongings as soon as he is back home. I am expecting him today. You'll have many more of the family that you must visit today if the soldiers are as close behind as you say. You will be better off riding a horse. Since we cannot take our horses you may as well ride mine." She hands him the sack of food she has prepared for him, "Follow me," and leads him back out to the barn.

"Where will you be sailing?"

"The Netherlands."

"Holland?"

"The Hollanders, Zeelanders, Guelderlanders, Frisians; la, I cannot say for sure who all, but the lowlanders are calling themselves a republic." She places a halter on the mare that she has ridden for so many years. "We are hoping this republic of the Netherlands to be a more civilized place to live than the wilds of America." She hands the reins over and tells him, "This mare loves to run. Let her set her own pace and you will cover ground much faster than those following you."

He hoists himself up, "Thank You Auntie." She watches him ride away on her dear companion of so many years. She consoles herself with knowing that she will have another to ride when they get to their new home. Now she must busy herself with loading all that is left onto the cart.

She is rolling up her makeshift bed when she hears horses in the lane and wonders, *can the thieving horde be here already?* She looks out the doorway and recognizes the two priests that are dismounting. These two have pestered her for ages, stopping by all the outlying households regularly to visit, and to share their beliefs, hoping to sway others'. "I apologize to you Sirs, but I am very busy today and cannot sit for visiting."

"Apology accepted. We are not here today to visit. We have brought you something." They are unbinding a parcel from the back of a heavily burdened horse. "The Cromwellians bring with them the Anglicans who are taking away our cathedrals for their own use." *How Ironic* thinks Mara. "We are forced to flee for our lives and we can only bring what we are able to carry with us. While clearing storage chests we have come across this drawer full of artifacts from a previous age. Though they are of no value to us, we have determined that it would be unwholesome to let them fall into the hands of these newly arriving vanquishers of the truth."

They hold out to her what appears to be a drawer with a hastily cut panel placed over the contents and held in place by a thick silken ceremonial cord. She tells them, "We are also fleeing and only able to take what we can carry. I am not sure if there is space for anything more."

"Well then, we will have to leave these artifacts here, for our horse is overburdened."

They are looking around for a place to set the drawer and its contents when she tells them instead, "Put it on the cart. We will see if we have room for it." She is familiar with the tales of how this order of monks have robbed the ancient holy mounds. She asks them, "For what purpose does your order hold these relics?"

"They should have been sent long ago to Rome where all *pagan* artifacts are stored away." He lifts his head boldly, "Wherever we have successfully replaced the false teachings with the one truth we have taken and hidden away the relics of bygone *paganism*."

"Ah, you are so certain that your truth is the only truth!" In the past she has held her views close, but her current mood has dissolved her civility a bit, "There are many peoples. Many Nations. Many Truths." Then she catches herself, stops her tirade and asks, "Where will you go?"

"The monastery at Portsalon."

"I wish you well," she says, "and from what I have been told earlier this day you'd best be hurrying on your way."

She fills the cart with all the day to day household utensils that she has saved for last, and closes the door of her home one final time. "No longer my home," she says as she spanks her hands to clear this dust of remembrance from them. She loads the chickens, nanny goat, and cat; all inside their travel compartments, onto the cart. She leaves all the barn doors and all the gates open, "No longer our barn, nor our pastures." She hitches her great white shire to the cart, and then before starting out for the beach, takes a long last look. There stands the storehouse that has been the center of their trading, now empty. Robert has hopes of establishing the same sort of trading business wherever they settle next. For now though, she is thinking of how she will miss all the visits from their neighbors who have been their customers these many long years.

This has been the home of her husband's family for generations. There will always be memories of raising their children here; children now grown and off to the Americas and likely never to be seen again. Looking toward where the land drops off she thinks of the stark winds of winter that blow in off the sea. There is the small garden that requires so much attention to grow here on this rocky ground. Yet, her heart swells with the love she holds for the life she has known here. Defiantly she says out loud to nobody, "Let somebody else attempt to make a life here on the edge of nowhere." She leads the big horse out to the main road, then turns her cart down the winding passage leading to the strand. It is a steep and tortuous path that is barely wide enough for horse and cart. It is a path that most sensible folk are loathe to traverse, yet Mara knows it well, having hauled cargo up and down its narrow course these many years. She knows how to angle the horse and cart around the tight inner corners, and she doesn't fear the vertigo-inducing drop-off of the outer corners.

The swallows that nest on these cliffs swoop around her. She is able to look down upon a raven flying by below. There are seals in the water where the stream that empties into the cove emerges from its chasm. "Will there be seals and tales of the selkie in our new homeland?" This melancholy thought brings to mind a sad old song that repeats itself in her mind. She stamps her foot, bringing the horse to a halt. She shouts, "I want to let this sadness go!" The echo from the cliffs across the way comes back to her, "... let this sadness go ... sadness go ... go."

From her current vantage point she is able to see out through the narrow space between the rocks that Robert will sail through. She scans the horizon for his sail, knowing he will be waiting for the tide, which won't be favorable again til this evening. Then she resumes her descent knowing that he will be wanting a signal fire burning as a beacon shining across the waves for him to follow into the cove.

♡♡♡

Robert's standard route has always been around the northern coast of the isle of Britannia, keeping away from sailing through the Sleeve at the South. The narrow channel that separates the isle's southern coast from the continent is patrolled heavily by the tyrannical Royal Navy. He grew up sailing this northern route, often used by smugglers, from his grandfather who passed this way to avoid tariffs. Robert carries on the tradition, not thinking of what he does as smuggling, but as a service to his neighbors. He supplies the inhabitants of the remote area where he lives with the niceties of life that city folk take for granted; wines, liquors, spices, sugar, mill ground flour, coffee, tea, silk, seeds, bulbs, and whatever else is seldom found readily available in these outlying hinterlands. His ship, christened the Tulip during the height of the continent's obsession with the flowering bulbs, flies the tri-colored flag of the Netherlands emblazoned with the VOC emblem. The Tulip, being a single-masted open sloop and smaller than most cargo ships in this new age of transport, allows him to sail alone. Few choose to sail alone fearing loneliness, which does not bother Robert. Aloneness suits him.

He is on his return voyage now, with the North Sea behind him, past the Orkneys, and into the Minch. The cold winds blow. Robert passes only local fishing boats, until the Hebrides where through his spyglass he watches the sailors of a Royal Navy frigate harassing the crew of a fishing boat. He maintains his pace as he continues his westward course toward the Atlantic and away from the Scottish coastal islands before finally turning southward for his homeland. The sun is setting when he first catches sight of Inishowen Head, which means he will not need to take his bearings by the stars this night, being familiar enough with this coastline so close to home. He sails past Trawbeaga Bay, continuing on to the harbor that his Grandfather had always referred to as Ríoga Cove.

Darkness settles in, and even though the tide has turned favorably for sailing through the narrow gap into the cove, Robert will only enter if he sees a beacon fire. There it is! Through his spyglass he catches sight of flames upon the beach. This bonfire will be a signal from his beloved, and for the fire to be so bright must mean that she is there tending it, "Won't be long now my Dear." That she is on the beach late at night keeping a fire going has him wondering. Under normal circumstances she would be home and he would remain out on the open waters until daylight. "Have the Cromwellians already stolen our home then?" He gazes up to the top of the cliff where he knows the house built by his grandfathers is situated back from the edge. He salutes the grand oak tree atop the escarpment, its silhouette standing out against the backdrop of the starry night. That old oak has been there since before the house was built and is the emblem emblazoned upon his family's crest.

He adjusts the lines on his foresail, then tugs the tiller to steer his ship through the narrow cleft that leads into Ríoga Cove. The English, these Cromwellians have been steadily moving across his homeland, casting his people out of their homes, and then moving themselves in as the new landowners. The fire burning there on the beach may very well be the signal that he no longer has a home to call his own. The main objective of this voyage so early in the year has been to procure a place to move into before they are among those who have lost everything. They had started planning for this after watching more and more of the English moving in and grabbing the homes and lands away from the good people of Éire. The rightful owners have been banished off to the west; the Burren and the uninhabitable islands beyond.

Robert has traded with a Dutch miller long enough to determine that the new Republic of the Netherlands is the choice for their new home. This voyage has taken him first to Norway where he obtains casks of beer brewed with clear mountain spring water to deliver to a regular customer in Rotterdam. Also from Norway he garners quarried blocks of basalt. His regular buyer of these blocks is the miller, who is also a builder. The miller operates a windmill powered sawmill, and for years Robert has returned home with cargos of milled lumber. This Dutch builder and miller, Philip van Haumann, has offered a place for Robert and Mara to live. Even though it is only a small hut sitting near the noisy sawmill, at least it is a place to stay while they establish themselves.

♡♡♡

Mara has a large beacon fire centered on the beach where it will be visible out on the waves beyond the narrow entry to the cove, and she tends another that is burning at the end of the quay to provide Robert direction to his mooring. She sits in one of their household chairs sipping a glass of wine, while gazing up at the star-filled sky and wondering how long til the moon-rise. The sun-bleached driftwood that is burning here on the stone quay spits and sizzles, causing her to wonder if she is actually hearing something out there in the center of the cove. She is hoping that it is the sound of waves lapping against the wooden hull of a ship. Then she hears the distinct splashing of whales, and by the noise figures it to be the local pod of orcas. Something has stirred them.

"Ahoiiieee!" Out of the darkness she hears Robert calling out to her.

"Halloooo!" She answers back liltingly. Ah, tis good to hear his voice again.

She watches as he lights a lantern at the stern, and another at the bow. Then he calls across the water, close now, "Do ye see me?"

"I do, and you'd best be lowering yer sail or you'll be crashing into the wharf!" They start right in with their teasing banter.

He lowers the sails. All around his ship, under the light of the stars, he makes out the slick round heads of seals gathering to welcome him home. "Hello my friends," he tells them, "have we interrupted your frolicking?" Then noticing how close he is to the stone pier he jumps to the tiller and twists it to dig in, bringing the ship admirably around and alongside the dock. He tosses the bow line to Mara, then scurries to the stern and jumps over the gunwale with the aft line. He barely stands from slipping the knot over the cleat and she has her arms around him, "Ho, my darling, I have missed you."

She withers into his embrace, "I am so very happy that you have returned home this night."

He leans back in order to engage her eyes, "Oh? Is this a special night?"

"If the English army and their horde of interlopers have not arrived at our doorstep this day, then they will tomorrow."

"Then it is true that they intend to take every home in *Éire* from the rightful owners, even to the farthest away and most desolate outposts such as this."

"Tis so, my Love." They hug one another fiercely, lost for a moment in the mixed emotions of grief and anger. The seals all around them begin a mournful keening. The owls in the rocks above them send out a matching *Hoo Hooing.* The pod of Orca, having followed Robert's ship into the cove, add their own lament, and it is as if there is weeping all around them. "Now there'll be no more sadness!" She releases her man, claps her hands rhythmically above her head and dances a clever little hop-jig. Robert takes her hand, spins her around and back into his arms, kisses her hard on the lips, and then lets her go and does his own less elegant version of the happy dance. She teases him some more, "Don't be wearing yourself out Sir for we have much to do this night."

"Oh, I was hoping for something warm to eat."

"Aye, as I figured, but consider first what we must accomplish so that we are ready to sail with the morning tide."

He looks up into the sky and gauging by the positions of the twinkling stars says, "It is just past the middle of the night." Looking at the crates stacked and ready for loading he says, "I am supposing that you have our Shire nearby for us to harness to the crane."

"Aye, that I do," as she directs his gaze to where the grasses grow tall on the beach.

There in the twilight he sees the great white beast, "Ach, I thought it was a ghost!" He laughs and calls out, "Stefan!" The horse raises its head and snorts, shakes out its mane, and then puts its nose back down into the grass.

Mara says, "I'll fetch him. There's a pan of stew there by the fire. It's not much, but it's warm." She pulls him close and kisses him lingeringly, and then turns and makes her way toward the shore.

He watches as she goes. She is wearing her rompers, the trousers that she sews for herself to wear when she rides. "Will you be riding him then?"

She turns, with her fists on her hips, "You know he is too tall and too wide for me. I'm wearing my rompers because I am going sailing. La, didja ever see a sailor wearing a dress?"

A half-sized moon rises over the hill that surrounds this sparse estuary availing quite a bit more light for them to work by. The two of them are an efficient team, chattering the night away as they load all their worldly belongings. The morning sun warms them up as they take a break to enjoy some coffee and a bite to eat. The tide has turned before the rising of the sun, and they know that they must soon be on their way to make it safely through the narrow gap that leads from the cove to the open waters of the Malin Sea. Robert is tying down the sailcloth tarps that cover everything now stored securely in the hold of the ship when he hears Mara say, "Here they are now." He follows her line of sight to the top of the cliff, where the narrow lane starts down, to see a host of redcoats beginning the descent, "Their horses look to be accustomed to steep terrain, but we still have a while." Mara removes the harness from the great Shire workhorse that has been a faithful companion for so long, and pats him on the hind quarter sending him to the barnyard where the left-open gates will allow him to feast on loose hay. Next they bring aboard the animals that will be traveling with them; the cat, the goat, and the chickens, lashing their traveling cages together just forward of the tiny crewman's cabin. Then they carefully hide a small chest, containing their personal treasures and heirlooms, in the false wall of the cabin, another smuggler's trick. They have let the fire die down and with a paste of charcoal ash leave a note scrawled in large characters across the rocks of the quay. ***SAOIRSE***, which is their word for Freedom: something they will not allow to be taken from them. The lines are loosed from the dock cleats and the hoisted sails immediately fill with a favorable wind. The sound of shots fired comes from the direction of the descending redcoats, but to no avail for the distance is still too great. They both stare about them longingly as their homeland recedes. Mara makes a ceremony of removing her boots and then banging them together knocking off the soil of the land they leave behind. Robert has seen her do this one other time: when she left her family and the county where she had grown, to start her new life with him.

♡♡♡

The HMS Cooper, a slave ship accustomed to the warmer southern environs, is now sailing the colder northern waters surrounding the Hebrides. The Royal Navy is currently at war with the Navies of all the nations of Europe and is in desperate need of sailors. This captain and crew have been assigned the duty of plundering the fishing villages of these northern islands for able-bodied men willing to volunteer. They have collected many of these fishermen; willing or not. The most unwilling of the volunteers are locked in the hold, where the seeping cold damp and lack of food tend to shift even the most defiant attitudes toward compliance. Captain Derek is watching, from his command post on the quarterdeck, a hazing imposed upon the newest batch of *volunteers* by the seasoned deck hands. Cruel pranks are delivered hardest upon those who wail the loudest. His quota is nearly filled and he is anxious, along with his crew, to be away from these cold northern straits.

Turning the helm over to his first mate the captain descends the ladder, his gloved hands sliding smoothly down the rails, his feet nary touching a step. On the deck below he proceeds toward the crowd of unruly sailors who all immediately stand at attention, except for the initiates focused upon cleaning the offal that has been repeatedly dumped on the deck for them to swab over and over again. "Hmmmm ..." muses Captain Derek as he walks by with nothing else to say to his men. He wears a skull cap that barely holds in a wild fringe of hair hanging loose to his hunched shoulders. He keeps his hands settled comfortably deep inside the pockets of his long woolen coat, passing by without returning his men's salutes. The visage of this unkempt captain leaves most wondering how such a man has risen to his position.

He continues making his way across the deck, then hops up a ladder to the next deck, and another, where he arrives at the door to his personal cabin. He unlocks the door, and then once inside locks it again: this is his private chamber and he abhors interruptions. He sits at his table, opens the drawer of his desk and withdraws his hashish pipe. After smoking he sits back in his chair, awaiting the lightness of heart, even though he seldom ever feels that lightness anymore. He settles instead for a pale numbness.

He turns his thirty minute hourglass so that he will not be too long away from his duties. He then pours himself a glass of bourbon and stands looking out across the roiling swells. He shuts down his thoughts but the silence does not last long before he is dwelling again upon how he dislikes everything about this life he is living. It is a pointless cycle of thought that leaves him disliking himself. There is still sand remaining as he sets his empty glass back in the cabinet. He leaves his cabin and takes a circuitous route back to the helm.

Upon his return, and after checking the traverse board, he asks for a report from his first mate. "A sloop flying the VOC flag sails off the port side Sir," tipping his head to indicate a speck in the distance. Captain Derek pulls his spyglass from an inner pocket of his coat and raises it to peer across the waves. He brings the single-masted ship into focus and then scans the waters ahead.

To his first mate he says, "We will want to cut off the little bugger. We cannot allow these bloody smugglers their thieving." He slides the scope back inside his coat. "That dinky insignificant bucket is indeed flying the flag of our nation's current enemy, hah, yet is haaardly a warship." Now wringing his hands greedily and eyeing again the traverse tracking their course, "Aha, the rose shows that we are already set to close the gap. Well done, but we do not want to alarm the captain of that scow, so for now we will ease over gently until after nightfall. We'll set our course at a more direct angle once we can no longer be seen, and be there to o'ertake 'er at daybreak!"

"Splendid Sir, shall I tell the men?"

"Certainly! And," now feeling lighthearted with the prospect of an adventure, "give them all an extra jar of whiskey."

"Sir, yes Sir. Thank You Sir."

♡♡♡

Robert is noticing fewer fishing vessels than usual whilst passing amongst the islands of the Hebrides. Now in the wider channel of the Minch he spies an English frigate sailing out from within the straits, "Must be the same ship I witnessed harassing fishermen when I was by this way a few days ago."

Mara asks him, "What interest does the Royal Navy have so far north?"

"They are up to no good." He points the Tulip west, nearer to the Scottish coastline intending to stay out of the strong westerly current. He is keeping a watch on the English vessel and is not overly surprised to espy its change of course in what looks to be an attempt to cut him off. Wanting to be first to the Nord Zee he opens his sails to the wind, listing dramatically while skimming along at an exhilarating pace.

Mara braces herself close to the animals and sings to them soothingly in hopes of diminishing their dismayed reaction to this tilting world, "*A leanbh mo chléibh gon-eiri do chodhladh leat*," child of my heart sleep calmly. After a while the creatures are quiet and she has fallen asleep there next to them. The ship sails gracefully on.

As the sun descends Robert reels in the mainsail line a bit and allows the sails to flatten. The deck rights itself. He brings out his navigational tools and sights off the first stars that are visible while the shade of land is still discernible in the dusky dim. He is establishing the course he will be following through the night. He makes note of the compass bearing. He gauges the distance of the English ship that remains at full sail and is certain that it intends to cut him off. His calculations lend him to believe that he will reach the Nord Zee before they will.

Mara awakens and Robert shows her on his map where their progress has put them. "Here?" She asks him, pointing at a spot in the straits near where he had pointed. "Are there not tales of blue kelpies that swim in these waters?"

"The *fear gorm.* Yes."

"The blue men that swim like dolphins." He has told her of seeing these creatures, this aquatic race that so resemble humans.

"Aye," he smiles, "I have seen the blue kelpies swim in these straits, but they've never allowed me close enough to see them clearly. Always faraway."

"I hope I get to see the *fear gorm.*"

Robert opens the sails again. Their pace quickens and soon the Tulip is back up to speed.

♡♡♡

Captain Derek had remained at the helm, steadily taking new readings and calculating his ship's progress toward the inevitable overtaking of the smuggler's sloop. He had finally gone to his cabin for a few hours of sleep. As the sun rises he is at the helm again scanning the expanse surrounding them, but does not at first catch sight of his quarry. He fetches his spyglass and soon discovers the puny vessel so near to the shore that its visage blends with the rocky cliffs. Through the darkness he has kept his course safely away from landfall allowing this freebooter in his dinghy to capture the lead. "Damn the knave!" He scans what lies before them knowing that the Orkneys lie ahead, "We may still have a chance to catch this scoundrel." Turning to his Mate, "Set course to steer him through the Orcadian strait. That will put him within range of our cannon."

"Yes Sir!" The mate is remembering that the mandate of this voyage designates the northwestern waters of Scotland, leaving the Eastern coast to others. For a moment he considers commenting that sailing through the strait of the orcs will lead them into the North Sea, out of bounds of the area stipulated by their current directive. Being a sensible man, and not wanting to stir the ire of his Captain, he keeps his thoughts to himself.

As the day progresses they pass quite a number of Orkney fishing boats, possibly enough to complete their quota and allow them to return home, yet the Captain, in his determination to thwart this smuggler, stays his course. The crew, thick-headed and bad-tempered after last night's extra ration of liquor, grumble amongst themselves unhappily as they pass by the potential completion of their mission and the subsequent turning for home. "A fool's errand," some are whispering, "a sloop will out-maneuver a frigate. What is our Captain thinking?"

♡♡♡

Morning brings a calm sea and rain. Robert has spread a tarp to provide dry shelter for the animals. He sits with them now beneath the tarp. Mara is by him sleeping. In this calm moment he allows himself to grieve the passing of the life he's known. He had not bid a proper farewell to the home of his ancestors. Rather than looking back in pity though, he'd rather imagine the good things ahead. Rather than saying that we are too old for this he likes that there'll be some adventure in life, rather than the same old routines.

Instead of distressing himself thinking about the tiny shack next to a noisy sawmill, he imagines that his Dutch friend has found a more agreeable dwelling. La, he allows himself to imagine something very nice. A home that suits them perfectly.

When there is enough daylight he rises to take his bearings. He is pleased to discover that they are still on course, yet it is no surprise for there has been no change in the wind. Determining that the swells are calm enough he brings his longscope out from the cabin. He trains it toward the English Frigate and hones in on the quarterdeck where he catches the captain looking through a scope right back at him. The Englishman lowers his scope and raises two forefingers to his eyes and then turns them toward Robert. I see you. Then he performs a vulgar gesture. Robert lowers his scope. "The bastard is making threats."

Mara has awakened and is taking his arm, "Does he worry you?"

"He thinks to catch us in the narrows. Twill not be so. We might have to take evasive action."

"La? Evasive action?"

"It may be a ploy. There could be another English frigate awaiting for whatever this one drives through the narrows. They may hope to box us in. We will not want that to happen."

"What is our plan of action?"

"We can outrun them, but that would cast us off course."

"And we do not want our pets at sea longer than necessary."

"Nor you, my Dear."

"Right." She agrees. On occasion she has travelled with him, yet she is ever uneasy on the open water. "So ... our plan?"

"Do you remember me telling you that I have rebuilt my grandfather's *ballista*?"

"That giant-sized crossbow? Yes, I recall that you made some improvements. Have you been practicing? Can you hit a faraway target," she looks to him warily, "from beyond the range of their cannon?"

"The plan is to set a trap for this bastard to sail into."

She follows him as he reefs the mainsail. "Are you slowing us down?"

"Only enough for this plan to work. Then he uncovers and assembles the *ballista*. It is, as Mara had said, an oversized crossbow made of wood and iron and nearly as wide as his ship. After testing the workings of the crank and the gears he looks back jubilantly at the shrinking gap between them and their pursuers. He then gets Mara to assist him in rolling a barrel of flaxseed oil up a plank and over the aft gunwale. Before releasing it overboard he loosens the bung so that the oil will spread out across the surface of the water. They watch as it recedes away behind them closer and closer to the English vessel. He then instructs Mara, "Please bring a lit candle, for we will need to set flame to this torch." He is rubbing his palms together briskly in boyish anticipation.

Back with the flame Mara asks him, "How often have you had to do this sort of thing?"

"First time." He has set a heavy bolt into the iron channel of the behemoth, its tip wrapped in oil-soaked sailcloth. He then proceeds cranking back the cord, requiring all of his strength, until it latches. He points out to her where to touch the flame when he gives the signal. "You will want to watch," he tells her grinning broadly. He holds out his thumb at arms-length determining his range. He makes an adjustment to the angle, then with a heavy mallet in his hand. Shouts out to her, "Now!" She touches the fire to the bolt setting it alight, then he slams the mallet down on the latch releasing the missile. Watching with anticipation as the fiery bolt flies a graceful arc. It lands in the water near the oil barrel, which has drifted within close range of the English ship. At first nothing happens, but before long the sheen of oil that surrounds the cask catches fire giving the impression that the waves are burning. Then the wooden casket is afire heating the remaining oil. They see the barrel burst before hearing the *WHOOOMMMPPH* of the blast. Oily flames are splattered all over the exposed hull of the English ship.

Mara, watching through the scope is aghast, "Oh my. Oh my. Ohmyohmyohmy," she lowers the glass, looking to her man tentatively, "They'll not be able to stop the fires."

"Tis the fate of a foolish captain to lose his ship at sea. Let's hope there are lifeboats enough for his crew."

♡♡♡

Aboard the HMS Cooper Captain Derek is dumfounded by the gall of this pipsqueak to have fancied the preposterous concept of taking on a frigate of the Royal English Navy. "Bring her around broadside while he is within range of our cannon." Then as an afterthought, "Get these fires put out!" Sailors are already dumping hastily filled buckets of water over the gunwale attempting to stop the flames. The water only spreads the burning oil. Other sailors have manned the bilge pumps while their mates attempt to direct the stinking rot toward the devouring flames. One of the ship's boats is lowered and from down below sailors in the boat are doing their best to splash seawater up in a futile effort to douse the expanding inferno.

Captain Derek, confident that his crew will extinguish the fires, continues to watch through his spyglass as his foe's sails unfurl to catch the wind, "Get this hulk turned! They are getting away! Prepare to fire the cannons!" The flames rise up over the rail before him. He steps back away from the heat. Looking around he is at last realizing that his entire crew is battling an out-of-control inferno. Now he understands why his orders to bring the ship around have not been enacted. He takes a last look at the receding sloop that has brought about this unforgivable downfall, and while shaking his fist declares, "You'll have not seen the last of me!"

The prisoners in the hold, are released by an older sailor, a man who like these captives, began his service with the Royal Navy after being snatched from his own fishing boat out of Galway Bay. Once on deck the prisoners, witnessing the sorry state of affairs, begin throwing anything that might hold them afloat into the sea and then jump overboard, liking their chances of enduring the cold waters over the unlikelihood of surviving this burning disaster. More and more of the English sailors are doing the same; tossing over barrels and crates filled with the ship's supplies, hoping that there will be something floating for them to hang onto when they are forced to abandon ship. A few of the ensigns have joined in the task of turning the ship toward shore, hoping that a closer proximity to land will ease the amount of time to be endured in the shivery sea water. The ship's boat that had been lowered in the effort to fight the oil-spattered flames has filled rapidly with evacuating sailors and is now rowing away in an effort to escape being swamped by the rush of bolting mates. The other ship's boat has sailors shinnying down its lines even before it has splashed down on the surface of the waves.

The Captain, in a rare show of bravado, takes the helm, sending his first mate scurrying after all the others vying for any remaining positions aboard the departing pinnace. Standing at the great wheel doing his best to steer toward shore he is nearly thrown off his feet when the cover of the closest hatch is blown open by the forces of heat and flame raging belowdeck. The entire ship suddenly lists dramatically, forcing Captain Derek to grip the wheel as the deck tips out from under him. Dangling from the teetering ship's wheel over empty space he casts a final glance in the direction of the disappearing sloop that has brought about this disgrace upon him and the nation he serves. He shouts defiantly to that unknown captain, "You are now and forevermore the sworn enemy of the Royal English Navy!" The ship's wheel breaks free, dropping him sputtering into the chilling water. His grip of the great wooden wheel keeps him from sinking. He looks around at all the other floating debris until he catches sight of a barrel of the navy's whiskey which he determines to be serviceable enough to hold him up and out of the water. Upon reaching the large wooden cask he throws his arms over it and pulls his body up, but the barrel rolls taking him with it and providing him with another frigid dousing.

♡♡♡

Robert watches the burning ship with mixed emotions, surprised at how circumstances have conspired his participation in this conflict. While there have always been conflicts and wars fought all around him, he has previously maintained a neutral attitude which has allowed him to remain a non-participant. He wishes to disengage and to sail free.

Mara, still watching the doomed ship through the lens of the spyglass, has her own mixed emotions; feeling anxious for all those despairing sailors, yet also feeling a sense of pride in having dealt such a blow to the oppressors. Lowering the scope now, the scene is shrunk to a plume of black smoke on the horizon. As she scans the sea around them she notices a ship off starboard, between them and the shoreline, sailing north. She raises the glass again and upon sighting the British flag furled on its mast tells Robert,

"There is the frigate that would have cooperated with the other to box us in."

"We could have sped away before they had set the trap."

She moves to sit beside him, "Are you having misgivings for what we have done?"

"Aye, this world provides enough for all: there is no need for war." She hands over his spyglass and he takes a look across the waves, "At least those who survived the fire will welcome the arrival of their own navy." They are pleasantly distracted by a passing group of dolphins. He stands, leaving the tiller to her, and then fills two tankards with a potent concoction of beer and whiskey. Handing over one of the tall mugs to Mara, they toast, "To us!"

They are silent for a bit, then she laughs out loud, "La, I must tell you my Dear, that was a spectacular accomplishment. When that barrel of oil exploded I nearly fainted in surprise. I had no idea that what you had planned would be such a sight to see. I will remember it forever!"

"Shall we do it again?" he asks, suddenly shifting away from his brooding.

"Heavens no! It is too frightening! La!"

"What would our ancestors think?"

His remark sparks in her a memory of the dreaming she had awakened from on the day of his return, "They visited recently."

"Our ancestors? Have you dreamed again of Éire's Queen and King?"

"Um-hmm. I had played my great harp before lying down to sleep. Then, when I became aware that I was dreaming I was visiting with them. We were all seated upon our thrones dressed in furs and finery, with jewels and gold circling our hair." She pauses, reaching up to turn his cheek so she can gaze into his eyes, before continuing, "You were with me

Rob." She often brings him into her dreaming, the same as she has attracted him into her waking.

Robert reaches into memory, for he shares this desire for shared dreaming, "Ah, yes; it is coming to me." A quizzical look appears from his eyes, "Is it a foretelling?"

Verifying that he is remembering the same as she had dreamed, she tells him, "They showed us two other necklaces of Golden Hearts identical to the necklace that we bring with us." His bewildered expression has her laughing.

"It is hard for me to imagine," thinking of the magnificence of her necklace of golden hearts, "That there could be more than one."

Her charming musical laughter brings the dolphins out of the water again.

♡♡♡

As the days pass by. Mara grows restless. She busies herself weaving on her small loom, but it is not the same as sitting at home weaving with the stark beauty of the cove outside her windows. She hopes that their new home will have windows and a pleasant scene to look out upon. In Holland the land does not rise up. There are no mountains. Robert's description of a timber hut set on logs does not instill in her a sense of contentedness. As they sail through the traffic of the coastal shipping lane their progress slows, and then slows even more as they move into the wide expanse of the River Rijn. It takes two days for Robert to weave the Tulip through the vast array of ships waiting in line to enter the Port of Rotterdam. "I have been here when there were so many ships, so close together that none were able to move. A complete impasse. I am glad not to be sailing into the port. We will sail past them all." As they move further up the river they pass a moorage where a dock, and a windmill sit amongst the homes of a settlement situated at the entrance to a canal. "Look. There is a magnificent loading crane." He is pointing and explaining, "A shaft from the windmill turns the wooden cogs that raise and lower the boom. Tis a mechanical wonder."

"You would like to have yourself a crane like that." She has heard him tell of these windmill driven cranes.

The afternoon turns out to be warm, and even though there are clouds scuttling across the sky, there is no rain. It is a big sky. There are no mountains, nor even rolling hills; only water and flat land. Mara sits atop their cargo watching the passing shoreline. Robert, feeling a bit drowsy, lets his eyelids be softened by the warmth of the afternoon sun.

Sailing this wide river which is much smoother than the sea, they grow accustomed to the quiet sound of the ship skimming along easily. They grow used to the sound of the wind blowing across the lowlands. They become used to the sound of the rain as it spatters on their hats and coats. They are used to hearing the calls and watching the variety of birds passing by. They have passed by noisy gristmills, with Robert explaining the windmill's inner workings. They have passed even noisier oil mills. "There are rows and rows of rods stamping up and down turning the seeds to mash."

"Ach, it is a terrible ruckus! Is the sawmill we will be living next to as loud as this?"

"Almost."

"Oh dear," she moans.

Later in the afternoon they begin hearing something that grows louder as they get closer. It is a steadily repeated whoosh, whoosh, whoosh. There is an accompanying ticking, and underlying it all is a deep thumping, along with a rumbling rubbing. The hum of all these sounds drones on and on and on. Mara is scanning both shorelines through the mist, but she cannot see what is causing all the racket. She finally asks Robert, "What is that noise? Is that another sort of windmill?"

"That, my Dear, is a windmill driven sawmill," he answers. "It is Philip Haumann's mill, and shortly we will mooring at his dock. We have at last reached our destination. Here, you will want this," holding out to her a tuft of sheep's wool, "for stuffing your ears to deaden the sound."

Leaving Poland

There are chickadees flittering in the bushes here at the summit of the mountain pass. They are a cheerful group enjoying these warmer days of springtime. Now that the snow is mostly gone from these mountains these tiny black-capped birds are seeing horses with riders again. Now there is even a team of horses drawing a wagon. These horses are larger than any of the animals that call this mountain wilderness home. They stamp their hooves boastfully; proud that they have arrived successfully at the summit after many days of climbing. The wagon they have brought behind them is brightly colored and sits atop six wide wheels. These horses have pulled the wagon off the roadway and have stopped. The chickadees watch four fledgling humans jump out of the back. The flock of little birds flutter around the wagon, the horses, and the people before they fly off announcing to all that there are visitors in the forest.

The family that has disembarked from the big bright wagon stand in awe of their surroundings. From the direction they have come the land drops into a vista of mountains, and in the direction they intend to go the land drops into another vista of mountains. The nearby peaks that rise above them are still topped with snow. Indeed, throughout the day they have crossed patches of snow in the shadowy portions of the roadway. Up until now the road has been rugged and barely passable in some places because of the mud, the old ruts, and the debris that has sloughed off the hillsides. They stand now upon the wide flat paving stones where an ancient Roman road begins. The children are examining the pavers. The oldest son Razs is amazed, "Wow. These are huge! This is Awesome!"

"They are so smooth," his sister Kirin rubs the toe of her boot over the edge of a paving stone, "like the worn steps of a tower."

"Our wagon's wheels will no longer be sinking in the mud." Their brother Vejz pumps his fist.

"I love this place," gushes the youngest, Audrae. She is standing at a large fire pit and looking around at the flattened areas where tents have been pitched. "Looks like folks camp here all the time."

"Folks have camped on this spot for hundreds of years, or thousands, or like, forever." Her father says, "Even I have camped here before."

"This is the farthest you have ever been along this road?" asks his wife Annia. "So tomorrow the route will be as new for you as for the rest of us."

"Right!" He answers, "Now, boys do you want to take care of the horses, or would you prefer to scrounge up some firewood?"

The two young fellas look at each other, happy to be given the choice, "We'll get wood for the fire," and off into the trees they go.

"I'll help with the horses," offers Kirin already loosening a buckle.

"I'll get water," Audrae tells them while pulling a bucket out from a storage box between the axles. "There looks to be a spring right over there."

They busy themselves removing the harness from the team of horses and leading them to graze upon new grass that has sprung up where so recently there has been snow. Annia reaffirms, "So the roadway from here on is paved?"

"Yes, paved and downhill." Her husband Renaldo answers, "Let's hope it is not too steep."

With the horses tethered, the fire burning, and dinner being prepared the family begins speculating about how cold it might be tonight. Razs informs them, "It is a clear sky so it will be very cold."

"Without clouds we will see more stars," Vejz says. "We'll see the Milky Way." He hears something, "Shhh! Listen." Having their attention, "What's that? Is there someone coming up the road?" So far today, they have seen no one else.

They all peer down the pavered road. Sure enough, there are two riders making their way up the steep cobbled roadbed. Renaldo shouts, "Hallo!"

Both riders look up and wave, "Hallo," they answer, "*Guten Tag*!" They are leading a third horse saddled with gear. Even though there are warnings of brigands along this road, these men are well outfitted and respectfully dressed, seeming to pose no threat. They stop and dismount.

Renaldo introduces himself, "Greetings. I am Renaldomus Gedimin." He then introduces the rest of his family, "My wife, Annia, and our children, Razs, Kirin, Vejz, and Audrae." Each curtsies or bows as they are introduced. "We have chosen to camp here for the night, and we would be honored for you gentlemen to join us."

The two newcomers, one a tall burly man, the other a short slim fellow, thank him and tell him that this is their intended bivouac for the night. "We are scouting ahead for a group that is planning an expedition over this pass," noting that the Gedimin's wagon has made it thus far, "and are pleased to see that the road is ready." They report that the road that they have traversed, the road leading down from here into the valley, is clear of snow, "Although there are places where water from the melting snow runs over the pavers."

As they set up their tent the big guy tells them, "My associate is a rider for the postal brigade, and I am a minister of the Westphalian Society for Peace." He looks around before adding, "We worked together on the treaties of Westphalia." This man speaks well; he is an orator and used to speaking eloquently.

Renaldo is impressed, "The treaties ending the wars."

"Well, the treaties have not entirely ended the wars, but they did bring representatives of all the countries to one table."

He is called out by Kirin, "But they didn't all sit at one table!"

"Right you are, my dear!" Laughing a great belly laugh the big guy slaps his partner's shoulder, "We are amongst a well-informed crowd here my friend!"

"The members of the two religions would not sit at one table," fills in the postal carrier. "So the Catholics gathered in Münster while the Protestants met in Osnabrück. I was one of the many to carry proposals back and forth between the two conventions."

"A two days ride for most," admiringly commending his friend, "ridden in a day by the riders of the express brigade."

"Wow. Cool." All the family members are envisioning themselves riding a fast horse on an important mission.

Annia asks, "Is the Society for Peace still active?"

"Oh yes, my dear lady," speaking in his deep baritone as he dips his head in deference to her, "we are currently preparing to bring a delegation of the Polish-Lithuanian Commonwealth to a meeting with the invading Swedes so that borders that have been agreed upon will be honored."

"It will be a great accomplishment," the postal rider infers, "to convince the Swedes and the Russians to honor the terms of the treaties they have signed!"

"It will be nice when everybody agrees to get along," Kirin says wistfully.

♡♡♡

After the evening meal Razs, Vejz, and Audrae are poking sticks deep into the fire's red coals and then sharpening the charred ends on the rocks surrounding the firepit. The postal express rider has joined them, bringing his own long straight stick to sharpen. After performing animal calls for their entertainment he is now attempting to teach the kids these same calls. They are being noisy. Inside the wagon Annia and Kirin are practicing lessons by candle light. The taller diplomat, organizer of peace negotiations, walks out on the point where Ren sits watching the last colors of the day fade into the night. "Mind if I join you?" Ren is startled and makes as if to stand. "Do not bother standing for my sake. I apologize if I have startled you. I hope that I have not interrupted your contemplation." He takes a seat, then noticing that there is a steep drop off, scoots a little way back from the edge.

Renaldo slides back so that he does not have to turn around to visit. He points across the tops of all those mountains toward a line of dark clouds, tinged purple by the setting sun, "It looks as if we may have some clouds moving our way."

"Um-hmm." He does not pursue the topic of the weather, instead asks, "If I may be so bold, I must say that I am fascinated by you and your family, and intrigued by your brightly colored home on wheels." Because Renaldo is slow to answer he continues, "You and your family are well-mannered, well-educated, and well-dressed. Your wagon and team of horses are of the finest quality." Renaldo continues to watch the sky as more and more stars appear. "Your surname is a close match to the royal Polish lineage."

Renaldo turns to face the older man eye to eye, "An astute observation. I suppose your position as a diplomatic emissary has you acquainted with the domestic affairs of many nations."

Chuckling deprecatingly he answers, "The wars brought nations together as allies. Nations that have warred against each other have now joined against a common foe." The man speaks with practiced eloquence. "Your nations of Poland and Lithuania have formed an alliance against the common enemies of Sweden and Russia. I am very interested in the form of governing adopted by this alliance, this *Serene Commonwealth*."

Renaldo waves away a moth, "You assume correctly that we are Polish. Is it your interest in the government of the Commonwealth that has you traveling over these mountains?"

"We intend to bring together a delegation to meet with the Swedes, who are breaking the terms of the treaty they signed at Westphalia. I am sure you are aware that they have invaded the northernmost portion of your commonwealth."

"A lot of good, these treaties eh?"

Familiar with this sentiment the ambassador answers optimistically, "The treaties are something new and will take time before all nations agree upon the importance of respecting borders." They sit silently for a bit. It is dark enough now that there are bats flying overhead: flickering shadows passing by against the backdrop of the stars. "Tell me if I understand correctly: in your *Republic* the king is elected by representatives of the people?" For an answer Renaldo nods yes. "The former rulers willingly stepped aside allowing these newly elected 'kings' to rule?" Again Renaldo nods yes. "How does all this impact the lives of commoners?" Renaldo flashes a bewildering smile, barely discernable in this dim light so far away from the fire. "Or should I be asking how has all this impacted the lives of these former rulers' families?" At last Renaldo laughs out loud leading the diplomat to ask, "What?"

Renaldo sighs. He looks up at the wide band of the Milky Way. "My grandfather's brother was King. I grew up, and have raised my family, at court." A sudden cold gust blows up from the canyon below rustling the branches. "I have served as a judge for the King, a judge sent by the King's advisors to administer justice wherever there was a dispute to be settled." He is not used to talking about himself, but continues, "I grew to love the travel. I love passing through nature. I love sitting under this star-filled sky."

"So now you share your love of adventure with your family?"

"Our shared love of adventure. Our shared love of travel. Our shared desire to live common lives away from the busy city."

"Common?"

"I believe, as you seem to believe, that the vast majority of people do not require the protection of laws. Most folks wish to get along agreeably with others. Integrity is all that is required. I like thinking that all humanity is inclined toward integrity. Most common everyday people live their lives with integrity. In our travels we hope that along the way we will share in the lives of common everyday people." Renaldo rises from his seated position in an easy quick movement, then extends a hand to the older gentleman offering him assistance up from the ground.

Thinking of this family of royals traveling amongst commoners the diplomat tells Renaldo, "I am reminded of a fable about a king and queen disguising themselves as peasants in order to live easier simpler lives."

♡♡♡

Annia awakens earlier than the others, as she does most days. She feels the brisk air on her nose. She can tell by the dim light coming through the caravan's windows that the sun is not yet high enough for full daylight. She has been dreaming again of riding a wonderfully fast horse across a wide open landscape. It is a dream of another lifetime: an era of riders carrying very little with them. On this cold morning she is grateful for the warmth within this hulking wagon, and grateful for the heavy horses that pull the wagon, and grateful to be away from the confines of the city, and grateful to hear the morning chatter of these high mountain birds. She dresses and pulls a knit cap over her head and a tightly woven shawl around her shoulders, then steps quietly through the door and out into freshly fallen snow.

Walking toward the firepit she hears the black-capped birds of yesterday and greets them, "Good Morning chick-a-dee-dee-dee," mimicking their call. A crowd of the little birds flitter around her, as well met friends. She has previously befriended birds like these in other places. She likes to think that she is recognized now throughout the species. So that even though she may have never encountered these individual birds, the familiarity is shared within all their kind. "It is nice to have friends wherever we go. Chick-a-dee-dee-dee." Even with the snow all around there remains a warm and dry center in the firepit that she is able to stir into life. Then with a few small sticks she has flames again. Looking up she perceives the sky is clearing, and that there is sunlight touching the hilltops. She determines that by the time they have had something to eat and hitched the horses the snow will be melted and they will enjoy another sunny spring day.

She fills a kettle and sets it on a rock near the flames, then while it warms she strolls out to the spot where her husband had sat whilst visiting with the minister of peace. Ren has passed on to her the gist of the conversation, and what had particularly struck her was the comment about the legend of royals living as commoners. From the history of her ancestors she has been taught that in ages past Gods and Goddesses visited this earth disguised as commoners. And that some still visit by being born as a human baby and experiencing life first hand. She has been further taught that these celestials have frequently chosen to be born into her own family's royal line. Newborns are often given names reflecting this belief: thus her full name, Deviannia. She has been used to a morning dance practice, yet here beneath this pink sky of the sunrise amidst the snow all around she is happy to sing her morning prayers quietly to herself. She is interrupted by the postal rider calling out, "Your water is boiling away. Would you like me to move it from the heat?"

"Yes please, that would be wonderful. Thank you." Walking back to the fire she tells him, "I will be brewing coffee. You are welcome to have some."

"Oh, don't mind me M'lady. I'm used to caring for m'self."

M'lady. "Please Sir, there is no need for such formality. We are everyday people."

His eyes grow wide. His eyebrows arch higher on his forehead. His mouth drops open, "Oh M'lady! I daresay that I am able to distinguish members of the aristocracy." While watching her pour the hot water over the coffee grounds he gathers his thoughts, then speaking in as dignified as possible tone, "You and your family are all so well-mannered. You speak evenly and clearly. You carry yourselves with confidence. Most telling though, is that your offspring are well-educated." He stops himself and bows to let her know that he means no disrespect, "beggin' your pardon if I have spoken too boldly." He is nearly down on one knee in obeisance.

"Stop!" She laughs, "Get your cup. I do believe this coffee to be nearly ready."

♡♡♡

Before long the minister and the postal rider are standing with Annia and Renaldo at the campfire, each holding a steaming cup of hot coffee. All around them the melting snow dripping off the branches makes a staccato rhythm. The sun's rays are opening up miniature yellow blossoms, bright lavender clusters, and diminutive white bells in the grasses all around the campsite. All manner of clouds pass by overhead; billowy clouds, followed by longer flat dark-bottomed clouds, followed by wispy fluffs, and followed by hurrying masses that momentarily hide the sun. "Oh, brrrr, it gets cold whenever the sun goes behind a cloud," Annia shivers.

"Yes indeed!" The tall orator happily delivers the proverbial weather cliché, "Yes indeed, there is every sort of weather in the springtime here in the mountains," a calculated pause, "all in the passing of an hour." He laughs, encouraging everybody else to laugh with him. Then he generously throws out an offer that he does not foresee being accepted, "Your route from here is quite steep. We can stick around a while if you require any assistance." After a moment's pause he continues, "Oh, but surely you will not need us, so we'll pack up and be on our way."

"We appreciate your offer." Renaldo answers, "We've got a handle on this." Then to Annia, "How about us? Shall we hitch the team to our wagon and be on our way?"

"I'm ready to go."

The younger Gedimins remain inside sleeping while their parents hitch the team. Annia and Renaldo put four horses at the front of the wagon, and two at the back for holding the wagon steady on the steep portions of road ahead. The children have risen from their beds and are out and about as all is finished up. The Gedimins are ready to go as the two diplomats are also mounting up to be on their way. Farewells are bidden and these two wayfaring groups set off in opposite directions. It gets exciting right away as the heavy caravan rolls down the first steep incline. The two horses hitched at the back of the wagon are well trained and know to dig in and lean their weight back into their breech straps. The youths are out and taking turns walking alongside the horses. Sometimes they like to hoist themselves up onto a horses' back and will ride rather than walk. The ancient roadway is really quite an extraordinary feat of engineering. Hillsides have been cut away making corners wider. Steep terrain leveled by traversing the roadbed crossways of the mountain's flank. Where there would be washouts the engineers have lain drainage beneath the road's surface. After the initial drop from the summit the grade maintains sensibly and the team of horses enjoy an easy pace.

By late afternoon they have descended from the steepest portion and are now passing the wilderness dwellings of the men who cut down the trees of the forest. Their route is now littered with the bark scraped off the logs that have been dragged along this way. The road rises and falls, meandering through a forest so thick that the road has become a very narrow passage with barely room enough for the wagon. Audrae asks, "What will we do if we meet somebody going the other direction?" Barely after she has asked, they are startled by the sound of rapidly approaching hoofbeats. They are at a bend in the road and so unable to see what is coming toward them. Ren is pulling back on the reins to slow the wagon as three riders come around the bend at full pace. All three are forced to reign in hard. Their horses' front feet come up and down in a frenzy. The wagon's team stops instantly, shaking everything loose inside the wagon, and now dance nervously nose to nose with the horses of these riders, who are attempting to resituate themselves after being jolted nearly out of their saddles. Their horses are loaded as if on their way home from market. Contents of loosely bound bags of goods are now spilling out. Overwrought chickens that have been slung over the horses' flanks with their feet tied are squawking wildly, with wings flapping frantically. Each of the three riders is attempting to hang on to a wooden cask under one arm while struggling to control his horse with the other. Two of the chickens break loose and while one runs back the way it has come the other is up and tearing the hat off a rider's head and then is flapping toward the dancing horses of the wagons' team. Audrae, seated on a lead horse's back, reaches up and is able to capture the poor scared creature and bring it down into a safe embrace.

Renaldo and Annia standing up from the driver's bench, are both thinking it is strange that these riders carrying so much are going so fast ... unless, "These must be bandits! They are being chased by those they have stolen from." They have both come to the same conclusion. Meanwhile these riders, that seem to be in such a hurry, are seeing no way around the wagon. They start hollering "*Aus Dem Wag*," wanting this wagon out of the way. There are turnouts along the way, but none nearby. Ren does not see the point in backing the wagon. Besides, the generally accepted rules of the road grant him the right of way. So he mischievously flicks the reins for the team to move forward. The rider's horses, being no match to the much larger beasts, turn in an effort to get out of the way. The riders are kicking heels into their horses' flanks, yanking viciously on the horses' reins, and cursing wildly as they spin round and round spilling loot all over the road. Ren and Annia cannot help but laugh. Audrae, hanging on with her knees, is still holding the hen whose cackling reminds her of laughter.

"*Aus Dem Wag*," shouts one of the riders as he is still trying to settle his horse. Razs, Vejz, and Kirin have squeezed themselves around the wagon and made their way up next to their horses to see what the commotion is all about. They are totally amazed at this standstill. "*Aus Dem Wag*," the burly rider is shouting over and over. He is sounding quite agitated. Razs sees him reaching for the flintlock in his waistband and hurriedly reaches down and grabs a rock. Straightening up, he slings the rock at the fiend who now has a firearm pointed in the direction of his parents. Razs' well-aimed missile hits the side of the man's head with enough force to knock him out of the saddle. As the fellow hits the pavers his gun goes off, setting the startled horses to bucking and spinning again. Now all three of the ruffians are on the ground as their horses race away in the only direction they are able to go.

The children, hedged in close, settle the team horses easily enough. Ren hands over the reins to Annia while asking offhandedly, "What was it he was shouting?" Carrying his staff, he leaps lightly over the horse's backs and landing on the ground near these three troublemakers he shouts, "*Aus Dem Weg*. Get out of the way yourselves!" Kirin, who has grabbed another staff moves forward next to her father and pokes one of the brutes as he is attempting to rise, hard enough to convince him to stay down.

Audrae who is still sitting on the back of a lead horse and still holding a chicken asks, "La, what do we do now?" Everybody else is wondering the same when they hear the rumbling of rapidly approaching horses. Razs and Vejz have joined their father and sister, wielding their own heavy staffs. The bandits make as if to flee but think differently after being forcibly jabbed by these staffs. The bandits' confused horses are being chased back by a group of riders, all brandishing some sort of cudgel. The three rider-less horses, once again trapped with nowhere to go, are now stamping and bucking and neighing. This new group of riders come to a halt and because of the ruckus remain in their saddles wary of dismounting into this melee. It is a standstill. Nobody is sure of what is going on here.

Now it is Annia who skips out over the backs of the wagon's horses tapping Audrae on her way, "We need to settle these poor beasts." They hop over the lead horses' ears landing nimbly in the fray, and easily gather up the loose reins and calm the three horses. One of the new riders dismounts. Walking forward tentatively, unsure of this situation until Annia tells him, "We are travelers on the road and not in cahoots with these hooligans. It would appear that they are thieves that have stolen from you. We do not wish to interfere with their apprehension. Our desire is to be allowed to continue on our way." She hands over the reins of the two horses she has charge of, indicating for Audrae to do the same, then moves back toward the wagon. Ren and the boys are coaxing the team to back the wagon away allowing room for whatever justice will be served here.

"Danke," this man tells Annia while accepting the reins from her and the chicken from Audrae. The rest of the posse riders dismount. They move forward menacingly waving their clubs and staffs. Each takes a turn poking and kicking the three on the ground. Ropes and straps appear and the three are tied and then gruffly tossed over the saddles of their horses. As what is left of the stolen goods are retrieved the same man that had spoken his thanks bows to the Gedimins and thanks them again, "Danke, Danke, Danke," bowing each time. "You have done us a great service and we would be very grateful if you will choose to stay the night in our humble village and allow us to show our gratitude." He bows again.

Annia accepts, "We will be pleased to share your hospitality. Lead on good Sir."

♡♡♡

The forest opens up and now the road follows a creek that will eventually become a river. There are homesteads with gardens watered by ditches leading from the little river and there are fields of sprouting grains, orchards just past blossoming, cows, sheep, pigs, horses, mules, and chickens. All appears orderly and well cared for. The men of the troop take turns riding alongside the travel-wagon pointing out the prosperity of the land. They are proud of their bounty. They tell of rebuilding now that the wars are over. "A few of the mercenaries that came to fight the foreigners' wars have hung behind. They complain that with the wars ending they are left without jobs. Such are the three apprehended today," explains the man who is currently riding along beside them.

It is early evening when they arrive at the village. The hearty odors of cooking waft on the breeze. A crowd of children run out to greet the procession and quickly begin taunting the three troublemakers, who are already miserable from the bumping they have endured slung over their horses' backs. The village is upstream from the confluence of two small rivers forming a wide expanse of narrow channels and sandbars. The rolling foothills rise all around. The Gedimins are instructed to park the wagon in the village square, and the horses allowed to feast on the grass growing there on the commons. The prisoners are taken away and tied up near the riverbank, presenting an easy source of mud for the younger village children to heave at them. The older children of the village eagerly introduce themselves to Razs, Kirin, Vejz, and Audrae. Dinner is a feast served on long tables under a communal roof.

After dinner an old timer asks Renaldo, "Now tell us sir, if you do not mind, where you are headed in your bright fancy wagon."

"We are following this road. Perhaps we will eventually see Amsterdam."

"Are you chasing tales of easy fortunes to be made in the lowlands?"

Ignoring what seems to be a bit of the rancor that mountain folk traditionally hold toward lowlanders he answers, "Actually, we are interested to see the windmills. We are fascinated by what we have heard of them. Great tall machines they are."

A man of his age tells him, "The road of pavers that you have been driving has long since been washed out here, but still continues once across the river. This time of year the water may be running too high for your wagon to get across."

"How deep is the water?"

"Let's go take a look." They all stand and follow this fellow who is explaining, "Where the pavers of your road have washed away the river is wide and shallow. There are sand bars separating the main channel and a couple other smaller channels."

There is disagreement among the men of the village about whether or not the high water of the spring run-off will allow a crossing so early in the season. But there is an answer for that argument, "It is running too high and fast this late in the day, but early in the morning it will be low and slow enough. You'll see." Off they go to inspect the river crossing.

Renaldo gauges the depth of the river uncertainly. There are places that look deep enough to put his wagon's axles under water, possibly deep enough to float his wagon away. He tells the men, "I would be wary of attempting a crossing with the river at the level it is now."

Another fellow who believes the river can be crossed tells him, "It still gets cold enough at night to stop the snow's melting long enough for the river to drop. The water will be considerably shallower early in the morning. You'll see.

Besides, there'll be all of us here to keep you from floating away."

"Okay then, we will be ready to make the crossing early in the morning."

♡♡♡

The men return to the tables where many of the villagers have brought out instruments and are playing music while the others sing. After a while someone asks the Gedimins to teach them some new songs, songs they have not heard before. Razs gets his zither, Kirin her flute, Vejz has a drum, and Audrae a set of hand pipes. Annia plays a harp and Renaldo another zither. They are able to perform a few songs that the villagers have never heard before, and different versions of songs that they are familiar with. The villagers like their music and many of them are dancing and singing along. It is a regular party.

When at last the revelry settles down and the conversation grows quiet, one of the teenage girls that has been sharing tales with Kirin and Audrae asks Annia, "Please tell us the tale of," uncertain of the name, "Kupala."

Annia scans the crowd and receives nods of encouragement; everyone is interested to hear a new tale. She has lain her harp aside, but now picks it up again and begins a quiet simple melody. The harp's strings, strummed so eloquently, have a soothing dreamlike quality that acts like a lullaby on the gathered crowd. She begins the tale, "Our ancestors believed there to be many Gods and Goddesses, and that these celestial beings will occasionally visit us here on this earthly realm. One such Goddess is named Kupala, and she abides in water; in rivers, lakes, and rain." Annia coaxes the sound of rainfall from the strings of her harp, magically drawing the attention of all her listeners.

She is interrupted by the same girl who had asked before, "Tell us of Kupala's Eve."

Annia smiles, "Kupala's Eve is at the cusp of spring and summer. We are taught that on this solstice night unattached young women and unattached young men may find a mate." She whispers now, "Some like to believe that those of age are allowed one night of love-making without the usual consequences." Tis a fantasy for many. Annia's fingers fly across the strings of her little harp. She is gazing up into the starry sky. She continues, "This is the tale of one particular maiden who walked into the forest on Kupala's Eve seeking her mate. It is safe for her to walk in the woods on this night for it is the one night each year that the fern flowers bloom. The fern flower is a flame. It is wonderful to imagine walking through a dark forest illumined by tiny flames." Now her fingers' trilling of the harp's strings allows everybody to envision a nighttime forest alight with many tiny blooms of fire. "This fair maiden, wearing a wreath upon her head, follows a lighted forest pathway to Kupala's Mere. As tradition dictates she and the young man that has been waiting for her wade into the lake beneath the moonlight, the starlight, and the mystical light of the fern flowers." Annia sweeps the harpstrings over and over. Everybody feels their hearts beating a bit faster. "The Goddess Kupala appears from across the lake. Her presence radiates with even more light. Splendid in her beauty and grandeur, she transforms the maiden's wreath of evergreens into a wreath of Golden Hearts. Then Kupala presents the young man with a sphere; a golden orb that hums wondrously." Annia pauses her telling of the story, while playing the chorus of a lullaby that tells this same tale. It is an enchanting interlude that she repeats, allowing some in the crowd to be off to bed. Annia begins telling the tale again, "There are those who believe that the wreath and the orb remain here with us still. That the wreath has become a necklace of Golden Hearts, and that the orb has the power of dreaming." Now Annia's harpstrings surprise everyone with a crescendo of tones that leave all who are listening feeling sleepily happy and satisfied.

Annia scans the crowd hoping as ever for a spark of familiarity with the subject of the Golden Hearts. She has been bequeathed a necklace of Golden Hearts and the accompanying Orb of Dreaming. Her heirlooms have been passed down through her family over the ages. She has been taught that there are two more identical necklaces, and that the three are destined to be joined together.

♡♡♡

Morning is heralded by the rooster's "Er-er-er-er-Errrrrr." The sound wakens Renaldo. He breathes in and smiles at the wonder of yesterday's events. He smiles at the warmth and comfort of his bed. He smiles at the presence of his beloved Annia next to him, and the presence of his beloved children sleeping in their own beds nearby. He smiles at his happiness. He smiles at the prospect of rolling this caravan that they call home across the wide gravel beds and sandbars of the river. He knows that as soon as the sun rises the snow and ice will begin melting and the river will rise. It is a cycle repeated every day of every springtime. "Er-er-er-er-Errrrrr," calls the rooster. Ren slips quietly out of bed and quietly out the door. Standing in the cool morning air he puts on his jacket and walks to the river to see if the water level has dropped as considerably as he has been told.

There are a couple of men his age already standing at the river's bank; one of them has been there keeping watch over the prisoners, while the other has arrived to take his place. They each greet Renaldo and are pleased to point out to him the much lower water level. They also point out the clear morning sky, "The sun will warm things quickly. The water will rise quickly. You will want to ready your wagon quickly." They laugh.

Renaldo tells them, "I have explained all this to my family. They are prepared to rise early." Now looking back he sees his two boys hopping down from the wagon and making their way over to where he stands.

The two village men greet Razs and Vejz, "Good morning young fellas. You are early to rise."

Both nod and greet the older men, "Good morning sirs." Then they ask, "Will we make it across?"

"Yes. I believe so," answers their father. "Are your mother and sisters out of bed?"

"They are." Vejz is looking over at the three prisoners, still tied, and pitifully peeking out from under the blankets thrown over them. Then he asks the two villagers, "What will become of them?"

"They will be invited to work off what they have stolen. And if they are willing to change their thieving ways will be invited to become members of our land-holding." Then speaking a little louder, for the hooligans' benefit, "And if they are not willing then they will be tied to a log and thrown in the river." The speaker winks at the boys including them in his jest.

Renaldo joins in, "Where we come from they would be handed over to the army and given the chore of cleaning latrines and hauling slops."

"Rest assured, if they choose to stay here they will be given the most disagreeable chores while being closely watched; and locked up each night."

"Fair enough," pronounces Renaldo, then to his sons, "let's be getting the horses hitched to the wagon for our early start." As he is walking away he turns his full attention to these two men of the village, and touching two fingers to his brow casually salutes them, "Gentlemen." It is an old habit.

While the family hitches the team to the wagon a crowd gathers at the riverbank. There are mostly children and dogs, but there also riders on horses, prepared to assist if necessary. Kirin and Audrae station themselves on the backs of the team's leaders, Renaldo and Annia sit in the driver's seat, while Razs and Vejz hang off the back, ready for any unforeseen circumstances. The sun is now peeking over the mountaintops and a few wispy clouds are forming in the azure sky as the signal to move is given the horses. When they reach the river's edge they pause momentarily, bidding farewell to these village folk gathered here to watch. Renaldo signals the go ahead to the horses. The team has no qualms about traipsing into the river. The wagon's great wide wheels crunch heavily over the gravel of the riverbed. They make it easily across the first shallow channel and now the horses' shod feet sink into the soft wet beach as they pull out of the water onto the first sandbar. The horses lean forward keeping the momentum as they cross the soft ground, and then regain their ease once back in the water again. The accompanying villagers, even though the team and wagon are experiencing no difficulty in the crossing, remain close. The horses enter the main channel. There is first a shallow bit before the deepest section where the current flows strongest. The water is suddenly deep. The girls, riding the backs of the lead horses call out in unison, "They are swimming!" No sooner have they made this announcement when the wagon begins drifting with the current.

"Hold on!" Annia shouts, but in the same instant the horses have reached the shallows on the other side and are again pulling the wagon. It shivers as the wheels roll onto firm ground again. There is one more sandbar to cross before a final shallow channel. The scariest part had only lasted long enough to be a thrill. The crossing has taken very little time so far. They cross the last shoal onto a sandy beach. The horses grunt up through a narrow cut of the river's embankment then pause where the roadway of pavers begins again. Renaldo jumps down and, with the boys, inspects the under-carriage. All is in order. The wagon is surrounded by village folk who have crossed on their horses to guarantee a safe crossing. These well-wishers and the Gedimin family all bid each other farewell.

♡♡♡

The road does not directly follow this winding River Main, but instead takes a straightened route centering in this wide valley. Although the river is ever close, fields and pastures separate it from the ancient roadway. Mountain ranges rise to the right and the left of the river's valley. This road has been here a long time. This area has been settled and prosperous for a long time. "How many did it take to build this road?" Razs and Vejz are sitting up front with their dad.

Vejz laughs at his brother, "How many what? How many years? How many men? How many of these huge flat rocks? And where did these big flat rocks come from?"

"Must have come from a quarry."

"So there would have had to be a crew of men cutting the rock out of the quarry, and another crew of men hauling the rocks to make the road, and a crew of men laying the rocks down; building the road. With all these crews of workers there would have to be crews of cooks to feed the lot."

Now their father joins in, "There would have been crews of overseers to point out to the stone masons specifically where to place each paver." He laughs sarcastically, "And there would have been crews of better cooks to cook better food for these elite crews." The boys share sideways glances; this is their father making bureaucraticisms. "Yes, history tells us that for hundreds of years the Romans kept thousands of people employed building these roads."

"Dad." Razs says, "They were not employed. They were slaves."

"Not serfs. Slaves." Vejz adds.

"Anyway," Renaldo says, "It took an awful lot of people an awful long time to build this road."

"Well, they should have built a bridge back there."

"Rivers change their courses over time. Or maybe back when the road was being built that section was too close to the frontier for spending anymore on a road to nowhere. Looking at the map I see that we will be crossing a bridge at Frankfurt am Main that is said to be as old as this road."

"Is that where we are going to catch the ferry?" It is Razs asking now. "Do you really suppose there is a boat large enough to carry our wagon and our horses down the river?"

"We have been told that it is a great big river and that there are great big boats," Vejz is not sure if he likes the idea of being on a boat that size, or a river that wide.

"I am looking forward to seeing this River Rijn," Ren tells his sons, "if there is a ferry large enough to carry our horses and wagon down river, then I think it is an adventure that we cannot pass up."

"Whatever."

The bridge over the River Main is wide enough for them to stop in the middle and look over to the water far below. Again it is Razs asking, "How many did it take to build this bridge? It must have taken forever!"

Audrae leans over farther to get a better look. Annia keeps a hold on her daughter's sleeve, "Please don't lean out there so far, it is such a long way down."

Kirin, while looking down at the river flowing below, feels a strange sensation like she is moving, "Oh I do not think I can look any longer. It makes me dizzy." But she continues looking. It is thrilling.

Following the directions they have been given they arrive at the ferry port to find a ferry that has enough room for their horses and wagon. Ren drives the team and wagon across a wide gangway onto this ferry which is a deck of heavy timbers set atop a log raft. There stands a mast at midship that will hold a wide sail. A long tiller extends off the back. There is another wagon and two carriages already onboard. All the teams of horses are relieved of their harnesses and herded into a corral at the back. There is a covered area with tables and benches for the passengers, and where some of them will sleep.

There are rooms for the crew and a small kitchen where two women cook and pour drinks. The crew consists of two men and the Captain. It is surprising how swiftly the river's current carries the large raft. Audrae asks the Captain, "Why do you not raise the sail?"

He laughs, "Are we not going fast enough for you?" He laughs again before answering, "The sail is for the return trip." He laughs some more. She is discovering that this captain punctuates nearly everything he says with laughter. She likes him.

Later Audrae is standing by as the two crewman cast a fishing net and she asks them, "What sort of fish will you be pulling in with your net?"

The larger of the two winks to his mate, "Today we are hoping to bring in *wassernymphen*."

"Vassanoomf? What sort of fish is that?"

They are laughing; enjoying their joke. The other tells her, "There are nymphs that swim this river and live in underwater gardens."

The big guy tells her solemnly, "You had best stand back for they are vicious." Both men are holding back their chortling, and failing miserably.

Audrae decides to counter their teasing with a bit of her own, "Do you intend to eat these water nymphs?"

This question has them snickering again. The smaller fellow drops his voice to a confiding tone, "Oh no my dear. We hope to collect the bounty."

"Ya. Sure," his partner tells her, "A bag of gold for every one of these frightful blue bogies!"

One of the women comes out of the kitchen and dumps a pan of dishwater over the side. She smiles to Audrae and asks, "Are these two teasing you?" As she dips her pan in the water she says, "I bet they are filling you with stories of the wicked water nymphs." She stands with a full pan of river water. As she walks away back to her kitchen she tells Audrae, "Do not believe anything they say. The little blue nymphs are sweet hearted creatures."

"Oh, oh, oh. She is a contrary girl, that one," They are shaking their heads. "Sweet hearted is not how most folk describe the *die Najaden*." The shorter fellow is frowning sternly now, while his belly quivers with the laughter he is attempting to hold in. "I must warn you to never stand close to the edge. These creatures will reach up and grab your ankle and pull you over into the depths!"

Audrae stomps her foot, "I will not be scared by your ridiculous stories!" Oh, they like this spunky girl. When they pull in their net it is filled with salmon. "Not the blue nymphs you were hoping for?" She taunts them. They laugh.

The next day comes in raining, followed by two more days of rain. The low clouds hang on the hills. There are many old castles nestled upon these hillsides. Many have crumbled. Many others stand as neglected stone walls with only emptiness where the wooden roofs and floors had been. There are many boats that travel this river. There are many land-holdings along the banks of this River Rijn. The ferry docks twice to let off other wagons and carriages. The last stop is Nijmeegs in Gelderland, and this is where the

Gedimins leave the ferry. It is raining. There is mud everywhere.

Leaving Amsterdam

A jay, one of many living in the trees that grow along these canals of Amsterdam, leaves the branch it has been perched upon and flits down to a drain spout where there is always a puddle to drink from. After getting a drink it flies to the roof over an upper story gable where it can look at a windowsill where nuts are sometimes left out for it to eat. The sill is empty. The jay follows an impulse and flits over to that windowsill and peers through to see what is inside. It sees the person that puts the nuts on the sill, so it taps its beak on the glass. The person does not move, so the jay taps the glass again.

Dirk, entranced by this necklace of golden hearts, is broken from his reverie by the tapping at his window. He shakes himself out of his stupor upon realizing that his jay friend has been tapping at his window for a while now. Opening the drawer where the peanuts are stored he takes a few, then walks over and when he opens the window the jay flits back again to its gable-top perch. Dirk places one of the peanuts in the palm of his hand, then holding it out for the little bird says, "Come on back over here. You take this one, and I will leave a couple more for you on the sill." Dirk has been feeding this jay often enough that it is not long before it flits over, perches on his thumb, grabs the nut, and then flies away. "There ya go my little friend." He lays the other two peanuts on the sill before closing the window and turning back to where the necklace remains spread out on the table. He wonders aloud, "How long have I been gazing at this incredible necklace." He feels all abuzz, outside of time, like awakening from dreaming; has his imagination gone loopy? He picks up the necklace, inspects it some more, and passes it back and forth between his hands; it is a most amazing thing of beauty. This necklace, *whoo*, for a while there, it seemed as if he has held it before. It is easy to imagine, or envision, this necklace around the throat and over the collar bones of a most beautiful woman: it is almost as if he has seen her, perhaps in a dream, a dream of an angel; the jewels matching the colors in her eyes and the glow in her cheeks, and the dark gold complementing her shimmering hair. Summoning his will, tearing his attention from this wonder, he gazes away. Looking out through his window; the trees, the rooftops, the clouds, and the sky shine with a clarity that he has not felt for so long. This vibe stirs him into deciding to leave Amsterdam: now. As he stuffs his few extra clothes into his satchel it feels like he has already packed. A feeling or a memory? As he fashions a sash from a long silken scarf he experiences the same sense of having already wrapped the necklace in the scarf and then tying it around his midsection. It seems like he has already done this but cannot remember when it could have been.

He retrieves, from a hidden recess at the back of a drawer, a wallet with the money that he has saved. The wallet goes into his coat's inner pocket, with its chain attached to a ring sewn onto his vest. The last thing to do is deposit what is left of his peanuts on the windowsill, then with his satchel over his shoulder he is down the narrow steps and out the door. The heightened sensibility that he feels, since the enthrallment of the golden hearts, draws him along in a sense of wonder. He wishes, now more than ever, that he had his horse. He had left home with nothing but his clothes, a few of his painting supplies, and paper for sketching. He hasn't touched any of that. He hasn't felt in the right mood to paint until now, but he cannot paint now, he is leaving.

He is noticing that everything that usually bothers him about the city is not bothering him today. People rushing urgently past do not stir urgency in him. He sees the sameness of the buildings, the sameness of the clothes, and the sameness of expression on peoples' faces and the sameness does not bother him. *Where are these feelings coming from? I feel so satisfied.* If it were not such a crazy notion he would say that the necklace has evoked this comfortable sense of well-being. It is a strange sensation to think that an object is somehow alive, and so pleasant to be with.

At the outskirts of the city he decides to stop somewhere for a bite to eat and to perhaps get some food to carry with him. Here is a farmers market with most of the stalls already standing empty due to the late hour of the day. During his interlude with the necklace he had lost track of time. He is still feeling pleasantly disoriented. He is able to get a nice bit of smoked ham, and a triangle of cheese from a farmer who breaks from packing up for the day to do one last bit of business. Across the way is a brewer's booth where he sits down for a mug of dark lager and a kebab snack. The proprietors are a dark-skinned couple. That they are here doing their own business signifies that they are not slaves. *Everybody should be free.* As Dirk sits enjoying his beer and his dinner another couple arrive bringing a drum and a wooden soundbox that has tightly stretched strings. As they get going with their music the serving woman comes out from behind the counter moving sinuously to the beat of the drums. Dirk wishes he knew how to dance like that. As if there is a pre-arranged meeting time more folks arrive and soon there is a happy crowd. More of them bring drums, sound boxes, and flutes; they are having a party. Dirk is enjoying all this, although it is odd to be the only light-skinned person in the crowd. Before leaving he gets a jug of the dark beer to take with him, and now his satchel is full and he is thankful for its wide straps as he slings it over his shoulders.

While he had sat there with other things going on around him he had forgotten about the necklace of golden hearts. As he makes his way along this canal that leads to Utrecht, while admiring the homes and the farmlands, thoughts of the necklace move far to the back of his mind. He likes this time of day and wonders if he will walk through the night. He spies an idle windmill with its sails set intermediately, signifying the need for a millwright. As he nears the place he makes out unusable equipment left in disarray all around; broken wheels, discarded masts, split shafts, cracked millstones, and even unused timbers left to warp and twist. Across the way sits the miller's home, equally surrounded by junk. It is how some people live. He considers peeking inside the windmill to see what repairs it needs, but the squalor keeps him walking. His father's mills have always been keep up with an emphasis on order, and his own years as a millwright have provided him an appreciation for orderliness.

But, he is no longer a *molenaar*. That life is behind him now. After Donar, his mentor, friend, and employer had passed away last summer his world had completely gone awry. His grief had him constantly vacillating between sadness and anger, with neither suiting him. He was unable to find solace in any of his old familiar activities, was even unable to get along with his family. So, one morning last fall he had packed a satchel and set out walking with no predetermined destination. It had been easy getting rides, and he soon found himself in Amsterdam. In the flourishing commerce of the city it was easy to find work, and easy to find a place to live. But, leaving everything behind had not brought him solace, nor did the city life fill the emptiness inside him. His overall dissatisfaction is what had led him, only a couple days ago, to thieving. Knowing that he was risking everything had not deterred him, that is, until today. And now, here he is with his satchel on his back, leaving it all behind once again.

Dirk continues on along the canal in the dim light that remains after the sun has set. Walking past another windmill, this one well kept, a friendly dog comes running out barking its greetings. He stops to pet the friendly creature and hears a voice calling from the miller's home, "Hallo."

He straightens up from scratching behind the dog's ears and answers back and waves, "Good Evening."

Walking toward him now the miller asks, "Where are you walking to so late in the day?"

"Nowhere in particular."

"Ah, the easy life. Have you a place to sleep?"

"I had not thought of it. Maybe I will walk all night."

"Well, you are welcome to sleep here the night. And I have a job that you could help with in the morning. My wife will cook you breakfast. How does that sound to ya? A comfortable place to sleep and a bite to eat in exchange for a bit of simple labor? You are not afraid of a little work are ya?" This man has friendly eyes and a big smile.

"OK, that seems like a good offer."

"Good, good, very good. Come along then." As they begin walking down the drive the dog barks and spins around joyfully before running ahead leading the way.

"Are you not wondering what sort I work I have in mind for ya?"

"Well, seeing as you are milling corn here I am imagining that you will be having me move sacks of meal."

"Ah, you are a bright lad." He shows Dirk to the bed in the windmill and leaves him to it for the night.

♡♡♡

The morning after arriving home from his long sea voyage Nicklas Voorhaven is lying awake in his bed appreciating having slept in his own room, which has been cleaned and freshened by his landlady. She has placed a vase of freshly picked flowers on the dresser by the window. He is feeling particularly rested from having slept without the constant motion of the waves. He is reluctant to rise from the comfort of his bed as he is thinking of all that needs his attention this day, with priority to his looking into the disappearance of the priceless necklace that was inappropriately seized from his belongings. He also wonders how soon he will be able to leave Amsterdam to visit his mother and father, hoping that their fortune has improved from when he had last seen them. Maybe he will even feel inclined to visit his brothers living in Paris. Will any of them be interested to hear the tale of his voyage? Or that he has come home a wealthy man? He could easily skip ever seeing them again, but considers it his duty to stay in touch with his family.

As he is lying there contentedly imagining his schedule for the day there is a knock at his door and so he jumps up anticipating his landlady arriving with coffee and biscuits, oh and perhaps some sausages, "Mmmmmmm." Instead, when he opens his door it is not his landlady, but a slim young man, a Frenchie by the looks of that floppy cap. "Hello," there is something faintly familiar about this young man's features, "I thought you would be my landlady with breakfast. Do I know you?"

The young fellow, surprisingly strong, pushes him backward into the room, closes the door, then says, "Klas, it's me. Trinjntje." Somewhat taken aback, Nicklas wants to ask why she is dressed this way, but she speaks first, "I had to sneak away. There is too much going on. There are too many people after me."

Nicklas suddenly realizes that he is standing there in the presence of a woman, his employer, with only his nightshirt and so proceeds to disappear behind the screen to clothe himself. "Trinjntje, have a seat whilst I dress."

"You cannot call me by my name, I am dressed as a man."

"No, you are dressed as a boy. With your size you do not pass as a man."

"Pffft. Trifles. Few will notice. I am wearing pants and boots and a hat," and with a defiant lift of her chin, "I am even carrying a knife; a man's knife in a leather sheath on my belt." Pulling back her cape she exposes the jewel-handled blade for Nicklas to inspect, "See!"

Nicklas, with only one leg down through his new trousers, peeks around the screen to view what she is so proudly displaying and loses his balance, landing clumsily on the floor. Amidst Trinjntje's giggling there is another knock at his door. He jumps up stuffing his shirttails into his pants, still barefoot and his hair still mussed from sleep. Shushing her from giggling in an attempt to present an appropriate display of decorum, he answers the door.

His landlady bursts through with his breakfast tray loaded with a pitcher of beer, two glasses, plates of biscuits and steaming sausages, "I heard your guest arrive as I was preparing your morning repast, so have included enough for both of you." Setting the tray on the table she turns smiling to Nicklas, "It is so fine to have you home at last dear boy." Her eyebrows go up as she appraises him from head to toe, "Oh, but you are no longer a boy are you?" She turns her gaze to her boarder's guest, and then back to Nicklas inquiringly, "Are you going to introduce me to your friend?"

Momentarily caught off guard by all this upheaval so early on his first day home Nicklas begins explaining before he has had time to devise a story, "This is my," noticing the beret on Trinjntje's head, "nephew. One of my brother's sons, here from Paris."

"Trin," Trinjntje introduces herself, filling in for her flustered friend. Then, speaking as a Frenchman would, "I happen to be visiting Amsterdam, when to my surprise, I hear that the very ship Uncle Klas has been traveling upon is here in port. So, la, I tell myself I must stop by for a visit, and how lucky I am to have arrived in time for breakfast. Thank you very much." She brushes past the landlady and snatches a biscuit. She is ravenously devouring her bread while filling a glass with beer for herself. Washing down her first bite with a long swig, she then immediately reaches for a sausage. She plays her role accurately.

Nicklas is surprised by the way she has used her childhood nickname which passes easily as a boy's name. Even more fascinating is the way she has lowered the tone of her voice while speaking as a Frenchie would. He has the impression that she is familiar with portraying this deception. He almost laughs out loud at the way she is tearing into her food and drink, not at all her usual dainty manner of eating. The older woman also notices the food disappearing from the tray and remarks, "If I haven't brought enough for the two of you feel free to stop by the kitchen. There is always more." With that said she is on her way, but stops in the doorway and turns to Nicklas with a wink, "My daughters will be most pleased to have a handsome man such as yourself stop in with a kind hello." And then she is gone.

"Trin," says Nicklas as the door closes behind his landlady, "that's very good, like you have planned this." He fills a glass for himself and commences to put together a sausage biscuit sandwich, "Now, tell me please what this is all about."

Trinjntje takes another bite of sausage and another sip of beer and then whisks off her hat, tossing it on top of her bag there on the floor.

"Your hair! You have shorn half the length of your hair."

"It will grow back soon enough." She tosses her head laughing, "It was getting too long anyway. It feels good this length." She has removed her cloak, "these clothes feel good. I like wearing trousers. I love that as I walk through town I am given so very little attention. You men do not realize how difficult it is to be a woman."

"Is that what this is all about?" Exasperated, he sits.

She takes a seat. "You were probably long gone yesterday afternoon when I was finally allowed to disembark."

"I heard there was a large crowd."

"A fair portion of that crowd still remains outside the gate of my parent's estate."

"What for?"

Her expression is that of a wide-eyed doe caught unaware. "I wish I knew." Then, "As long as I am home the attention I receive makes life miserable for my parents. They feel that they need to protect me. I like being on my own: unprotected. I do not wish to burden my mother and father. So I have disguised myself and run away."

Her clothes fit her well and she seems familiar with her role, "You've done this before?"

"Yes." She leans back in her chair, "I used to go out often dressed this way so that I could be a normal everyday person rather than a well-known and talked about personage."

"How long do you plan to carry on this charade? I imagine your father will surely have soldiers out looking for you. And where will you stay in the meantime?"

"This is where I was hoping you would help me," she tells him as she sits up straight again, flickering her eyelashes very un-boyishly, "I remember you saying that you will be going to Utrecht, or is it Antwerpen? I can travel with you. It will be great fun! But we must leave soon. Immediately. As you say, there will be soldiers looking for me." Then a shadow crosses over her expression, "There are already people looking for me, as you saw yesterday aboard the ship."

"Yes." *Those uppity lawyers.* "You should not worry about those people. The Spaniards and their hateful inquisition are gone. We are a nation of free people."

"My Mother and Father are upset about the band of people at their gate. That is why I cannot stay there. I am expecting the crowd will go away once they find out that I am gone. My folks can get back to their everyday lives again. The charge filed against me is some outrageous trumped up claim that I am bringing back stolen contraband, like I'm a pirate. Arrrghh!" They both snort cynically. "Furthermore, my father fears that this charge is an attempt to sully his good name with lies. There are those who will pursue this as an opportunity to smear him and the Company."

"I understand why your parents are upset." He stews for a moment, then adds, "I understand why you would choose to leave."

"It seems best for me to disappear for a while." They sit quietly for a bit, until Trinjntje breaks the silence again, "It will soon be breakfast time at home and my absence will be noticed. My father will be worried for my safety and will immediately give the order that I be found. He probably has a hundred men at his beck and call." She has her eyebrows up as high as they will go and her eyes wide, showing with her expression how unstoppable her father can be. "So, we have very little time before we must be away from Amsterdam."

"Away from Amsterdam," Nicklas muses disappointedly. "We have only just returned, and there is so much to do; business I must tend to, and friends I long to visit."

Although, his few friends are in Antwerpen where he had grown up, or Utrecht where he had last attended school. "And fresh food to eat, and fresh beer to drink." He pauses upon noticing that she has her eyes closed feigning to not be hearing what he is saying while shaking her head. "Surely you can find a place to hide here in Amsterdam for a day or two."

"I guess I'll have to leave on my own." Pouting. "Or perhaps I can find someone else willing to help me." Finished bemoaning her fate she stands, pulls on her beret and steps across the room toward the door.

Nicklas notices that although she has picked up her bag and has a hand around the doorknob she is not turning it. He is wondering if she will really charge out, and wondering what he will do if she does. His feelings are torn, his thoughts are in turmoil, for even though he is technically her employee they have worked close together for so long that they have become friends. On the other hand; his wages have come from her father, even the bounty from the cargo he has been allowed to bring back has been through the good graces of her father, Director Olmsfeld. Oh, what to do? "Trinjntje wait!" He implores, "Please give me a moment to sort this out. Surely you have had some time to put together a plan, but I've been awake for only a bit and this is a lot to sort out. It's just me, ya know, plain ol' simple me. I'm a bit slow sometimes."

She lets go of the doorknob, returns to her seat and sits down. She is smiling her familiar mischievous smile, "Oh, Nicklas thank you. It will be an adventure. We'll have great fun."

A fun adventure does not exactly describe how Nicklas is imagining this endeavor, but at least Trinjntje has not rushed out the door. "Now please allow me a moment to think about what must be done and how we will go about taking care of all we need to do." His heart is fluttering as he is reconsidering his feelings toward this woman across the room from him. She is at least ten years older than him. His love for her is like ... what? A sister? He had never had a sister. She is beautiful, but he does not desire to be with her as a lover. "I will do what I can for you as a friend. You are a dear friend. We must leave behind our M'lady and her assistant relationship. That is the only way I can act against your father's desires."

"If he knew you are with me he would be happy that I am not alone. You do not need wages anymore anyway, the goods you have brought back will make you a rich man. Besides, it has been nice having you as an assistant, but I think it will be even nicer now that you are my friend. Friends are very wonderful."

"As for me being rich," he points out, "the goods that I have brought back are sitting in the VOC warehouses and have yet to be sold." The subject that is really bothering him comes next, "Trinjntje," speaking gravely now, "there is something else that I need you to know." His heavy tone takes some of the brightness out of her eyes. "The necklace of Golden Hearts that the Prince presented to you as a betrothal gift is missing."

She responds vehemently, "He refused to accept that I would not marry him. Then he refused the return of the necklace." She stands and begins pacing, "Evidently nobody has ever refused his Royal Intentions. He did not believe, nay, would not accept that his offer was being rejected. He wanted me to be his first wife. I do not want to be a wife." She is staring out the window, "I take that back. I do want to be a wife, but I have yet to meet a man that I will marry."

Remembering the incident, Nicklas adds, "Even his royal clan refused to take back the necklace when I attempted to return it for you. It was almost as if they wanted it gone." It had all seemed so strange, for the necklace is indeed a thing of great value, yet the royal clan had been very clear regarding not wanting the tainted item back. "You did not want the necklace. The prince and his family did not want the necklace. Nobody seemed to want it. I had no choice but to stash it away in my cabin. It was stolen by the VOC clerk that signed off my paperwork."

Waving a hand while tossing her head, "Now it is gone. You are free of that burden. What's to worry about?"

Thinking that she clearly does not understand the value of the item; she never seems to understand the concept of things holding value, "OK." He throws his hands up, "OK. That is settled." At least he will not have to meet with that smarmy clerk and his overgrown thug sidekick. "OK. As for the issue of my cargo being sorted and sold," he pauses, further collecting his thoughts and as Trinjntje begins saying something he holds up his index finger indicating for her to shush, then finishes, "the Company will sort and sell for me all that was brought back as per the contracts that I signed yesterday. My gains will be deposited into my account where interest will be paid and my wealth will grow of its own accord. Ah, the glories of this modern age." He beams, "and that settles that." Once again he pauses, and once again Trinjntje begins in a rush to say something, and once again he raises his index finger shushing her while he closes his eyes in concentration. "What else is there requiring my attention?"

It seems such a long wait to her that she rises from her seat and walks over to him wondering what is going on in his mind. Bending down she brings her face closer and closer, as if the proximity will allow her to look inside at his thoughts. She is staring at his closed eyes from inches away when, with his thoughts finally in order, he opens them and is so startled by her nearness that he tips backward in his chair landing with a thump on the floor. She gasps with her hands to her mouth, "Oh Nicklas are you OK?"

He stands up, dusts himself off, and says to her, "Let us be on our way."

♡♡♡

Cornelius Janszoon, no longer a ship's captain, no longer a servant of the *Verenigde Oost-indische Compagnie*, no longer in charge of anyone or anything other than his own self and his own private affairs, sits in the dining room of one of the most recently built hotels of this boom town that Amsterdam has become. Director Olmsfeld, his brother-in-law, had dropped him off here yesterday at the conclusion of their business. A dubious business meeting it had been, with the Company offering him a higher salary, more shares, more of whatever they could offer, including a variety of other positions, in a final attempt to secure his continued trustworthy services. Telling them to stop wasting energy, he had unabashedly discarded all offers. The board of directors, thinking that he intended to idly pass his life away, had told him they will keep the offers on the table for a year. He clearly informed them that he is not retiring to an inactive life, but that he is moving forward into a well-planned and executed business venture. They had even pretended to be interested and congratulatory when he explained that this pursuit had begun many years previous. But alas, to these men, leaving the Company is akin to treason.

Those many years ago he had invested, with a group of others, in an endeavor intending to drain away a large portion of marshland situated along the Kromme Rijn River. Because it is a long-term project many of the original investors have sold out. Janszoon's advocaat, a forward looking man, has bought up those shares on behalf of his client, putting the captain in the position of being the major shareholder. Cornelius feels extremely lucky to have this accountant who is so well versed in the machinations of the new economy. When Janszoon had last been in Amsterdam, over two years ago, he had visited the property and witnessed for himself the glorious drainage mill already turning the marsh into quality farmland. At that time he had determined to have the land farmed rather than dividing it into plots as originally planned. At that time he had also commissioned a house and a horse barn to be built for himself along the river's edge, and this is what has him so excited to be on his way.

His morning reverie is interrupted by the arrival of a troop of VOC soldiers. Janszoon watches through the dining room windows as the leader dismounts and rushes in, stopping to scan the room then spotting the Captain and rushing to his table. He halts and salutes, "Captain Janszoon, Sir." The captain stands returning the salute. He was introduced to this soldier yesterday, a self-important vainglorious type. "Your niece, Trinjntje Olmsfeld, is missing. Director Olmsfeld has directed us to seek her whereabouts. We are checking with those of you who have been her traveling companions for clues as to where we might find her."

"Trinjntje Olmsfeld is of legal age and I believe that gives her liberty to move about as she chooses," replies Janszoon "unless, of course, there is evidence of foul play. I left her yesterday at her parent's home, after being escorted by a full troop of armed soldiers," looking through the windows to the street outside, "perhaps the same band out there awaiting you now." This last bit is said with irony, for the soldiers of the VOC are a presence wherever the Company has a stake and are not to be trifled with. Janszoon is all too familiar with the heavy-handed tactics of the VOC armed troops.

Unflinching, the Colonel continues with his interrogation, "Have you seen Miss Olmsfeld this morning, or do you have any knowledge of where she might be found, or whom she may have gone off with?" He hesitates for a moment, then clarifies, "Is there a love interest that may have spawned an elopement?"

The patrons seated at the surrounding tables are all listening unabashedly now as Janszoon answers, "Her love interests are her plants, her music, and her acrobatics. She is, as far as I know, a totally self-absorbed woman." Looking around the room with regards to the attention this conversation is receiving; even the kitchen help can be seen peeking out, He continues, "Wherever she goes there are men falling in love with her, and she is continually turning down proposals, even proposals from princes," then adding another jibe, "even proposals from soldiers the likes of you."

Now the Colonel creases his brow giving a very stern expression before explaining, "Captain Janszoon, you are aware that there are charges filed against Trinjntje Olmsfeld by an organized group of citizens who do not share your tender feelings toward her. Some of these concerned *citizens* may even be of a frenzied nature intolerant with the slow rolling wheels of the law."

"Pah! She has broken no laws!" exclaims Janszoon heatedly. "The wars are ended. The treaties signed. Those who would have previously attempted to enforce such frivolous charges have been sent packing. I am led to believe that these are peaceable times and that we live in a realm of freedom for all." Noticing that all the room is listening he raises his voice as he carries on, "Our homeland is considered to be the wealthiest in the world. Here we enjoy the best lifestyle of any I have seen in all my travels. We are free people! Why is there anyone unhappy enough to wish harm upon anyone else?" He is enjoying the attention of the room as he makes this speech. Now hoping to divert further scrutiny away from his niece he carries on, "We, all of us, want to focus on our good fortune, on our wealth, and on our freedom to do as we please while happily allowing others the same!" pausing for effect before declaring, "**I stand firm.**" Evoking what has become a national motto brings all who are seated to their feet clapping their hands and cheering him on. Now looking the soldier square in the eye he finishes, "You are only following orders, but I say, leave the woman, my niece, alone." With a nod of dismissal, pleased that he no longer holds a position that requires him to salute, he places his hat on his head and makes his way across the room and out the door.

As he walks along he smiles at himself and the little speech he has delivered. Spouting the motto of stubbornness is a habit he has developed as a Captain not wanting his authority to be undermined. He ponders that liberty and freedom for all means a kinder world for everyone. The soldiers race past him goading their horses with urgency. "Where the devil is that girl," his niece, "that woman?" Having been her guardian during this past voyage he is still in the protective mode. She has long been past the age to be called a girl, yet she is such a whimsical spirited sprite that he thinks of her as a girl, so trusting in her outlook toward others. Being the only child of wealthy parents has provided her every opportunity for learning, and she has proved an avid student attendant to the best tutors. She has studied and is even proficient in all the scientific trends; botany, astronomy, physiology, and even philosophy, having had a bout of tutoring from Descartes himself. She is adept in Latin, enough to attend academic lectures were she a man. Being a scholarly woman is enough to earn disfavor from amongst the puritan factions. Remembering the crowd stationed along the roadway yesterday he is prone to believe that she is seeking her solitude, and he hopes she finds what she is looking for.

As his stroll takes him past the dam he lets go of all these bothersome thoughts. He is determined to enjoy this special day. It is a beautiful spring morning and he is setting off on the adventure of his long held dream.

♡♡♡

Nicklas does not need to pack his bag because he has not unpacked since arriving home last night. So he buckles the straps and as they leave, he glances back wistfully at the room he has so looked forward to these past months. On their way out he informs his landlady that he is off again and not sure for how long, but that he will keep her posted. After bemoaning the fact that neither of them currently owns a horse to ride, they aim themselves toward the coach station. Trinjntje remembers the *Koetshuis Inn*; travelers can stay the night, get a meal, and catch a coach. It had always been one of her favorite places to sit and watch the parade of people coming and going. "It is a beautiful morning for a stroll," she tells her companion, "I am particularly pleased to be out walking freely after being cooped up aboard the ship for so long." Nicklas seems to be lost in thought. "At least we are out and about enjoying the sunshine, even if our dream of being home is not playing out as we have imagined."

Nicklas says nothing leaving Trinjntje to wonder if she has over-reacted to the circumstances of the previous day. It was so exasperating and confusing to be finally home where she should be able to move about as she pleases, only to have it not be so. She was feeling the pressure of the world to be something different than she is. She likes herself. She does not want to be different. *Why is the world the way it is?* She had not liked feeling that way, so she had attempted to shift her thinking. She had reminded herself that all those other folks are well intentioned and believing in their hearts that they are doing what is best. Alas, her attempts to turn her thoughts in a more loving and forgiving direction failed while she was not feeling love or forgiveness. She was feeling hurt and angry. Last night, still feeling hurt and angry, she had trimmed her hair, donned these men's clothes, and snuck through the estate fence. She had continued feeling hurt and angry as she walked the city's cobbled boulevards through the early morning hours. Now that what she has done is sinking in she is feeling frightened and foolish; unfamiliar feelings spawning unfamiliar thoughts. "I'm sorry Nicklas for getting you into this quandary. I acted impulsively from my horrible mood, and now it is all catching up to me and, Ohhhh, I have gotten you involved in my big mistake!"

"Have no pity for me." He's beginning to think that this situation might be better than the option of returning to his position as a clerk. Wishing for something cheery to tell her, "I remember the red robed Bengali monks chanting that a*ll pity is self-pity*."

"Are you telling me to stop feeling sorry for myself?"

He looks at her sideways with hooded eyes, and once he is certain that he has her attention, twists his mouth while crossing his eyes, sparking immediate laughter from her. "I am telling you to stop feeling sorry for me. I'm a big boy now. You did not force me against my will, unless," he flashes a comical expression of horror, "this is some of your m-m-m-magic." He then stretches his arms out in front of him while his eyes stare blankly forward, "Oh Mistress, I am your slave. What evil deeds will you have me do today?"

She giggles, and slaps him for his humorous insolence. "Stop it!" Giggling some more. "No. Don't stop." Now they are both giggling contagiously. When their silliness seems to have subsided she asks him, "We told your landlady that I was a cousin, no, I mean nephew. Which was it? Oh, it does not matter, that story will not hold when you introduce me to your family."

"Hmmm. What to do?" His devilish expression is a clue that he is about to make another ridiculous comment. She gives him her full attention as he tells her his first idea. "You could dress yourself in a full robe, and cover your head and face and I could tell everyone that you are my Persian servant who is not allowed to speak."

She slaps him again, but then plays along, "Then at night around a fire I can drop my robe revealing my fine brocade dancer's costume and," stretching her arms above her head, wrists bent, whilst gyrating her hips, "perform some of that wiggly dancing you so appreciate!" Teasing him back and reminding him of the belly dancers that had enchanted him.

"Oh my goodness, that will start a frenzy!" Guffawing uproariously while at the same time remembering that while he had been digging plants for her to bring home she had been taking lessons from those dancers. "You did learn to wiggle your hips like that didn't you? But we had better be thinking of something less scandalous." Meaning something less likely to evoke the ire of those already after her for unsubstantiated misdeeds.

"OK. How about if I paint my face white and wear a long silken gown like those beautiful girls of the farthest eastern Asian realms?" she suggests slyly.

"Oh yes. That will have the added bonus of keeping you out of sight most of the time; put away like a doll. Isn't that the way those women live? Like dolls?" Again, while he had been busy potting specimens to be brought home she had been learning about completely different aspects of the culture. "Here's an idea. I will don a suit of armor while you run along beside me as my squire."

"Oh, that'd be great. You can attack windmills!" So he tucks his head, makes as if to be holding a lance and charges forward, trotting in a silly characterization of a prancing stallion. "That," she tells him, "is beyond silly. You need help my friend." Their laughter is interrupted by the sound of real horses, many of them, charging up behind them. Looking toward the approaching sound they are confronted with the sight of a mounted troop of soldiers rushing at them, "Klas," tugging at his arm, pulling him toward the side of road and out of the way of the charging horses, "we are about to be discovered." The riders slow, but do not stop. "Don't look, maybe they won't notice us," her voice wavers.

Nicklas watches as the soldiers pass, "Do you really suppose this many men would be sent after you?"

"The Company Guard," she says, "sent at my father's behest."

Not seeing the dress, nor the long hair of the woman they are searching for the riders barely slow and continue on their way. "Well," says Nicklas, "if indeed they are looking for you, then your disguise is working in your favor." He peeks at Trinjntje where she has stopped in her tracks, then watches as she tears the beret off her head, throws it down and kicks the dirt. With her fists clenched, jaw set, and brows furrowed he hardly recognizes her. He has never seen her angry. "Trin? Are you going to be OK?"

She stands immobilized. Nicklas picks up the soft hat and brushes off the dust and the dirt. He holds it out to her, but she does not immediately take it from him. When she finally snaps out of her trance, she grabs her hat and while crushing it in her hands says pointedly, "They think they have outwitted us." Now she gives herself a shake, consciously relaxing her shoulders, and brushing off the hat some more before placing it on her head. Smiling a wan smile she tells him, "When we arrive at the *Koetshuis Inn* they will be already there and waiting, and probably inspecting the occupants of each coach as it leaves. They are most likely also inspecting barges heading upriver as well," now her voice rises to a subdued sort of shriek, "and they will have probably sent ahead to cohorts stationed in the outlying communities to watch all arrivals." Her eyes widen even more and her mouth becomes an O. "Ooooooh, we are going to have to walk."

Assuming a cavalier pose she finishes, "La! Luckily I am wearing comfortable boots." Giving herself another overall shaking until she once again looks to be the radiant sweet tempered woman that Nicklas is familiar with she tells him, "I relieve you of any obligation that you have accepted on my behalf. I will travel alone."

Nicklas closes his eyes while calculating how long it will take to walk to Utrecht and what would be the best route, the least guarded route, when he hears a recognizable voice addressing him, "Nicklas Voorhaven." It is the familiar tone of Captain Cornelius Janszoon, "fancy meeting you here. Are you on your way out of town so soon after arriving home?" Shaken out of his calculations, he opens his eyes to Janszoon's greeting and sees that the Captain has recognized Trinjntje, despite her disguise. Nicklas is feeling a rippling sensation in his belly that renders him speechless.

"Uncle," Trinjntje speaks crossly, "Has my father commanded you to be a part of the search?"

Evident by his bemused smile, Cornelius is savoring the moment. He is quite fond of these two, his niece and her assistant. His first inclination, that they may be eloping, is confounded by Trinjntje's outfit and shortened tresses. "First off," he tells them, "I am no longer at the beck and call of the Dutch East Indies Company, nor have I ever been subject to your father's dictions." His eyes sparkle as he witnesses the relief showing in their faces, then he adds, "I did have a discussion a short while ago with an obstinate soldier who is employed by the VOC and subject to your father's directives, who is in fact, carrying out a search for you."

Janszoon is dressed in his new blue coat and hat, the same as yesterday. Trinjntje admires his trendy outfit, then for the first time realizes that Nicklas is likewise dressed in new clothes; and very cool boots. "Wow. Look at you fine gentlemen so stylishly dressed. I stand abashed in your presence. Me: in my vagabond outfit."

Ignoring what she has said, and changing the subject, "Sir, if you do not mind me asking," Nicklas addresses the captain, "How is it that you are allowed to leave your captaincy? Er, Is there not a stringently loyal brotherhood of Captains? Is it not against some code of honor to leave such an exalted position? Not to mention that you come from a long line of sea captains stretching back since time began."

"Really Nicklas," Trinjntje scoffs, "since time began???"

"Time," laughs Janszoon, "is no longer of any importance to me." The bells of the city's clock towers ring eight times. It is still early. "Yes Nicklas, I fit somewhere in a long line of sea captains; surely not the last. My father, along with his brothers and cousins, and before them, my grandfather and his father, and on and on, were sea going adventurers." He looks up the road in the direction he is going. "But alas, sea captains of this current generation must follow prescribed courses and are expected to keep within a close timetable. For me, it is repetitious and drab. There is no adventure." Standing here now, considering the circumstances, his mind floods with possibilities. Though he has been looking forward to this time ahead of him, he has also wondered if he will actually enjoy the solitude. Now, the thought enters his mind that *perhaps if he offered them a ride...*

In the interlude Nicklas asks, "So what are your plans from here, Captain?"

"First off," straightening his lapels and appearing to be very pleased with himself, "I am presently on my way to take possession of a new carriage with a pair of sturdy horses, and from there I am hoping to make it to Utrecht before darkfall. Then on to my new home tomorrow."

"Your new home?"

"Oh yes," nodding and tugging at his lapels some more while puffing up his chest a bit, "on the bank of the Kromme Rijn River."

"Are you capitalizing on the drainage? Will you have your own windmills?" asks Nicklas eagerly. He has secretly envisioned such an endeavor for his own self.

"Very astute of you my--" Janszoon catches himself before he nearly calls Nicklas a boy, "my good man. Very astute, indeed. That is, in point of fact, my plan. We already have one mill sailing and have a polder with crops being grown where before there has been a marsh." Now he leans toward them for emphasis, "and there is a new house and barn for me." Straightening up he gives a final tug at his lapels and a forthright nod.

"Well done Captain Janszoon!" congratulates Nicklas.

"Indeed well done Uncle Cor," coos Trinjntje.

Realizing that he has been standing here visiting for too long Janszoon tells them, "I have an appointment. I must be on my way. Since we are aimed in the same direction shall we walk together?"

"Let's do," answers Trinjntje.

"OK," Nicklas agrees, still wondering about those soldiers that are now somewhere ahead. "Do you really intend on making it to Utrecht today?"

"Postal couriers make the ride in a day."

"On a fast horse."

"It will most likely be after dark when I arrive at my lodgings."

"Uncle?" Trinjntje asks apprehensively.

"Yes?"

"A major consideration for my sudden improvised departure has been that my presence is an added burden upon my parents. And so, I hesitate to ask a favor, I would not wish to impose myself upon you."

"Well then, my dear Trin, before you ask, allow me to make an offer."

"Oh? What would you offer?"

"That you ride along with me. I am speculating that the destination for your morning walk matches mine; that you intend to catch a coach. Am I correct?"

"Yes. But, if the place is being watched by soldiers, then we dare not be there."

"I suggest that the two of you circumnavigate the *Koetshuis Inn* while I complete my business there. Then we will meet up somewhere along the way past the outskirts of the city. We will all enjoy the comfort of my new wagon."

Nicklas, who has been silent since they have begun walking again, now speaks up telling Trinjntje, "I believe your uncle has presented a sound plan. I suggest that you accept his offer. Oh, that is, unless you wish otherwise."

She does not answer and in the extended silence a surprising gust of wind has them all grabbing their hats. Overhead they hear a raven's low warbling and looking up see it being tossed sideways by this sudden wind that now subsides as mysteriously as it has arisen. The blue sheen of the raven's black feathers, as it regains equilibrium, is an impressive spectacle for it is a very large bird, definitely not a common crow.

"Whoa!" from Nicklas.

"Indeed!" Janszoon agrees.

"OK," concurs Trinjntje, "It is settled. We will all travel together."

♡♡♡

"Wake up sleepyhead." Dirk opens his eyes and sits up. The miller that had invited him in last night with the offer of work is telling him, "The barge man will be here soon and you'll be loading these sacks of *gierstmeel*, like we agreed last night." Dirk yawns and is rubbing sleep from his eyes,

"Come into the house for some breakfast." Watching the man turn and go, Dirk jumps up and follows the miller into the house where he takes a seat at the table. The kitchen smells wonderful. A steaming mug is set before him, "This will help to wake ya up."

A full plate of bacon, fried potatoes, and scrambled eggs is likewise set before him by the miller's wife. "If this doesn't fill ya I can cook more."

"Thank you." He tells them, and as they both sit and begin eating he digs in also.

It is quiet while they are eating. A large long-haired cat moves itself next to Dirk's chair, *yeow?*

"He'll get the scraps when we are done," the woman says to Dirk, then she tells the cat, "you know better than to beg at the table. Be off with ya now." The furry thing gives her a look, then walks across the room and jumps up onto a windowsill. The miller's wife turns back to Dirk and tells him, "You are saving me a lot of work this day. I am usually having to be up above working the hoist while himself," she lifts her chin indicating her man, "does the lifting and packing down below."

"So you'll be saving me a lot of work too," fills in the miller, "as I'll be upstairs taking it easy with the hoist while you'll be outside packing the bags of meal to the barge."

These good folks are teasing each other. Dirk tells them, "I have been too long in the city. I can stand some hard work. It will be good for me."

"Is Utrecht your destination?" she asks.

"For now," he answers, not offering any more information.

"Well then," says the miller as he stands, "I'll get started hoisting some of the bags down so you can get started moving 'em out to the landing. But, finish eating, there is no rush."

Sitting there in the kitchen after the miller has gone back upstairs Dirk, hoping to be a gracious guest, wonders what he can say. A loom sits across the room where the cat has gone, "That is a fine loom you have there."

"Ach. I mostly weave only course cloth. Sacks for what we grind."

"No linen then?"

"I would not know how to handle such fine thread. No, I am used to the hemp," nodding her head sideways directing his gaze to stacked spools in the corner, "nothing fancy for me."

Dirk acknowledges by bobbing his head up and down, not able to think of anything else to say. He scoots his chair back and stands, "If you will excuse me Ma'am, I will be getting to work. Thank you for the delicious breakfast."

"You are excused and you are welcome." She has a wonderful smile and bright green eyes, "I can tell by your manners that you have been brought up well. We are pleased to have you as our guest." She dips her head to him. This is the atmosphere of home. He misses home. He misses his ma. He misses them all. He bows to her, then is out the door just as a loaded pallet is settling down from above. He releases the hook, waves an all clear signal to the miller and then picks up the first sack and carries it over to the landing.

It is still quite early when the barge arrives. The barge man waves and calls a greeting to the miller up at his hoist who waves and calls back, "We've got a man to do the heavy lifting for us. I will do my best to keep up with him. Maybe you will have your barge loaded early enough for you to make it to Utrecht before dark." They have done this often and they are old friends and happy seeing each other. The barge is pulled by a heavy brown horse with a blaze upon its forehead. The other half of the barge crew is a long-legged collie. Once the barge is secure to the dock a command is given and the horse settles in to sleep. The collie lays down next to the horse, at first attentive, but soon its head drops between its paws, also asleep.

For a while the barge man carries the bags of *gierstmeel* from where Dirk has been stacking them on the landing and lays them in a tidy row beginning the task of filling the barge. When he catches up to Dirk he asks, "How much is the miller paying you?"

"A place to sleep and a meal, so far."

"I will pay you what'er he pays you if you will stack 'em in the boat for me."

"Fair enough. I've got nothing better to do."

They shake on it. "Don't overwork yourself."

Dirk picks up another bag, slings it up on his shoulder and walks the fifty steps it takes to get to the landing. From there he steps over the side of the barge down to the flat bottom. He continues placing the bags in the order the bargeman has begun. As one end of the barge fills and sinks lower in the water the other end floats higher and higher. After the barge is filled halfway the high end of the boat starts coming steadily down with the weight of each successive sack. Dirk has long since removed his coat and vest and sash. It has been a while since he has done work like this. He feels good.

There is an inquisitive river otter living in this little side channel that is dug-out from the canal. After a while of watching Dirk go back and forth she brings out her three pups who are soon scrabbling up and down a muddy trail that leads from the towpath into the water. When there is only room enough for a few more bags he sees, as he steps out of the barge, the mother otter coming to shore with a wriggling salmon clenched in her teeth and he laughs at the sight of her little ones racing after her. The miller and the barge man help with carrying the last of the heavy bags. As the last one is laid into place they slap him on the back and tell him, "Well done!"

The miller hands over a coin to Dirk, "I hope that is equal to what you are used to being paid for a day's work."

"Oh sir that is more than enough for a day's wages, besides I have worked less than half a day."

The old timer winks as he elbows his friend the bargeman, "I am hoping that this old fart has made his usual offer of matching what I pay."

The old fart holds out a coin of like value for Dirk, "Here is what I promised you for your help loading," and then shaking Dirk's hand firmly, "if you will ride along with me to Utrecht I will pay the same amount again for your help with the unloading."

Schoonhoven Landing

Amidst the deafening noise coming from the sawmill Mara and Robert secure their ship to the dock. A sign attached to a piling announces in carved out lettering 'Haumann Landing'. The many buildings, besides the saw mill, are evidence that quite a lot of enterprise goes on here. From the stone wharf a path leads them along a thin strip of land; an earthen dike held in by wooden pilings. On one side of the path is a pond filled with a cluster of logs awaiting to be sawn. A wide wooden ramp leads up from the pond into the vast inner workings of the mill; where all the noise is coming from. The saw mill is a very wide building that has a turning windmill on top. The dike path leads them over a canal emptying into the river. They stop at the center of the walkway atop the canal's lock. Robert points out for Mara, "There is the home of Philip and Beatris Haumann. Next is the home of their older son."

Robert is using his loudest voice while telling her all this. They both have fluffs of wool stuffing their ears to block out the noise. Mara asks him as loud as she can, "Is that another sawmill?" She is pointing at a miniature version of the large sawmill.

"What?"

Louder this time, "Is that another sawmill over there?"

"It is their wood working shop. The windmill on its roof powers a smaller saw, and a wood-shaping machine."

"Oh yes," remembering something he had told her, "That must be where the looms are built."

"Looms," hoping that she is hearing him, "and other household furniture." A mist is now descending from the low dark clouds overhead. "Those cabins over there are for workers."

"Will one of those be for us?"

"Yes."

"Hmmm." Well, he had told her that their temporary home would be small. They continue across the bridge and follow the track, then up a wooden walkway leading to the door of the main house.

They are greeted at the door by a smiling Beatris Haumann, "Robert. It is so nice to see you again." She slips her feet into wooden clogs and steps out, "You must be Mara. I am very pleased to meet you."

Mara says, "Hi," not sure how she feels about yelling at a new acquaintance.

"Philip will be finished up soon. I will show you where you will be staying." As they are following her toward the row of cabins the mist turns to rain. They pass the first cabin and she tells them, "Our second son stays here in this cabin, even though he is has not been around for a while." They pass two more, then she explains, as they turn up the walk of the fourth cabin, "This place has a shed out back for animals," turning to Mara, "Robert told us that you would be bringing a nanny goat and chickens."

Mara nods, "Yes, they will be so happy to be on dry land again."

"La," Beatris laughs, "not much of anything dry around here!"

As they are shown inside the little hut Mara cannot help but ask Beatris, "How do you put up with the dreadful noise?"

"The noise?" She waves it off, "La, after you are here for a while you'll no longer notice it."

"See," Robert tells Mara, "you will get used to it."

"Oh dear me I hope so."

Beatris assures her, "When Philip finishes for the day the noise stops," there is barely room inside the hut for all three of them, "we serve dinner at the house shortly after. You will please join us. We can get acquainted." Then she is out and away.

Robert and Mara embrace and hold each other close. No words are spoken. They are each feeling a bit disheartened by the tiny abode that for now is their home. "How about I get a fire started, then we will bring the animals," Robert suggests.

"Yes. Let's hope they will abide their new surroundings." Looking around at these walls, "This is not much larger than a tent."

"This is only temporary. We can think of ourselves as itinerant vagabonds."

"As a sailor you are used to being an itinerant vagabond," she reminds him. "Once we have the animals ashore, let us bring over only the bare essentials. Hopefully we will not be vagabonds for more than a night."

"Right." The room has a loft for sleeping, a table for two, and a hole in the wall with a chimney. Everything to start a fire is handy. Robert sets a spark to a handful of tinder, then adds kindling. "A fire will dry the damp, and warm the place while we fetch the animals. I think there is enough room in here for all of us."

"Will you bring the animals inside?" She feigns exaggeration, "La, aren't you the sweet man?"

"Whaaaat?" He stands up, arms out, palms up imploringly, "We cannot desert them in a cold unfamiliar shed!"

They walk the path over the canal and out to where the Tulip is moored. They don their raingear, even though they are already soaked from this rain that has blown in so quickly. Robert carries back the cages that hold the cat and the chicken. Mara walks the goat on a short leash. Upon their return the fire is indeed warming and drying the air inside their little hut. Robert leaves Mara with the animals and traipses back along the ever muddier path to the dock. He returns with as much as he can carry, "I hope this will be enough for the night." Mara is seated comfortably on a chair close to the fire with a hen in her lap, her goat at her feet, and her cat curled as close to the flame as it dare. "La, such a happy home." Amongst what he has brought back is food for the animals and a small cask of beer. He is filling a couple of glasses when the drone of the saws changes timbre, as it does between one log and the next. It is more than the interval between logs though. Instead of the sound of the saws biting into another log the pounding stops and there is silence. "Ahhhhh. They must be done sawing for the day."

"Tis a blessed silence. Dare I remove the wool from my ears?" She has her raingear hanging to dry and has scraped the mud from her boots. Robert does the same, and then sits down with Mara close to the fire. The room is a bit foggy from the steam rising off their wet clothes.

There is a knock and the door opens, "Hello Robert," a blonde haired man with a round beard steps in and looks around, "I am glad to see that you have it warm and dry." He introduces himself to Mara, "I am Philip Haumann. Please come over to the main house for dinner. We can get to know each other." He sees the boots drying by the fire and points to the carved wooden slippers by the door, "Save your nice leather boots. Wear these clogs when you walk over." He turns, "I'll be on my way. Dinner will be soon." Out the door he goes.

"That was very quick. I see why you like him. He is like you."

"Like me?"

"Quick and to the point."

"Okay, I get it. Now, let's try on these wooden slippers."

"Clogs." They each slip their feet into these shoes made of wood and slog over to the main house. Just inside the entryway is a space to hang coats and leave muddy clogs. The dining room is large and there is an assembly gathered for dinner. Besides Philip and Beatris there are five men, and a woman; sawmill help and a house maid. All are seated at the table awaiting the arrival of the two new guests. Platters of meat and dishes of vegetables are passed around. Plates are filled, then emptied with nary a word said except for, "Please pass that platter," or, "would you like some of this?" It is a congenial crowd, and a tasty meal. There is a fire in the kitchen and a fire in the living room. All is warm and inviting.

The walls are adorned with paintings handsomely mounted in molded wooden frames. Noticing a similarity of style and subject Mara asks, "Who is the painter in your family?"

"Our son, the youngest. He will paint night and day. When he runs out of paper he makes his own."

"He makes his own colors too; by crushing berries and flowers, or pulverizing rocks and shells. Sometimes mixes them with egg, sometimes with turpentine."

"Such a talent. I have never seen such a study of birds."

"He loves birds. Says they talk to him."

After dinner, and the hired hands leave for their own cabins. Mara and Robert sit at the big table sipping wine. Philip tells them, "Our oldest son is away working on a construction project."

Beatris adds, "Our youngest, the painter, has left without telling us where he planned to go."

Mara looks to see if Robert will say anything, but he encourages her to speak, so she tells them, "Our children are grown and have children of their own. They are off to the Americas. We receive posts, but will probably never see them again." She says this matter of factually, without apparent sadness.

Robert says something to fill in the silence. "They felt there was no way at home for young folks to thrive." Shaking his head, "now the new landholders leave us no choice but to leave."

Philip, while refilling glasses informs his guests, "I can show you a vacant home tomorrow. It is a ways up the river and there are actually three vacant homes for you to choose from. It is a drainage project with three windmills. For each mill there is a home. It was a robust enterprise undertaken by an old fellow that had made his fortune selling tulips. He got in right at the beginning of the craze and then had to find something to invest his money in." Philip and Beatris exchange a glance leading Robert and Mara to likewise exchange glances wondering what is being left unsaid. "I was the contractor hired to build the windmills. Eventually, instead of a marsh there is now a polder with acres of farmland, and a pleasant little lake held back with a dike. Each of the three mills has a house and the old gentleman always had members of his family and friends living in them." Another glance is exchanged. "To get there takes an hour or two on horseback."

Robert asks, "Is it on the river? Could we sail there?"

"Oh sure," Philip smiles. "It is an old river landing with a stone wharf. We can sail your ship with my little boat tied behind, then I will row myself back home if you folks decide to stay."

Mara cannot help herself, "What of the tulip farmer and his family?"

"Alas, the old man passed on last summer. His family and friends all liked to visit, but never really liked living out here, and so have all returned to city life." Anticipating further questions, "The property, up until recently, has been held up in probate court and stands empty." He pauses, sips his wine, looks to his wife, then breathes in deeply as if he is unsure of how to continue. "The whereabouts of the man who has inherited the property are unknown, leaving me in charge for the time being. I am hoping to find tenants. It is not good for homes to be left unlived in, and not good at all for those windmills to stand idle. With all this rain that little lake will soon overflow its dike."

"Okay." Robert stands, extends a hand to his wife, "We will take our leave and be ready to sail in the morning. We thank you for the wonderful meal."

♡♡♡

Ferrying their caravan down the river has left the mountains behind. Setting off from the ferry dock at Nijmeegs they continue following the River Rijn toward the Nord Zee. Since reaching the lowlands it has been raining, "At least it is not snow," sighs Kirin.

This flat landscape is not very appealing to these folks, having lived their lives in the mountains, "Even if the clouds lifted there is nothing to see," grieves Razs as he pulls back the curtain again, peering out the window of their caravan, for about the thousandth time today. He would rather be outside of the wagon, but this rain and this mud, "Our father had a brilliant idea widening the wheels of our wagon; otherwise it would be mired in this muck up to the axles. We would be stuck forever."

Audrae groans as she scrubs mud off her most beautiful boots, "What do the people who live here wear on their feet to withstand this slippery sloppy mud?" She is worrying that they will never come clean. "The sun must shine occasionally," she throws up an arm in despair, "else how could all these grasses be growing the way they do? Taller than me."

Vejz, wanting his siblings to know that he is not bothered by the rain, the mud, or the flatness of the land tells his siblings pedantically, "If this is where we are going to live, then we will eventually be getting used to it: so you all might as well start getting used to it now."

"Shuut Uup. Go back to sleep!" The other three shout in unison, while tossing whatever is available in his direction.

Outside, driving the wagon, Renaldo speaks his thoughts out loud, "Wouldn't it be nice to find a dry stable for our horses tonight?"

Annia, holding a sleeping cat within her oilskin cape nods ahead toward an arrangement, in the near distance, of a series of Windmills, homes, barns, and sheds, "Perhaps the folks living there will allow us the use of a barn." Looking up she notices a ray of sunlight shining through a gap in the clouds, "Well, there is the first sunshine we've seen in a few days. Let's hope there will be more." Opening her cape for the cat to see the bit of sunlight, "Look kitty, some sunshine. Maybe there will be some dry dirt for you to dig in."

They are all feeling the need for dryness. They have been traveling beneath a dense cloud cover, and there has been plenty of rain. Still thinking out loud, Ren laments, "Just when I think the rain has stopped, I feel the drops landing on my cap again."

Annia responds with her own repetitive thoughts, "Water everywhere. We are following this enormous river, and there is all this marshland, and there are all these canals! Water, Water, Water. We must be getting near the ocean for it to be as soggy as this."

"There may be some dry land up ahead where those windmills are."

Their oilskin capes and wide brimmed hats keep the rain off, but still, the moisture has seeped inside and underneath, dampening clothes and spirits alike. Renaldo's hopes for shelter at this next settlement seem unfounded as they get closer and see no sign of life. There are no animals in the pastures. There is no light shining out from the windows. There is no smoke rising from the chimneys. They stop in front of the home nearest the road; there are more houses and buildings and windmills further back. The dock on the river brandishes a sign with carved letters spelling out 'Schoonhoven Landing'. Renaldo hands the reins to his wife, "I will see if there is anyone about and if there is a dry spot for us." Stepping down and going to the back of the wagon he opens the door where all four children are pulling on boots and jackets anticipating release, "Please wait inside while I go up to the house." He closes the door upon the sullen expressions of his children.

He knocks on the door at the front of the house and when there is no response he goes around to the back, calling out, "Hello. Hello. Anybody?" Stealing a glance through a window he notices that it is mostly empty inside. There are herbs growing in the kitchen garden that have been left untended. There are flowers blooming in beds where they are outnumbered by the weeds. He heads toward the large barn, calling out again before opening the door, "Hello. Hello. Anybody?" Opening the door to the immense stable, he sees that there is an open area easily large enough for their little home on wheels, and there are stalls enough for all the horses. It is dry and clean and smells of hay.

He is startled by the ruffling of feathers. He looks up. Perched high in the rafters are two owls, white-faced birds with blinking eyes, *Ooh-hoo-hoo*, they say.

"Welcome friends. My apologies if I have wakened you." It is a pleasant omen: a barn with owls has fewer rodents.

Ren asks the birds, for there is nobody else to ask, "May we share your barn this night?" Both birds spread their wings wide and drift down from the rafters, circle where he stands, and then lift themselves back up to their perch. "Okay then, I will take that as an invitation. Thank you." He feels good about this and will bring the wagon and the horses inside. Tomorrow they will seek out neighbors and, who knows, maybe this place is available for new inhabitants. He swings open the great doors and sets them to remain open. He is impressed by the heft and balance of these doors, and by the fine detail of the hinges and latches. Walking out the drive to inform his family of their good fortune he is pleased that it is not presently raining. There is even some sunshine, and far off across the wide river is a partial rainbow. He opens the back door of the caravan and tells the children, "We will stay here for the night. Please be patient and stay inside a little bit longer until the wagon is in where it is dry. Then to Annia, "I'll leave the driving to you." She nods affirmatively. "There is a turnaround, and we can back the wagon inside." The team of horses recognize that they are near a barn and are prompt about bringing the wagon around, and steady as they back into the great open space within. They smell hay in the dry air. Barely past the threshold the children have the door open and are hopping out even before the wagon is fully halted. They are overjoyed to be finally out of the confining inner compartment. Ren tells them, "We are not alone." They follow his gaze to discover the two owls gazing wide-eyed down at them.

Together they all join in unharnessing the team, then with buckets and water and brushes clean the accumulated mud off the horses' legs and bellies, finally getting each one into its own stall with a share of grass and a bit of grain. Audrae, allowing herself the privilege of being the first to explore tells them, "This barn has a room with a desk and chairs and empty racks for tack. There is even a little stove, but there is no wood for building a fire."

Pointing toward a neatly stacked pile of turves Vejz tells her, "They don't burn firewood here, they burn peat."

"A fire of sod?' she asks, for that is what she sees.

Picking a couple pieces off the top of the stack, he motions for her to follow, "Let us see how difficult it is to get this sod burning," then with a questioning glance toward his parents, "that is, if it is allright to start a fire." They each shrug to one another, then give affirmative nods, eager themselves to see how a peat fire burns. While the two youngest set about getting the fire burning the two older siblings help with hanging lines and draping all their things to dry.

Success with the fire prompts the warming of dinner. When the meal is finished and the bedding laid out in the little storage room they sit basking in the radiant warmth while relishing being dry through and through for the first time in days. "Mom," inquires Kirin, "it has been so very long since you have brought out your globe," referring to her mother's heirloom.

"Yes, it is so warm and dry and dreamy here," concurs Vejz, "I feel that the charming pursuance of the orb would fit in splendidly with this comfortable ambience." He prides himself in his vocabulary.

"You should talk like other people talk," Audrae teases her brother for his choice of words.

Mimicking her voice, "Be like everyone else," he jests, "says the girl who flaunts her unique one-of-a-kind style."

Ren agrees with Kirin's suggestion, "This does seem like a good moment for the orb," then teases, "otherwise Vejz and Audrae will be teasing one another in their dreams."

Annia had already been considering the orb; the object that, together with the necklace, has been passed down through generations of her mother's family. Both items are imbued with qualities of enchantment. The Golden Orb tends to ease thoughts, and provides deep sleep accompanied with pleasant dreaming. "I will fetch it," she tells them as she rises and hands her goblet to Renaldo for a refill. She leaves the room with candle in hand. The goblets they are drinking from this evening are a matched set of Slovakian crystal. The bottle of wine, a special vintage, has been carried with them in anticipation of an event such as this. They are all hoping that they have found a place to stay for a while; perhaps even a home.

Annia returns, carrying the plain wooden reliquary that holds her family heirlooms; a necklace of golden hearts and a golden orb. She sits herself cross-legged on her mat with the box beside her. She sips her wine, and then setting aside the crystal goblet, raises the rounded lid of the chest. She takes the velvet bag holding the necklace and sets it aside for now. She then withdraws and unfolds a cloth of unnaturally fine weave, revealing a map of the starfield. Next, from the chest, she withdraws a saucer, and places it in the center of the map of stars. Lastly she eases out the globe itself, releasing it from its soft velour pouch. It is a fist-sized golden sphere that shimmers in the candle light. Cradling the orb lightly with the fingertips of both hands, she extends it forward. When it is within a hands-breadth of the dish it is drawn out of her grasp by some inexplicable force, and with a barely discernable snap, seats itself into the hollow center of the saucer. The two items, now together, are the size of an apple in a custard dish. From experience they all know what will happen next, so candles are extinguished as they all lay their heads upon their pillows and pull their covers up snug. In the darkness and the silence the orb's faint humming begins. As the sound crescendos they witness its steadily brightening glow. The orb transforms from the original golden sheen to a frosty mist. The hum stops. The orb clears and becomes crystalline; radiating a colorful aura that has them all sensing safety and comfort.

They feel the familiar sleepiness that the crystal ball provides; an all-pervading ease. They know that they will sleep well, and be splendidly aware in their dreaming. As each settles in under their covers Annia begins the litany learned as a girl and practiced throughout her lifetime; as her mother and her grandmothers before her had learned and practiced. "Our sun, moon, and stars shine light through us. Our Earth shines light through us. Our own light shines through us." Altogether, their breathing lightens. "The wellspring of love bubbles up from our hearts." Their pulse softens. "Light as spirit. Spirit as life. Every living thing is alive with light. Everything is alive." It feels wonderful to imagine light in everything; the animals, the plants, the rocks, the rivers, and all the empty spaces in between, not empty, but filled with light. "Imagine that we are dreaming our lives." All are asleep. In restful slumber their dreaming begins. The secret of this golden orb is that it inspires vivid dreaming, and consequently vivid waking.

As Razs becomes aware that he is dreaming he focuses upon swinging out on a rope that hangs from a branch over the river. He feels the excitement of letting go and the thrill of flying through the air, except in his dreaming he does not splash into the water below. Instead he remains suspended, or surprisingly, as he rolls and dives then ascends again, he realizes that he is flying. It is not flying as a bird flies: there is no effort, nor flapping of wings. His heart bubbles forth with joy as he follows a thread of light. There is always another thread, and another to follow. He gazes toward where he desires to be and then there is a thread to carry him there. When he shifts his gaze he shifts his direction of flight. He is moving along by simply wishing toward where he wants to be. He feels happy and free.

Kirin becomes aware of the sun's warming light as she is dreaming of floating gently and easily on a river's current. She skims along the smooth surface, buoyed afloat with the love bubbling forth within. This river is bordered on both sides by thick forests. Then the water is splashing as the river tumbles through a narrow channel strewn with boulders. Even though she is tossed to and fro across the frothing foam of the cascading current she is confidently trusting that there is only fun here. It is exhilarating to be skirring through the rapids. She reaches another calm stretch: some colorful ducks zip past. Oh, there are more rapids ahead! Never has floating on a river been so easy and fun. She is happy and free.

Vejz discovers, as he wanders between aisles of shelves, that he is dreaming a cosmic library: an archive of knowledge, known and unknown. Shelves stretch in all directions. Shelves that are as tall as the sky and filled with books bound more colorfully than any he's ever seen before. It is a most magnificent library; more spectacular than any he has ever before visited. Books that match his interest reveal themselves to him. There is a book that shows what is inside his body, and a book that shows what is inside his earth, and a book that shows him the vast universe that he is a part of. There are books showing him what has yet to be discovered in the waking realm. There is a book showing him that the purpose of life is to feel happy and be free.

Audrae is at the top of a muddy river bank when she realizes that she is dreaming. Instead of feeling loathing for the slimy mud she feels exuberance as she laughs and slides belly first down the slippery bank into the water. Her momentum carries her out into the current where she surfaces and, rolling belly up, luxuriates in the warm sunlight, but not for long. She flips over and is paddling her sleek furry body back to shore before the current can carry her away. She scurries up the bank again chasing after her litter mates. Upon reaching the top they all slide and splash down again as they have been sliding and splashing all morning while their ma sits nearby, grooming herself and loving the fun her pups are having. They are all happy and free.

Renaldo is seated in the little sailboat that he thought he would never sail again, having left it behind, but then remembers that he is dreaming as he skims across the smooth surface of the lake. The wind has blown away his hat so his hair is free. In this glorious setting he has no care whether his hair will tangle or twist. He nears the shore and the boat slides smoothly onto the sand. With graceful fluidity he is out of the boat and feeling the warm sand between his toes as he rushes toward Annia waiting for him there. They often dream together. As they embrace and kiss tenderly two slim figures step out of the shadows of the forest and into the bright sunlight of the beach. They are very tall and have glowing bodies covered with lavender colored feathers. They beckon for Renaldo and Annia who follow along a path meandering between the trees. Sparkling lights drop flickering from the branches, transforming into frolicking sprites whose infectious giggling has Renaldo and Annia giggling along and feeling happy and free. The lavender celestials raise their arms and the forest sprites settle. The breeze slows. The two, radiating love and joy, speak as one, "Love each other and be happy. There is no need to wonder why you live or what you are supposed to do, for there is nothing more important than to Love and Be Happy!" They transform into bundles of silvery threads; filaments of light. All the little sprites, become flashes of light again flittering off and away into the forest from whence they have come. Annia and Renaldo, feeling happy and free, are filled with trusting certainty that even in their waking there is happiness and freedom.

♡♡♡

Morning arrives with sunshine lining the edges of the clouds orange and yellow. There is a gentle breeze. Higher up the wind is moving those orange tinged clouds briskly across the sky. It is the noise of Renaldo opening the doors and leading the horses out to the tall grass that awakens the others. They roll up their blankets and gather just outside the huge barn, surveying their surroundings in the full light of morning. The big doors are opened wide to allow the fresh air through all the clothes and blankets still hanging there from yesterday. The nearby Windmill stands tall against the sky. Looking down the drive that leads away from the river there are two more windmills, each with an accompanying home and numerous sheds. A canal running in line with the three windmills empties into the river. Far away, past the third windmill, there is a lake shimmering in the morning sunlight. Catching movement out of the corner of his eye and turning around toward the wide river, "Look," Razs says. A fair-sized ship is gliding in alongside the wharf. Its sails are lowering. Two bearded men jump from the ship onto the stone quay, each carries a line, and each ties that line to a cleat; fore and aft. A woman wearing trousers hops easily over the gunwale. These three walk up the ramp that brings them to the top of the pillared breaker wall. Upon seeing the family watching from the barn they wave and call out, "Halloo."

Renaldo answers back, "Halloooo," then reaching out to gather his family, "Let us go introduce ourselves." They meet on the roadway separating the windmill from the river. Renaldo is the first to introduce himself, "Hello and Good Morning to you. My name is Renaldo Gedimin, and this is my family. We are pleased to make your acquaintances," testing his language skills, hoping his words are understood.

The heavier of the two men steps forward returning the greeting, "How do you sail today?" Noticing that these folks are foreigners, "Pleased to meet you. I am Philip van Haumann, and I have with me two guests from the land of Éire," extending an arm to one side, "Robert," then to his other side, "Mara."

Renaldo introduces his family one by one, "My wife Annia. Our oldest, Razs. Our daughter, Kirin. Our next in line, Vejz. Our youngest, Audrae." Each curtsies, or bows, as they are introduced. "We have come from over the mountains. We have been traveling across the Germanic lands and have taken a ferry down this huge river." Then admitting that they have trespassed, "We have taken advantage of the dry barn for the night--" he is interrupted by Haumann.

"And well that you should," Philip smiles, "'tis a shame for these buildings to be sitting here empty and unused."

So Annia asks, "Why are these homes and shops standing empty, and these windmills idle?"

"Ah-hah," begins Haumann, "allow me to give you a brief history." He has a genuine smile and everyone is happy to listen as he points toward the river, "Of all the wharves along this river, this particular wharf has been called Schoonhoven Landing for as long as anyone can remember." Now directing them all toward a square of stones, next to where they are standing, which clearly outline the foundation of a building that had once stood here, "This was where the landing's storehouse stood. Not very far upriver from here is a track, roadway if you will, that leads inland to the township of Schoonhoven, which is a half-day ride on a good horse." Now, winking and speaking conspiratorially he fills them in with the rest of the story, "This landing once held the reputation as a haven for Smugglers."

"La!" Says Robert, "Our home port, Ríoga Cove, has the same reputation of being a safehold for smugglers." Catching all eyes on him he quickly adds, while holding up his hands innocently, "Not me! Oh no. I'm no pirate. I am willing to pay all tariffs." He points to the VOC flag at the top of his ship's mast. "There, you see? I am registered."

Haumann laughs for he knows Robert to be an honest man, "This landing, built upon a mound ages ago, after having sat empty and unused for," he shrugs, "who knows how long, provided a great opportunity for the right person to come along intending to drain the marsh. That person was a man named Donar van Eyck. A very fortunate man, one of the few, who survived the tulip madness by selling off at the height of it all."

"Tulip Madness?" asks Audrae.

Philip looks at all the faces and sees the same questioning look. "I am not sure if I know how to explain the tulip madness except that it arose from bankers scheming to trade tulip bulbs. Er, well that is, bulbs that had not even yet been grown. Getting paid in advance at ridiculously high value. Over-valued futures." He laughs, "There is no explaining the things that some people will do. Donar van Eyck though, did understand, perhaps better than anybody else. Most tulip investors lost all their money, but he came away with a fortune. Donar was not a banker, no, he was a farmer, a true lover of the land. After purchasing the property of Schoonhoven Landing he contracted with me to have the mills built and the marsh drained. He endeavored to have his family join him, and they often did visit, but would never stay for as long he wished. He had no wife, nor any children of his own, but he had many brothers and sisters. And nieces and nephews. Alas, Donar van Eyck passed on last year, leaving his wealth to his family, and this property to his *molenaar*."

Renaldo asks, "Are you the molenaar? Has he left this property to you?"

Laughing now, "Alas, no. I am merely acting as agent for the current owner."

Mara starts walking, "Well then, let us discover what is available. I do believe that I am encouraged by what I see so far."

Philip invites the Gedimin family, "You are welcome to follow along with us. There are three available homes here. It will be serendipitous if two of these empty homes are being lived in before this day ends." They set off as a group while he continues his commentary. He is a talker, "This is the first mill of the *Molengang*," pausing to assess the crowd, then explaining the term, "windmills lined up in order. Over the years these three mills have operated together to drain the standing water away, leaving this vast *Polder*. Wonderful farmland. This first windmill, *Windhoek*," pointing out to the others the nameplate above the entry, "drained this section of land that we are standing upon. Then the next drained down some more, and then the third. All three mills work as a team; a *Molengang*. Down past the third mill is a dike holding back the lake." He raises a hand beckoning all of them to follow; the teacher confident that he has explained everything perfectly.

Vejz, ever the inquisitive one, asks, "Windhoek is this windmill's name? So, then each has been named? What are the names of the others?"

"It is tradition to name a mill, just as ships are given names. And like ships, we call the arms that catch the wind sails."

"Why are these sails not turning?" Kirin wonders.

"The marsh has been drained these many years now. Whereas many mill owners have refitted drainage mills for other purposes, Donar did not want to be disturbed by the noise. He enjoyed the idyllic life. He was a nature lover." Then to Vejz, "Oh, and to finish answering your question; the next mill, the center mill is named *Windmidden*, and the third, down by the lake, is *Windweg*."

Noticing curtains in the upper windows of the mill, Ren asks, "Do folks live inside these windmills?"

"Oh yes, indeed. The lower level has the canal running through where the scoop wheel does its work lifting the water. The second level up has a kitchen and loom. The third level has beds. The cap is where all the gears are."

Amazed at the size of the machine, Razs asks incredulously, "And the sails connect to the cap and the cap turns to match the direction of the wind? Does the whole top of the windmill revolve?"

"Yes. That is the job of the *Molenaar*. Sometimes the mill owner will operate his own mill, but usually hires a *Molenaar,* which is a millwright, to keep the sails turning and all the inner workings cared for properly."

The group leaves the windmill and now as they are walking toward the house Renaldo finds himself walking along with Robert and asks tentatively, "So, you recently left your home in Ireland?"

"Yes. Sad as I am to say it, we have left behind the lives we knew. The current circumstances rather forced us away. How about you?"

"Yes. We have left our home. For general principles. Primarily, we found ourselves without a home and determined it to be an opportunity to move away from the crowded conditions of the city."

Opening the door of the house, Philip bows while extending an arm graciously through the entryway, "Ladies first." Annia and Mara, without stopping to look at anything else, head straightaway to the beautifully crafted loom, bumping each other as they coincidently seat themselves. Behind them Philip explains, "My son builds looms in his factory. Donar has one in each home and in each mill. I think he hoped that somebody in his family would take up weaving and decide to stay here keeping him company."

"This looks to be set up for linen," Mara muses.

"Do you weave with linen thread?" Annia asks her.

"I am used to hemp or wool. Sailcloth and winter clothing."

"We occasionally weave wool, but mostly linen."

"Donar farmed flax here in hopes of producing the linen thread for these looms," Philip is still talking while directing their attention through the windows at the fields beyond, "and those long sheds were built for drying the stalks." Chuckling now, "He would hire crews for harvesting and to ret the stalks in the canal. The odor being so horrible during the retting that his relatives would stay away for the season. And then there was the hammering of the stalks for the thread. Geez," shaking his head while laughing to himself at the memory, "alas, another failed attempt. None of his family wanted to live here during the processing of the flax."

The women, while listening to his story, are appraising the view out these windows. In this corner of the house, where the loom sits, there is a magnificent panoramic view of the fields, the river, and the sky. Each of them is imagining sitting in this well lighted spot weaving. "I like it here," Mara says, "I can be happy here."

Robert agrees, "I like it here. The dock is perfect, and I can rebuild a warehouse on the remaining foundation. Perhaps even carry on as before."

"Can you add a loading crane to the wharf?" Mara wonders.

He looks speculatively to Haumann, who answers, "I can ask the proprietor." Rolling his eyes up, giving him a bewildered expression, "When I see him next. Whenever that will be." Changing the subject, "Shall we move on? There is still much to see."

Approaching the barn and admiring the six stately horses of the Gedimin team, "Your magnificent horses resemble the quality Donar was so proud to have here in his stables. He had fine heavy horses for pulling his coaches, and many excellent light horses for riding."

"We are used to having horses for riding." Annia says, and then to her children, "and yes if this be our new home we will soon have horses to ride again."

"Hallelujah!" Audrae peels, bringing laughter from everyone else. "I've had enough of riding in carts."

"La, a girl after my own heart," Mara laughs, then reminding Robert, "I will also be needing a horse to ride."

When Philip had first set eyes on this Polish family and their colorful caravan he had wondered if they were vagrants, but now that he has gotten a better look at their well-bred horses and their elaborate home on wheels he is certain that these are steady folk. He directs them to follow along the drive past the long stable toward the second windmill rising majestically up to the sky. All around them the flax grows tall. "This second windmill was my younger son's second home. When he was a boy growing up I would send him to help Donar with the miller's duties." He remembers how Diedrik had ridden back and forth whenever the wind changed. "Then, as he grew older, the old man began paying him directly for his services, and allowing him the living quarters of this windmill; *Windmidden*." Speaking wistfully as he opens the door into this second mill, "They became great friends: my son and that old man."

Each one of them walking through that door see that the rounded inner walls of this windmill are covered with sketches and paintings. It appears to be the daily practice of years on display. When they are all inside Philip tells them, "My son, Diedrik, is a painter." Spreading his arms wide, "These are examples of his work."

"It is like a gallery," Kirin coos.

"He must paint every day," Vejz remarks.

Mara remembers the paintings they had seen last night, "You told us that he makes his own paper and mixes his own paint?"

"When he has to. He makes good paper with a smooth finish. As you can tell by this sampling of his work, he often runs out of paper and colors."

Ren, standing before a series of pictures showing houses in trees connected by walkways along the branches says, "This is very interesting. People living in trees."

Philip explains, "Donar collected myths. He was particularly fond of the legends of the forest people. Diedrik, sharing his interest, often painted how he imagined it must have been when humankind lived in trees."

"The forest people?"

"Our ancestral predecessors built their homes in the trees. In the olden days, before mounds and dikes, living in trees would have been the only reasonable way to survive the springtime floods, or the high tides of the Nord Zee. Our ancestors revered the forests and have always been woodcutters, shaping whatever they needed from wood. Even wore wooden shoes; a tradition that continues on to this day."

There is a large section of the gallery devoted to paintings of birds. Coming to a series that are all similar Audrae shouts out, "Whoa, look at this. There are pictures of people riding on the backs of eagles." She turns to Haumann, "Are there birds this size around here?"

He laughs, charmed by this question, "Diedrik wishes there were." Now bringing their attention to a series portraying a wild-haired fella with a great big smile, "these are of the old man himself; Donar van Eyck." They all crowd around and admire the artist's skill that has set sparkling glints in the eyes and light-heartedness in the man's smile.

"He looks happy," comments Mara.

"He was always happy." Philip moves them along, "Let us be on our way." They move on and inspect the Windmidden home and are fascinated by the upper gables that allow sunlight to stream down into the living area making it bright and cheery. "I remember Donar considering having the upper windows set with colored glass, but a niece living here at the time disapproved: said something about not wanting it to be churchy in here." In the long open space there are work tables and chairs, a cooking area, and beds separated by a partition. There are lots of windows. Daylight streaming in makes it light and bright and welcoming.

At the third windmill, *Windweg*, the home is situated very close to the lake which is held back here by another timber pillared dike. Philip notices to his dismay, "The water level is nearly up to the tops of the timbers. These mills should be turning now."

There is a wooden dock with an overturned boat resting there. The house sprawls with additional wings and rooms. There is an inner courtyard with a fountain. Audrae tugs her mother's sleeve whispering, "If we lived here we could all have our own room."

"This is where most visitors stayed. This is where they held parties," Philip tells them. "There were always servants in the kitchen," he directs their attention to a separate room full of counters and cupboards and a sink. "Most times of year there were men working the fields and needing a place to sleep," pointing to a plain square barrack between the house and the mill. "Donar loved having other people around him. His workers were as much his family as everybody else that visited here."

The Gedimin family gather in a huddle with their heads together. Philip moves outside. He sees Robert and Mara also have their heads together. He stands apart, giving them all a moment to themselves. He walks down by the lakeshore and looking again at the water level knows that these windmills need to sail, need to drain down the level of this lake. He wishes Diedrik were here. Diedrik had always done such a fine job of keeping these mills in order ever since he was young. Ah, he had been so aggrieved when the old man died. Then so lost when the probate officials had claimed the place and made him leave. He had not been himself back at home; always angry, then leaving without a good-bye. He misses having his son around.

"Philip?" Robert's voice startles him out of his reverie. "We are wondering about a few things."

"Yes?"

"We have decided that we would like to live here, in the first home, the one closest to the river and the wharf."

"Ah yes, the Windhoek home. Splendid."

"Can we move in today, or do we have to file papers with lawyers?

"Yes, you can move in today. No, there are no papers or lawyers."

Renaldo calls over, "We accept your invitation to live in this lovely home by the lake."

"Splendid! Splendid Indeed!" Rubbing his palms together. "Since you will all be staying here, there is a favor I have to ask of you before I leave today." He receives quick approvals all around, with everyone eagerly anticipating his request. "I want to make millers of you all. Let us get these Windmills sailing so they can drain the lake down to its summer level." He is met with excitement, especially from the adolescents. "We will have to begin where we started, at *Windhoek*," pointing back toward the river, "the windy corner."

As they walk the distance of the property Philip begins their instruction, "A *Molenaar's* primary focus is to know which direction the wind is coming from. How do you suppose he does that?"

A lifetime of sailing has given Robert a natural tendency to recognize the direction of the wind. As a young sailor he had been taught to keep watch of the triangle flag at the top of the ship's mast, and so he has already noticed that at the top of each windmill is a wind vane. He nudges Razs, who happens to be walking next to him, and points up to the top of Windmidden, "Do you see that little rooster up there?"

"It is standing on an arrow above the points of the compass. It is like vanes I have seen at the top of the pointy towers of the highest buildings." Razs remembers watching the direction of the wind, "Sometimes knowing where the wind comes from gives us a clue as to what weather to expect."

"A wind miller always knows the direction of the wind." Philip then continues by asking another question, "Have you ever noticed the clouds high above moving faster than the breeze that you feel down here closer to Mother Earth?" His students crowd closer. "The wind is fascinating. You want to always know which way the wind is blowing. The wind is your hobby."

Vejz is reminded of the hill he used to climb every day, "It seems like the wind is always blowing at the top of a hill."

"The wind is indeed awesome."

They arrive at Windhoek, the windmill closest to the river, enter and climb the stairs up to a door opening out to the platform that circles the entire structure. Philip leads them around this upper story walkway until they are standing at the interstice of the tail pole and braces. He stops at a wheel that is taller than he is. "This is the capstan wheel," placing his foot on one of the spokes of a large wooden wheel, "it turns the cap. The sails move with the cap when it is turned." He asks them to watch and remember as he releases the anchor chains and the spoke chain. He invites them all to turn the capstan wheel. They all try. It does not budge. "It may be stiff after setting in one position for so long." Stepping onto one of the wheel's spokes, he grunts while dropping his weight into his feet, and the entire apparatus moves. Once it has started moving he steps up to the next spoke and the next, like climbing a ladder, until he is centered over a different set of anchoring posts. "What do you think? Are the sails set properly now to catch the wind?" His wide-eyed students are thrilled by what he has accomplished.

"So does the cap need to be turned every day?" asks Razs, wondering how often they will get to do this.

"Sometimes a miller will reset his mill many times a day, but I will not expect you to do that."

"Actually," Renaldo tells him, "I think we all like the idea of climbing up here and jumping on that wheel."

"Ahhhhh, natural born *Molenaars*. La." Philip leads them back inside. "You will want to climb up and look at the workings of the gears and the brake blocks someday, but for today let us get these sails turning. Once down the stairs he points out something else he intends for them to remember, "This is the brake rope. The miller grasps it firmly with one hand while loosening it from the cleat with the other," he checks to be certain that they are all watching what he is doing while he does it, "and then by letting go of the rope the brake is released and the sails are free to turn." After loosening the brake and the wind is turning the sails, the large center post begins to spin, turning the gears that revolve the scoop wheel, and as the scoop wheel turns, splashing water from below to the channel above, the sluice gate opens allowing the water to flow out toward the river. "And there it is, we have the first of the three windmills turning. Two more to go."

All of these newcomers stand in awe admiring the workings of this giant wooden machine with so many moving parts turning in unison. Outside they gaze in wonder at the gracefully turning sails. Robert says, "They catch the wind the same as the foresail of my ship."

"Interestingly," Philip, a man who always has a story, tells him, "I have been told that the shape of these windmill sails, and the shape of a ship's foresail are both designed after the pattern of a bird's wing."

"Right," agrees Robert, "I see that."

They move on to the other windmills. Philip has them all take turns. Explaining to them not to worry, "These windmills practically run themselves." Although nobody had to sign any papers, before he leaves Philip does bring out a pen and paper to record their names, "So if the authorities come asking I can tell them that you are not squatters." Then he rows away downriver leaving the rest to begin unpacking and moving in.

The Kikker Gat Public House

Cornelius Janszoon is pleased with how circumstances have come about on this first morning of his life away from sailing. His coincidental meeting with Trinjntje and Nicklas has him wondering how his plans will change, yet remaining optimistic about everything working out. Having them ride along will provide a diversion without having to alter his plans. He rationalizes their behavior to the emotional lag one feels upon returning home after an extended voyage. First time passengers aboard ship are always warned by seasoned travelers to expect a few days of funk upon reaching the end of a long voyage. So, he tells himself, the two youngsters require a few days to settle down; he, as well, may need a few days to settle into this new life he is embarking upon. Trinjntje and Nicklas have split off for now, to meet up later outside the city. Cornelius arrives at the *Koetshuis Inn* as a fully loaded carriage is departing, presenting an amiable lull of activity. The troop of soldiers have been here and gone, leaving two soldiers stationed as lookouts.

The *Koetshuis* is more than a coach stop: they also have a long standing reputation for building fine coaches and trading quality horses. Business is thriving in this good economy. Cornelius enters and introduces himself to the hostess at the front counter. She tells him, "We are expecting you Captain." She flashes him a bright smile, "Please wait here. I will be right back." As she disappears through a doorway he looks around the large dining room. About half of the tables are full and the aroma wafting from the kitchen is making him wish that he had waited to eat here. La, but then he would not have met those two runaways. His hostess returns carrying a tankard decorated with a painting of the *Koetshuis Inn.* She hands it to him with a big smile, "Our finest brew Sir. The mug is a token of our appreciation. There is a young man outside with your new cart waiting and ready to go." She allows him to take a drink from his new mug before taking his arm and leading him through the bustling room.

Out the back door and down the steps awaits his coach. It is a clever new design that has an enclosed bench up front and an open deck behind. A canopy extends over the bench for keeping out the rain, and rises up in front of the knees for keeping out the mud. There are two windowpanes behind the bench allowing the driver to see what is behind. There is storage space beneath the bench that will always be dry. Behind this little cab is a deck equipped with side rails. Under a tarp there are boxes, kegs, and sacks filled with everything a new pantry will need. Janszoon's sailor's trunk is also there under the tarp.

The young fellow that greets him is holding a clay jug which, like the mug Cornelius is already carrying, has a picture of the *Koetshuis Inn* painted on its side. "Greetings Sir," he bows to the captain and presents the jug, "May I present to you a complimentary flagon filled with the same tasty brew that is in your cup; brewed here by our *Koetshuis* brewers. I will set it here," placing it under the driver's bench of the new wagon, "so you will be able to refill your mug easily." He smiles and tips his head, he squints one eye half winking, "Now let me acquaint you with this fine little wagon."

"Wagon?" Questions Janszoon, "is that what a coach this size is called?"

"A coach," the youngster tells him pedantically, "is fully enclosed."

"Wagon," snickers Janszoon, "sounds like a child's toy."

"What you have chosen, Sir, while too small for commerce and too open for the Gentility, is well suited for a gentleman farmer. It has an under carriage strong enough to carry a heavy load, yet soft enough to give it a remarkably smooth ride. You will especially appreciate these springs holding up the driver's bench." This man is proud of what is built here. "We are very pleased to have found these horses for you, Sir. We hope they are exactly what you wanted. They are bred from a line out of the province of *Perche*."

A pair of tall black horses are harnessed to the wagon. "They are magnificent." Janszoon introduces himself to the two horses, rubbing their noses and withers, while examining their legs and telling the great beasts, "You are handsome and strong. You will be my guides. We will be friends." He inspects his wagon, and looking under the tarp is pleased to see all that has been arranged there as per the directives of his accountant. He is feeling as giddy as a child; reeling from the splendid outcome of his plans. He steps up and seats himself comfortably on the driver's bench. Releasing the brake, and with a shake of the reins, he is on his way.

It seems that his business at the coachouse has taken only a short time, but he travels along the canal path quite a distance before catching up with his two traveling companions. He finds them with a group of children that are showing off whatever is inside of the basket at their feet. He sets the brake and jumps down to see for himself. The children are all telling him, "We have some very nice kittens. They catch mice. If you take them all we'll let you have the basket." Nicklas and Trinjntje each hold a kitten and there are three more mewling away in the basket.

Cornelius asks the children, "Do you have food for them?" One of the girls holds up a jar of milk. "Okay," he says as he takes the basket of kittens and the jar of milk. Placing all snugly in the space beneath the bench, "I have always imagined cats walking along the rails in my stable. I have not had pets since I was a youngster. These kitties will be fun." Feeling even more like a kid now he waves for Trin and Klas to join him on the bench, "Let's go!"

Trinjntje and Nicklas put their kittens in the basket with the rest and stow their bags alongside. When they are all settled and Cornelius has the little wagon moving again, he hands his empty tankard over to Nicklas, "Please be so kind as to refill this from the jug beneath your seat." When the mug is filled and being handed back he waves it off, "You first. We will share and celebrate together." They each drink from the tall mug while admiring the splendid scene of the *Koetshuis Inn* painted on the outside.

As Trinjntje hands him the mug she says, "My dad has a collection of these mugs; one for every carriage and cart he has ever purchased. The painting has changed over the years to match the growth of their business."

"La, is that your reason for buying this wagon?" Nicklas jokes, "So that you will have your own collection of *Koetshuis* mugs?"

They all laugh. The two horses toss their heads whinnying a staccato, *Ee-ee-ee-ee-ee*, laughing along with them.

"Are your horses laughing too?" Trinjntje asks her uncle.

A crane standing in the canal, startled by the laughter, lifts off squawking, *ah-eh-ah-eh-ah-ah-ah*. It sounds like laughter too. It sails ahead on wide spread wings to where more cranes are calling the same, *ah-eh-ah-eh-ah-ah-ah*.

"There, you see," Nicklas pronounces, "laughing is contagious. Everybody is laughing."

"Is that something they taught you in school?" Trinjntje pokes him in the ribs. He squirms away ticklishly.

Nicklas," Cornelius commands, then realizing he is using his captain's voice, softens to a friendlier tone, "Nicklas, where did you go to school?"

"Yes. Tell us. Were you a disruptive force in class?" She teases him some more.

"Why do you ask me that?! Do you think me a troublemaker? School was boring. As a child, I stymied my tutors. I was always ahead of them. In exasperation my parents sent me off to a proper academy in Paris."

"What did you study there?"

"Goofing off, mostly." He snorts, "I excelled in mathematics. I enjoyed the life sciences. I did well with the philosophers, but, was never able to accept that any one explanation described everything."

"Questioning the philosophers makes you one yourself. Is that not the scientific method?" Janszoon considers himself to be a bit of a philosopher.

"Yes, always asking questions is how I learned to stay out of trouble."

"So, you are a troublemaker?" She continues teasing him.

"School was too easy and boring. I was overjoyed when I was finally old enough to move up to the University at Utrecht."

"Are you a graduate?"

Scoffing again, "If I had graduated from the University I would not have been employed as a clerk."

Almost afraid to ask, Trinjntje queries him, "What happened?"

"My father served on the board of directors for the Port of Antwerpen." He lets that information sink in. "It was my second year at the University when the treaty of Munster closed off all traffic on the Scheldt River, shutting down the port of Antwerpen, leaving my father without a post and diminishing his assets considerably." Sighing regrettably, "My parents could no longer afford my tuition, nor did they want me returning home adding to the household expense."

Trinjntje remembers, "So many lost their livelihood. So many had to leave Antwerpen. So many came to Amsterdam."

"I was among that great crowd, and that is how I came to be a clerk in the office of the Director, your father, and consequently to my meeting you, *Mejuffrouw* Olmsfeld. Funny how life provides the most unique opportunities." This last bit is said with a touch of cynicism. "Enough about me. Tell me Trin," using the version of her name that matches her disguise, "what have you done that has so many chasing you?"

"I do not wish to talk about me."

"Give us the short version Trin," coaxes her uncle, "please."

"Okay." She breathes in deep while sitting up a bit, "When I was a little girl I had lots of friends." Both men remain silent while she gathers her thoughts. "It was very disappointing for me to discover that no one else could see my friends, nor believed that I had any friends. I was diagnosed with an over-active imagination." Another pause before she continues tremulously, "My parents told me to keep my *invisible* friends a secret."

Cornelius tells her, "I remember a visit with your mother about this."

She looks at him sideways, "There, you see, I am a troubling influence. I need to leave them be."

Nicklas asks uncertainly, "Do you still have these invisible friends?"

"Yes."

"Are they here now?'

"Yes." A tiny black bird with a red patch on each wing lands on the rump of one of the horses, peers around, then flits off again. Trinjntje watches it fly away while determining if she wants to talk about something she has never spoken with anybody else about; well, except for that rouge priest. She tells them, "Everybody has a group of these friends with them always. I do not know why I see them whilst others do not." Both men look at her. She looks back to each of them in turn. She is not joking or teasing.

"Are they spirits?"

"Spirits, memories, dreams," she sighs, "perhaps someday science will discover how to explain that this familiar world we are so fond of is not the only world." She slides her arms through theirs, "Perhaps someday science will discover where thoughts come from. Or prove that our Earth lives and breathes and thinks." They are passing a succession of these little black birds, with their red-striped wings, perched on the tops of the tall grass. The birds are taking turns, as the first one did, alighting on one of the horses' rumps for a moment before flicketing off again. "So, I am different," she tells them, "which seems to frighten some, La, while intriguing others." Releasing her companions' arms, she slaps her hands on her knees while kicking a rhythm with her heels. "Now that I have told you my secrets; you are my accomplices. La-ha! Where is your mug Uncle Cor, let us drink a toast to our alliance!"

"To our alliance," he raises the mug high, drinks, and then handing it over says, "Ever since those two tattered lawyers came aboard intending to serve you a summons I have wondered what case they claim to have against you."

"Oh, that; okay. I do not want to bore you with the long version. So let's just say, a year or so before I left Amsterdam aboard your ship on my botanic expedition I received a request to attend an inquisition. Because the Spanish no longer rule, and the laws have changed, someone meeting the criteria for inquisitioning cannot be simply arrested as before. Those desiring to inquisit are now required to ask; thus the invitation."

Nicklas is astonished, "So, let me get this straight: you were invited to your own inquisition?"

"Right."

Janszoon says, "I remember hearing that your father brought in a priest to perform the inquisition in your home,"

"He did. A priest that is actually no longer a priest who serves as Librarian for the University of Utrecht."

"Was it Professor Calderon?" Asks Nicklas, remembering his short time at the University.

"Yes. Did you know him?"

"I was in the library a lot. I liked him. I thought he was cool; but you say he is an inquisitor priest?"

"No, he is not really an inquisitor, but he does hold the credentials required by law to act as one."

"Oh, this is rich, by whose law? Is it the law of the church, or the law of the republic?" Captain Janszoon is used to the law of the sea, and is unfamiliar with other laws.

"The law of," Trinjntje, sounding exasperated says, "whatever! It does not matter!" Trinjntje is starting to think that these two are having too much fun with her story. "This priest, Calderon, who is no longer a priest, visited Amsterdam and interviewed me every day for a week. He followed all of the prescribed procedures and documented our meetings according to the requisite criteria. And when he presented his council to the court the case against me was dismissed."

"So, let me guess, an appeal was filed. Right?"

"Oh, Nicklas, you are a genius. It turns out that this priest, Calderon, is a rogue with a dubious history. The appeal demands that both sides shall choose together whom shall perform the rights of inquisiting."

"And that is when your father's lawyers held things up long enough for your botanic expedition to be arranged," finishes Janszoon, putting all the pieces together.

"Gone, but not forgotten. They have been waiting." Nicklas has also put the pieces together.

"But," she holds up a finger making a point, "I must confess. Even without this trouble," she laces her arms through the arms of the men she sits between, "I did not want to return to the confinement of home, but I was scared. Now, even though I am pestering you, I promise that neither of you will be responsible for my well-being. I intend to live on my own. Soon."

♡♡♡

After his morning of packing and loading sacks of milled grist Dirk is happy to relax in the sunshine. The bargeman has walked ahead to the upcoming lock to check if it is set for his barge's passing. He has left his collie to manage. The dog keeps a steady pace just ahead of the horse. Comically enough, every time it spots a frog or a toad in the grass or on a rock, it will hop off the towpath chasing the errant creature into the water. It yips a couple times before it returns to its duty. The dog has a rule that these water creatures must be in the water, just as it keeps the horse following the rule of steady motion. A practiced thought pops into Dirk's artistic mind; that the image of the dog bent forward yipping as the frog hops into the canal would be fun to paint. He has his painting supplies with him, even though he has not painted, or even sketched, since leaving home. He has a packet of his flax paper and another with his cakes of color, and a smaller pouch with a bowl and some brushes.

He fills the bowl with water from the canal, then dipping a fine-tipped brush and wetting his cake of brown he begins at the corner of the page practicing the outlines of the horse's flanks. Over and over until he is satisfied that he will be able to present the shape of the horse when he is ready for the full scene. He rinses the brush. Now wetting his cake of black he begins with loose strokes that he hopes will catch the busy attitude of the dog. He wants to present the nature of these animals working. He wants to capture the light-heartedness of the dog each time it breaks from its duties to play at chasing off the pesky reptiles. He fills his page with these practice strokes. He trains his arm to feel the brush-stroke and then to repeat the stroke that captures what he wants to show. He turns the page over and continues his practice strokes, combining them now for the image of the horse plodding along the towpath, and the image of the dog as it delivers the yelp that sends the startled frog hopping. He dips his wet brush into his emerald cake of color, then slashes a long curve of extended legs that he hopes will characterize the frog's frantic leap away from danger.

He fills the back of the sheet, then setting it aside pulls a fresh sheet of his flax paper. It is this love of practicing that had originally roused him to consider making his own paper so that he would never run out. After practicing all the components for this scene; the horse, the dog, the frog, and how they will be situated with the towpath and the canal, he is ready to start on the full scene. With a fresh sheet again, he sketches light strokes of outlines. Then in a flurry, not wanting any of his colors to dry before he has finished with them, he paints the entire scene. He completes it quickly because of his practicing. He is pleased, but sees where he can improve, so paints the scene again and again. Soon he has copies of the scene surrounding him, with the edges tucked between the sacks of meal to keep them from being carried away on a visiting breeze.

As the barge approaches near enough to the lock for the collie to recognize the bargeman it runs forward, but is stopped with a spoken signal that sends it rushing back to stop and sit directly in front of the horse. The horse, familiar with this routine, stops. The momentum of the barge carries it past the horse, putting slack in the lead line. The collie leaps onboard to retrieve a line tied off the tail end. As the slack on the lead rope runs out and tightens the horse leans its mighty girth back, dropping down its hind end, slowing the barge to a stop. The collie jumps to the bank with the rope in its teeth and digs in to keep the back end of the barge from drifting out away from the bank. The lock's gates, that appear so tall from below, open and another barge moves out. After the other barge has passed, the bargeman maneuvers this one into the lock. Familiar with the process, Dirk hops ashore and closes the gates that will hold the rising water, while up ahead, the chutes are raised that let through the water that is filling and raising the lock up again. It is teamwork. It is fun and feels good.

While waiting for the lock to fill the bargeman checks out all the sketches and scenes. "You are a very good painter." Then he asks, "Have you apprenticed with a master?"

"Not a master painter, emmm, I worked for an old man who encouraged me."

"And did he supply you with lots of extra paper? Hah?"

"Well," Dirk has little practice answering questions about himself, "he gave me the idea of making my own paper so that I would always have plenty in supply."

"Do you make paper out of rags?"

"Ummm. No." Most paper comes from rags. "That would be linen paper. I make paper with flax, before it is ever spun into linen."

Picking up one of the practice pages, filled with rows of miniature preliminary sketches, the bargeman rubs the paper's edge between his thumb and forefinger, "It is very smooth paper." He is impressed. Scanning the pages he notices the progression, "These sketchings show how the final painting started." He picks up the best of the completed scenes and compares it to the sketches. "Remarkable. You have caught a perfect likeness. The scene has me ready to hear the plop of the frog on the water."

"Please keep those sheets you are holding if you like."

"Really now?! I would think that you would have buyers for artistry of this *calibre*."

"Um, nope. I do it for fun." They both laugh as the collie jumps from the path to the bank with a yip, sending another frog out where it belongs. "Collies like to keep busy. I am like that. Always wanting something to do. Painting is something that I really like to do." While he has been busy he has not thought of the necklace of Golden Hearts hidden away in his sash.

♡♡♡

Trinjntje has moved to the back of the wagon and is sleeping comfortably atop the tarp. Cornelius allows Nicklas his thoughts. Moving along easily at a steady pace on a sunny day tends to set the mind at ease. They pass farmland with crops of grain that are past the sprouting stage, and are now turning the fields an effervescent green. They pass bogs where turves are being dug from freshly drained peat. They see rabbits and pheasants in the grasses. A fox runs across a faraway field. Some of the farmsteads have sheep, others have cattle. Nearly everyone waves to them as they pass. There are all varieties of small birds, water fowl, and winged hunters.

It is a pair of these hunters, birds of prey, which Janszoon watches now. Hovering by catching the wind in their wings. Captain Janszoon is a master whose lifelong study has been the catching of wind currents. He is able to put any wind into a sail. He has learned from legendary captains, and he continues his learning even now from this pair of kestrels. He has watched similar small-sized eagles everywhere he has ever sailed. He has always marveled at these agile creatures whose long sweeping wings allow them to swiftly turn, or to suddenly dip. Cornelius has long recognized how the shape of a sailing ship's foresail matches the shape of this bird's long slim wings.

One of the birds he has been watching suddenly folds its wings and drops at such an amazing velocity toward the ground that it surely will fail. At the very last possible instant the bird spreads its wings out flat, drops its legs, and grasps a snake with its claws, then rises again with the wriggling snake clutched in its talons.

"Wow!" shouts Nicklas next to him. "Did you see that bird drop out of the sky?"

"Yes. It knew, from way up there," pointing, "where that snake was. Now look." The bird has landed on a branch of a long dead pine. It deals a blow that finishes off the snake, and proceeds with its meal. "This has me remembering something from many years past."

"About a kestrel?"

"About a Jayakartan wise man."

"A Jayakartan wise man?"

"Before the arrival of the Dutch East Indie Company the port city of Batavia was known as Jayakarta. There were many years that my ship weighed in at that port."

"And there was a wise man?"

"A wise one, yes. Said to be reincarnated every generation. Sometimes a man, other times as a woman. Said to be in direct communication with a realm beyond our own."

"Do you mean that he talked with Spirits?"

"More like Spirits talked through him."

"So you went to see this wise man?"

"I had been told that people wait in line to speak with this oracle. Was told that anyone can ask one question."

"Oh yeah? So, what did you ask?"

"I have long been fascinated by eagles. Just as this kestrel dropped from high above to snatch the snake out of the grass, sea kestrels will drop from high above to pluck fish out of the waves. I have always wondered at the nature of a creature's vision that allows it to see from so far above." Cornelius seldom tells of this event, "So I asked the Jayakartan Wise One how is it possible that a feathered huntress from so far above can know so clearly the position of her prey." He is warming to the telling of the story now, "I traveled to the jungle temple of the Wise One, the Oracle, with an interpreter and waited in line for nearly a full day."

After I was deemed admission and my interpreter had relayed my question, the incarnated Oracle rose from his seat and waved for me to follow. He led me to an outdoor balcony and from there called out into the sky, *hoo-Yah*, mimicking the sound made by kestrels. He repeatedly called out *hoo-Yah, hoo-Yah,* and then changed it up a bit, *hoo-Yah-ahh, hoo-Yah-ahh*. Then holding up his arm as would a falconer," Cornelius shows Nicklas by raising his arm bent at the elbow, "to my surprise and delight a golden feathered kestrel landed there on his sleeve. The Wise One, without speaking, brushed the back of his fingers along the kestrel's brow outlining the eye socket and then cupping his hand to his own ear to show me the similarities of shape." Janszoon showed what he was describing, "He was not merely caressing the bird, but was showing me the answer to what I had asked. He would repeat the motion, outlining the bird's brow then cupping his ear, while looking me in the eye to be certain that I understood what he was showing me. Eventually it occurred to me, and I understood, he was showing me that a bird's eyes are also its ears. That for these birds, sight and sound are one and the same. A bird hears as it sees and sees as it hears."

"Do you think that the kestrel just now heard the snake from way up there with its eyes?"

Cornelius nods, "I believe so."

Ahead of them now is an intersection with a sign pointing the way to Utrecht. As Cornelius steers his wagon toward that direction, "Wait Uncle Cor," an awakened Trinjntje calls from behind, "I do not want to go into the city."

"I have lodging reservations for the night," he answers while pulling in the reins.

The wagon stops and Trinjntje jumps out of the back. She reaches in under the seat for her bag, "You go ahead. There will soldiers of the company guard watching all arrivals."

Nicklas tells her, "Your Uncle's route tomorrow will not bring him back this way." Turning to Janszoon he says, "I am thinking that the two of us could take a roundabout route and then meet up with you tomorrow on your way out of Utrecht."

"You are familiar with this area?"

"While attending the University I would come out this way with friends on holiday. There is a horse path along a smaller ditch that will eventually intersect with the road you will traveling tomorrow. We can meet you there."

"Where will you sleep?"

"Well, the last time we came out to this area we slept under a lean-to roof attached to the wall of a small windmill. It must be there still." They all agree that it is a good plan and part ways, as they had earlier in the day. Cornelius is following his intended schedule, while Trinjntje and Nicklas follow a short-cut that bypasses the city.

♡♡♡

The barge that has brought Dirk to Utrecht passes through the city until it reaches a long wharf with easy access to nearby warehouses. The bargeman leaves to make arrangements and returns with a crew who form a line from the canal to their wagon. Dirk hands a sack over to the first in line who passes it on to the next in line. They get a break when the wagon is full. It returns filled with casks that are rolled into the barge and set in rows where the sacks had been. Back and forth. They are finishing up when the bargeman returns. He pays Dirk what he had promised, thanks him, and then tells him, "The public house where I ate dinner seems to be short on help. If you are interested," pointing to the nearest intersection, "follow this road a ways until you see the sign for The *Kikker Gat*." He smiles.

"That is a strange name for a public house."

"I know. Right? A frog's hole does not sound very enticing, but the place is run by a man named Kikkert. With frog being his name: it is a play on words; a ridiculous pun. And get this; his last name is Verboom, so he goes by the nickname of Boomkikker."

"Treefrog?"

"That's it." The bargeman shakes Dirk's hand, thanks him again, then as a final thought tells him, "Go through the alley in the back. You will find a door there that leads into the kitchen. Good Luck young man."

Dirk follows the directions he has been given. He is able to see the bright sign from a distance. A caricature of a grinning frog wearing tails and a cocked hat, carrying a walking stick, on a background of yellow: a smiling sun. Looking in from the walkway he sees a large open area full of tables, and there are more seats at the bar. The man behind the bar turns around. He has a bald, rather pointed head, small ears, and a thick neck. He laughs at something said to him, displaying a wide gash of a mouth. His hearty laughter convinces Dirk to meet the man. All the tables and all the seats at the bar are full so he decides to go around to the back. He finds the alleyway easy enough. There is a smaller version of the bright yellow sign here. He looks into the kitchen and sees dishes piled high, verifying what he has been told about the place being currently understaffed, so he knocks and enters, "I have been told that you may need some help?"

"Oh, indeed we do," the busy women says, then calling to the front of the house, "Boomkikker!"

The big man peers around the wall, "Yes?"

"There is a man here that you need to talk with."

The Pubman takes a look at Dirk, then he looks back to the front before tossing his towel and coming around to the kitchen. He gives the woman, must be his wife, a look; she nods vigorously back, so he asks Dirk, "Are you looking for work?"

"Yes."

"Can you start now?"

"Yes."

Turning to his wife he asks her, "Where do you want him to begin?"

She points toward a tub filled with dishes, surrounded by stacked cooking pots, "We need plates and silverware."

He reaches out his long-fingered hand for Dirk to shake and introduces himself, "Kikkert Verboom," then gesturing with his eyes, "and my wife, Rhetta." She nods, but does not stop what she is doing. She, like her husband does not seem to have much of a chin. Verboom is looking back now awaiting the completion of the introductions.

"Dirk."

"Is Dirk your full name?" Suddenly stern. Arms akimbo. Knuckles at hips.

"Diedrik, Sir." Eye to eye. "Diedrik van Haumann. Dirk is a nickname."

"Okay Dirk," pointing a long arm extended by long fingers, "there is an apron." Now pointing with the long fingers of his other arm toward nearly empty shelves that are meant to hold all the dishes, "We need some clean plates and bowls to serve dinner to our guests."

"And knives and forks and spoons," chimes Rhetta while handing over to her husband a full tray of meals to be carried out front.

Dirk tosses his bag, pulls on the apron and goes to work. He fills the large sink with water that flows from a bamboo pipe leading in from a wooden barrel standing on stilts just the other side of the wall in the alley. He no sooner gets started when Rhetta sets a large tray for him to fill saying, "Four plates, four bowls, and four sets of cutlery. And as soon as you have got this, some tea cups please." She moves off and it goes like this, at this accelerated pace, through the evening.

After a while Kikkert brings him a mug of beer, "Here you go. I noticed you are looking thirsty. Are you hungry?" Admiring the progress that Dirk has made so far, "Let me bring you something to eat." Dirk likes the taste of the man's brew, but he stays focused on scrubbing dishes. Kikkert returns again with a bowl of beans and a sandwich, "Here you go. Take a break and feast on this." Moving a chair over to the cutting board, "Have a seat." Dirk wipes his hands on his apron, sits down, and takes a look at what he has been served and wonders, "You must have a stove out front besides the fires here in the kitchen?"

"A small fire. Enough to keep a pot of these sausages and beans warm, alongside a tea kettle and a coffee pot."

Dirk bites into the flavorful sausage sandwich. The sausage is hot, the bun has been slathered with a sauce combining mustard and horseradish. There is a relish of chopped vegetables over the top. It is delicious. He asks

Kikkert, "You keep this always ready? So a wharf-man or a clerk with only a short lunch break can come in here and get served instantly?"

"Oh yeah," very proud of himself, "and when they work late after dark and all the other kitchens are closed, Boomkikker," patting his chest, "will have pork and beans. Ya see," talking secretively now, "I always keep a pot o' molasses flavored beans warm. My specialty." He says this last with a flourish and a wave while straightening himself up to his full heighth, which is incredible. Dirk likes this tall lanky tree frog fellow.

♡♡♡

This ditch that Trinjntje and Nicklas are following has no water in it. They determine that water might flow in it later in the season for irrigation. Their path borders a polder that must have been drained long ago. They are enjoying the pleasant breeze that is blowing across the plain and rustling the tall grasses. The little black birds that have been keeping them company all day are now perching among the branches of the tall shrubs. They are warbling their whistles and twittering their scritches; noisily adding a joyful enhancement to the evening.

Nicklas walks along silently while Trinjntje sings. He is used to her clear voice; his cabin aboard ship was directly below her's. He is used to her drums and zither and wonders what she will do without them. She is playing her flute, which easily fits in a pocket, as a chorus between each verse of the silly song she is singing. "I love to dance, dilly-dilly, I love to sing." She blows a riff through the flute. "When I am queen, dilly-dilly, you'll be my king." The flute repeats its stanza. "Who told me so, dilly-dilly, who told me so?" Again with the flute before she finishes, "I told myself, dilly-dilly, I told me so." He has heard ribald versions of this tune sung in taverns, and repeated by the sailors aboard ship, but she sticks to the child's simpler, and sweeter, version.

Nicklas notes the windmill up ahead that is their intended destination. Not wanting to interrupt her singing he waits for the interval between verses, "Here is our stop for the night." She stops her singing and turns to him with the radiant smile that he is used to, but that has been missing for most of this day.

The windmill's sails are halted at the idle position. The grasses all around have grown tall. There is a pond covered with lily pads and algae. "It looks abandoned."

A tall heron wading through the green water stops suddenly, snatches a frog from below the surface, then tipping its head lets the frog slide down its long throat. "That is one less frog we will be hearing tonight," he says while crossing the makeshift bridge of planks laid over the irrigation ditch. One of the planks is rotten and breaks under his weight, sending him sprawling. "Oh! I am such an oaf," standing and brushing where the grass has stained his new trousers green. "Geez," he grumbles.

"La! You are no oaf."

The grasses are matted down beneath the lean-to roof where he had intended to sleep, "It looks like deer sleep here." They try the door, and finding it unlocked, enter the old mill. Besides the water-wheel, there is a table and two chairs in front of the shuttered window.

"The floor is dry." She says, then asks, "Do we dare sleep inside, or will we be thrown out as trespassers?"

Nicklas pushes open the shutters letting in the dwindling light of dusk. "I would think that if someone were planning on using this space for themselves," inspecting the enclosed space with this new light, "they would be here already." Next to a closet full of tools and grease brushes he finds a stoppered cask of oil which he uses to fill the lantern that has been left sitting on the table. There are matches in the table's drawer and now, with the lantern lit, the high ceiling makes the space seem quite expansive compared to the low-ceilinged cabins they have grown accustomed to aboard ship.

Trinjntje pulls a broom from the tool closet and busies herself sweeping the floor and brushing away cobwebs from the window frame. "It is quiet here."

"It probably will not be so quiet after dark and the frogs get started."

"Wouldn't it be fun if the sails of the windmill were turning?"

Nicklas, like every boy growing up here, is familiar with the basic operation of a windmill, "Probably all we need to do is release the brake." Pointing out where the brake rope is wound about its cleat. "What can go wrong?"

"Let's go check the direction of the wind." He follows her out and watches as she tosses handfuls of grass above her head while paying close attention to how it falls. "The wind is coming in sideways to the sails," she announces disappointedly.

Walking around to where the tail is anchored Nicklas wonders, "How long since this cap has been turned?"

Trinjntje, admiring the capstan wheel, exclaims, "It is just like the wheel of a ship!" Watching him unhook the anchor chains she asks, "Will it budge?"

Stepping onto the platform he says, "We'll see." After releasing the chain that has held the wheel in place for so long he grips a spoke and pushes. Nothing happens. He climbs up onto the wheel, and using all his weight and all his strength he is able to get it moving. He calls out, "Tell me when we have the sails lined up with the wind."

Trinjntje tosses up another handful of grass. "Now!" She tells him. "You've got it."

He has to inch it back a bit until it is centered between two anchor blocks. He sets the chain on the wheel, then sets the chains on the blocks before announcing, "That should do it."

She has already rushed inside and released the brake rope. There is a groaning of gears in thickened grease as the sails begin to turn. She comes running back outside with her expression lit up like a child's, "Oh Nicklas. Hoo-Ray!" She spins in a circle with her arms stretched wide, "We made it go! We made it go!" She takes his hands and leads him in a dance. "We made it go, we made it go. Sing with me! We made the windmill go." They continue dancing like a couple of silly kids in the lee of the sails. Before long the night sky is filled with stars. Now the pond and the bit of forest surrounding it have come alive with the nightly serenade of the frogs, along with the occasional hooting of an owl.

♡♡♡

Cornelius Janszoon sits himself down at a small table amidst many family-sized tables in a merrily boisterous dining room. He crams his bag under his chair and drops his coat and hat into the table's companion chair. The Proprietor shows up with a quart before Cornelius has barely sat down, "I apologize again Captain that you had to do your own stable chores."

"Quite allright Verboom. These are new horses to me, so it is good to have had the opportunity to get to know them and to say thanks for their work this day." He drinks from the glass that has been set before him, "Tis a fine brew. A fine brew indeed."

"Our house brew," pointing to a brightly painted sign that reads *KikkerBier Bierbrouwerijj* and displaying the same jaunty frog as the sign out front. "You would not think that anyone would want to drink something called frog beer, but we cannot keep up with the orders. Are you ready for something to eat?"

"Yes, please."

"Begging your pardon again Captain for any delays you may experience this night; we have been shorthanded of late," looking toward the kitchen, "although, a while ago a young man showed up to help us out."

Cornelius surveys the roomful of happy diners. He is unused to dining alone. A ship's captain's duties include hosting the evening meal. Over the years the conversation around his dining table has always been a source of enjoyment. He has visited with adventurers, politicians, scholars, scientists, and representatives of the Company ever moving from port to port. Sitting alone at the dining table for his evening meal is something unfamiliar for him. At the table next to him sit three gents whose appearance has him wondering what they have in common. There is a flamboyantly dressed fellow with trendy facial hair that is in need of a trim. Across the table sits a more seriously attired colleague with a neatly trimmed beard, wearing a black frock coat. Sharing the table with these two is an Asian, looking out of place in a business man's suit and a thick plait of black hair. Cornelius smiles to himself, for he has hosted many dissimilar guests in his time, and is fond of the varied conversations arising from each person's particular interests.

Kikkert returns with a tray of four dinner plates asking Cornelius in a jesting tone loud enough for the three patrons at the next table to hear, "I hope these professors are not unduly disturbing you." Now that he has their attention, he introduces them to his guest, "Sirs, Captain Cornelius Janszoon will be staying the night with us."

They all stand abruptly and bow to the captain. "Most pleased to make your acquaintance Sir," the flamboyant gentleman with the pointy whiskers on his chin is first, "Henricus Regius at your service."

"Honored to meet you Captain," from the bearded man wearing his hair pulled back, "Paulo Calderon." Calderon? Could this be the man Trin had spoken of? The ersatz inquisitor.

"Lu-Tang, of Huaxia," the Asian's moustaches wiggle as he speaks, "there is room here at our table if you would care to join us." His smile is genuinely inviting.

Cornelius has stood during the introductions, bows now that they are complete and speaks, "I will be happy to join you." Looking to Kikkert questioningly, "unless that would cause extra work for you and your shorthanded staff."

"La, I appreciate your consideration, but actually it makes no more or no less work, in fact it is as I have intended. I have brought all your dinners and it suits me to set them all down at one table." Still talking while distributing dinner plates all around, "We do not want our captain eating alone." Books, parcels, and correspondences are shuffled, making room for the fourth setting. Cornelius sits at the freshly cleared spot as Kikkert tells them, "I am able to serve your dinners sooner than expected. Our new kitchen helper has us caught up, saving you the wait of my having to wash dishes." He laughs heartily.

"Captain?" Asks the man who had introduced himself as Henricus.

"Please call me by my given name: Cornelius."

"Ah, then, Cornelius, have you previously known the pleasure of Boomkikker's hospitality?"

"Boomkikker?"

"His nickname, Kikkert Verboom: frog in a tree."

"La, Treefrog. I have stayed here once before Henricus."

"Hendrik. Call me Hendrik."

"Very well then, Hendrik, I stayed here a couple of years ago when I was first getting started on my current project."

"Is your ship harbored in Rotterdam or Amsterdam?"

"Ah. It pleases me to say that I have no ship." Picking up his glass for a toast, "I am, as of yesterday afternoon, no longer actively serving as a ship's Captain."

They all raise their mugs joining in the toast. "You seem young to be leaving the active life behind," comments the tall bearded one, Calderon.

"I am embarking upon a new and exciting endeavor."

"Please tell us of your plans," Lu-Tang requests. Cornelius explains briefly the details of his drainage venture. The Asian comments wistfully, "I have been tempted to forego my position with the University so that I may pursue the life of a windmiller."

"Oh, indeed; and what position do you serve at the University?"

"I lead instruction in the Philosophy of Movement; Inner Alchemy."

"Kung Fu?" Janszoon asks, "On one of my voyages we had an adept of the Wudang School traveling with us as a passenger."

"I teach the Wudang style," Lu-Tang tells him.

"Splendid!" Turning to the others he asks, "And do you gentlemen also lecture at the Academy?"

"I am a professor of medicine," states Hendrik.

"I am librarian," states Calderon.

Tis indeed the same man thinks Janszoon. "I am honored to be sharing a table in such knowledgeable company." Raising his glass to them, "Enough of our introductions, now pray tell me, what discussion were you having before I interrupted."

"I was telling them," Hendrik holds up a slim volume, "of a new process for determining quadrature."

Knowing that many mathematicians take pride in the quickness of their calculating, even going so far as gambling over who is quickest, Cornelius asks, "Do you wager on your skills?"

Hendrik tips his head and clears his throat, "Ah-Hem, It might be construed as impertinent for a lecturer of the Academy to gamble." Answering neither yes nor no.

"You may be thinking of another master known to do quite well demonstrating his geometrical prowess at the gambling tables," Lu-Tang fills in, "you may have heard of the fellow; René Descartes?"

"Oh yes, I have heard of the man's prowess at the tables," then adding, "and I have heard of his views, which many deem heretical."

"Oh, well," Hendrik wears a sour expression now, "I mistakenly agreed publicly with something the man said, and as a result have been barred by the Academy from lecturing on philosophy." Rancor shows, "In my effort to clarify my position there has ensued an ongoing argument."

Knowing that this is an unpleasant topic for his friend Calderon refers the captain back the original question, "Instead of gambling tables Hendrik is more interested in mortuary tables, focusing his lectures upon human physiology."

Hendrik sheepishly nods, "La, tis so. I lecture on the nature of anatomy while dissecting cadavers."

"Oh indeed! A worthwhile endeavor. Somebody must do it!" Referring back to the slim volume, "you mentioned quadrature. From what I have studied, these geometric principles for measuring the area of objects are similar to the methods we use for calculating distances at sea."

"I believe you are correct in that assumption, and it is the same with the study of astronomy," fills in the librarian, "which, I believe, originates from the calculating that is been used at sea. As a sea captain you have to be ever aware of the positions of the planets and the stars. I personally theorize that much of modern science stems from skills applied at sea for ages."

Noticing Calderon's Spanish intonations while remembering what Trinjntje had said about the man Janszoon asks, "Have you always been a librarian?"

Calderon swallows the bite he has been chewing, and then sips from his wine glass while his two associates watch him closely, awaiting his answer. "Before assuming the role of archivist I was a priest." He mouth forms a tight smile, then he finishes, "Circumstances have led me toward the more scholarly pursuit of archiving all manner of reference materials."

"I hope you will forgive me if it seems that I have unduly pried into your past. My reason for asking is that your name came up in a recent conversation that I was having with my niece, whom I believe you may know: *Mejuffrouw* Trinjntje Olmsfeld."

Calderon's face lights up, "A delightful woman. Yes. It has been a couple years since our consultation. I hope that she is doing well."

"She is well. She traveled aboard my ship on this last voyage. She was contracted by her father's Company to bring home botanical specimens."

"And so she is home now?"

"She is here in the Netherlands."

"I am always amazed at how small our world has become," remarks Hendrik gleefully, "la, it seems that everybody has something in common with everybody else!"

"Everything is intertwined," states Lu-Tang matter-of-factly.

"Indeed," muses Janszoon, thinking about the way other lives have entwined with his this day.

Ancient Maps

After transferring their household belongings from the Tulip to their new home and arranging everything to suit them Robert and Mara are pleased with what they have accomplished. The bed, wardrobe, and chest of drawers are in the larger of two rooms at the back of the house. Their table and chairs sit at the middle of the house's great room near the cooking counter and the shelves filled with dishes. Her large loom is set up in the corner by the windows, where the house's original loom had been. Her large harp sits in a corner, while her smaller harp sits upon her loom's bench. There is a rocking chair, where the cat is sleeping upon a soft padded seat, and a comfortable settee where they are now seated appreciating what they have accomplished.

Having put nearly everything in place yesterday, now this morning they turn their consideration to the drawer that the fleeing monks had left in Mara's care. Robert asks her to explain again the circumstances that have left this package in their possession. She tells him of her last day in Éire. "The redcoats bringing the settlers that would be stealing our homes were getting near. So I was busy clearing out the house before the soldiers and the squatters arrived. I had determined that I could not wait for your return to move everything down to the wharf. My first visitor of the day was one of the nephews warning me that there was no time left. I sent him on his way riding our roan." She gives him a stern look, "I am determined to have a horse to ride again soon," he nods, agreeing that will be so. "The two monks arrived next. They were fleeing from their monastery because the Anglicans are taking over the cathedrals and friaries. In the process of saving their own liturgical objects, they had come across these artifacts from an earlier time stuffed away and forgotten in a drawer. For reasons that are beyond my ken, they brought the drawer to me: to us. At first I told them, "No," that we did not have room, but they were determined to leave it whether I accepted or not."

"So, this drawer holds relics of our past?"

"Of a bygone era. Yes, that is what they said."

He carefully unties the knots in the ceremonial rope that holds the screen over the open top of the drawer. "I would think that there is a more appropriate use for this fine silken altar rope."

"They probably had to use whatever was handy in their rush."

As he lifts the screen of wood that has been tied in place to hold the contents of the drawer inside they are surprised to see that it is something more. The thin wooden slab has a painting on the side that had been turned down. It is a remarkably well-preserved portrait of a haloed woman playing a harp.

"That looks like my harp!" Mara gasps as Robert holds it up for a better look. The lady of the portrait possesses a celestial beauty. The ornate styling of her harp so closely resembles Mara's large heirloom that it may indeed be the same. "And she is wearing the necklace!" She gasps again. Around the queen's throat is a necklace of Golden Hearts identical to Mara's heirloom necklace.

"There is something different about the harp."

"There," Mara points to the top of the painting's harp, "That looks like a globe inside a crown. I wonder if my harp used to have a crown and orb at the top of its mast." In the painting the queen and her harp have a glow around them. "There is an aura surrounding this lady and her harp."

"She must be a saint, or else, a dream." They like to believe the legends of celestials visiting this earthly realm; whether it be in waking or dreaming.

"Do you suppose she is of my ancestral line?"

"She is playing what appears to be your ancestral harp, and is wearing your ancestral necklace of Golden Hearts." He hands the painting over to her for closer scrutiny. "Let's see what else is in this drawer."

She carries the painting over to a bare spot on the wall, "It would look nice hanging here," and holding it up against the wall at eye level, "tis lovely, how old you think it is?"

"Eh?" He answers distractedly, "I would not know, but look here," unrolling parchments, "these are maps. I wonder how old these are."

Setting the painting down, she looks over Robert's shoulder, "The marks look to be of the old style."

"Aye," now unrolling another and recognizing it for what it is, "this is a star map used by sailors."

"That would be from your ancestors. They were the navigators."

"Navigators and adventurers." He unrolls a map of familiar landforms showing a dotted line connecting what is clearly Éire, through the straits and across the Nord Zee, to Norway. "This must be a few hundred years old. It looks to be a map of the route between Éire and the Sognefjord; tis the very route that I travel.

"What is this that you have uncovered?" She reaches in and lifts out a wooden bound book. "The cover has the runes of the old language," and flipping through the vellum pages, "it is a story. There are pictures," flipping through the few pages, "and here is another map." She shows him the page.

"Hmmm. Look at this," comparing the map that had been unrolled to the map in the book, "this book's map shows the Sognefjord again. There is route marked from the end of the fjord leading into the mountains. I wonder what these runes are here at the end of the route." He turns the page and there is another picture of a stone tower with cliffs rising up behind it. Beneath the picture are the same runes that are on the map. Robert flips the pages back and forth to compare that the runes are the same.

"The Sognefjord is where you go for the quarry blocks."

"Aye, and the light amber beer brewed from high mountain spring water."

"That beer you have been delivering to the buyer in Rotterdam for so many years?"

"Aye." His regular route takes him to Norway for quarried basalt building blocks that he takes to the lowlands to trade for milled lumber. From the port of Vik, where he gets the quarried blocks and the kegs of beer, he also trades with a monastery of ascetics who carve runes in glacier stones. "I am hoping to return there soon. I want to bring home building blocks for adding to this wharf. I should be able to bring home enough to put a tower on the wharf that will support a loading crane."

"Are you not getting ahead of yourself?" She asks wryly, "We will be needing a few things done around here before you are off sailing again."

"Okay, we will get a horse for you to ride, and another to pull a wagon, and we will get a garden planted, and, ya know, there is maybe not so very much for us to do." She can tell that he is already calculating how soon he will be able to get away on this next voyage. "I will make copies of these maps to take with me. There is an old fellow in Vik who may be familiar with this trail leading up the mountain."

"There are things that we need. We should visit the market of this nearby town that Philip told us about. Maybe we can find a horse trader there."

There is a knock at the door, the oldest son of the Gedimin family peers in, "Good morning."

"Good morning Razs."

"My parents are going to market. They want you to know that you are welcome to ride along."

Mara tells him, "We were only now discussing making that trip ourselves. Tell your parents that we will be happy to go along with them."

"How soon should we be ready?" Robert asks.

"They were hitching the horses to the cart when they sent me to fetch you. I imagine they will be by here shortly." Robert and Mara jump up and quickly get ready to go.

Annia is driving the cart and invites Mara to sit beside her on the bench. The rest are in the back. They are all sharing the details of their new homes.

"Moving from our cramped travel wagon into our sprawling new house has been quite easy," Annia tells Mara. "We have little to move, and besides the house is furnished as well as a manor home would be." They are living as well as always.

Renaldo tells Robert, "The main house is large and has been added on over the years. The additions have been built around a large oak, leaving a courtyard in the middle."

"There is a huge kitchen," Kirin says, "with extra counters and extra cupboards; all filled with dishes, glasses, cups, and silverware. Pots and pans hang on the walls. There is a flat-top cooking stove that has an oven."

"We have a large sitting room," Vejz says, "with seating enough for a crowd. If we pushed the furniture out of the way the room could be a dance hall."

"Pa and Ma have the big bedroom that is part of the original house," Audrae tells them. "We all have our own rooms, with windows looking out into the courtyard."

"I love, love, love the kitchen," Annia says. "It is a dream come true to have a kitchen of my own. I have always lived where there has been kitchen and wait staff and have never been able to do much of my own cooking."

"La, well then you will also learn to enjoy the sweeping and mopping," Mara teases.

Kirin says proudly, "We have already swept and mopped. La, I am hoping that baking cookies will be more fun."

"We will need eggs for baking," Audrae tells her, then announces, "We shall be bringing home laying hens."

"She loves chickens," Annia tells Mara, "when she was still very young someone gave her a hen to hold and the sweetness of its countenance beguiled her. La, for a while she carried that hen in her arms wherever she would go."

"There is a little boat for us to row out on the lake," Vejz says, "and we found fishing poles in the toolshed."

"I will catch more fish than you," boasts Audrae.

"You do not always have to outdo everybody else," laughs Renaldo.

"Yeh, there are lots of poles," Vejz teases her, "we can all catch fish."

Robert says, "Was this cart in your barn? It is very nice."

"It is a nice cart," says Kirin, "but I want my own horse to ride." Everyone agrees.

Mara holds up the bridle she has brought with her, "I intend to bring home a horse today."

Annia says, "Good for you," then while shaking her head at the flat landscape, "Will I ever get used to this? There are no mountains," and asking, "are there mountains where you come from?"

Robert answers, "There are hills; not what one would call mountains. It is a rugged landscape. It is not at all flat like this. Oh no, this is more like being out on the sea with light swells in every direction."

Renaldo says, "Where we come from there are mountains. Tall rugged beautiful mountains." Then to his children, "Imagine if it were the other way around; what is it like for flatlanders to visit the mountains that we are used to." Then to Robert, "What sort of horse are you hoping to bring home today?"

"Ask Mara. She is the one that cannot bear a day without riding."

Mara turns around, "Do not let him fool you. He loves horses."

Vejz speaks up, "but you are a sailor, and there are no horses at sea."

"I am not only a sailor. I am a farmer, and a merchant, and a fisherman," then he laughs, "but mostly I am a lay-about," and he laughs some more.

Renaldo laughs along with him, "La, sounds like we have a lot in common." Busy folk like to kid themselves about not being so busy, but others rarely believe them.

They reach the walled village of Schoonhoven by midday. It is not market day, but there are a few stalls selling fruits, vegetables, and flowers. Audrae even finds some chickens to take home. There is a supply shop where they find flour, salt, and sugar. There is a blacksmith who is also a horse trader. Mara is pleased to find a lovely black mare for riding and a heavier horse for pulling a cart or a plow. The blacksmith's wife has a cow with a calf that she is willing to let go. Annia tells Mara, "We would like to have a milk cow, unfortunately we have never done the milking."

Mara answers, "I can teach you," then teases, "And you will also be learning how to make butter and cheese."

Robert, overhearing them says, "Mara loves her animals, they are her pets."

"Oh," Kirin says, "I love animals too! I want a cow. I want to learn milking and how to make butter and cheese." They return home leading the cow and calf behind the cart.

♡♡♡

Deciding not to leave the windmill's sails turning overnight, Trinjntje and Nicklas had set the brake before climbing up the ladder into the sleeping loft. Nicklas had hoisted himself into a top bunk and Trinjntje had lain herself down on a bed by the open window. After lying there in the darkness for a bit Nicklas asks, "Trinjntje?"

"Yes."

"I keep thinking about what you said; that we each have a crowd around us."

"I do not see them always and I seldom see the crowd of others, but I know they are there. It is like dreaming; sometimes we remember our dreams, but not always."

"Well, a few days before my Oma died she was seeing a crowd that nobody else was seeing; mostly her family that had gone before her, but she also saw angels. At least that's what she told us."

"Dying is similar to dreaming, except that when you wake up you are a baby again."

"Oh," not sure what to think of that, "that is nice to know." He is quiet for a moment, then, "Hey, about tomorrow."

"Yes, what about tomorrow?"

"After we meet up with your uncle, you will not really need me for anything, so I could go back to Amsterdam, or I could go on to Antwerpen to see my folks. But, ehhhh, I would rather go along with you guys. Would that be okay? I want to see Captain Janszoon's new estate."

"I get the impression that Uncle Cor is very happy, even relieved, to have us along. He is not used to being all alone."

In the morning they set out walking. The dew is so thick that they are walking barefooted to keep their boots from getting soaked. They see Janszoon's wagon across the field before they have reached the road, and run to stop him before he passes them by. He laughs when he sees them running across the field carrying their boots and their bags. They all arrive together. He asks, "How was your night?"

"Delightful," Trinjntje is the first to answer, "and how was your night?"

"I enjoyed a full evening of stimulating conversation."

"We both fell asleep early to the sounds of frogs' ribbetting, crickets' chirruping, and skylarks' tweedling." Nicklas laughs, "The natural sounds are a surprisingly effective inducement for sleep."

"I made the acquaintance of three gentlemen who are professors at the University of Utrecht and we stayed up late talking of some most fascinating topics. When I finally made it to my bed I was asleep at the instant my head rested upon the pillow."

"That is nice Uncle Cor. We did something way more fun."

"Oh, tell me then, what did you do that so rivals my own experience?"

"We became millwrights. Nicklas turned the windmill's cap to put the sails properly facing the wind, and then I loosened the brake and we watched them turn. We made the windmill go!"

"La, so now you are windmillers. Very nice indeed. The caretaker living on my property is also the millwright, so he will be teaching me how to keep the sails turning. Besides that, he is also a glassblower, and he has been busy making windowpanes. The plans for my new home have mullioned windows in every room, including a large open space that has a high ceiling and gables, with windows, all round. It will be a home full of light. I am very excited to see how it has all turned out."

"Are there furnishings? Do you have a table? Have you a bed? Or is your home empty?"

"Trin," he scolds her, "with all my planning do you suppose that I would have forgotten anything that you are asking about?" They are teasing each other. "Over the years I have filled a warehouse. I always dreamed of doing what I am doing now. All those stored away items from all over the world have been shipped to my property, and all of those marvelous things await in their crates to be unpackaged and placed around the house. There are tables, desks, bookshelves, beds, wardrobes, lamps, chairs, and coatracks. There are paintings, statues, and all manner of decorum. There are utensils; all the pots, kettles, and skillets to fill the many cupboards of a large kitchen. There is a magnificent dining table with matching chairs. There are sideboards and dishes to fill them. Oh, I am brimming with the anticipation of seeing it all."

"Well done Uncle Cor!"

"Indeed. Well done. Now my anticipation is piqued."

"I am happy to hear that Nicklas, for I am thinking that I can use your help for a few days, or even more if you are so inclined. Why, there is probably enough to keep the both of you busy for at least a fortnight."

"Are you intending to make slaves of us? What did I tell you Klas?" She pokes him, "he needs us."

"At your service Captain Sir." They have a good laugh.

They are travelling on a well-used roadway that follows the River Lek. The sky above them is mostly clear, yet darker clouds can be seen far off. They pass a gaggle of cranes. These elegantly graceful birds seem to have taken an interest in the little wagon; and are flying a parallel path with it out over the water. The horses, moving along with their own elegant grace, are responding to the cranes' gurgling calls of *er ah-ah-ah-ah* with their own similar sounding *ah-eh-eh-eh-ah*. The horses and cranes trade their calls back and forth. At least that is what the riders in the wagon are hearing.

Actually the cranes are good-naturedly taunting the heavy beasts, "We usually see grand horses your size hitched to much larger loads. Are you vacationing? Eee-AhHaHa."

The horses answer back, "We have pulled heavy loads for enough of our lives. Harummmph-mmmph-mmmph."

"You could be pulling barges. The slow pace would suit your age. Eee-AhHaHa."

"And be bothered by the likes of you all our days? Hehehehe. Hehehehe."

This final bit of banter has them all sharing a laugh, "AYEEE-Yee-Yee. AYEEE-Yee-Yee."

"Are they talking to each other?" Nicklas asks, then adds his own attempt at mimicking that last call, "Ayeee-yee." The cranes turn all together now and fly back the way they have come.

Trinjntje slaps Nicklas on his shoulder in fun, "Whatever you were trying to say has chased them away!"

"What did I say? I did not chase them away!"

Making up lyrics she sings, "What did he say? What did he say? With a hoo and hey he chased them away. With a hoo and hey they all flew away!" Then she has her flute out and the morning flies by merrily. The great horses maintain their wonderfully smooth cadence while showing no sign of tiring.

Remembering that Cornelius had mentioned visiting with professors where he stayed last night in Utrecht Nicklas asks, "Tell us Sir the names of your dinner companions; mayhap I was fortunate enough to have had one or more of them for an instructor during my time attending lectures there."

"Oh certainly. The most talkative of the three, and the most outlandishly dressed, is a doctor of physiology by the name of Henricus Regius."

"That would be Professor Henrik! He is a favorite. I do believe that he wore a new outfit every day. He is a veritable trend setter of fashion."

Laughing, "He was indeed dressed splendidly. Another at the table is a native of the Far East; Huaxia. His name is Lu-Tang and he teaches a uniquely eastern philosophy."

"Kung-Fu?" Trinjntje asks. "I spoke with the acrobatic dancers that entertained us in Formosa. They explained to me that balancing thoughts with posture is the goal of every devoted dancer. They call this balance Kung-Fu."

"Well my dear, you will have the opportunity of discussing that with Lu-Tang. He has accepted my invitation to visit. He is considering a windmill of his own." They come to a bridge and cross the Lek and are now following the river back on its opposite bank. "I believe that you may know the third man at the table. He is not an instructor, but is the University's librarian."

"Calderon?" Trinjntje's eyes light up. "Is it Paulo Calderon?"

"Yes." Cornelius, noting the way she has lit up, "It seems that you have more than a passing interest in the man."

Now blushing, "Yes, I suppose I do. I feel a strong regard toward his kindness."

"I have the impression that Professor Calderon has lived a life of varied experiences."

She explains, "He told me that he is from a wealthy family and, being a younger son, was entered into the priesthood at an early age. He traveled to New Spain and served his order there. But all did not go well for him. He did not tell me what happened, only that he returned in chains."

"Entering the priesthood from a wealthy background would have given him a modicum of privilege. Most monks lead lives of hard labor, much the same as sailors; they are provided a place to sleep and food to eat," a sideways glance before finishing, "and hard work from dawn til dusk."

"Be that as it may," she continues telling Calderon's story as she knows it, "after a tribunal was held the charges were dropped and he was posted as an archivist assigned to the underground vaults in Rome."

"Sounds like a prison sentence to me," scoffs Nicklas.

"When his term came up he chose to leave the order."

"Which stains a man's reputation almost as severely as excommunication," Nicklas says, "few people are willing to openly step away from the church."

"Not only the church," the Captain tells them, "the directors of the VOC did not believe that I would have the audacity to leave. Nobody quits the Company!" He laughs. "But I say, Professor Calderon's countenance does not reflect bitterness, in fact, he seems more interested in the pursuit of research materials than anything else."

"He has put together one of the finest libraries in all of Europe."

"Perhaps I can arrange a visit," sighs Trinjntje wistfully.

"Ha. He'll not be remembering having ever met a vagabond named Trin." Nicklas laughs at his own joke. They all laugh.

It is mid-day when they pass through the gate of Captain Janszoon's estate. There is one tall windmill with its sails turning, and a second still under construction, evidenced by the builder's scaffolding and only three completed sails. Cornelius parks his wagon in the yard between the house and barn, "Let us take care of these horses and then we will look at the house." They enter the barn which is huge, with stalls enough for many horses.

Trinjntje sets the basket of kittens in the corner of a stall, "We will need a bowl for their milk."

An unfamiliar voice tells her, "There is a cup in the grain bin that could be used," it is the caretaker who has come out to greet the newcomers.

Cornelius introduces everybody and tells the man, "I have brought help to get things properly situated in the house."

"That will take some doing. I lost count of how many wagons delivered crates here. All is sitting inside. You will see that there is hardly room to move."

After getting the horses taken care of they make their way to the house and find what the man had described. The house is filled with shipping crates. "There, you see Nicklas, we have our work cut out for us."

"Aye Sir. Shall we get started?"

♡♡♡

It takes Dirk, or rather Diedrik, as he is going by more and more here, only a few days to catch up with the chores and to become familiar with the routines of the Kikker Gat Public House. His inside chores include washing dishes, clearing tables, sweeping and mopping floors. Boomkikker and Rhetta are fastidious about cleanliness, "Having everything clean keeps the vermin out. It is our reputation for cleanliness that draws in our honorable clientele." Outside Diedrik takes care of keeping the stable clean and caring for those honorable client's horses. His duties also include hitching horse to cart for making deliveries, stockpiling turves, and garnering supplies. His room in the barn, while keeping him readily available to late night arrivals, provides a comfortable bed and a quiet spot to be alone. With each day he grows fonder of his new post, its owners, and the revolving crowd. Indeed, the patrons drawn to Kikkert's establishment include a bright mix of students here in Utrecht to attend lectures at the new university, business men prospering in this burgeoning economy, families visiting the city; and there are the regular boarders that call the Kikker Gat home.

Above the brewery, which stands next to the stable, live the brewer and his wife. He is a tall broad orange-haired fellow, and his wife is equally tall, broad, and orange-haired. He stays busy with the brewing chores while she does all the laundry for the Kikker Gat. They both sing as they work; she will be above singing while hanging sheets to dry and he will be below harmonizing while raking barley over the roasting floor.

There are three steady boarders that Kikkert refers to as the three wise men because of the fact that they are all employed at the Academy; now known as The University of Utrecht. The most flamboyant of the three is Henricus Regius, known to most as Hendrik, a professor of medicine and a philosopher of the Cartesian persuasion; although he seems to be currently embroiled in a disagreement with the famous philosopher. The next of the three is Paulo Calderon who is librarian at the University. He is a Spaniard, and is rumored to have learned his archivistical skills in Rome while still serving as a priest. The third, a man from faraway Huaxia, is Lu-Tang and he teaches a variety of subjects at the University. He explains Huaxian culture to aspiring businessmen, religions of the world to eager philosophers, and a training discipline that he refers to as *Inner Alchemy*, although most refer to it as Kung-Fu.

Each day is a similar routine for these three professors. Mornings, instead of stopping for breakfast, each one grabs a prepared bag, filled with food and drink, and is out the door and on his way. Evenings, they settle in together at a table in the large dining room, where Kikkert, once they are all three present, serves their dinner. After the meal they remain, sometimes til late, and often joined by other scientifically-minded folk, discussing all the latest theories. Diedrik finds himself drawn to these scholarly discussions, lingering while clearing nearby tables, or listening from the kitchen.

During a quiet afternoon while Kikkert has stepped out, leaving Dirk in charge behind the bar Professor Hendrik walks in earlier than usual, his coat is colorful brocade, his hat is draped nonchalantly over his unbound hair, and his trendy van Dyck beard is nearly obscured by several days' growth of stubble. He carries himself as a man that enjoys being himself. He sets his empty lunch bag, with the sound of an empty bottle inside, on the bar with a smile, "Good Day to you Sir," pausing while Diedrik checks the shelf behind the counter where posts and parcels await, picking up and handing over a bundled collection addressed to Henricus Regius. The knot is untied with a flourish and the posts riffled through. Looking up with a pleased expression he says, "Much of the progress in the sciences becomes available by comparing results with others who likewise are engaged in the processes of scientific discovery," said while waving the bundle of letters that he holds to ratify his point. "Mmmmmmm," he asks with quizzically raised eyebrows, "May I have you bring me some goats cheese and rye crackers with a pint please?" He takes a seat at a table near the front windows and tears into the posts he has received. Hendrik is devoted to the 'Academy of Letters', the unofficial exchange of new thought that educated folk from all over the continent participate in. Dirk delivers the beer, and a plate filled with cheese and crackers. "Thank you my good man," Hendrik says genuinely, "this snack will tide me over til the evening meal."

"With pleasure, Sir." Diedrik likes Hendrik and wonders what it would be like to attend his lectures.

Kikkert returns, thanks Dirk, and suggests he eat something now before the evening crowd arrives. Calderon is the next of the professors to return home for the evening. He carries himself easily, as if his duties of the day have been light rather than burdensome. Calderon, unlike Hendrik, has his hair secured neatly and his beard trimmed evenly, "Good evening Boomkikker." He politely removes his hat and gently sets his empty lunch bag on the counter. He stands unbuttoning his coat while Kikkert fills a tankard with the lighter brew favored by those once accustomed to warmer climates.

Kikkert sets the full pint on the counter along with a wrapped parcel, "Just one package today and by its size I am guessing it to be a book." Teasing now, "Will we be soon collecting all of your library's deliveries?"

Calderon takes the proffered parcel and tucks it under his arm smiling at the pub man's jest, "If it is what I expect it to be, it is not a thing I would have in the library," feigning distaste, "but something that suits Hendrik's interest." He carries his mug and parcel with him to the table where Hendrik sits eagerly reading some missive most likely describing the entrails of the latest cadaver dissected by one of his many correspondents. Depositing his coat in an empty chair Calderon tells his friend, "This may be what you have been waiting for Hendrik," opening the parcel with a small blade, then with a flourish, "Yes it is; a copy of Shakespeare's Hamlet, as per your request." Now he scrunches up his nose in mock disgust as he drops the manuscript on the table, "Remind me again why you have an interest in such as this." He is among those who find the English bard's plays to be trifling and contrived.

Hendrik, thoroughly immersed in what he is reading allows Calderon time to sit down, and time to spread cheese on a cracker, and time to idly stroke the little gray cat that has followed him and is now sitting on his lap. Finally pulling his attention away from the missive he has been so absorbed with, Hendrik looks up with a blank expression, and taking in his friend's presence at the table and noticing with surprise the well-thumbed transcript laying there on the table, he snatches it up, "Wonderful!" He excitedly opens it, "Ah, this must have belonged to the actor playing the lead; all of Hamlet's lines are underscored! Brilliant!"

"It was available for purchase because it was an understudy's copy," Calderon tells him wryly, "and again I ask," pausing long enough to be sure that his friend is listening, "why?"

"Oh, emmm," Hendrik stops his flipping through the scenes, and looking up startled, "What was your question?"

Before he can answer a flurry of guests enters from the street. Coming in at the back of this group is Lu-Tang who has held the door and who now waits for the way to clear. He wears a long cape with its hood pushed back, forming a ruff behind his head. He turns to his companions across the room and, upon seeing his friends watching, smiles while raising his eyebrows and sliding his eyes sideways indicating the crowd that is holding up his progress. When he finally makes his way past he sets his lunch bag on the counter. Kikkert is busy greeting this new bunch of diners so Rhetta comes out from the kitchen to welcome the Huaxian. While she fills a pint glass he removes his cape and tells her, as she is sliding the foamy glass toward him, "I am most appreciative, Dear Woman, for the excellent bag of food that you prepare for me each day."

Rhetta wearing her hair in a thick braid down her back, as does Lu-Tang, tells him, "Tis my pleasure to serve you, and tis a pleasure to be appreciated," while sliding her eyes toward the group her husband is busy with, "By the looks of it, you three may be waiting a bit before your dinners arrive."

"We will be fine." He turns toward the table where his companions are seated, but then, having remembered something, he turns back before Rhetta has disappeared again into the kitchen, "Oh! Will you ask Dirk to stop by please? I have a favor to ask." She nods. "Thanks!" He is hoping that Dirk will be able to drive him to Captain Janszoon's new estate.

Calderon, seated with his back to the windows, and Hendrik on the bench, have stayed their conversation while watching all this. There are greetings all around as Lu-Tang joins them and relays Rhetta's message that they may be waiting a while for dinner.

Calderon starts back in where the conversation had left off by asking Lu-Tang, "Do you remember our moony associate's request," waving his hand toward Hendrik hinting as to who he is referring to, "that I procure for him, if possible, a copy of the script for one of the English playwright's *dramas*?" Speaking the last word derisively.

"I remember his oft retelling of a play he has seen many times." Hendrik travels to Paris often, and even to London on occasion, and has seen versions of Shakespeare's plays whenever possible; some plays more than once. "What is it Hendrik," he asks, "that you wanted with this particular script?"

Calderon leans his head back laughing, then with forefinger raised, "The very question that I have asked, and am still awaiting an answer to."

Looking up absent-mindedly, "What did you ask?" Hendrik queries, still holding the script that has him so preoccupied.

Head back and laughing again Calderon points out to Lu-Tang, "It is a winding path sometimes," twirling an upheld finger, "to an answer from our nutty friend," They both turn expectantly toward Hendrik as he shouts excitedly.

"Yes! Here it is! I have found the passage." He slaps the script with the back of his hand, then leans back into the bench, "but first, allow me to explain."

"We are all ears."

"While in Paris at a conference of physicians, there was an English troupe at a nearby theatre."

"You were so enthralled with their performance of Hamlet that you attended each night that you were in Paris," Lu-Tang reminds him, hoping to ward off hearing the entire plot again.

"Yes. I sat through it enough to become familiar with some of the most brilliant lines."

"Have you in mind the thought of forming a troupe of players?"

"Oh, no," wagging his head at the idea, "Heavens no! Please allow me to answer your question." These two always tease him. He does not mind; rather enjoys being teased.

Calderon grins at Lu-Tang, "Be careful not to distract him, or he will forget the question and we will never have the answer."

"Indeed. If you two are finished I will explain," Warming to the story now while smoothing the pages of the open manuscript with his palm he begins, "Whilst tending to a cadaver in the laboratory with a group of students watching it is common for someone in attendance to spout off some crude remark. It helps to ease the tension, you know, to laugh a bit."

Spouting a cadaverous remark, "Are you feeling blue?" Calderon asks snickering.

Lu-Tang joins in, "Such a ghastly shade of pale," while pinching his nostrils and pursing his lips comically.

"Don't bother," Hendrik waves them off, "I have heard them all." He's laughing and enjoying his friend's jesting. "So anyway, at the moment that I am ready to make the first incision, one of the students present has an epiphanic moment and, rather than the usual, begins spouting verbatim, a line that seemed familiar to me," now holding up the folded back script while pointing emphatically toward an underlined passage, "and here it is. *What a piece of work is man! How noble in reason, how infinite in faculty, in form and moving--*"

"*--and moving*" Calderon interrupts, mimicking a wise cracking student. Lu-Tang snorts.

Hendrik raises his eyebrows, then finishes, "*--how express and admirable.*" Slapping the page with the back of his hand, "the upstart knew these lines. The fellow received applause. In my lecture hall. Disrupted my orative. Even took a bow right there in front of the cadaver." He goes into a fit of giggling rivaling Calderon's chortle. "Come to find out," Hendrik gasps, "the lad claims to be a nephew of the English playwright … hoohoohoo ... borrowing from his uncle's works whenever a chance arises."

"You gentlemen seem to be enjoying yourselves." All three turn, and then stand up in the presence of the woman before them.

"Anna Maria," Lu-Tang greets her while clearing coats from a chair, "Please join us."

The only woman to attend lectures at the Academy, albeit from behind a screen, takes the proffered seat; she often joins this crowd for the evening meal and discussion. "Pray tell me what has you all chortling so." Hendrik holds up the Hamlet manuscript, to which she asks, "Regius, are you planning to start a theatre troupe?"

Closing his eyes while shaking his head, "No." His friends are having another laugh on his account.

"We have already asked him that question. He has told us, with the help of the manuscript, of his lecture being interrupted by Shakespeare's nephew," Calderon explains.

"We are uncertain if he is disturbed more by the fellow's breaching of his lecture, or by the fellow's spouting of the lines without giving credit where credit is due," Lu-Tang tells her.

Reaching across for Hendrik to hand over the manuscript, "What speech was used to interrupt?" Well versed in many languages, she reads what he has pointed out, "It is a common sentiment, another instance of the writer plagiarizing whatever suits him." She is among those confounded by the English playwright's popularity. "Perhaps the young man was not referencing Hamlet's soliloquy at all, but is familiar with the true source of the quote: Montaigne."

"Oh, this again. Your argument that there is nothing new under the sun," Hendrik quips.

"A line used in a sonnet, but originally from Ecclesiastes," Calderon points out another noted case suggesting the bard may be stealing some of his lines.

"Well said Sir," congratulations from Anna Maria, who has taught herself the Hebrew and Arabic languages in order to more fully understand the bible.

The discussion is interrupted by the arrival of their dinners. Dirk holds the large tray while Kikkert sets a plate before each guest. Once they all have their dinners before them Lu-Tang asks, "Have you a moment Dirk?"

Dirk turns back to the table at the same moment that the woman seated there turns and they each instantly recognize one another. "Anna Maria," he gasps.

"Diedrik," she extends a hand to him. He bows and kisses her fingers. "I have missed visiting Schoonhoven's Landing since Donar's passing. Are you no longer a molenaar?"

This wonderful woman before him had visited Donar often. He tells her, "I am taking time away from the windmilling."

"You know each other?" Lu-Tang asks, then turning to Dirk, "and you are a windmiller?"

"He is a fine molenaar," Anna Maria tells them, "and a fine painter as well."

"Well Dirk, or rather, Diedrik, I have a request of you."

"How may I be of assistance, Sir?"

"I am in need of a driver, and if Kikkert is able to spare you for a couple of days I would be most appreciative if you will accommodate me."

"I believe that can be arranged."

"I have developed an interest in Windmills and I am considering a windmill of my own. Captain Janszoon has invited me to inspect his home and mills, and I am in contact with a windmill contractor, Philip van Haumann."

"Yes, my father." He cannot help but notice the rapt expressions on their faces upon hearing this news.

"Your father? Oh, yes, well, he has posted me with news of some vacant windmills that I may be interested to see."

Anna Maria begs the question, "Would that be Schoonhoven Landing?" She shakes her head unknowing. Dirk scans the room wishing to be anywhere but here, "I have tables to clear, but we can work out some arrangements."

"Thank You."

Before he is altogether gone, "Diedrik?" He turns to Anna Maria, "How is your painting?"

"Emmm, I have been distracted, but I was able to do some sketching the other day."

"Oh, you must paint: It is balm for your soul."

"Yes." He nods and hurries away. As he clears another table his thoughts tumble upon themselves. If he is to take on this assignment for Lu-Tang then he will need to contact his parents, for he will not wish to show up unannounced. Back in the kitchen at the sink he is remembering Anna

Maria's visits, and how she and Donar would sit up late discussing theories of science and philosophy; subjects normally reserved for the company of men. He is remembering the life that he had so enjoyed up until a season ago. Through the window he sees riders arrive and dismount, so he slips off his apron and goes out to care for their horses.

The conversation has diminished at the professors table while eating. Hendrik passes the salt to Anna Maria and speculates in his thoughts, as always, when will more women be tutored in Latin, and thus be able to attend lectures, as this woman claims will happen. Lu-Tang refills his wineglass while wondering about what he has discovered regarding the young man that is doing chores here at the Kikker Gat. Calderon, while savoring the asparagus slathered in buttery sauce, contemplates broaching the subject of traveling with Lu-Tang on his windmill tour. Anna Maria considers teaching Diedrik the art of etching now that he is living here in Utrecht. He could present his drawings and his knowledge of birds to the world. Behind the counter and in the kitchen Kikkert and Rhetta are each appreciating having this attentive young man working for them and yet, knowing inside, that he hides something, for why else is a trained millwright performing menial chores in a Public House.

The Proper Heiress

Boomkikker is checking the cart for the tarpaulin that he has instructed Diedrik to take along with him on this windmill tour they have arranged for Lu-Tang, and upon finding it stashed away beneath the driver's bench says, "Ah, good, tis wise to be prepared for rain." Three days ago, as these preparations were first set into motion, Diedrik, not wanting to arrive unannounced, had posted a note to his parents and paid extra to the courier for the guarantee that his message will be delivered before tomorrow. The planned route has them arriving at Captain Janszoon's later today, and then a quick jaunt over to Schoonhoven Landing where they intend to stay the night. With an early start tomorrow they will be able to stop at his father's sawmill for a short visit before continuing the remainder of their journey and arriving back in Utrecht before darkfall. The jitters of returning home that had at first plagued Diedrik have subsided. Is he finally getting over the grief of Donar's passing, or is it the presence of the Golden Hearts hidden within the sash beneath his coat that has settled his nerves? As he is checking the horse's harness Lu-Tang arrives carrying a small satchel and appropriately, an oilskin cape and wide-brimmed hat. "Good for you," Boomkikker tells him, "you come prepared for rain."

"My apologies," Lu-Tang tells them, "there is a slight change in our planned arrangements."

"Ungh?" Both the innkeeper and assistant have everything settled and ready to go. The slight change becomes evident as Calderon and Hendrik rush out the door into the stable-yard wearing travel clothes and carrying their own satchels and rain gear.

"Tis a school holiday, and this little road trip will be the inspiration necessary for the refreshing of our spirits," halloos Hendrik.

Kikkert makes a dash toward the kitchen telling Diedrik, "You will be needing more food and drink."

"NoNoNo," Calderon calls him quickly to a halt, "We have agreed that we will only be allowed as fellow travelers so long as we do not hold up the departure time, nor cause any other unscheduled delay." Then climbing into the back of the wagon and seating himself next to the already snug Hendrik, raises a hand and with a parade wave pronounces to all, "We are ready whenever everybody else is."

Kikkert and Diedrik regard each other with quizzical smiles, then Diedrik climbs up to the bench next to Lu-Tang, gathers the reins, clicks his tongue to the horses, and bids *vaarwel* with a wave. Out of the alley they are occasionally slowed by the early morning traffic, but driving becomes easier as they leave the business district behind. The two wayfarers seated in the back chatter away. Lu-Tang sits quietly, taking in the sights and sounds, until they are beyond the city's boundaries. Now passing through a rural landscape of fields and pastures he says, "This reminds me of my childhood home."

"You will be seeing my childhood home tomorrow," Diedrik tells him, "and tonight we will be staying where I lived and worked for many years."

"I am interested to meet your father and mother," Lu-Tang says, "My parents were potters," he continues, "of porcelain. Not the magnificent vases brought back on your merchant ships, but the everyday bowls, plates, pitchers, and serving dishes found in every home."

Interested, Dirk remarks, "There is a porcelain guild in Delft."

"Indeed," They return a wave to the man surveying the world from his doorway, "My father kept us busy digging and sifting the clay, churning the slip, and filling the molds," Lu-Tang casts a glance toward his bench mate ascertaining his interest, "while he kept the fires beneath the ovens hot enough to properly temper the castings."

"It was the same for me growing up." They turn to one another sharing a look. "My father kept us busy fishing logs from the pond, feeding them up the ramp, then keeping them butted end to end to be pulled through the saws. When we weren't needed in the sawmill he had us stacking and re-stacking boards, or carving cogs for the gears of the windmills he was building."

"You had one other brother." Lu-Tang states, "My parents had many children. When the monks came recruiting for the monastery it was no great hardship for them to let me go; the work would still get done." They are momentarily distracted as a rabbit scurries miraculously across the roadway between the horses' hooves. "That is perfect timing," he laughs, then continues, "I was told that it is a great honor to represent our village as a novitiate but, at the age of twelve it did not seem so wonderful. Wudang Monastery sits at the top of Wudang Mountain, high above the lesser monasteries. There are twenty thousand steps up the mountain," Lu-Tang smiles at the astonishment he sees in Diedrik's eyes, "and for the first four years of my apprenticeship I followed the path of that stairway each day; carrying a load up and bringing another load back down."

"Up and down twenty thousand steps each day! Whoa!"

"It takes some getting used to. It was the beginning of my training in the discipline of Internal Alchemy."

The chattering from behind the seat has been still for a while, and now Calderon speaks up, "I was also taken off to a monastery as a youngster, but instead of climbing steps I learned to write, or rather, to copy. Hour after hour, day after day, I scribed copies of liturgies, copies of canticles, and copies of biblical extracts. I can still recite verbatim many of those passages I copied so many times over and over and over."

"La," smirks Hendrik, "I was sent to military school; trained to be a soldier. My aptitude for calculating assigned me a commission in the quartermasters' corps so, although I traveled with the army, I never did serve in battle."

"Pardon me Lu-Tang," Diedrik asks, "You mentioned *Internal Alchemy*. Is there an External Alchemy?"

"A very perceptive question," answers Lu-Tang. "External Alchemy focuses on the ability of a chosen few, the Wu, to interpret what the Spirits of Nature have to say."

"Did you say the 'woo'?"

"Those who proclaim themselves wizards because of their ability to speak with Spirits." He tips his head inquisitively until Dirk nods his understanding. "Inner Alchemy," he continues, "teaches that everybody has that ability."

Calderon says, "That is what the Mystics teach," then adds derisively, "I would say that priests are our version of the Wu."

Hendrik, not wanting to get Calderon started on the subject of the priesthood so early in the day begs of Diedrik, "Please stop at the next presentable public house. I would like to stretch my limbs ... and perhaps acquire some refreshment."

"Okay, will do." Then back to what they were talking about, "I would have gone crazy climbing up and down that many steps every day for so many years."

"You would not have gone crazy. I have noticed wherever I have been that people generally repeat the same daily routine for a good portion of their lifetime without going crazy. I have discovered that it is not the task, but one's attitude regarding the task."

"Riiiight," laughs the young man as he pulls the cart off the road into the foreyard of a pleasant looking inn.

"We will be quick," says Calderon who is leading Hendrik at a brisk pace. They are inside only a short time when the Spaniard steps out carrying a loaf of bread and a two gallon cask. Hendrik follows with a string of sausages and a triangle of cheese, but has stopped in the doorway continuing his conversation with someone inside the room. Calderon jumps into the back of the wagon and tells Diedrik, "Go ahead, Hendrik will be there talking all day if you wait. When he sees the wagon moving he will come running. He will not let you leave without him."

So Diedrik gives the horses the signal to move along, and as soon as their hooves begin to move and the cart's wheels are turning Hendrik comes running, hallooing all the way across the yard. Catching up with the wagon he jumps and rolls in. Holding up a spigot for the little cask of beer, he smirks at Calderon, "Were you forgetting something?"

♡♡♡

Mara and Robert have settled comfortably into their new home. Their barn now holds additional goats, a few sheep, a rooster and some hens, and horses. They enjoy having the windmill turning, but leave the mill-tending chores to the Gedimins, who make a game of keeping the sails going round. They have a patch of garden planted with vegetables, and the weeds have been cleared out of the flower beds.

After further scrutinizing the drawer's contents Robert and Mara have determined that there could be information regarding her harp and necklace at the tower marked on the timeworn maps. Robert is a fine painter, and he has made copies of those maps, copies of the book's pages, and even a copy of the painting of the celestial harpist; leaving all the originals safely within the drawer. He has been to upriver trading posts filling the Tulip's hold with merchandise, and is now sailing downriver toward the North Sea. He easily slips through the many ships awaiting entry to Rotterdam's harbor, thankful that, not having business in this port, he is able to pass by.

This passage from the North Sea into the Port of Rotterdam takes days and there are ships from all over the world awaiting their turn. Among those in line as Robert passes is a frigate that has been reconfigured from its original design and is now garishly dressed out with larger than usual cabins for people wanting to travel in style from port to port. Where there had once been space in the hold for commodities there are now cabins contrived for comfort. At the helm of this cruise ship is the recently de-commissioned Captain Derek; the famous fool that lost his ship to fire. The sinking of the HMS Cooper is a well-known embarrassment. His family's influence, having saved him from being court-martialed and subsequently hung, has also assigned him this ignoble position as titular captain aboard this aging and over-sized yacht. He has only a minimal command over a few actual sailors, and has the unfortunate distinction of flying the flag of Britannia through foreign waters and into ports where the Royal Navy is an unfriendly rival. Captain Derek keeps an ever vigilant eye out for the ship that he blames for his ruination. He clearly remembers the Tulip; that devil spawn responsible for his disgrace. He tells himself that the only possibility for him to ever regain his dignity will be for him to capture and bring to trial the pirate that had firebombed and sunk his ship. And so he watches. He particularly watches now where there are so many ships in his view. Then he notices, from a distance, the outline of a sloop the size of what he is looking for, and it is flying the Dutch VOC flag. He raises his glass to his eye, and feels his heart pound upon his ribs, beholding that it is indeed the ship he has been watching for. It is the Tulip! Without thinking he shouts the order, "Turn about!" Excitedly he repeats the command, "Turn about, I say. Set course to overtake that miserable cur!" The slovenly First Mate, unkempt as usual, turns his heavily hooded eyes toward his captain, but makes no move to alter the ship's course. Stymied again by this ineffectual posting as a figurehead captain Derek throws his cocked hat down in frustration, barely able to halt his fit before stomping it flat.

"What was you going to do, Sir," asks the Mate derisively, "toss some of the fancy cherry candied crumpets at 'em? Ha, Ha, Haha!" The man's wise-cracking is a further reminder to Derek that he does not hold the authority of a true naval captain. He bends down, picks up and dusts off his silly hat, bemoaning again that the dress code does not allow him his preferred skull cap.

The shouted command and the Mate's loud guffaws have drawn the attention of those passengers wandering the deck. Captain Derek hears a woman asking from behind him, "We are not really turning around are we Sir?"

With an extreme measure of resolve Captain Derek turns to the young lady, who is dressed in finery and holding a frilly umbrella to shade her made-up face and daintily coiffed hair, and knowing that he must be civil, bows while offering his apology, "Upon sighting yonder pirate," stretching his arm directing her attention toward the passing sloop, "I was overtaken with memories of past conquests." Then he pantomimes humility while bowing deeper, "My apologies Madam."

"Oh," looking toward the sleek ship he is pointing toward, she comments, with an affected shake of her head, accompanied by a flutter of lashes, "it does not look like a pirate ship." Derek removes the hankie from the breast pocket of the garish uniform he is required to wear. He wipes his brow in the most gentlemanly manner he is able to embellish, consoling himself as he is wont to do whenever he is forced to communicate with *these people*. She smiles, raises her eyebrows, and flutters her eyelashes while shaking her head in bewilderment, then further consternates the captain by asking, "Why must our ship wait in line behind all the other ships?" He looks away. His eyes roll up into his forehead. Noting his First Mate's belly shaking with stymied laughter, He wonders is there any remote possibility for this dilettante to ever understand the nature of the procedures recognized and enforced at sea. Not to be put off she asks, "Will it be very much longer?"

He has no answer. He cannot discipline her. He cannot confine her to her quarters. He dare not risk saying anything, wary that it may come out as an affront. He raises his spyglass back to his eye and watches the receding Tulip while bearing silently the indignity of his circumstances.

♡♡♡

Keeping the conversation going as the morning passes Diedrik asks Lu-Tang, "What made you decide to board a ship and travel here?"

"I did not travel here aboard a ship," pausing long enough for the younger man to turn his way, "I walked."

"Is that a long way? Like, how far is it?"

"Not how far: how long." Lu-Tang laughs, "The Overmaster of the monastery called me aside one day and after telling me that I had completed my development at

Wudang, he suggested that I walk westward. Basically, he told me to begin a new training by walking another four years." He turns in his seat checking on Hendrik and Calderon, no longer chatting away, but listening. They each wave him on, encouraging him to tell his tale. "There are many tall mountains to walk around, and many cultures at war with their neighbors to walk around, and inland seas to walk around, and deserts that I should have walked around. And there are many, many: too many large sprawling cities. After four years had passed I found myself seated in the main dining room of an establishment that we are all familiar with," pausing again for a moment before continuing, "seated at a table next to me was a rogue priest, serving as librarian for the recently established University, who deemed it imperative that his academy take on an Oriental Master in order to add flair to the school's curriculum." Tossing a hand in the air he says, "Enough about me. Tell us if you please Diedrik, why you have chosen the city life."

"I did not actually choose city living. I only wanted a change." He gathers his thoughts. "When the man that I worked for passed away I moved back home with my mam and pap. I did not know what I wanted, so I left." Unused to talking about himself, he halts.

"Where did you go?"

"I went to Amsterdam. The land of opportunity and all that. I hired on as a dock hand. I did not mind the work, but the hours that we worked were determined by the tides. Ships that come in on the tide need to be ready to sail out on the tide. I never imagined that there are so many ships sailing the oceans."

Each of the professors are thinking of what they have heard regarding the inconstancy of dock work. Most dockhands are itinerants that work only long enough to earn passage to the Americas. Hendrik asks him, "Were you planning on traveling across the Atlantic?"

"I considered it, especially after the dock boss put me to tallying."

"You have training in the keeping of accounts?"

"My father taught me calculating. He even taught me what he could of Latin, in hopes that I might attend University." This interests his companions. "Clerking is easy enough; actually somewhat boring. Adding up columns of weights and measurements in order to calculate as much cargo as possible to fill the hold of a ship."

"So, you know geometries?" They are impressed.

A kestrel dives out of the sky, with an audible whoosh, into the deep grass nearby. Having missed its prey it circles back up into the sky where it hovers once again. "That little falcon is one of the fastest birds in the sky," Diedrik's arm is raise pointing out the hovering bird, "but I do not think it is quite as fast as a peregrine."

"So, you have also received training in the natural sciences?"

Noting that they are nearing a junction, Diedrik answers distractedly, "it is not difficult to determine which the hunter is and which is the hunted." He sees that this is indeed the road that he wants to take, "We will take this short-cut." It is a smaller, less traveled way and soon has the two riding in the back of the wagon jostled over bumps and tumbled by ruts to the point that they choose to walk. The springs beneath the bench smooth out the bumps, so Lu-Tang chooses to remain seated there rather than walking with his friends.

Bouncing along, Lu-Tang presses Diedrik to carry on with his tale, "Clerking did not suit you?"

The young man takes a look at Lu-Tang, then after checking behind where the other two are absorbed in their own conversation, takes a deep breath before saying, "I will tell you, but it is in confidence, for part of what I have done lacks dignity."

Lu-Tang glances behind them observing that the other two are out of listening distance, then assures Diedrik, "I am honored that you will take me into your confidence."

"I did not like sitting at a desk for so long," he begins haltingly, "nor having to answer to the orders of superiors that cared nothing for me." He raises his eyebrows questioningly, perhaps wondering if anybody else ever feels this way. "It is enough for others to drink and gamble away the time when they are not working," shaking his head, "but that does not suit me." Rearranging himself on the seat, postponing what comes next, "When I was not working I usually ended up sitting alone on a bench in the square watching the people passing by."

"People watching is fascinating."

"Oh yeah! Yeah, great when there is nothing better to do," agreeing, "but I was noticing, emmm well, what caught my attention, ehh, or rather the circumstances that surprised me most were the sneak thieves, the dippers, the wallet lifters." There. He has said it. He steals a glance at Lu-Tang, seeing that he is focused directly forward, expressionless, not encouraging him to continue nor, aghast at what might come next. "What intrigued me was not their methods as much as their targets." This does bring a look of interest from the man seated next to him. "It is kinda fun to watch 'em snatch a wallet from the inner pocket of some snobbish looking cad as he strides along with his nose up in the air. Or, for one of them to distract a fastidious fop whose belly has his coat stretched to the limit, while another is detaching the man's shoulder bag."

"So you tried it for yourself?"

Taken aback by how easily he had been read out, Diedrik confesses, "Yes," surprised that he is telling this, "Yes I did, and with three lifts I had more than I was being paid for a week of clerking."

"Ah, exchanging drudgery for thrill. That is not such a bad trade-off."

Perplexed by the Huaxian's opinion, yet encouraged, "I took the next day off, enjoying my new life of leisure," wondering how to finish without divulging the nature of his stolen prize, "but after making another lift with such ease," now embellishing a bit, "I was struck by the absurdity of my actions. I could get myself thrown in prison!" There, it is done. "So, I returned to my room, packed my bag, and left Amsterdam. A day later I was catching up on the dishes in the kitchen of the Kikker Gat."

They wait at the end of their shortcut for Calderon and Hendrik to catch up and jump back in the wagon. Diedrik tells them, "We are getting close," two raptor mates are screeching overhead, "Osprey." They all watch the two birds circling over the river, then gasp as one of the pair drops suddenly. There is splash, then the eagle rises from the surface of the water with a large trout clutched in its talons. Diedrik tells them, "The osprey's outer toe is reversible; same as an owl. I imagine that it makes quite a difference when holding on to something as wiggly and slippery as that fish."

"There it is again," pronounces Hendrik, "your avian knowledge. Did your father teach you about birds also?"

"I have a portfolio of bird paintings. Given to me by a woman that you all know."

"Anna Maria?" asks Calderon incredulously.

"Yes, she purchased the book at auction. It is incomplete; the artist passed before completing his life's work. She imagines that I will finish it."

"I am familiar with that book," Calderon tells him, "Anna Maria outbid the University. It would have been a fantastic addition to our library." He gets a sheepish look from Diedrik.

Hendrik is watching the eagle on its perch, through a set of twin scopes, as it tears apart the fish. "Augh! Grishy!" He shivers away the morbid vision. "Eeeew." Dirk turns and upon seeing the modernistic marvel which Hendrik holds to his eyes experiences a spate of envious desire. He considers asking for a look through the bi-noculars, but he has recognized the Captain's windmill ahead.

Pulling into the drive and past the turning sails, he stops the wagon in front of the house. The three scholars are greeted by Captain Cornelius Janszoon from his doorway. He is waving for them to come inside. Diedrik has been here before, occasionally assisting his father and brother. He leads the wagon over to the barn where he is greeted by a man his age who introduces himself, "Hello, I am Nicklas Voorhaven. You will find brushes and feeding sacks inside," directing Diedrik's attention through the barn's doorway."

"Okay, thanks," Diedrik introduces himself, and they work together getting the horses unhitched and into the barn for brushing and feeding.

Inside the house Cornelius Janszoon has a large table spread with plates of meats, cheeses, bread, fruit, and desserts. He carries on in grand fashion explaining the ease of how all this has come together, "For the most part my ideas were presented by my solicitor to the contractor, who then made everything happen magically," Said with all his fingers waggling. "Now that I am living here I am practicing to be a molenaar." He stands before a wall of windows. Out of those windows is a serene garden with cobbled pathways. There is what appears to be a slim young man transplanting seedlings into rows. Janszoon, looking out at the scene tells them, "I am lucky to have someone here with a green thumb to fill in my gardens."

After they have eaten the Captain offers to show off his working windmill. As he leads them out Calderon begs off, "If you do not mind Captain, may I walk your garden instead?"

"By all means." Janszoon waves him off wishing him well, then carries on with his enthusiastic presentation, "There are two reasons for having this windmill built so very tall," as they get closer they are forced to crane their necks as they gaze upward, "The winds blow stronger up there," now directing their attention to his barn and two-story home, "and I am allowed to have taller buildings without the worry of blocking the wind." He waves his hands in circles. He opens the door and Lu-Tang enters. Hendrik peers inside, but after taking a look he steps back shaking his head vigorously declining. The Captain comments, "You will miss the grand view from above."

"Not for me! Oh no," shaking his head some more and grimacing, "Not me. I like to keep my feet on the ground," stomping his boots in the dirt. "You two go ahead. I will see how Diedrik is getting along in the barn." He walks away as Cornelius and Lu-Tang climb the stairs.

Calderon has walked around the house admiring the freshly planted gardens. As he is strolling along a row of sprouting corn he hears footsteps behind him, and turning, sees the young man he had noticed from inside the house, immediately realizing that this is not a man, and surprised even more that he knows who it is: Trinjntje Olmsfeld. Though it has been more than two years, their eyes meet in mutual recognition and simultaneously each asks the other, "What are you doing here?"

There is a long moment of silence. He is feeling the same sensations that he had felt a few years ago when, as a non-partial intermediary, he had interviewed this woman. "I beg your forgiveness. You do not need to tell me what you are doing here. I spoke in surprise."

Holding out her hand to him, "I too, upon recognizing you, spoke in surprise. Greetings Professor Calderon." She is also remembering those days. This man is different from others. Her heart is fluttering. "I gather that you are accompanying this man who is interested in building, as my uncle has, a windmill to drain a swamp to create new farmlands?"

He squeezes her hand tenderly and bows affirmatively, "Yes, and I am so very pleased to see you again." Ah, she is as beautiful as ever, "You are wearing your hair in a different style."

"La, yes." She tips her head triflingly, "I am masquerading as a young man; a vagabond."

"Are you hiding?" He asks. She nods, yes. They search each other's eyes. "Is there anything I can do? Is there anything that you need?"

She nods again while reaching out to grasp both of his hands in hers', "Please get word to my mother and father that I am well." She looks up at the passing clouds, then back into his eyes, tentatively she adds, "Only that I am well. They do not need to know where you have found me; that I am staying with my uncle."

He wonders what is going on. She does not tell him. "I will send a post to your parents upon my return to Utrecht." Considering how pleasing twould be to correspond, he tells her, "I would like to hear from you. Post me; care of the University. Let me know how you are doing, what you are thinking."

"I would like that." He smiles back at her. She notices how his smile lights up his indigo eyes. They notice that Hendrik has returned and Diedrik is getting the horses ready to go. "*Vaarwel* Paulo, til we meet again." She surprises him, and herself, by kissing his cheek.

"*Vaarwel* Trinjntje," walking to the wagon feeling lighter than before.

Diedrik and Nicklas are hitching the horses to the wagon, Hendrik ambles round and round muttering, "Crazy fools, climbing to the top." Meeting up with Calderon, he points to the wooden stage circling the mill, "I did not want to walk up all those stairs." The Captain and Lu-Tang can be seen way up there on the windmill's staging, "Not me though. Nope. Not going up those stairs," slapping his hands in a gesture of wiping away something unwanted, "I do not care for high places or empty spaces. Nope. I am keeping my feet right down here on solid ground." Smiling now with exaggerated smugness.

Diedrik pulls the cart out of the barnyard and onto the drive waving up to Lu-Tang that it is time to go. By leaving now they will get to Schoonhoven Landing before darkfall. When they are all in the wagon and thanking Captain Janszoon for his hospitality and bidding him good-bye they make their way out the drive and following another canal.

For distraction Dirk is counting birds, an old favorite pastime, including the falcon and osprey seen earlier as one and two. There is a grebe, number three; he watches it dive, then waits expectantly for when and where it will resurface. He hears the croaking of an egret, number four. It unfolds its great white wings and rises from the water to fly alongside.

Sitting next to him lost in his own thoughts, Lu-Tang is inspired by Captain Janszoon's enthusiasm. It had been thrilling to stand up above looking out over the land. It would be fun to sleep up there. He would like living in a windmill, at least for a while. Contemplating leaving his life at the University, the reasoning behind this tour, while admitting to himself that wherever he goes he will only stay there a while. He longs for the life he had as a walking nomad.

Feeling sanguine after his meeting with Trinjntje in the garden, Calderon's thoughts turn to ancient tales of the *Enlightened* who walk this earth. He had archived countless manuscripts, written in the first known languages, which tell of Celestials walking amongst us. His heart tells him that Trinjntje is ethereal enough to be Celestial.

Hendrik is appreciating what Captain Janszoon has, and foresees himself leading a similar life after he has had enough of lecturing. Lulled by the turning of the wagon's wheels he drifts off dreaming of creating the home of his fancy. Imagining his family's crest, wings of freedom over a wreath of ivy, carved into the lintel.

♡♡♡

Out on the open sea Robert chooses to sail outside of the main shipping route. There is a thick cloud cover hiding the stars, leaving him only the compass for plotting his course. He follows a generally northeastern line, dozing for a while, then awakening, checking and adjusting his bearing, and then dozing again. Through years of sailing on his own he has developed an instinctual confidence with this continual process of waking and dreaming.

Morning arrives, the clouds lift, and as he calculates his new bearings he remembers mythical tales of the land beneath this water. Some say that this area, now covered by the waters of the North Sea was once a part of the continent. There is a tale of a gigantic wave washing the land away, scouring out and filling this basin. He has heard of colossal waves washing away coastal villages, but a wave massive enough to form this sea, "Twould be a wave of unfathomable proportions indeed." If there is any credence to the myth, then there are remains of civilization beneath these swells. "A forgotten civilization. A bygone era." His attention is drawn away by a pod of pelicans flying overhead. They all dive simultaneously, then skim along the surface scooping with their pouches from a school of fish that must have been visible from above. They settle there on top of the swells tipping their heads up and down; draining the water from their bills, and then swallowing the fish. These are the everyday moments of life at sea that Robert loves.

As the day passes the pelicans stay with him as he crosses into the Sognefjord; although tireless in flight, many have perched themselves along his ship's gunwales. He enjoys watching their silhouettes against the backdrop of the fjord's steep hillsides. In the distance there is snow remaining on the mountaintops: there is always snow on top of some of these mountains. He wonders if the trail he hopes to follow will take him as high as the snow. As he is nearing the end of the fjord and the port of Vik the Pelicans leave him to join with thousands of their kind gathered on an offshore rock

Upon mooring, the first order of business is dispensing of his cargo. There is a merchandiser who wants all the barrels of oil, bolts of cloth, crates of spices, and bags of flower bulbs. He trades casks of Dutch beer for casks of Norse beer. He negotiates with the quarry for the granite blocks he has come for. He visits the commune where the rune stones are carved and arranges to have a quantity delivered to the wharf. The dock crews will have the cargo he has brought with him unloaded tomorrow. The building blocks, kegs of beer, and rune stones will be loaded the following day. He has a three day mooring, which he hopes will allow him time enough for his planned hike to the tower.

On the edge of Vik is the public house Robert has chosen as a base for his adventure. The proprietor's grandfather sitting on the porch greets him, "Hallo." This centenarian's bright eyes shine with the sunny outlook of satisfied living. He stands and firmly shakes Robert's hand while calling through the door to bring a quart for their new guest. "It is good to see you again my friend. I am hoping that your life is prospering."

"Aye, tis good," taking a seat Robert tells the old fellow, "You are looking as spry as ever."

"Yes, I am happy. Every day is good."

"Greetings Sir," a grandson brings the mug of beer for Robert, then upon seeing the backpack asks, "Will you be having a room for the night?"

"Aye, I will." Glancing over he is disappointed to see that the older gentleman has dropped off to sleep, "Oh, I was hoping to visit with your grandad about the past."

"Have no worry, he never naps for long and will be awake soon enough and happy to visit."

This porch is pleasant, a gentle breeze rustles the leaves of the trees in the yard. A distant cawing can be heard, and looking up to a rocky ledge Robert watches crows returning home from a day of foraging. After a while the older man stirs, perhaps the draft has tickled his beard. His eyes are once again open and bright, giving him the look of having had a good laugh. He asks, "What is the news of the world?"

Robert laughs, "The wide world is as ever." Disregarding news of Kings and their armies or nations and their navies, he withdraws the copies he has made and hands over the map that shows the passage from Vik into the mountains. "A collection of old maps have been left in my care and this is a copy of one of those maps."

The old fellow recognizes what he is looking at. "You will not find this trail anymore," he tells Robert, "it lies beneath boulders set loose when the side of the mountain slid off." Scratching his chin now, "Must have been eighty years or so ago; I was still a youngster." His eyes close and his smile is a wide grin as he contemplates his bygone youth. "I followed that trail as a boy with my Da and his brother." Robert hands over the sheaf of papers holding the meticulously copied cover and pages of the book from the drawer. Recognizing again what he is looking at, "Ah, the *Tale of the Tower.*"

"You are familiar with it then?"

"Indeed." He leans back in his chair, resting the papers in his lap, and closing his eyes, "This tower is legendary, though few remember it anymore. We hiked that trail and we visited that tower." Spoken wistfully. Eyes closed, and drifting away into sleep.

The grandson, standing in the doorway behind Robert says, "I can show you where that trail begins. It follows this stream," tipping his head referring to the sound of running water coming from behind the house "but the trail is all grown over and ends where the stream comes out from beneath the boulders of the *skritha.*"

"*Skritha*?"

"The landslide that Grandda mentioned."

"Surly there is a way over the rocks."

"Ach, no reason to. That path on your map would lead almost to Vinje Parish, but the ridge at the top is too steep; besides there is a much easier trail that goes around instead of over the mountain."

From across the porch the boy's grandfather, with eyes open again, tells them, "The trail on your map ends where a lake sits in a bowl surrounded by steep cliffs. The tower and its walls sit near the shore of that lake." Closing his eyes and nodding his head, remembering the scene, "it is the most beautiful region of this entire world." Opening his eyes again, he smooths his hand across the illustration from the cover of the book that shows the tower with the cliffs rising behind. "The outer wall has crumbled, yet the tower remains and is dry inside." Robert hands over his copy of the painting showing the golden haired goddess seated at the harp. Upon seeing the picture the old fellow stands straight up. His face wears an expression of pure awe. As he drops back down into his chair he hugs the painting to his heart.

A few moments pass in silence. An orange cat walks along the porch's rail, hops down and slides itself along Robert's pant leg, then rubs its furry cheek against the boy's knee before jumping up into the old man's lap and curls itself for sleep. The old fellow absent-mindedly strokes the cat. His eyes open and he holds the picture up for another long look. "The inside walls of the tower are covered with a tiled mural. This picture is of that mural, with this lady at its center." He breathes in deeply and then releases a long sigh before continuing, "I remember clearly the moment that she came alive. We all heard the strings of her harp."

The young man says to his grandad, "I have never heard you tell this story before."

"Everyone scoffed when my Da and his brother told the story," he scowls uncharacteristically, "so they stopped telling of the miracle; and made me promise to never tell of it either. The remembering has been hidden for so long that I may have forgotten." He tells Robert, "I thank you sir for reviving this memory."

♡♡♡

Captain Derek's cruise ship, after finally docking in the port of Rotterdam, where it was only allowed a short mooring, had made the exchange of passengers a rushed affair. The port authorities wanted the mooring available for important, revenue generating traffic. Now, days later, arriving in the Port of Amsterdam, they are greeted quite differently. One of the passengers aboard this ship holds enough influence that they have been escorted directly into the Port after navigating the shallow waterway called the IJ. They have been granted two days mooring. The quartermaster's crew are already off and about the business of refurbishing for their continuing voyage: next stop

Kopenhagen. The passengers, eager to get away from the confines of the ship pass the captain, standing at the top of the gangway ramp, as they disembark. Derek gives them little attention, focused instead on planning a visit, later today, to the offices of the Dutch East Indies Company hoping to discover information regarding the ship whose captain he so determinably seeks for revenge.

The important emissary, whose presence had allowed them this quick moorage, has already disembarked, another passenger, the princess Saarika, a passenger that has kept to herself, stops before Captain Derek. She is wearing a patterned scarf wrapped around her neck and over her head, a long sleeved cloak that extends below her knees, and loose leggings that cover the tops of soft leather boots. The captain looks up, for she is taller than he, as she extends her hand, which he takes in his, "Thank you kind sir for getting us here safely." As she withdraws her hand she leaves a sizable golden coin in his palm.

This is a first for Captain Derek, befuddling his already befuddled thoughts. He is so taken by her grace and her generosity, and so unaccustomed to having kindness directed toward him, that he stands spellbound for a long moment before finally remembering to bow deeply, "Always at your service M'lady." When he straightens up she is already halfway down the gangway and now there are other passengers, with their noses haughtily lifted, passing by. He slips the coin into his vest pocket thinking that this may be enough to replenish his dwindling store of wine.

Saarika reaches the dock and is greeted by port authorities seated at a makeshift tariff desk set up beneath an impromptu awning that is comprised of two poles set in barrels supporting a VOC tri-colored flag draped over a rope. They want to see her papers. Because her family has traded with Europeans she is familiar with this language and these procedures, but she pretends to not fully understand. "What papers do you wish to see?" She knows that these men are looking for money, trolling for revenue, and she is hoping that she does not appear to them as a worthy catch.

The official seated at the center, probably a mere clerk, yet responds to her query as if he is an important man, by first folding his arms significantly across his chest, then leaning back in his chair, and while noticeably pointing his nose skyward, allows himself to pronounce to all who may be illiterate to the customs of this land, "The Port of Amsterdam is an international port. We need to know if you are bringing illegal contraband across our borders."

Saarika gives pause. She is familiar with this type of self-serving bureaucrat. She smiles sweetly to the man while imagining reaching out with the toe of her boot to tip his chair over backward, "I have no papers. I have no contraband."

One of the other two seated here snickers for they have received instructions to greet this particular passenger with proper decorum, then holding up his copy of the ship's manifest tells her, while making it sound like a question, "You are the Princess Saarika?"

"There. You already know who I am. I know that there are no tariffs for an individual disembarking upon your shores carrying no cargo. I am a guest to your country. As a guest I expect a friendly welcome."

Normally anyone with the honorific of 'princess' would arrive with crates of extra clothing, servants, and even soldiers as body guards, but this woman, on her own and carrying so little does not seem worthy of further interest. Dropping his chair forward, and after making a check mark on his list, the snooty bureaucrat perfunctorily waves her off, "Be on your way."

She remains. Speaking directly to him, "I am seeking information that may require a knowledge of your company's records." Her gaze holds his eyes. "I seek access to docking manifests."

Her eyes hold this itchy functionary spellbound. At long last, recognizing an opportunity, he is compelled to withdraw from his vest pocket the silver case that holds his personal calligraphied card of introduction. He holds the calling card out for her to take, tips his head ever so slightly, and as she slips the card from between his fingers tells her, "Greely DeVoss, at your service." If it is a bribe that she is offering it is best to see her in private and not have to share with these other two men at the table.

Saarika, accepting the man's card, and pleased to see that there is an address says, "Thank you Sir. I will look for you tomorrow morning." She recognizes the address on his card, for it is the same as the address on the envelope she carries in her pocket that holds her letter of introduction.

She slides the card into the deep side pocket of her jilbab. She lifts her duffel and slings its long strap over her shoulder, "In the morning then," she tells him and is off while wondering if meeting this creepy little man will be a waste, and reckoning that it might be best to go directly to the person whom her letter of introduction is addressed to.

Having spent the last decade on the southern Huaxian coast, where her family's trading business serves as a go-between for the European traders of Formosa, she has dealt often with Dutch businessmen and Dutch financiers, but this is her first visit to the lowlands, and as she moves away from the docks she is pleased by what she is seeing of Dutch society. She locates a hostelry, a spa catering to women, and soon has herself immersed in a warm soothing bath. She has kept her hair tightly braided while at sea and now it floats luxuriantly around her head. It has been so long ago now since she received her mother's dire summons. She had sailed from her adopted homeland of Huaxia back to her childhood home; Djibouti. Her mother had told her the tale of her brother's brash usage of the golden heart necklace as a marriage proposal to a foreign woman. Because of the defiant woman's dismissal, the necklace had been deemed unlucky, and its return denied. That necklace of Golden Hearts belongs to Saarika by right of birth. Her brother had stolen it. Now she is hoping to track down and regain what legitimately belongs to her.

She brings with her a crown of golden leaves which belongs with the necklace of Golden Hearts. While visiting her parent's home she had crept into the secret underground temple that dates back to a creed revered by her ancestors. Standing before a tiled image of a Goddess seated at a golden harp and wearing the necklace of Golden Hearts, Saarika had deemed it necessary that her crown and the necklace be together again. So instead of returning to her home in Huaxia she has sailed to Holland. Many of the ships leaving the port of Djibouti are slave ships. She chose instead a commodities ship that dropped her in London where she booked the final portion of her passage. It has been such a long voyage, and now this hot bath water is melting away the discomfort of being pent up inside tiny cabins. After bathing she allows the bath house attendants to manicure her nails, braid her hair, and massage the accumulated tension out of her muscles. All the while they are marveling at the unblemished perfection of her ebon colored skin.

Saarika sleeps well and awakens to find her clothes freshly laundered. She is served Ethiopian coffee with her breakfast of figs and cheese. There is a light mist as she takes to the streets of Amsterdam. The address on the card that she was given yesterday takes her back to the wharf district and to the local office of the *Vereenigde Oost-Indische Compagnie*, which is not yet open. Through the windows of the eatery across the way she sees the miserly little man she has arranged to meet seated at his breakfast. She crosses, enters, and presents herself at his table. He greets her without rising, "Princess Saarika," pouring syrup over his waffles, "So you have decided to join me for breakfast."

"I have already broken my fast. Thank you. I am seeking someone who may have recently returned from a long voyage." She pauses, looking away while this vulgar man stuffs another forkful of food into his mouth before he has even swallowed the last. "It may not be necessary that you look through the manifests of recent dockings, for you may be already familiar with the name." She sets a copper coin on his table and pushes it with a long, elegantly manicured finger toward him. It is not much, but brings the promise of more.

He snatches the coin while dripping egg yolk on his chin. With his mouth full, he asks, "What is the name?"

"I am not certain, but I have heard others pronounce the woman's name as Treentja Oomfelt."

DeVos chokes and sputters. As the blood drains from his face he takes a long draught from his morning pint. Swallowing, patting his chest, and blinking his eyes rapidly as a bit of color returns to his face, "I do indeed recognize the name. There was a conflagration took place in port the day of her arrival." Saarika is wondering what sort of person she is following. "The woman you seek is wanted on criminal charges, but by forces unknown she has escaped those whose job it is to detain her." He stops to reach atrociously into the back of his mouth to loosen something from between his teeth, then after inspecting what he has found continues, "Before she had been home a full day she vanished from this city. Her family has many searching for her; all in vain. She has not been found." Looking up at Saarika, for she has chosen to remain standing, and covertly lowering his voice he says secretively, "It is believed by many that she is a witch." Chuckling to himself he sits back with a smug expression pasted on his face.

Saarika has heard enough. Although what he has told her is of no use, she drops a silver coin onto the man's plate, along with his card, before marching out the door. In turmoil, with her thoughts spinning, she wanders, stopping to watch the water spilling over the dam. She repeats to herself that everything is okay, and soon has regained her certainty. The mist stops, the clouds part, and songbirds greet the day. She returns and seats herself upon a bench that allows her to see when the VOC office opens for business. Coaches arrive and men in business attire enter. The bell strikes ten.

The letter of introduction that she carries in her pocket bears the address of this office she has been watching. She rises from the bench and enters, introducing herself and handing the letter, inscribed to Christophorus Olmsfeld, over to a polite young man. He indicates an upholstered bench where she can be seated while waiting, "Director Olmsfeld is in conference." Upon hearing the man's name spoken aloud she wonders if it is the same last name as the woman she seeks. The polite young man returns with a tray of tea and biscuits. *Ah, dignity.* After the unpleasantness of her earlier meeting this is a great relief to be served politely.

Before long one of the businessmen that she had seen arrive earlier steps into the lobby where she is seated, "Princess Saarika?" He extends a hand which she takes as she rises. He introduces himself, "Chris Olmsfeld, at your service." He bows and tells her, "I have concluded my business here until this afternoon. There is a coach waiting to take me home. I would be most honored if you will accompany me. We will be able to discuss your business away from the noise and distraction of these offices, and my wife will be most appreciative for you to honor us with your presence."

Ah, dignity. Standing and taking his proffered arm, "It will be my pleasure, good Sir."

The Tower

Inside Christophorus Olmsfeld's carriage, awaiting the opening of the gate leading into his estate, Saarika is perplexed by the presence here of a small rabble. Chris explains while pointing, "On this side are those who love her," mostly young men; some holding flowers, "On the other side are those who fear her," purists dressed in matching grey. "That our daughter is not here does not deter them; any of them." He shows her a dispirited expression.

"In other countries these people would be prosecuted."

"Yes, behold the liberty and freedom of our nation." Having passed through the gate and arriving at the home's front entry a servant holds up a hand for Saarika to take as she steps down. She thanks him, and as Olmsfeld steps down next to her he also thanks the man by name. As they make their way up the walk he explains, "Our servants are free to come and go as they please. They earn wages," justification from a director of a company citing major profits from the transport of slaves.

Saarika's family has also profited from slave transport. "I like to imagine that there will be a day when all are liberated and free."

Once inside Olmsfeld introduces his wife, "Doortje," not as tall as he is, "Princess Saarika," who is taller.

"Pleased to make your acquaintance," Doortje takes her hand, gently directing her toward the sitting room. "We will have some tea. Can I get you anything else?"

"I am fine. Thank-you. It is relief enough that the floor is not moving," reminding them that she has spent months at sea.

Tea is brought in and as Doortje pours, Chris tells Saarika, "I received a letter from your mother, preceding your arrival, which is a copy of the letter you presented at my office this morning."

"So you have been forewarned of my visit?"

"Your mother's post included a receipt for a sizable deposit into our company's bank, and a request that an account be set up for you here. All has been arranged as per her edict."

"Thank you, Sir." She sips her tea, gazes through the windows out at a large thriving garden. "My mother has beckoned me home from our family's Huaxia station where I have served as Director for ten years." Saarika's family traces their lineage to the former Sultanate, and though they no longer rule, they still control enormous wealth, and are still considered as Royalty.

Christophorus acknowledges, "My Company and your family have an amicable trade relationship."

"I have not traveled here for business related purposes." She sits straight and tall. "First, I must ask; have you a daughter named Treentja Oomfelt?"

Doortje answers, "We have a daughter named Trinjntje."

"A while back, two or so years ago, this woman Treentja Oomfelt, stopped in my family's homeland port." She pauses to allow verification.

The Olmsfelds share a look, then Doortje responds, "Trinjntje was gone over two years on an horticultural expedition," noticing the questioning look in her guest's eyes she explains, "She traveled to find, and to bring home, exotic plants and trees."

"Her ship did stop in the Port of Djibouti," Chris tells her, "for coffee bushes."

Princess Saarika had not imagined the way this scenario is turning out. "One of my brothers became infatuated with your daughter and deemed it necessary that she become a wife. He presented her with a betrothal gift, expecting her acquiescence." Does anyone ever fully understand another country's traditions? "Her rebuke was deemed as a stunning affront to his Eminence."

Christophorus sits up and leans earnestly toward her, "We received news of the incident, and we sincerely apologize for our daughter's behavior." He does not want to diminish his apology, yet attempts a feeble clarification, "She has very little comprehension of cultural mores," he swallows, then adds, "or, actually, what I should say is that she lives by her own set of standards."

Saarika smiles, hoping to alleviate his anxiety, "She must be a remarkable woman. I look forward to meeting her. Be assured that I have not followed her because of any supposed insult to my family, nor because of any disregard for traditional principles, shared or unshared." Her smile becomes wider at the matching looks of perplexity upon the faces of this sweet Dutch couple. "The betrothal gift bestowed upon her by my brother was not his to give. It is an ancestral heirloom that belongs to me. I have come to fetch it."

Chris and Doortje look to each other in wide-eyed wonder. "We know naught of what you seek."

"It is a necklace of Golden Hearts set with jewels."

"Oh," Doortje brings her hand to her mouth astonished, "She made no mention ... She was only here a day ... less than a day. Oh ..."

"Is it true then, what I have been told, that her whereabouts are unknown?"

"Yes. We worry for her."

"And is it true that she has criminal charges filed against her?"

"Rubbish!" Christophorus proclaims, "She has broken no laws."

"She is different, that is all," says her mother, "she is as innocent as a child."

Saarika feels tenderness in her heart toward these two loving parents. She wants their minds to be at ease, "I did not come here to stir trouble. I believe that everything follows an order, and this situation will remedy itself."

A servant appears announcing the midday meal. Doortje invites the Princess, "Will you dine with us please?"

"I will. Thank-you."

"Have you a place to stay?" Doortje asks. "We have room for you here if you like."

"I do not wish to trouble you."

"Oh, please. I can show you around. We can go shopping."

"Well," it is nice here, "Okay. While I sort things out."

♡♡♡

Robert, having slept well in the Vik hostelry, is awake early. He hears birds calling to each other in the branches outside his open window. Someone is stirring about in the kitchen below. He dresses and folds the covers on the bed. There is fresh coffee and a breakfast sandwich, and then he is on his way with the sun barely peeking over the mountaintop. He follows a little used road to where it fizzles out at a crossing. He wades through the water and follows the path that winds alongside this stream until it disappears into the overgrown brush. To continue he has to walk the middle of the streambed. Moving from pool to pool he catches glimpses of fish. He watches small dark birds on the rocks bordering the edges of the deeper pools. The steady burbling of the cascading water provides an ever present accompaniment to his sloshing.

Before long he is fairly well soaked, yet marches on, at last breaking out into an open glade he feels the warmth of the sun. A steep barrier of boulders rises up before him. "This must be the rock slide that the old man spoke of," thinking out loud, "*the skritha*." The stream emerges at the base of this rockslide creating a marshy wetland. Looking up he cannot see over this wall of boulders. He starts climbing. There are hoofmarks of some agile rock climbing beasts, "Mountain goats, and big-horned sheep." Occasionally he is able to follow the hoof trodden pathways. His neck and shoulders are feeling tight from constantly scanning upward. He loosens the stiff muscles by twisting to look back at the ever expanding landscape below him. The day grows warmer. He climbs on. Up and up he rises, reaching now for handholds and placing his feet carefully.

The steepness levels a bit and he is able to hop from boulder to boulder. When he finally sees over the top of the slope he is met with the scene of rocky crags rising higher. He stands on the edge of the wide gap in the mountainside where it had slid away. There is a long valley before him to traverse. There are sparsely forested rocky escarpments rising up on both sides. Once again he is following the stream. It meanders through a meadow of tall grasses on its way along this flat bench. The earth is soft and mushy and he often has to jump across branching channels of water. He notices muddy areas that appear to have been stirred by the hooves of large beasts, and expanses of flattened grass where they have slept amongst the gnarled alpine shrubs. He hears an animal call, *Eeeee-Uhn, Eeeee-Uhn*. He looks in the direction of the throaty chirping and sees a huge beast standing at the edge of a vast herd. "Alce," he speculates. Deer-like in appearance, but much larger. *Eeeee-Uhn, Eeeee-Uhn* The herd's outriders standing watch are calling to the rest of the herd that stretches away across the valley, a few hundred animals if he were to count them. Robert creates a picture in his mind to hold the memory of this scene. He moves on; he must keep moving for the valley is long.

It is late afternoon when he reaches the far end of the grassy meadow. Where the land begins to rise again he is grateful for the wide paths made by the Alce through the briars and the nettles. The trail climbs steadily past a roiling pool at the base of a tall fall of water. At the next falls the trail passes through the narrow space behind, taking him between the falling water and moss-covered rocks. The trail continues climbing. He passes three more waterfalls before arriving at a lake surrounded by forest and boulders. Looking back from where he has come he is astonished by how high he now stands above the meadow and the large herd grazing there. Looking further out from this vantage he realizes he is viewing the Sognfjord, and beyond out to the North Sea. He makes out the bare outlines of the isles with the orange fire of the setting sun as a spectacular backdrop. "Have I ever before climbed to such an altitude as this?"

He knows that he will need to make camp soon, but determines to follow the shore of this lake. Knowing that he will want a fire he begins picking up branches. There is another short steep climb up the side of yet another waterfall. Coming out on top is another lake. This larger lake sits in a bowl of steeply rising granite cliffs. He is able to hop across rocks where the lake empties into the creek he has followed all day. He passes through a sparse forest of short gnarled trees. He comes upon a tall archway of masterfully carved stone blocks. Through the arch, up against the cliff, stands the ancient tower. Robert does not need to compare this tower with the illustration he carries to know that he has arrived at his destination. He is eager to rush forward and to investigate, but the daylight is fast diminishing so he designs a firepit with a circle of stones and sets some of the gathered branches within. Before total darkness falls he is able to gather more wood for the night. He finally sits down by the fire where he has a view of the tower. The stars wink into sight above him. He recognizes familiar constellations and determines the directions from where he sits in relation to all else. As he munches on his dinner snack he speculates on what he will find tomorrow.

♡♡♡

Mara is at her loom rhythmically sliding her shuttle to and fro, from hand to hand, while keeping the heddle going back and forth with her feet. She has been at her loom for long enough today that her thoughts are wandering far away. She is happy here. The countryside is not as rugged as her former home, but the weather is similar to what she is accustomed to; lots of wind and rain. Robert is away. They are each used to being alone. Where her loom sits at the front corner of the house she faces a wide bank of windows that look out across the yard, the roadway, and the river. There are occasional travelers passing by on horses, in carts, or walking. Ships and smaller boats pass by on the river. Birds fly up and down the wide expanse before her. She imagines that she is at the center of creation with the entire natural world revolving around her. She is singing, as she often does while weaving, an old familiar ballad, when she hears a knock at the door.

"Mara," the two girls, her new neighbors Kirin and Audrae call out as they enter, "We have brought you a plate of cookies," Kirin tells her placing them on the table.

"What was that song you were singing?" Audrae asks.

"Was I singing?" Mara rises from her bench smiling. She is glad for company.

"You were singing something that sounded kinda sad," Kirin says searching for the words, "Britannia's briar, Éire's rose ..."

"Two lovers. N'er to be together," Audrae finishes. "We heard from outside. Who are the two lovers that will n'er be together?"

"The song is the tale of a young man and a young woman who come from different lands." She busies herself gathering her tea-pot, cups, spoons, tea, cream, and sugar, "Two lands that have always been at war with each other." With everything readied she lifts the kettle from its hanger over the fire and pours the warm water over the tea leaves in the little pot. "Isolde of Éire and Tristan of Britannia. Have you heard the tale?"

Wondering if she has heard correctly, "What is the name?" Kirin asks, "Isolt?"

"Yes, you've got it. Isolde."

Always wanting new songs to sing, Audrae asks, "Will you teach us this ballad? Please."

"It is a very old song, not a particularly catchy tune. It is from back in the days, ya know, when the king of Éire was ruler over Britannia."

"Is this a fable?" asks Audrae, thinking Mara is making a joke.

"Ahhh," smiles Mara, "Some will tell you 'tis fable, while others believe 'tis fact." She has been taught in her childhood that she is born of this line that had once ruled. "History is written by the conquerors." They are quiet then as the sand in the little kitchen hourglass sifts from top to bottom letting them know when the tea has brewed long enough. "Sugar? Cream?"

"Our father wants us to use honey in our tea. He says that there would not be sugar except for slavery."

"I can fetch the honey if you like."

"Oh no, please, may we have sugar in our tea?"

Mara fills their cups, then tells them the tale of the offspring of feuding nations. Kirin remembers hearing a similar story and says, "It is much like the play of the English Bard; the story of Romeo and Juliet."

"Right you are my dear, but don't let us get started tallying what the Brits have stolen from the Irish." They hear horses outside in the drive. Through the windows they see a wagon. "Oh. Philip Haumann said to expect visitors. Someone looking for a windmill to live in. Could this be a new neighbor?"

Audrae jumps up, "Shall we go out to greet them?"

"Let's do."

The horses are reined to a halt. Diedrik, back at Schoonhoven Landing after so long, is surprised to see a woman with a cascade of glowing hair come out the door of Donar's home. She is followed by two younger women that could be close to his age. Lu-Tang jumps down and rushes forward introducing himself with a bow, "Good afternoon ladies." They curtsy in turn. "I am Lu-Tang. I hope that our arrival does not come as a surprise." With the approach of his friends he proceeds with the introductions, "My companions: Calderon and Hendrik." He turns with an arm extended toward the wagon's seat, "and our driver, Diedrik." He has remembered to use the full name rather than the nickname.

"Mara," She introduces herself with a tipping of her head.

"Kirin,' while curtsying.

"Audrae," wide-eyed and eager.

"We have made arrangements with Philip van Haumann to inspect a windmill for possible habitation. We will be staying the night in …" sweeping his gaze from the nearest and down past the other two windmills, "whichever one is vacant."

"That would be Windmidden." Audrae tells them while pointing toward the next mill down. Then swinging around to point at the closest mill, "This is Windhoek, and way down by the lake is Windweg. That is where our family is living." Enjoying showing off her knowledge, "The three are a gang, a work gang. They all worked together to drain this polder. And now," sweeping her arms wide, "see what great work they have accomplished." She performs a spin on her bare toes. "This is a marvelous place. You will love it here!"

"Audrae!" Scolds Kirin, thinking that her sister is talking too much.

"La, let 'er be," soothes Mara, "will one of you fetch your Da and Ma please," then turning back to the gentlemen before her, "You will find a place in the barn," pointing toward the next barn down, "for your horses. The house and windmill are open. These girl's parents and brothers will be here shortly to show you around properly. After you are settled in I will be honored if you will join me for the evening meal."

Audrae has raced away to fetch the rest of her family while Kirin walks over, lays a hand on a horse's flank, and smiling pleasantly, tells Diedrik, "Follow me. I will show you to the barn." He knows his way, nevertheless, allows this pretty girl to lead.

Hendrik gallantly tells Mara, "We will be on our way then," doffing his hat once more, "until later Dear Lady."

She is tickled by the manners of this dandy, and tickled again by the sideways glances directed his way from the other two men as they each bid her, "*Tot ziens.*"

Tot ziens, Tot ziens, mimics a magpie perched on the roof of her house, *Tot ziens. Ah-Ah-Ah-Ah. Ah-Ah-Ah-Ah*"

"Whatcha chatterin' about?" Mara asks the bird, "with yer white wings and yer black tail. Whatcha chatterin' about? Eh?"

Eeeeeekh. Eeeeeekh. Eeeeeekh, the bird answers as it flies off to spread the news that company has arrived.

"She is talking to a bird," Lu-Tang tells Diedrik delightedly. He reaches the door that leads inside the giant machine that is called Windmidden, enters and makes his way directly to the steps that lead up. His friends follow him in, but stop upon sighting the array of artwork adorning the walls. Lu-Tang calls from the stairway, "Are you coming up with me this time?"

"Oh no! Not me. I will stay down here where I am comfortable!" protests Hendrik.

Calderon laughs at him, "You will be filling your lectures with tales of visiting windmills, but you will lose all credibility when having to admit to your adoring crowd that you are too timid to climb to the upper levels." He laughs again at the look on his friend's face.

Hendrik is assuming that since Calderon had not climbed Janszoon's stairs that he is reluctant as himself to climb these. "You are going up?"

"I have climbed more dizzying steps than these. At least there is a handrail." Up the steps he goes while remembering the vertigo inducing climb up the face of a Toltec pyramid. "Fear not."

Hendrik stews for a bit, arms crossed and toe tapping hollowly on the floorboards. "Okay," running to catch up, "wait for me then, I am right behind you." The hard soles of his boots clatter on the steps; these steep steps. He looks back to where he was standing a moment ago. The expanse from this height makes his belly flip-flop, so he looks up to see the others and the span sends his belly flip-flopping even more. So he stares straight ahead and distracts himself by counting the steps, "seventeen, eighteen, nineteen," he counts to himself, "twenty-seven, twenty-eight, twenty-nine," he always counts when he is nervous. He reaches the middle landing wishing that he were at the top, then begins climbing and counting again, "thirty-nine, forty, forty-one," focusing on each step before him, "fifty-three, fifty-four, fifty-five," because something about counting keeps his belly from flip-flopping, "sixty-three, sixty-four, sixty-five." When he arrives at the top he dares not look down.

Calderon, holding the door open for him, squeezes his shoulder as he passes, "Well done my friend!" They step out onto the landing and look out over the treetops.

While his companions stand at the rail overlooking the expanse Hendrik keeps himself flattened against the wall. He breathes deep to calm the heavy beating of his heart. A large crane flies by. He is astonished to see the detail of the bird's wing feathers and steps forward. When the bird is past he suddenly realizes that he is standing at the rail on the edge of an abyss. "That is enough for me." He backs himself against the wall while dramatically fanning himself and hyperventilating. The others watch him with concern. He slides along the wall to the door and down the steps he goes.

Upon finishing his rush down the stairs he pulls a hankie from his inner pocket and is wiping the nervous dew from his brow when Diedrik and four others closely his age come in through the door. "Oh, heh, heh, heh," he laughs feebly, embarrassingly wondering if they had heard him running full speed down the stairs, "I am not used to such heights. Em, excuse me please." Straightaway past them and out the door he goes.

The Gedimins ask Diedrik about his art hanging on these walls. "Yeah, I used to live here. It was Donar's idea to hang everything." Not wanting to talk about himself, Diedrik asks them, "So what has inspired your family to leave your homeland?" Razs, Kirin, Vejz, and Audrae look to each other, each waiting for someone else to answer. "Oh, pardon me," he quickly asserts, "I did not mean to be nosy. I apologize. I do not mean to pry into your affairs. Sooooo sorry."

They all laugh. "La, that is not it at all," assures Razs, "our father held an important governing position. When the King stepped down, allowing the people to vote, many of the King's family holding governing positions also stepped down."

Diedrik is hesitant to ask, but cannot help himself, "So, your parents are, like, royals?"

"Were royals," Vejz answers "now we are everyday people."

"Living everyday lives," Kirin smiles charmingly.

"Like everybody else," Audrae finishes.

Lu-Tang and Calderon come down, and after greeting Diedrik and the others, exit the windmill. They are met by Renaldo and Annia, who introduce themselves and walk with them to Mara's. After eating, they decide to do some singing, at first they sing familiar songs that they all know, later they teach each other new songs. Before they all leave for their beds Calderon makes a closer inspection of the great harp sitting in the corner. He is familiar with a harp like this, and upon closer inspection he determines that it is identical to the harp he remembers. He looks across the room to Mara who is watching him. Their eyes meet. He passes a hand lightly across the strings. They are perfectly tuned, as he suspected they would be. He senses the recalling of this moment; *déjà vu*. His eyes meet Mara's eyes again and in this extended moment their souls greet each other.

♡♡♡

From Amsterdam Captain Derek has navigated successfully through the narrow passages of the Skagerrak and the Kattegat. His ship is now docked in the fortified harbor of Kopenhagen. Turmoil is currently embroiling this region; evidently there are wars going on here. Their route plan originally had them sailing further into the Baltic, but with the revelation that a ship flying the flag of Britannia will most assuredly be sunk, their amended route plan has them returning from whence they have come. The warring armies have displaced many. Legions of these uprooted families have washed up on these shores. Some are eager to move on; many are hoping to find a way back to their homeland. The cruise ship's onboard accountant is greedily accepting more passengers, even though all cabins have been filled. Remaining open spaces have been assigned to those willing to pay for any opportunity available. The ship is becoming overcrowded: heavily overcrowded. Of these forsaken expatriates most are Estonians and Latvians; squeezed out from both sides as the armies of the Swedes and Russians have transformed their countryside into a battlefield.

It is cold here so Captain Derek is wearing his heavy dark coat and has replaced the official cocked hat for his favored skull cap. His dark visage is not enough to dissuade these nervous passengers from interrupting the navigational duties of his quarterdeck. So chains have been hung to keep them out, while hemming in the captain and helmsman. On his inspections below decks he finds people everywhere. He is hardly able to tread without having to step over somebody, or somebody's belongings. It has been determined through interpreters that many of these who have paid exorbitantly for their passage, intend to disembark in Amsterdam with plans to travel overland back to their homeland. Derek cares not for these folk, only that he wishes them off his ship.

Even after the ship has left the wharf it remains in the harbor awaiting the passing of stormy weather. There is general unhappiness and much disagreement amongst the passengers. The mood spills out to the over-worked crew. The galley repeatedly shuts down before all are fed. Captain Derek is being called upon to exercise his authority where he has none. He prematurely weighs anchor and sails out of Kopenhagen's harbor even before the weather has settled. The violent swells have the gunwales lined with pewking patrons, "Fewer requiring to be fed," the brute of a Quartermaster sniggers to the Captain.

The crew fights the wind and the waves until finally the weather settles and they have made it out into the open waters of the North Sea. The Captain is enjoying a rare moment of calm. There is currently no one demanding his attention, no one screaming for food, and no one asking for a doctor. He watches as the Galleymaster and the Quartermaster make their way through the mass of bodies on deck toward the helm. He turns away from these approaching pests, wishing that he had seen them sooner so that he could have hidden. He hears the rattling of the chains as they hop up the ladder. He hears one of them clearing his throat, "Ahem. Cap'n Derek, Siiir," warbling the honorific.

Before turning to face his tormentors he makes them wait while he nods for the helmsman to carry on. And then, "Yes. What is it now?" Speaking peevishly; these goons constantly bully him disrespectfully.

"Beggin' yer pardon, Siiir," the quartermaster begins while flashing a concocted smile, "on account of the overcrowding, Siiir, the ship's stores of drink have been depleted."

"That is not my problem. You should have planned better."

The thug turns to his partner grinning wickedly, "I tol' you he's an 'eartless bloke." On any other ship such words spoken within hearing range of the Captain would be justification for hanging. Captain Derek seethes impotently.

Now the Galleymaster speaks, "Our passengers, your responsibility as captain, Siiir, are desperately thirsty. They are demanding that something be provided."

Derek can tell where this is going, and he is not happy. "Share with them the crew's ration of whiskey."

"We was thinkin' more along the line of you sharin' from the kegs 'n casks 'n crates an' fine bottles tha' be hidden away in yer cabin," squinting menacingly, "Siiir."

Captain Derek ponders this a bit too long, prompting the Chef to step a bit closer where he suggests intimidatingly, "I wonder wot this crowd o' thirsty folk," swinging a fat arm to encompass the mass of humanity packed on board, "would do if they 'as aware tha' sustenance were bein' wifheld?"

"Why, I 'ud 'magine tha' they 'ud soon be an angry mob," says his nodding cohort, "and I'ud be 'maginin' tha' there 'ud be nuffing this paltry crew 'ud be able to do tha'ud be stoppin' an angry type mob from tossin' a presumed scoundrel overboard!"

Through all this the helmsman is staring straight ahead, barely able to keep his snickering contained. Captain Derek wishes that he could have these two thrown in chains, but knows that he has no allies on this ship's crew to carry out such an order. He unconsciously folds his arms while tapping the toe of his boot upon the deck. They have him bamboozled. "Very well," he mopes, then turning to the sailor at the wheel, "Stay the course."

"Aye Sir." There are no salutes exchanged.

He instructs the two hooligans, "Follow me, then."

Upon reaching his cabin door, and while placing his key in the lock, he tells the quartermaster, "I will be expecting full reimbursement for whatever stores that I am being forced to give up."

"Of course ya do, Siiir," said patronizingly while pushing Derek aside in the rush to enter. Each thug picks up a case of expensive wine, and on their way out tell him, "Ya may as well leave the door unlocked. Yer passengers will be requirin' the full lot, so we'll be returnin' for the rest a' wot y've got hidden away here," grunting, "Siiir."

♡♡♡

Robert awakens to the honking of geese. Looking out across the smooth surface of this little lake he sees a fish jump completely out of the water. It is daylight, yet the sun has not yet risen above the crest of the rocky ridge circling this basin. The air is chill. He stirs the coals of last night's fire, adds a few sticks and is soon enjoying a warming blaze. Another fish jumping prompts him to tie a hook and line to a long branch. As the sun finally shows itself he is cooking his catch, a small trout that had somehow survived living beneath the ice that must have so recently been covering this lake nestled here where the glaciers sit not so very far above.

Upon completing his meal he walks through the tall outer archway and follows the paved pathway to the tower. He notices now that the side of the mountain behind the tower looks to have been blasted away. What force could have carved out this arena, where the tower stands, from the basalt mountainside? The roof of the tower is covered with wafer-thin slabs of stone. Generally, only the walls remain of ancient fortresses; the wood of roofs and floors decayed long ago. This tower's roof remains intact; evidently girded with beams formed of stone. Before the main tower stands a smaller tower with what appear to be round-topped buttresses leading off from both sides into the mountainside. Inside this entry tower Robert stops, examining the foyer where he stands. There are archways in all four directions. Behind him is the arch that he has just passed through. The arch before him leads into the main chamber. Considering the two archways on either side, he determines that what he had thought were abutments are actually hallways leading off into darkness "I will check on those passages later." For now he walks through the elaborately carved archway before him into the spacious inner chamber.

It is a vast circular room with gabled openings high on the wall allowing the daylight to stream in and flood the inner sanctum with sparkling brightness. "It is so very clean in this chamber." He had expected the dust and debris of ages, but everything is swept and tidy. He calls out, "Is there anybody here?" For surly there must be someone; a monk or an ascetic hermit. He calls out again, "Hellooooooo." There is not even an answering echo.

Situated at the center is a massive boulder, in no way spectacular, yet clearly the focal point of the arena. As he wipes his hand across the stone he wonders, "What can be so very special about this rock?" He is astonished to feel warmth; not hot, but neither is it as cold as he assumed it would be. He lays both hands flat upon the smooth surface and definitely feels an odd sensation through his palms. A tingling moves up through his arms. He leaves his hands there while examining the walls that are adorned with the tiled mural told of by the old man. "Remarkable! It does match the painting."

Within a wide brightly colored band rising from floor to ceiling is the image of the celestial goddess seated at her harp. The intricacy of the tiled portrait gives her such a lifelike appearance that for a moment he has the impression that she is breathing and smiling, and that her indigo eyes are sparkling. "Gracious," he exclaims as he unconsciously drops to a knee and bows his head to her majesty. His heart flutters within his breast. He struggles to calm his breathing. Then, looking up, and noting how the jewels of her necklace sparkle, he wonders if he has been tricked by the light upon the image, "Magnificent." He is enchanted and loses track of how long he stays there drinking in the perfection. The goddess's harp is the same as Mara's inherited harp, except for the golden leaves holding an orb atop the harp's mast. The same difference they had noted in the painting from the drawer. He stands and dares himself to step forward. Touching the harp of the mural he certifies that its tiles are, "gold; pure gold."

Still believing that there must be someone else about the place he scans the room around him. Noticing that the mosaicked walls depict the image of a crowded ballroom filled with Celestials he asks himself, "Why have I not noticed them all before? Am I enchanted?" He rushes out. Standing in the outside air he breathes deeply until his heart has calmed. The sun is already past the middle of the sky. "Where has this day gone?" He hears a screeching coming from a nearby tree that stands taller than all the others. There is a large blue crested bird perched upon a lower branch. It screeches again, and is answered by another screech, and another; the tree is filled with the stellar jays producing an ever louder cacophony of screeching. Robert calls out, asking them, "Does magic abide here?" The birds' answer is silence. In this stillness he becomes even more mystified.

He retrieves the chalks and folio from his pack and begins sketching, hoping to capture the grandeur of the lake, the tower, and the mountain raising up behind it all. Then he heads back inside to sketch the wonders within. He draws a picture of the large unimpressive boulder hoping for a clue to its importance. Seated on the floor as he outlines the image of the harp-playing goddess he gets the impression that she is suspended within a wide ray of light shining up from the scarred boulder. He draws and sketches and colors. The afternoon passes. The inner chamber begins to dim as fewer sunrays stream through the lofty windows. He finishes one last drawing, then collects his chalks and rolls up his papers. He bids farewell with a long last look and is rewarded with another smile from the golden haired celestial.

Upon exiting the chamber he pauses in the foyer wondering again about where these other hallways lead. He stares deep into the darkness, and then calls out again to anyone that may be hiding there in the depths, "Hellooooooo." Are his eyes playing tricks on him again, or was there a wavering light matching the undulations of his call. He tries again, "Hellooooooo." Yes, there it is; the light matches the reverberating of his voice. He shouts, "Hello!" and is rewarded by a flash of brightness. He sets what he is carrying down on the floor of this atrium and steps through the archway to his right. "Is the sound of my voice causing these walls to light up?" Yes. He steps further into the dark hallway, "If I keep talking will I have enough light to find my way?" While he talks the walls glow. When he stops talking the glow diminishes. So he talks as he walks, "As my voice gets louder the light gets brighter. OH MY GOODNESS." His yelling creates blinding flashes. "Oops, I will keep the volume down. There, that is easier now. How far does this hallway go? I must have reached the mountainside by now, but it keeps going round. Are my senses addled? The distance and the direction would lead me to believe that I am circling the inner chamber." From outside the tower looked to have been built up against the hillside, and so this hallway must be tunneled into the mountain. "I am walking through an arched hallway that wends its way 'round the tower. There are no doors or windows. The ceiling is beyond my reach." He jumps up anyway. "OOF! I can almost touch it when I jump. OOF! Oh! And the color of the light changes when I make these different sounds." Changing his voice so that he is talking in a deep baritone, "When I deepen the tone of my voice the light becomes red and blue, and when I go deeper still, it is purple." Changing his voice to the other end of the scale, talking in falsetto, "When I make my voice very high the light is pink and yellow!" He suddenly emerges through an archway and there are his things. He has gone all the way around and now stands in the foyer where he began. "Amazing."

As he walks back to his little camp he attempts to gather his jumbled thoughts. "How will I bear to leave this enchanting place? Am I enchanted? Have I been ensorcelled?" Enchantment feels like a sweet magic while sorcery seems scary. Because he will be here another night he gathers more firewood, catches another fish, and watches the sky as the stars appear and become a thick mist of sparkling dust.

♡♡♡

The two day windmill tour had been a success; there had been the visit with Captain Janszoon, the overnight stay at Schoonhoven Landing, and then the midday stop at his parents' place. Now awakening in the little room inside the stable, Diedrik hears the easily recognizable chirruping of a red-breasted robin. It is not a melodic sound. It is a steadily repeated sharp chirp that reminds him of something his aunt would say, "Whoever thinks that birds are singing is crazy. Birds do not sing!" This noisy robin's incessant tweeting also reminds him of the many early morning rides on the back of his father's tall horse along the river road to Schoonhoven Landing. Robins were always there chirruping noisily. He figures that he must have ridden between his father's mills and Donar's mills a thousand times or more. Surely more.

He likes laying here in his warm bed knowing that it is still early and that he has time to enjoy being snuggled up so warm and serene. He is appreciating that Kikkert's horses will wait patiently to be fed. He is appreciating that his chores are easy and his employers are decent honest folk. He appreciates how enjoyable the last two days of visiting the windmills have been. He particularly appreciates the memory of his visit with his parents, and is once again staggered as he considers what they had told him. He feels the warmth of the jeweled Golden Hearts beneath his pillow and tells himself again that he must get this magnificent item back to its rightful owner; and yet he feels the hearts telling him that everything is okay.

A short while later he walks into the kitchen, bringing in the baskets of eggs and the cans of milk that have been delivered to the back door. He admires the tray of sticky buns full of cinnamon, sugar, and nuts. He smells the day's loaves baking in the oven. He appreciates this warm comfortable kitchen. "A fine early start you are getting this day Diedrik," chides Rhetta teasingly. She has already been up and busy since before daybreak. They share a smile and she tells him, "He," while nodding her head to the front of the house indicating Boomkikker, "tells me that we need more beans ground before he can brew another pot."

"Okay, I am on it." He scoops the roasted beans out of the bag with both hands and drops them into the grinder's hopper, then begins turning the wheel that spins the burrs that grind the beans for brewing. Boomkikker's brewer roasts these coffee beans on the same heated floor used for roasting the malt that goes into his famous *KikkerBier.*

"Good morning Diedrik," Kikkert is carrying the funnel he uses for brewing coffee, "still here, eh?" He lines the funnel with a fresh paper filter. Diedrik, not failing to notice that each of them has addressed him this morning by his full name, stops the grinding wheel while the drawer at the bottom is opened and the fresh aromatic grounds are scooped into the paper-lined funnel. "Thanks my good man." Although it had been late, Diedrik had mentioned to Kikkert that he had received news from his parents that may lead to his returning home.

Rhetta has his breakfast ready for him and being such a fine morning, he carries it out to the table in the courtyard.

He sets his plate and mug on the table, then seats himself. As he sips his coffee his thoughts return to the remarkable news that his parents had delivered to him yesterday. After his father had shown off the workings of his sawmills to the professors he had actually shut down the saws and braked the sails, bringing a seldom heard midday quiet. Then after their meal, during which Philip had answered Lu-Tang's many questions, he had politely shooed his guests out to look around on their own, explaining that he and his wife needed a moment with their son.

As soon as the three professors were out the door his parents had rushed him with hugs. His mother had lovingly scolded him, "Why did you not let us know where you have been? Ah, but look at you. I have missed you." Then releasing him she had told him excitedly, "We have something very important to tell you!" His father had lifted down a special bottle of whiskey, ordinarily saved for only the most important occasions. His mother had set out three of her precious crystal glasses. He had never been offered a drink of his father's finest before. He watched spellbound wondering what could possibly warrant this celebration. With the glasses filled his parents had held theirs up for a toast, and so he had held his up likewise. They clinked the rims of their glasses, and then each sipped. Diedrik, surprised that there is a whiskey so smooth, had taken another sip.

Philip, with bright sparkling eyes, had then told his son, "The probate court has released Donar van Eyck's estate."

His mother had rushed to finish, "His will entrusts Schoonhoven Landing to you! To you!"

Diedrik's mouth had gone completely dry. Picking up his glass, forgetting what it held, he had downed it all in one large gulp, which had taken his breath away and left him gasping. His parents had watched wide-eyed with big grins on their faces. After a bit he was breathing normally again and they talked about what he would do. They congratulated him. They handed over the legal summons they had been holding. He is to meet with an advocaat in Utrecht.

He has replayed this scene over and over in his thoughts while speculating as to how things will change. He had casually mentioned to Kikkert last night that he may be moving back home, otherwise he has told no one else. As he sits in the morning sunshine, while savoring his cup of coffee, he determines that he must be the luckiest man alive. Thinking back on all those years that his brother, instead of sharing the Schoonhoven mill-tending duties, had left them to him. Remembering the way Donar had found more and more for him to do until eventually, instead of riding back and forth whenever the wind changed direction, he was allowed the living quarters inside Windmidden. Now, instead of living in the mill, he is imagining living in the house; with its upper gables that let in so much light. It is pleasing that his father has been able to find tenants for the other homes and that those folks are all so nice. His train of thought is disturbed when the brewer opens up the loading bay doors of the brewery, reminding him that this is his day for delivering casks of KikkerBier to all the pubs around town.

♡♡♡

Robert wakes to the sound of water splashing and upon opening his eyes beholds the last of what must be hundreds of geese settling down on the surface of the lake. In this moment he also remembers that he has been sleeping a second night in close proximity to the mystical stone tower that has so thoroughly intrigued him. His memories of the previous day's experience have meshed with his dreaming, leaving him unsure if he is now fully awake. So he holds his hands up before his eyes, employing the traditional test, asking himself, "Am I dreaming?" Able to focus on the details of his palms and his knuckles he determines, "I must be awake." He tosses off the blanket and stands, surveying his surroundings. The stone archway leading to the tower beckons him for another look before leaving, "No," he tells himself, "I spent the entire day there yesterday. I have far to go today." His fire is out, and there are no coals to be stirred back to life; only ashes. He eats the remains of last night's meal. Determined to be on his way, he rolls his blanket and wraps it protectively around his folio of drawings, then slides it all into his backpack. He straightens up and swings his pack over his shoulders, startling the geese and setting them to honking. They lift off the lake in a wave of outstretched wings, only to settle back down again at the far end.

"Robert." Hearing the melodic voice startles him, here where he has supposed himself to be entirely alone. Could it be the caretaker at last showing himself? He turns and there within the archway of carved stone stands the harpist.

Dumbfounded, "Oh, I am still dreaming." Immediately raising and focusing on his hands, he looks beyond them and she is still there. She is tall with a bird-like countenance. Lowering his eyes again, his hands remain in focus. This tried and true test of concentration tells him that he is awake: not dreaming. His legs feel wobbly. He squats down on his haunches, still holding his hands out while looking toward her and wondering what can be occurring. She smiles a most beautific smile. Her eyes sparkle as no eyes he has ever seen. "There is no need for you to bow before us." She is taller than him; taller than anyone he has ever known. She has a radiant glow surrounding her.

Feebly he asks, "We?" Surprised that he is able to put words to his thoughts, another guarantee of wakefulness.

She is joined there within the arch by another, taller even than she. "We are glad to have caught you before you have slipped away."

"Caught me?" Robert closes his eyes and shakes his head. When he opens his eyes again they are still there. The space between him and where they stand in the archway is crackling. He does not feel threatened nor afraid yet, how is this so? He stands up again, and holds an index finger up, signaling that he needs a moment. They wait as he slips off his pack and strides over to the lakeshore. Cupping his hands and scooping up water, he splashes his face, his hair, then his face again, rubbing vigorously. But that is not enough. He drops to all fours and dunks his entire head into the numbingly cold water to ensure that he is awake. He stands, shakes the dripping water from his hair, wipes his face and beard free of moisture, and finally feeling assuredly cognizant and alert turns back around. The celestial couple remain, there in the archway, patiently awaiting his regimen of believability. They beckon for him to come closer. His rationally processing intellect attempts to put together all he has ever been told of instances such as this, but falls short of experience. He walks toward them. The second Celestial extends a hand introducing himself, "We are not Lords or Masters, nor are we Gods." His grip, as they shake hands, is firm and corporeal.

The Lady holds her hand out to Robert. He takes it, feeling its delicacy, noting the iridescence of her fingers as he humbly bows, "We are as you," she consoles him, "except that we perceive no separation between the realms; what you call dreaming and waking." She is not squeezing his hand, yet he could not let go even if he were so inclined.

Noticing the glow surrounding these two Robert realizes that standing here in such close proximity has him within the bounds of their radiance. Sharing their aura has him feeling the same as they are feeling; calm, certain, and happy. Discovering his voice he attempts to say, "I am very pleased --," but then realizes before continuing, that is all he has to say, "Very pleased, indeed." He is then able to step back, extracting himself from the shared glowing. He asks, "Are you aware of what brings me here?"

The taller of the two nods while answering, "Ohhhh yes. We are aware of what has brought you here." His voice, smooth and melodious reverberates within Robert, setting his body to tingling. "Your quest resonates with the eternal process that intermingles the realms. Tis not a coincidence that we meet here."

Not certain of the meaning in that answer, Robert turns to the other, "My Dearest holds a necklace the same as that which you wear: and plays a golden harp, nearly the same as yours."

"Yes," she knows, "these Golden Hearts not only look the same, but are the same." Upon witnessing his perplexity she adds, "You do not need to understand. Know that the initial code, the pattern, of these hearts and all that go with them is entwined throughout the realms. The Golden Hearts abound," raising a hand for her fingers to caress the hearts where they cross her collarbone, "they are links that are eternally connecting through the web of light."

"Indeed," now both speaking simultaneously, "these hearts, along with the harps, crowns, and orbs, form a network across all realms."

Their countenance, within the archway, disappears momentarily. Their visage returns with the two of them facing one another quizzically. Then, speaking again as one, "Have you more questions? Best be quick."

Without faltering Robert asks, "What is this tower?"

"Out of the vastness of the *Starfield* a seed was cast and fell to this spot. The tower has been built over the Star's seed, here where it planted itself." Their appearance is dimming again. Robert hears their voices, but cannot understand what they are saying. Then they are gone. The carved stone archway stands empty.

Inheritance

There are no cadavers currently available for dissection, so Hendrik's early laboratory lecture has been cancelled, leaving his morning free. He is taking advantage of the recess, and the warmer weather, at a table in the park. He is reviewing his notes for his afternoon lecture in which he will be explaining the use of the algorithmic slide rule. He primarily lectures on medicine and physiology, but occasionally fills in his schedule lecturing on the basics of calculus. The area of the park where he is sitting is busy with mothers and their children. The din of children's laughter is interrupted by a soft voice behind him, "Good day Professor Henricus"

Recognizing the voice he stands, removes his hat and with a sweeping bow greets the Academy's only female scholar, "*Mejuffrouw* van Shooman," admiring her serene expression, "I am so pleased to see you."

"May I join you?"

"Oh, indeed. Please." He removes a clean kerchief from his vest pocket and gallantly sweeps off a place for her to sit on the bench next to him.

His attentions bring a smile to her already sweet countenance. She begs of him, "Let us forego formality Hendrik."

"Agreed Anna Maria."

"It is a most beautiful day," birdsong trilling from the branches above draws her gaze, "the little bird agrees."

"Quite rightly so," Children run by giggling, "these kids agree also."

Seeing his slide rule and the many papers spread about she asks, "Working on your latest calculations?"

He laughs while shaking his head, "No. I sat down here with the intention of reviewing my lecture notes, but alas, I have been mostly daydreaming."

"Oh? Well then, I apologize for interrupting."

"No need for apologies," he replies with laughter, "visiting with you is the preferred distraction. There could be nothing better than a warm spring day in the park sharing a bench with a delightful lady."

She humbly tips her head in acknowledgement of the compliment, "I have begun something new and would be delighted to know your thoughts."

"An artistic endeavor? A new engraving? Another painting?"

"La," mildly shaking her head, "no," sweetly, "none of those." She gazes around the park, then looks back to him, "Lu-Tang is tutoring me in the art of Inner Alchemy." He nods. "So, with his assistance, I have begun a dictionary of his language. Comparing his alphabet to any that I am familiar with is a puzzle. In particular, he explains a process requiring the practitioner to sit still and to quiet thoughts. The closest word that I find in Latin is *enthymema*."

"A discussion without words," Hendrik translates, "begging the question of the distinction between the body and the mind."

"The accidental unity?" She teases him with the phrase attributed for the beginning of his feud with Descartes.

"La, do we really want to go down that path right now?" They sit quietly for a bit. The wind rustles the leaves. A mother calls for her children who have been running back and forth across the sward.

She muses, "A discussion without words is an interesting thought. Can there be thoughts without words? Do our minds cease to exist without words communicating our thoughts?"

"These are absolutely brilliant questions." He so admires this woman's intelligence. "Calderon may have something to say about this subject; he has devoted a section of the University's library to the writings of mystics."

"I know. That is so cool. Paulo tells me that mystics listen to the Spirit." She reaches out and picks up the slide-rule, "With our rulers, protractors, and compasses we are measuring the dimensions of everything that exists in our natural realm," a little quieter now, "and with our telescopes we are measuring beyond what has ever been measured before." Ever since the events of Galileo's trials and subsequent house arrest the subject of astronomy is not a commonly approved topic in all circles, so they keep their voices low, as some would mistake the mention of the astronomer's recanted views for a discussion of untruths.

Hendrik, looking up into the branches, cannot help but ask, "When you speak of the natural realm, are you referring to the physical and the non-physical? There is the physical body, which is quieted in slumber, and there is the non-physical mind, which you are attempting to quiet using Lu-Tang's Inner Alchemical style of meditating." He takes the slide-rule back, "Does there exist a separation between the mind and the body? Can one exist without the other?" This is the topic that lies at the crux of the argument between scientific and Christian beliefs; and consequently, between Hendrik's definition of the perception of knowledge compared to Descartes' concept of innate knowing.

She looks to him, aware that they are walking a dangerously thin line with this conversation. Perhaps that is why she loves visiting with this man, "Oh Hendrik, I tend to agree with what I have heard you say before, that we perceive, through our personal experience, what is true," she leans in closer, and with shoulders now touching intimately, she whispers, "I believe, as the Mystics do, that we all have a Spirit within, and that divine revelation is available to everybody." She sits up and breathes in, "I am beginning to believe that when we practice sitting still and quieting our thoughts that we are allowing ourselves, by listening, to become acquainted with the knowledge of our own personal Spirit, which holds the code of who we truly desire to be; the code for our happiness."

He is looking into the depth of her eyes and believing that she is a saint. He turns to the sound of frolic as a new crowd of kids run by, "Look at these children. What thoughts have they?" He laughs. "Are they expressing their Spirit?" He laughs some more.

"Be as children and the gates of Heaven open easily," Anna Maria laughs with him.

"Anna Maria van Shooman, you are an angel."

♡♡♡

Robert wakes to the sound of water splashing and upon opening his eyes beholds the last of what must be hundreds of geese settling down on the surface of the lake. In this moment he also remembers that he has been sleeping a second night in close proximity to the mystical stone tower that has so thoroughly intrigued him. "Wait!" It seems like he had already awakened. "I must have dreamed the other." His memories of the previous day's experience have meshed with his dreaming, leaving him unsure if he is now fully awake. So he holds his hands up before his eyes, employing the traditional test, asking himself, "Am I dreaming?" He tosses off the blanket and stands. He surveys his surroundings. The mountain rising up around the lake. The stone archway leading to the tower. His fire is out, and there are no coals to be stirred back to life; only ashes. Determined to be on his way, he rolls his blanket and wraps it protectively around his folio of drawings, then slides it all into his backpack. He straightens up and swings his pack over his shoulders, startling the geese and setting them to honking. They lift off the lake in a wave of outstretched wings. He remembers that they will settle back down at the far end of the lake. Will he remember more as the day goes on?

"Now, I must be on my way." He turns a full circle taking in the panorama of lake, mountain, stream, and tower. "Farewell to you all. I thank you, and I hope to return someday." He hops from rock to rock across the creek's headwaters. The trail is steep as it drops down off the mountain bench where the starseed shrine stands beside its alpine lake. "Starseed Shrine?" Wondering out loud where he has come up with that name for the tower. He takes the trail around the lower lake and continues past the other waterfalls, dropping steadily down through the narrow canyon. He sits and slides down a steep slope of slick grasses. He stays to the far side of the vast open meadow inhabited by the herd of *Alce*. The calls that are chirped from the outriders back to the main herd must not be calls of alarm, for they do not set the herd to stirring. Robert's passing is not considered a threat. He foregoes the idea of stopping to sketch the scene. As much as he enjoys sharing pictures of his travels, some things need to be witnessed firsthand.

He follows the stream as it meanders across this wide meadow. He imagines that he can see for hundreds of miles from this altitude. The curve of the horizon is the same as the view from the top of a great swell out on the open sea. The view grows ever more expansive until he reaches where the stream disappears into the boulders where the mountainside has sloughed off. Looking down from the top Robert is having difficulty believing that he had climbed up this steep slope of rocks. His rationally processing intellect is attempting to convince him to sit, take a break and ponder his best route down. His heart is telling him to keep moving, and so he does. At first he drops easily from boulder to boulder, but eventually he must turn himself around, grabbing handholds and reaching down with his feet to continue his descent. He exchanges his footholds for handholds. Sliding down this slope would not be as smooth as the grassy slope he had slid down earlier. He takes a break while a family of curious goats pass him by, hopping easily from foothold to foothold, with the kids playfully butting each other while never losing balance. "I wish that I were as surefooted." He is grateful upon reaching the bottom of the slide, the *skritha.* He sits on a moss covered patch of ground at the edge of the pool where the stream has emerged from within the rockslide. While munching on the last of his snacks he looks up bemusedly at what he has just descended. Had it been easier to climb up? Because climbing down was a harrowing experience. He does not sit for long. The lateness of the day encourages him to keep moving. The thought of a meal and a pint, or a couple pints, gives him something to look forward to. He thinks of the beer he will be drinking, brewed from this mountain stream. This stream whose source he has visited.

It is later that evening. After satisfying his thirst and his appetite Robert is sprawling languidly across the porch swing feeling empty-headed and comfortable. He is drawn out of his languor when the old man arrives to sit in his favored chair. The grandson follows with a blanket, but the older fellow will not allow being doted upon. The younger man turns to Robert and handing him the folded blanket says, "Perhaps you will be wanting this. It is getting chilly." Picking up Robert's empty mug, "Let me get you a refill."

Robert sits up and shakes himself into a fuller wakefulness. There is a cool evening breeze blowing in from the fjord and he is grateful now to pull his outer wrap, which he has been using as a pillow, over his head. He loves the warmth of this woolen hoody Mara has woven for him. An owl hoots its early call, *Ooh-hoo-hoo.* The old guy twists something that he holds in his hands making a high-pitched screaking. The owl calls again, as if answering, *Ooh-hoo-hoo.* The old fellow turns a mischievous smile Robert's way while twisting whatever it is he holds, repeating the screaking. The owl flies into the yard and perches itself on a low branch of a nearby tree, *hoo-hoo-oo.* It is close enough that from the porch can be seen its tufted ears and bright orange eyes. Now the old fellow puckers his lips and mimics the screaking, only softer. The owl responds with a similar sound.

"They are old friends," says the grandson, returning with Robert's freshly filled mug and sitting down with a full mug of his own. "Grandpa is anxious to know if you found what you were looking for."

Anticipating this moment, Robert has brought his folio of sketches with him. He scoots a little table over closer and then theatrically withdraws his illustrations, spreading them out on the table now situated between them. The old man's eyes sparkle and come alive. The younger man is likewise impressed by the quality of the artistry spread out here before him. "Thanks to your directions I did find what I was looking for." They view the sketches in order, using their mugs to hold down the rolled-up corners. There is the archway crafted of stone with the lake, mountainside, and tower in the background. Then there is the entryway leading into the tower, followed by multiple sketches of the inner chamber. Upon viewing the illustration depicting the mosaic of the harp-playing celestial the old fellow's eyes become watery and Robert tells him, “I will make a copy of this for you before I go.”

As he shifts the pictures from the colored image of the harpist to a page filled with a series of panels, rendered in charcoal, showing himself making noises that cause the circular hallway to light up. The older man stands straight up with his fists raised above his head in victory shouting, “Ja! Ja! Jaaaah!”

His friend the owl hoots a staccato, *Hoo-hoo. Hoo-hoo-hoo-hoo.*

Sitting back down the old man spouts, “I used to remember this hallway that lights up with the sound of voices. I forgot about this because I quit telling the tale.” The older man sighs serenely. “I thank you once again for restoring my memories.”

The following morning, while waiting for the tide, Robert paints the promised copies for the old man. His illustration depicting the harp-playing celestial is especially appreciated. The old man will not allow his grandson to accept payment from Robert for the nights spent there. Now, back aboard the fully loaded Tulip he is navigating his way out of the fjord toward the open sea. He loves the steep hills of this narrow passage, knowing that he can trust the skills of his inner sailor to keep him safely following the current that runs through this channel. In the warmth of the day he allows himself to shift into his familiar routine of dozing and waking; setting his course, napping, then upon waking, setting his course again. In his lifetime of sailing this routine has worked for him, sometimes even better than imagined: having awakened to discover he has corrected his course while sleeping. It is this routine of alternating his waking with his sleeping, and occasionally dreaming while awake, that had started him jokingly asking himself was he dreaming. He had first begun the test of looking at his hands when he could only instruct himself to do so awake. But now it seems that he has learned to do it dreaming. He trusts his inner self, which is his dreaming self, as well as he trusts his waking self. He trusts himself the same as he trusts the sea. He believes that the sea loves and protects all sailors, and that it is fear, not the sea, that sends men to the depths. He does not fear the sea. His intention is to enjoy the unceasing wonder of sailing. His foremost intention is to be happy.

As this alternating of sleeping and waking gets him through this day and into the night he awakes to a star-filled sky. "Starfield?" Where has he heard that term? The light of the stars against the backdrop of the night allows him to distinguish the outlines of the mountains rising to either side. While looking up into the night sky, gauging his course, he notices another star streaking across the sky. He has already seen quite a few falling stars this night and wonders why it is that sometimes there are so many more of these starseeds. "Star-seed?" When did he hear that term spoken? Now he remembers. His conversation upon the mountain with the ethereal pair returns to his memory. The celestials had spoken of the Starfield and of a Starseed. He asks himself, "Was I dreaming?" And remembers dousing himself to verify wakefulness. They had told him that the scarred boulder of the inner chamber was a starseed. If something that size is a seed, then the actual stars must be larger than he has ever imagined. As he remembers more of his discussion with the two star-realm citizens he wonders about them saying that their dreaming and waking are the same realm. "Perhaps it is my routine of waking while dreaming that makes visiting with them possible." He is also reminded of the intense dreams experienced by anyone hearing the melodies from Mara's celestial harp. More questions arise. He knows that he will not know the answers until his questioning mood has passed. "Why are there so many shooting stars streaking across the sky?" He decides that it does not matter why. "I will enjoy this while it is happening. Let the astronomers tell us why."

♡♡♡

Diedrik, knowing that he is expected to be dressed appropriately for his visit with the lawyer, has visited a clothier's shop. He did not want to dress in business attire, for he is not a businessman. He did not want to dress in the plainest black coat and pants, for he is not a clerk. He has purchased, and is wearing a rider's suit and pants, with tall sturdy boots. The pants fit loose in the seat and reach long enough to tuck into the tops of his boots. The tails and lapels of his blue brocade coat are wide and banded in a darker blue silk. His vest, of the same blue, sets off the gray shirt beneath. He wears a plain collar with the barest minimum of a tie. His cuffs are held by buttons rather than links. He admires his reflection in the shop windows as he passes. "Tomorrow," he tells himself, "I will buy a horse."

He arrives promptly at the prescribed hour and is ushered into a room where the advocaat is seated at a long table across from Donar's nephews, nieces, and cousins. They all stand to greet him. He exchanges pleasantries. He knows them all. The solicitor, a stony-faced man of funereal visage, is noisily shuffling papers and clearing his throat, indicating that he would prefer getting on with the business of this meeting. After they have all taken seats around the long table the lawyer begins, "As pertaining to the will of, now-deceased, Donar van Eyck." He stops reading and scans eye to eye with everyone before proceeding, "You, the family of said deceased, having already been acquainted with your portions of this will, have been asked, as per the directives of Donar van Eyck, to attend this reading today in a showing of your blessings toward all that will transpire." He stops reading and looking again from one to the next of all Donar's family until each has nodded acknowledgement.

He lays down the portion of the amassed papers that he has been referencing, then picks up another batch. Before he begins he turns his stern expression to Diedrik who nods, as the others have before him, assuring the man that he is all in. Raising up this next batch of papers the man begins again, "Concerning the property, hereby established as Schoonhoven Landing: which is comprised of one hundred twenty acres on a riverfront landing, three windmills, three houses, three barns, nine sheds, and four bird coops. Donar van Eyck doth bequeath said property to Diedrik van Haumann." The nieces, nephews, and cousins all together raise a ruckus, shouting out 'Halloos' and 'Hurrahs'. As some of them stand to congratulate Diedrik they are stopped by the pounding of the advocaat's fist upon the table; an impromptu gavel silencing the room. Although, Diedrik has been prepared for this news; the actuality of the moment has him stunned and there is a long silence before he looks up to notice the lawyer staring intently toward him, "Furthermore," the man intones, "a trust has been established that will serve Meneer van Haumann a monthly stipend for his continued avocation as Molenaar." The man licks his fingers to facilitate withdrawing a page from the batch he holds. He expertly spins the page before sending it sliding across the table toward Diedrik. A small tray holding ink and quill is set down at Diedrik's elbow by a clerk, undetected til now, but who has been behind him. "If you have any questions ask them now, otherwise sign at the bottom of the page."

Diedrik takes a look at the minute scribbling that fills the entire page, "This could take a while for me to read."

"Allow me to abridge for you Sir," the clerk behind him begins by placing a finger on the first paragraph. "Firstly there is verification that you are the person signing this page." Moving his finger down a paragraph, "Secondly, is verification that all prerequisites of the will have been met." Sighing as he moves his finger to point out the next paragraph, "This states that you are able to do what you will with said property; that there are no further stipulations upon you. And lastly," moving his finger once more, "This final paragraph signifies that all counsel is complete."

"Okay, thanks for that." Diedrik skims over the page anyway, and it does say pretty much what the clerk has outlined, albeit with a lot more words: pity the clerk that sat for who knows how long scribing these copies. By now the clerk has un-stoppered the ink, dipped the quill, and is placing it in Diedrik's hand. After signing on the line the sheet is whisked away as he sets the quill back upon the tray.

The signed document is handed over to the older advocaat who places it with all the other papers in his folder. "That concludes our business here. Good-day." He stands and leaves the room with his clerk following close behind.

"We have reserved a banquet hall and catered a meal for this day's celebration," the oldest of the nephews tells Diedrik, "Come along." They adjourn to a nearby hostelry where a splendid meal is served. Every one of Donar's family tell Diedrik a specific tale of how their Uncle had loved him. They all happily agree with Donar's decision to leave the responsibility of the property to Diedrik, leaving them to their carefree lives. There is a final toast after the meal and he is presented with a heavy sack of coins donated collectively from them all, with assurances that any further assistance will be available if ever necessary. They all depart in their dandified modern carriages, leaving Diedrik alone on the sidewalk, marveling at the amassed fortune that has allowed such wealth for so many; including him.

At last alone with his own thoughts he is dumbfounded by what this means for him. He can now afford to take a coach. He prefers to walk. With each storefront that he passes he thinks, "I can buy that now, I can afford that luxury, I can purchase that if I so choose," but he does not stop until passing a familiar pub near the University. He takes a seat outside at a table shaded by a sailcloth awning. The Pubman does not at first recognize him, then makes a show of his regal outfit when he delivers the freshly-drawn pint.

In his head he is starting the process of making plans. How long will Kikkert need to find a replacement? What will become of the years of wages saved by his father for him? Will he need an income producing enterprise? He will need to develop an entirely new perspective, for he is now a wealthy man. "Diedrik? Is that you? How splendidly you are dressed today!"

He immediately stands upon hearing the woman's voice, "Anna Maria, it is so very nice to see you." She holds out her hand to him in greeting. He has seldom needed gentlemanly manners, so it is a moment before he remembers that he is supposed give her hand a kiss.

She is enchanted by his innocence. She loves this young man. Donar had always told her that he would never be able to manage without Diedrik. Donar loved Diedrik as other men love a son. "You are dressed handsomely. Is today a special occasion?"

"Emmm, yes. Yes it is. May I beseech you to join me please?" He pulls a chair out for her to be seated.

"I am most pleased to join you." She takes the proffered seat. The Pubman is there offering her a cup of tea. Instead, she asks for a glass of wine, specifying a delicate white with a French-sounding name. Turning her expectant gaze now toward Diedrik she waits.

This wealthy woman, well-known in this town as a successful artist and scholar, had always been a close friend to Donar, and had visited Schoonhoven Landing often. He tells her, "I met this morning with Donar's advocaat for the reading of his will as it pertained to me." Her wine is served. She sips and nods her approval. She has the refined mannerisms of a lady. Her presence has a calming effect, and yet when he attempts to continue with what he was saying his voice catches in his throat. She waits. He sips and closes his eyes before telling her, "He left me the Landing," spoken in a rush. His emotions spill out of him now and his eyes become watery. She reaches across the table and squeezes his hand. Wiping his eyes with the backs of his hands, "You must think me a fool."

"Hush. I think no such thing." She withdraws a small kerchief from her bag and pushes it across the table to him. As he wipes his eyes she tells him, "Donar spoke with me of his wish to leave the Landing to you. He loved you."

His chest heaves. She waits patiently. "I apologize," before he can say more she stops him and reaching over with another hankie dabbing tears from his cheeks, as a mother would a son, she shushes him.

"It is good for you. You loved Donar. You miss him. He wants you to be happy. He wants you to paint. He wants you to be free. Enjoy yourself my dear." She calls the Pubman to bring Diedrik another pint. They sit quietly for a bit. "I encouraged Donar to leave his property to you in hopes that I will be invited to visit."

What she says breaks loose laughter from deep inside, "Of course you are welcome to visit!" He laughs, and sighs, and chuckles some more. Now shaking his head he tells her, "Anna Maria van Shooman, you are an angel."

♡♡♡

The library has been quiet this morning allowing Calderon the opportunity to finish processing a recent acquisition of books, manuscripts, and letters from the estate of a Parisien dignitary. He is pleased with what he has accomplished and is considering taking a break when, looking up, he notices a young scholar walking his way. He straightens up from his work as the young man greets him, "Good day professor. A fellow correspondent," referring to the Republic of Letters, "has forwarded a post that had been forwarded to him, which is a copy of a correspondence reviewing Descartes' 'Discourse of the Method', and I am wondering if the library has other such reviews available."

"Ah, if the review has sparked your interest the library has the book."

"Forgive me sir, but reading a book in its entirety can sometimes be rather tiresome."

"Depending upon your interest in the subject matter, yes. Reading a book allows you to develop in your own imagination a personal viewpoint, while a review provides someone else's opinion of the subject matter."

"Rather like the professor's view one receives attending a lecture."

"True, I suppose, regarding less objectively oriented speakers. If you are interested in Descartes' Method, then you may be interested in the writings of Honoré Fabri." Calderon has led the young man across the room, removed a slim volume from the shelf, and now hands it over. "Fabri theorizes that mathematics prove what will probably happen. Postulating that nothing is ever absolutely proven."

"He is a probabilist?"

Calderon has walked back across the room and stopped in front of a case of large drawers. He opens one and points out a file, "Here we have an assortment of letters; some endorsing and some refuting Probabilism."

"How can one consider a probability as proof?"

"Questions like that are answered by reading the book."

The man is not put off by this mild scolding, "Thank you Professor."

Calderon turns back toward his workstation, but is accosted by another, a familiar scholar, "Good day Professor. I beg of you a moment of your time."

"What is it? Er, rather, how may I be of assistance?"

This man's interest lies not in the sciences, but in literature. "Professor Hendrik has allowed me to borrow his copy of the manuscript for Hamlet, the play by the English bard."

"Are you considering producing the play for a Utrecht audience?" This man has written, produces, and performs lead in a presentation that is enjoying a long run at the city's playhouse.

"Heavens no. If one wishes to watch Shakespeare performed they need only attend any weekly carnival. Ha! No, my good man, I am now looking for a translation of Homer's Odyssey for the purpose of comparing the two."

"Deception and revenge are not your usual topics." The man's play are lauded for his humor. It is why his performances are so popular.

"Indeed! La! I am considering the possibilities of satirizing these themes that, unfortunately, continue to perpetually dominate all literature from ancient times to the modern day."

Leading the man to a far corner, "We have the Odyssey in the original Greek. We have it translated into Latin, by Utrecht's own lady of letters. Of course, we also have German, Dutch, French, and English translations." Noticing, through the windows, the arrival of a postal rider leaping off his horse, tossing the reins over a branch, and now rushing through the library doors he hands over Anna Maria's Latin translation and excuses himself.

The rider, scanning the roomful of scholars, notes the distinguished fellow moving toward him and rushes forward, "Professor Paulo Calderon?"

"Yes."

Withdrawing a folded post from his shoulder bag, "A message for you, Sir. I have brought this from Amsterdam, and am betoken to return this day with your reply."

The folded page has the Olmsfeld seal. "I posted news to this man only yesterday." He had notified Trinjntje's parents the day after returning from the touring of windmills.

"This is his reply, Sir. He will be awaiting up for me this night to deliver your response."

Calderon removes his coin purse from his vest pocket and hands over enough for a meal and sends the man in the direction of a nearby pub. "Allow me enough time to read this and to compose my acknowledgement."

"An hour then, Sir."

Calderon moves into his office area, closing the door so as not to be disturbed, breaks the seal and reads.

My Dear Calderon. I thank you for news of our daughter. We are greatly relieved that she is doing well. Please be assured that my wife and I intend to honor her desire for privacy, and only wish her the best of our love. I write because there is a matter begging her attention. A visitor has arrived in Amsterdam seeking council with Trinjntje regarding the whereabouts of an important family artifact: a necklace of golden hearts. This foreign ambassador seeks the return of this cherished heirloom, implying that it was gifted mistakenly. I assure you, and consequently assure Trinjntje, that her privacy remains utmost in our concern.

The messenger delivering this missive is entrusted to bring your reply directly to me. I thank you for your immediate attention to this matter. Christophorus Olmsfeld.

Calderon's thoughts surge with ideas of how best to resolve this situation. Forwarding this message to Trinjntje will add another two days lapse before he has a reply. Will she be ready to return to Amsterdam? Does she have anything to wear besides her vagabond outfit? Could he take a day to ride and deliver this message himself? He decides on a plan and writes back to Olmsfeld.

Christophorus Olmsfeld. It is my hope that this message finds you and your wife in good health. Your daughter is currently residing a half day's ride from Utrecht. I am willing to make that ride, delivering your message personally, and upon my return I will forward to you her reply regarding this foreign visitor and the alleged heirloom artifact. You can expect my report of her response in two days' time. Regards, P Calderon.

He folds and seals the missive with his own personal seal. Opening his office door he finds the messenger already waiting. He hands over the sealed missive, adds another coin as thanks, and asks, "How late will it be when you reach Amsterdam?"

The man is already moving toward the door. "It will be after dark."

Paulo finishes up what he has been working on and makes arrangements with his assistant for the following day. Considering the possibility that Trinjntje may wish to answer this summons personally, she will need somewhere to stay. Knowing that the Academy has quarters for visitors, he makes a stop at the University clerk's office and arranges a reservation for one of the vacant residences. On his way home he stops at his regular stable and arranges for a fast horse to be ready early tomorrow morning. He then makes his way to a dress shop that Hendrik recommends over any of the city's tailors. Upon arrival he stands outside looking in through the storefront windows thinking what a totally feminine environment he is about to enter. He takes a deep breath and walks trepidiciously through the door into the shop. Inside there are two women pinning and stitching at a dress hanging over a woman-shaped frame. One of them leaves off what she is doing and greets him, "Good day to you, Sir. Are you lost? We do not have many gentlemen shopping here. We specialize in women's apparel." Her teasing does not ease his trepidation.

"I would like to purchase an outfit to be worn by a woman."

"A full outfit, Sir?"

"Yes, emm, you know, a dress ... and whatever else it is that is worn with it."

Smiling mischievously she prods him for a bit more information, "In what size, Sir?"

He holds his arm out before him, palm down and level with his collarbone, "She stands about," raising his palm up to his chin, then raising it up again level with his nose, and still not satisfied brings it up to the height of his eyebrows, "this tall."

"Okay, follow me. A gift? For a special occasion?"

"What? Emm, no," he thinks that he must sound like a fool, "It will be for every day, but nice, you know, good quality."

She leads him to a rack of colorful attire, "What color is her hair?"

What color is her hair, "Oh I suppose it is brown, light brown, yet red in the sunshine."

"Auburn? Brunette?" The questioning look he gives her leads her to try something else. "What then is her favorite color?"

Oh, so many questions, "The last time that I was with her she was wearing green." It had set off her eyes.

"Like this?" She asks while holding a light colored flowery thing.

"Em, no, a bit more like the next one."

"This is a nice choice, and is the style that is popular this season." Seldom are men in her shop, but from experience she knows that they need reminding. "A pair of shoes? An overcoat?" She directs him through the shop. When at last he has finished with all the choices, she gathers the undergarments, and a headscarf. She folds everything and slides it all into a bag adorned with carrying handles. "Will that be all, Sir?"

"Yes, thank you." She hands the bright bag over to him, "It has been a pleasure serving you, Sir." Her impish smile has him wondering what she is thinking. He nods to her, and then to her partner who surprises him with a wink. He rushes out the door hoping to never again visit this, or any other, dress shop. Leave womanly things to women.

♡♡♡

Cornelius Janszoon's architect has incorporated a pleasant watercourse that runs through the greenhouse and then alongside the covered patio offering both utility and tranquility. Trinjntje has been puttering away all morning appreciating the pleasant sound of the running water and also the ease it presents as she rinses the variety of greens that she has gathered. She also has a tomato, a cucumber, and a few radishes; all to be sliced and tossed with the greenery for a luncheon salad. She is currently thinning a row of carrots, creating a second row from what she pulls up, while saving a few to top her salad. She hums as she works, totally immersed in the simplicity of her task. A little wind catcher that she has created from the glass blower's discards makes a gentle tinkling sound in the occasional breeze.

Moving on to her next task of transplanting melon seedlings from the greenhouse to the garden, she thinks back when she had planted these seeds while wondering if she will still be here to taste the fruit. She has begun thinking that her time here, although pleasant, may be up. Nicklas, feeling the same, has informed her that Janszoon has loaned him a horse, and that he will leaving for Amsterdam tomorrow. His advance notice allows her time to consider riding back with him. She had told him, "I do not want to return to Amsterdam." After finishing in the dirt she rinses her hands in the flow of the little watercourse and dries them on the apron she has sewn for herself before removing and hanging it to dry. She has considered fashioning herself a dress, but stubbornly sticks to masquerading as a man; not sure why. Taking her basket of salad fixings, she exits the greenhouse, and as she passes the string of glass shards she reaches up and brushes them with her fingers restarting the tinkling that she so enjoys.

She has been out here alone all morning, so is surprised when she hears, "That is a charmingly beautiful sound."

Recognizing the voice, she is surprised, "Paulo! What brings you here?"

"Your uncle told me that I would find you out here."

"No. I mean what brings you back? It has been only a few days since you were here with the others."

"Well, as per your request, I did post a note to your parents apprising them of your good health."

"Oh. Thank you."

"Your father has replied. I bring you his message. There is a bit of urgency to his note."

"Uh-Oh. Is everything allright?"

He hands over Olmsfeld's missive. "That is for you to determine."

She places the folded letter in her apron pocket and with a gesture invites him to follow, "Come on inside. I am preparing us a salad."

"I left Utrecht early, and I will not be able to stay here for long if I am to return before darkness."

"Okay." She grabs him by the hand and makes as if to drag him behind her, "Come along then." At the patio door Cornelius and Nicklas are slipping off their clogs before entering the house. Trinjntje, likewise, slips off her clogs. "We will all have a meal together, that is," turning to her guest, "unless you are in such a hurry that you cannot sit for an hour?"

Her teasing flutters his heart. Sitting down to remove his boots he replies in a playfully begrudging tone, "An hour then."

Janszoon asks Trinjntje, "What does your father have to say?"

Setting out a cutting board for the vegetables, she answers, "I have not read the note yet."

Her uncle takes the knife from her, "I will do this. You will read that message, and not be keeping this kind man waiting overly long while you prepare your answer." She stares back at him defiantly. He gives her a shove, "Oh please. Stop being so stubborn!"

Without moving away she removes the note from her pocket, unfolds it, and reads, then shouts, "Oh Nicklas!" He looks up from where he is filling glasses. "It is about the stolen necklace."

"What stolen necklace?" Questions Janszoon while looking back and forth between the two.

Thinking of his planned departure, Nicklas offers, "I can make visiting your father my first priority upon my arrival in Amsterdam," adding, "I will explain the details of what happened."

"What stolen necklace?" Barks Janszoon a second time.

Trinjntje looks beseechingly toward Nicklas who begs in response, "Am I to tell this tale?" She nods pleadingly. As he delivers the full glasses of beer around the table he says, "I will have to start where this all began." He waits as Trinjntje takes the knife back from her uncle and pushes him toward his seat at the table, then begins chopping and slicing at a frantic pace, Nicklas gets started, "Do you remember, Captain, whilst in the port of Djibouti, taking Trinjntje to dinner with the sultan's family?"

"Yes, and then the next day their fool son accosted her expecting that she become one of his wives, attempting to seal the betrothal by adorning her with a necklace. Janszoon tells Calderon, "Trinjntje defiantly pushed him away before he was able to fasten the clasp, foiling his attempt and leaving the necklace at her feet. So insulted was the prince that his guards had to pull him away before he was able to draw his sword."

"Draw his sword?" Calderon asks.

Janszoon explains, "It is beyond their culture's traditional propriety to reject such an offer from a prince, and beyond the pride of a prince to accept the return of a betrothal gift." Raising his eyebrows he finishes, "In fact such a breach of etiquette toward one of such rank and standing would allow for swift retribution."

Trinjntje, working furiously at her salad, stops long enough to blurt out, "What was I supposed to do?" The three men, looking to one another, all wonder how such a sweet woman is able to stir up such controversy.

Janszoon tells her, "By all rights afforded him he could have beheaded you on the spot without fear of recompense." Trinjntje huffs, but adds nothing more; deferring back to Nicklas.

"I took the necklace to the royal estate," Nicklas begins again, "where I was not allowed entry, in fact they threatened to jail me if I did not take the thing away."

Janszoon finishes, "I found out about the unfortunate event when we were given the order to leave the harbor at once." Turning to his fuming niece, "So, Trin, what has become of this necklace?"

Trinjntje sets everybody's salad before them while saying regrettably, "I would not take it either, leaving poor Nicklas holding it."

Nicklas repeats this phrase, "Poor Nicklas," sardonically, "now poor Nicklas is wondering why your father is asking about the necklace."

"Wait," interjects the Captain, "you said something about it being stolen."

"Yes, my fault," bemoans Nicklas, then explaining to Calderon, "On the morning of the *Gouden Leeuwin's* arrival in Amsterdam, two creeps in suits came aboard, even before docking, intending to arrest Trinjntje. I waited around to see the outcome of that confrontation," shrugging to Janszoon, "and then, upon returning tardily to my cabin, found a company clerk already going through my things." He drinks from his glass and sighs, before continuing, "I was eventually able to present my papers and have them signed off, but it was not until after the thieving clerk was gone that I discovered that the necklace was no longer where I had it hidden away."

Trinjntje rushes to finish, "Then I showed up at his door the next morning and pulled him away before he had the opportunity to report the theft. I did not think it mattered anyway. Better off gone. But now …" she scans the faces around the table, "… my father tells me that the prince's sister has arrived in Amsterdam seeking the necklace." There is silence all around. The silence extends while the men allow her to gather her thoughts. She finally speaks resignedly, "I should meet with her." She removes her table napkin from her lap, stands, and with a forlorn wringing of her hands says, "I do not wish to go to Amsterdam. Paulo," beseechingly, "may I return to Utrecht with you, and make arrangements to meet her there?"

"Yes," he answers, "and with the possibility in mind that this would be your choice I have taken measures." He stands, retrieves the shopping bag from his satchel and presenting it to her, "I hope you will not think me presumptuous, but I have brought a set of women's clothing for you to wear."

"Oh, Paulo, that is too kind." Accepting the package, "La, you really should not have done this."

"Oh, well done Calderon, my good man!" Captain Janszoon claps his hands. "It will be a pleasure to see this woman dressed properly again." He is shooing her away while telling her, "Get yourself changed while I put a saddle and bridle on your horse. You two will want to be off and on your way."

Calderon is waiting with Cornelius and Nicklas when Trinjntje comes out of the house dressed in her new clothes. "Everything fits splendidly." She spins around showing off. She gives her uncle a hug, plants a kiss on Nicklas' cheek and hops onto the horse's back, and as they ride away she waves. They ride steadily until about halfway when they stop to rest the horses and she tells Calderon, "I find it remarkable that you brought this wonderful dress for me. It fits perfectly. And these boots are so comfortable; such soft leather. But what most surprises me is that you remembered the headscarf and the undergarments." Her raised eyebrows question him saucily.

"I had some help. The dress shop lady chose all that you would be needing, and wanted me to tell you that she would be delighted to assist with any necessary alterations." He is thinking that she does look splendid, and so tells her, "I am quite pleased with the outcome."

"Oh, well, I must visit this shop and thank this lady properly."

"I have also taken the liberty of arranging a place for you to stay."

"Oh, nice. Is it close to where you live?"

"It is closer to where I spend my days at the University."

"Oh good. We will have the opportunity to know each other better."

"I look forward to that."

There is still some daylight when they arrive at Calderon's stable. He returns the horse he has ridden and arranges for her's to be kept. They stop for a light meal and a pint at the public house situated around the corner from the cottage he has reserved for her. He then escorts her to the reserved residence and when they arrive at the front door tells her, "I have been told that there is a lantern and matches on a table just inside the door." He waits outside while she enters and lights the lamp, calling in to her, "There is also a bin of turves and bucket of tinder for starting a warming fire as well. If you can manage that on your own, then I will be on my way. It has been a long day."

Returning to the doorway with the lighted lamp, "Thank you Paulo," she says, standing at the threshold a step above him. Reaching out and touching his cheek she says, "You are a dear," then leaning forward she kisses him tenderly on the lips; surprising them both.

♡♡♡

Trinjntje, finding herself alone for the first time in ... Ever, scans the room in the lantern light. Discovering the bin of turves she starts a warming fire, which gives the place a sense of being lived in. She finds a small cask on the board in the cooking area. On the shelf above are glasses. She fills one and is pleased with the light colored wine. In the desk drawer she finds a sheaf of paper, ink, and quill. As she sits to write she listens to strains of organ music, a hymn, coming from the cathedral across the way. An evening service.

Her note to her parents advises them that she is well, and now residing in Utrecht for a time. She informs them that she will be pleased to speak with the princess, but asks that their meeting take place here, for she has no desire to be the cause of further turmoil in Amsterdam. She tells them that Nicklas Voorhaven, reminding them that he had traveled with her as her assistant, will be calling upon them soon and will be able to explain the details of this unfortunate occurrence.

She awakens early after sleeping well. She is quickly up, dressed, and out the door to find a courier's office that can get her note to Amsterdam today. Upon finishing her business she strolls through an early morning market picking out some apples and cheese for a snack later. She enters a small public house for something warm to drink and a bite to eat. The place is crowded with young men; clerks on their way to their desks, scholars on their way to lectures, and contractors on their way to building sites all around this burgeoning city. She hears excited talk, amongst the crowd, of the remarkable number of shooting stars they had all seen last night.

Her next stop is a bookseller's shop that she had noticed across the way while sitting at her table. She then wanders the neighborhoods looking for advertised vacancies. It is a pleasant morning for a stroll. She finds a branch extension of her Amsterdam bank and establishes an account asking for funds to be transferred. Nearly back to her cottage she stops at a wine merchant's shop, a baker's shop, and a fish stall. When she returns to her guest house with all her purchases it has begun raining again. She feeds the fire, pours herself a glass of wine, and fixes a plate of fruit and cheese, then sits down with her new book. Coming from the cathedral are strains of music, though not a hymn, soothing all the same. The organist is practicing an ethereal melody.

Coupled with the sound of the rain it broods a pleasant melancholia. She begins reading her new novel, a light romance taking place at court in Paris; she is asleep before finishing the second page.

In her dreaming she has exchanged her humanness for her felinity. She wanders where she will, through an alleyway, along a canal, then hopping up and over storage crates to saunter along the top of a garden wall. Leaping to an overhanging tree branch and climbing higher while ignoring a squirrel's scolding, until from high up in the tree she is able to hop over to a rooftop. Walking the roofline, bounding over a set of chimneys, until reaching the edge she looks across the chasm to the next rooftop. Collecting herself, then bounding across the gap to a balcony perched on high where she discovers a dish of scraps and a bowl of milk set out for her. She is not interested in the food, instead settles herself on the cushions of the old weathered chair under the eaves, and begins her grooming.

The Thief

The day after seeing Trinjntje leave for Utrecht with Professor Calderon Nicklas rises at first light and is on his way shortly thereafter. He and Cornelius had discussed their relief that Trinjntje has discarded her disguise, and is living up to the promise that she made on that first day; she is on her own. Not only is he relieved that she has moved on, but also relieved that he is now comfortably able to move on. Cornelius has loaned him the horse that he is most familiar with, the horse that he has been riding nearly every day, loving its smooth gait and frisky nature. The breeding papers list the horse's name as something fanciful, but Cornelius allows Nicklas to call it Trueheart. The horse picks up on his rider's light-heartedness and steadily increases its pace until it is loping along expeditiously. With few stops, the distance dwindles quickly away. It is late afternoon when Nicklas arrives at the Koetshuis Inn, stables Trueheart, and then sits for a bite to eat and a pint before walking the rest of the way into town. His landlady is surprised and delighted to see him, "La, you again! Gone away to sea for two years, and then gone anon after only one night. You vanished! I hope that you will be staying more than one night before you are off and away again." Holding up a finger signaling him to wait, she goes into her office and returns with a missive. Handing it over she tells him, "Twas the parents of the Olmsfeld darling, your employer, left this for you shortly after she," wiggling her eyebrows up and down, "and you, disappeared. I was asked to deliver this to you personally. So here it is."

"Thank you."

"I informed them that I did not know of your whereabouts, nor who you were with; just that I have not seen you." Her two adolescent daughters are peeking around from behind her. "The Director and his wife seemed to be under the impression that you had absconded with their daughter." Her expectant look tells him that she is waiting to be filled in with the particulars.

He looks at the Olmsfeld seal on the folded page while wondering what to tell this woman. Smiling, he delivers a rehearsed reply, "I arrived home from my sea voyage to discover a pressing circumstance requiring my immediate attention."

"Family? I hope that all is well."

"Well? The most pressing issues have been resolved. There is still more to be dealt with." He is distractedly fanning himself with the letter that she has just delivered him.

"Best wishes with all your concerns," she wishes him. "All other correspondence awaits you upon the table in your room." The girls have come from behind their mother and are ogling him unabashedly as she asks, "Will you still be here for breakfast in the morning?"

"Yes, thank you *Mevrouw*."

As he dismisses himself both young ladies curtsy and tell him sweetly, "*Tot ziens* Nicklas."

As he climbs the stairs to his room he is thinking that both the girls are quite nice. Upon entering and dropping into his familiar old chair he relaxes comfortably with his eyes closed, not wanting to think about the business that he must attend to. He rouses himself to read the letter addressed to him. He breaks the seal. The note is short and direct: *Please share with us any news you may have of our daughter, Trinjntje. We are most grateful for your prompt assistance. Sincerely, Christophorus & Doortje Olmsfeld.* He hears the bell toll the eight o'clock hour. He needs a bath and fresh clothes before presenting himself, and determines that if he is quick it will not be too late to take care of this business with the Olmsfelds tonight.

He bundles the clothes he will wear and heads for his bath house, and then after a quick bath he is feeling ready to visit Trinjntje's parents. He walks out along the second canal and rings the bell at the gate of the Olmsfeld estate, surprised at the troublesome crowd still here so late. Rather than a servant, Christophorus Olmsfeld comes to the gate himself. It has been a couple years since these two last met. They greet each other, but the gate is left unopened. Nicklas withdraws the letter, from his coat pocket, that requests this visit. Olmsfeld, recognizing the missive says, "You have been slow to answer our appeal," still not opening the gate.

Nicklas thinks he understands the man's reluctance to invite him in, yet is still a bit peeved, "I have been away. I have only just received this ***appeal.***" He does not wish to be rude, but he is getting the impression that coming here has been a waste of energy. "I have ridden all day. If you prefer, I can meet you tomorrow. I know where your office is." He tips his head bidding farewell and turns to be on his way amidst the sound of rapidly approaching hoofbeats.

A courier on a sweat-drenched horse rides up. Withdrawing a folded page from his bag the man calls out, "Christophorus Olmsfeld?" Chris reaches through the gate and the note is handed over. The courier rides away as fast as he had arrived.

"Voorhaven, please wait," Christophorus beckons as he is opening and reading the note. When he finishes he opens the gate telling Nicklas, "This note is from Trinjntje, writing from Utrecht. She tells us that you will be able to explain this situation to us. So, please come through." His eyes are still cold.

Nicklas, still peevish, makes no move. A woman's voice calls from the house, "Who is it Chris?"

"We will be right there, my dear." He changes his commanding tone when he speaks again, "Please, Sir. Forgive me. Come in. Come in please, we are anxious to know of our daughter." He calls back to the house, "We have a visitor, Doortje. Another visitor." As he closes the gate and escorts Nicklas toward the house he justifies his reluctance, "Is it not strange for a man to arrive home from a long voyage at sea, bringing with him a valuable cargo, to suddenly disappear? And that my daughter, who has traveled on the same voyage, also goes missing." They reach the steps, walk up, and at the door he makes the introductions, "Doortje, this is Nicklas Voorhaven." Then to Nicklas, "My wife Doortje," then referring to the tall slim figure standing behind his wife, "and this is our houseguest, Princess Saarika, visiting from the Sultanate of Djibouti."

Nicklas, having let go of his peevishness bows honorably, "I am pleased to make your acquaintances." Noting that he is still being eyed suspiciously, and still not being invited fully into the home he stirs up within himself the fortitude to explain, "I am a friend to your daughter. Please believe me when I say that she came to me for assistance in her endeavor to escape those wishing ill of her." There is something familiar about Doortje Olmsfeld, and then he remembers that she is sister to Cornelius: Captain Janszoon. "It will please me to bring you up to date of her circumstances."

Chris and Doortje are caught up in a wordless exchange when Saarika interrupts, "I will see about finding us some coffee." As she glides away Doortje steps back, gesturing for Nicklas to come in. He follows her through a foyer into a sitting room brightened by lanterns scattered profusedly around the room, and warmed by a glowing turf fire.

Christophorus points Nicklas toward a sideboard that holds a tray filled with decanters and glasses, while taking his wife aside and showing her the note that has just been delivered. Nicklas chooses a decanter filled with what he hopes to be a fine whiskey and pours a generous splash into a glass. Across the room Trinjntje's parents whisper back and forth. Nicklas sips while appraising the elegant room. The princess returns, accompanied by a servant carrying a tray filled with a carafe of coffee, cups, and biscuits. The room is silent as Saarika fills a cup for each of them. She seats herself at one of the table's high back chairs. Nicklas takes a seat in another of the table's chairs. The Olmsfelds come over and add sugar and cream to their coffees before seating themselves at the table. At last, with all eyes expectantly upon him, Nicklas begins. "I will try to be thorough while keeping this brief." Followed by a concerned silence. "The very first day following our ship's return Trinjntje came knocking at my door; so very early that I was still abed. I did not even recognize her at first. She had trimmed her hair and was wearing a disguise. She had made herself up as a vagabond; dressed as a man. She explained to me that she needed to escape, that she felt imprisoned, and that she no longer wanted to be locked up for her safety. She was overwrought."

"We did not lock her up. Was she referring to us?" Doortje asks her husband.

He looks to Nicklas, "I did tell her that it is not safe for her here, and that she should plan on staying within the confines of the estate for her own safety. I had no intention of imprisoning her. Did she feel that she was a prisoner while aboard ship?"

"Everyone feels imprisoned aboard a ship," comments Princess Saarika.

Nodding his agreement Nicklas turns back, "She arrived at my door that morning determined to flee." He sips from his coffee cup before continuing. "I must say that her greatest concern is for you, her parents. She worries that her presence brings turmoil into your lives."

"Ohhhh!" wails Doortje. Christophorus wraps an arm around her shoulder and pats her soothingly while staring directly at Nicklas menacingly.

Taking a sip of whiskey before continuing, "I am not sure how, but she convinced me to help her to leave immediately." Christophorus is still staring at him ominously. Nicklas feels like he is walking a tightrope. He reminds himself that this is a powerful man. "As per her request I will refrain from telling you where we have been, only that I told her goodbye yesterday as she was leaving for Utrecht with Professor Calderon." Now he turns to the princess. Even sitting she is so very tall. Delicately balancing his words he asks, "Am I to understand that it is the necklace of Golden Hearts that has brought you here?"

"It is," she tells him. Her voice carries resonantly, "Have you brought it with you?"

"Alas, I have not." The tension in the room is thick and heavy. "The necklace has been stolen."

Christophorus stands abruptly and barks, "What have you done with it?"

Nicklas stands equally abruptly and barks back, "Not I, Sir." Realizing that he must settle himself, he breathes in deeply before finishing, "I believe that the thief is a VOC clerk. A member of the Port Regulator's office." The two men stand defiantly, neither to be the first to give way.

"Explain your accusation."

"The morning of our ship's arrival saw an officer of the VOC escorting two advocaats determined to take Trinjntje back with them as a prisoner. I, concerned for her, was not in my cabin upon the arrival of the dockmaster's clerk assigned to confirm my cargo manifest. When I returned to my cabin he, accompanied by a personal guard besides two of the ship's sailors, was already going through my things. It was not until after they were gone that I realized the necklace was missing."

It is as if a dark cloud has moved into the room bringing with it a chill. Christophorus moves to tend the fire while Doortje sees to the lanterns. Saarika sits with a surprisingly amused look upon her face. Nicklas is seated again, wishing he were anywhere but here, "I had planned to make a report of the theft, but Trinjntje, so intent to be gone from Amsterdam, convinced me to let it be."

Olmsfeld, businessman that he is, tells him officiously, "Let me look into this. Do you recall the clerk's name?"

"From the signature on my manifest," Nicklas remembers only the first name, "Greely?"

Olmsfeld swears an oath under his breath, "Greely DeVoss!" He spits the name. "That scoundrel is nothing but trouble! If it were not so late I would be after him tonight." He turns apologetically to the princess, "I will do what I can first thing tomorrow morning."

She smiles, "I thank you all. I am eager to see how this unfolds."

♡♡♡

Diedrik returns to the Kikker Gat intending to catch up on the chores that have been neglected while he has been away visiting the lawyer and luncheoning with Donar's family: and then there had been his incidental meeting with Anna Maria. Before he enters the barn Boomkikker calls to him from the kitchen door, "Dirk," he says, then stopping to appraise his dignified outfit, "or is that *Meneer* Dirk? You are dressed so fine!"

"Well," he teases back, "My friends call me Diedrik."

"Okay. Diedrik it is then." They each take account of one another for a moment before both speak at the same time, voicing the same words, "I have news for you." They laugh, and then they both speak at the same time again, "You first." And now they laugh again. "Okay," begins the Pub owner, "a young couple stopped by this morning asking for work, and remembering that you had warned us that you would be leaving, and because your chores have been piling up this morning in your absence, we have asked them to stay."

"Splendid!" Diedrik is surprised and delighted at the timing of this young couple's arrival. "Rhetta will be pleased to have a woman to help in the kitchen."

"La, you are taking the news very well."

"My news then. I have been to see an advocaat this morning. It turns out that I am a beneficiary in my former employer's will. He has left me his windmills and the polder they sit upon."

"Congratulations!" Kikkert reaches out and grabs Diedrik's hand shaking it vigorously while slapping him on the shoulder. "That is great! We have always thought that your life was intended for more than the simple work we have here."

"So the arrival of this couple to take over my duties is serendipitous; all has turned out well for us. I will clear out my room in the barn. There is other business for me to tend to this day, but I will return to stay the night, that is, if you have a room to let."

"Indeed," turning to go back inside, Kikkert pauses, then asks, "What will you do with yourself as a landowner?"

"I was *molenaar* for the man who has passed and left his property to me, so I will be doing pretty much what I have been doing all along. Hmmm, except that I will be living in a house instead of a windmill. La, it turns out the old man was as fond of me as I was of him."

Kikkert, standing with arms akimbo, casts a silhouette in the open doorway. "I am very pleased for you," he says before turning back inside to his own splendid life.

Diedrik packs his satchel, leaving it sitting just inside the barn to pick up later. He makes his way to a horse trader where there is a horse that he has had his eye on. He returns that evening on the seat of a new wagon being pulled by that most beautiful honey-colored gelding. He has made many stops along the way filling the bed of his wagon with the supplies he will be wanting upon his return to life at Schoonhoven Landing.

In the morning he bids *vaarwel.* Rhetta has teary eyes as she hugs him. Boomkikker has loaded a cask of KikkerBier into the wagon. It is a mostly sunny day with white fluffy clouds floating above as he follows a canal out of Utrecht to the River Rijn. Nearing his parents' home he stuffs his ears with wool as the noise of his father's sawmill gets louder and louder.

He explains to his parents the specifics of the will and invites them to visit once he is settled. He retrieves his things that he has stored here; clothes, paints, and books. His most important possession, the thing he has longed for most, is the illustrated folio of birds that Anna Maria has tasked him with finishing. On his way again, following the familiar river road that he knows by heart, he is relieved when he is far enough away from the sound of the dropping saws that he can remove the sheep's wool from his ears. He plays his familiar game of counting the birds that he sees along the river. Overhead are the eagles. Perched atop the cattails are the red-winged blackbirds. The ravens soar through the trees on their long daily treks. Herons stand on thin legs in the shallows. Geese in formation pass by honking. Swallows swoop acrobatically over the river's surface chasing bugs. The pheasants and quail call out unseen from their nests in the grasses. Oh, how he has missed this.

At Schoonhoven Landing he pulls into the drive and waves to Mara who is at the door. She leaves her doorway and is walking over so he stops. Her unbound hair cascades in waves around her shoulders. "Hello Diedrik," she greets him, "back so soon?"

"Hello Mara" turning toward the river, then back to her, "I see no moored ship. Your man has yet to return?"

"Aye, right you are." Looking over his cart load of goods she inquires, "Looks as if you are moving in."

"Yes indeed. That I am." He looks down the way, then back smiling, "I will be residing at Windmidden."

"Tending to things for your father?"

"Emmm ... no," thinking that he will eventually get used to his new status, "actually, my father was stepping in as landlord for me in my absence."

With a slight twist of her head and a widening smile she remarks, "La. That is a fine bit of news. It will be a pleasure having you as a neighbor."

"Likewise." He tips his head to her while clicking his tongue to the horse and moves on down the lane. He takes care of setting his new horse out to pasture and moving all his things into the house. There is much more to do, but before the sun sets completely he climbs the ring of stairs inside his windmill. Standing upon the stage, looking out across the land and the trees and the water, he makes a horn of his hands around his mouth and brays as loud as he possibly can, "AYYYYEEEEOOOOOOHOOOOO!"

Then again, "AYYYYEEEEOOOOOOHOOOOO!"

And again, "AYYYYEEEEOOOOOOHOOOOO!" All the birds in all the surrounding trees are squawking, twittering, and chirruping at the sound, wondering what is going on. Down the way at *Windweg* the Gedimins stand outside their door looking up at him in wonder. From *Windhoek* Mara is wending her way down to see what he has stirred up. He waves and shouts out to them all, "Halloo Neighbors!" Back down the stairs he goes. He engages Razs and Vejz to help him roll the barrel of KikkerBier out of the wagon and into a cradle at the back door of the house. He invites everybody to fill a mug, then after a toast explains his new situation. He offers another toast to them, expressing how happy he is to have them all living here with him.

"Will you put us to work?" Renaldo asks.

"Only if you want to."

"What would you have us do?" Annia asks, her long silken hair flowing smoothly from beneath her scarf.

"Oh, I don't know." Looking around for things that need attention, "the flax is ready for scything."

"Will you have us harvesting?"

"Will the retting be done here?" Audrae asks, then making a face, "and will it stink terribly?"

"Have you done this before?" He smiles, then decides to set her up with a tall tale, "There is always a wind blowing here that carries the horrendous smell away."

"Okay," laughs Razs, "now if you expect us to believe that the smell of retting can be blown away, then you will also believe me when I tell you that the sun will rise twice tomorrow."

Vejz joins in with a jibe of his own, "Or that the moon is made of cheese." They are all laughing.

"You guys," chiding her brothers, Kirin tells them, "stop teasing."

Diedrik enjoys their kidding; it makes him feel like he is part of a big family. "No need to worry about me," he says to her noticing, as he had before, how pretty she is, "besides, I think it was me that started it all."

As darkness sets in lanterns are lit and he shares sausages and cheese. Good food, good beer, and good conversation allows them all to get to know each other better. They begin to notice, sitting out here beneath the night sky, that there are frequent shooting stars. The discussion turns to stories of falling stars. It is agreed upon by all that they are seeing more tonight than any of them has ever seen before. Mara wonders out loud, "As many as there are, I imagine that Robert may be seeing them also." It gets late, so his guests leave him for the night after expressing once more their happiness at his being here. He carries in a few turves and starts a small fire, not because it is cold, but to clear away the mustiness. He busies himself putting things away, sweeping the floor, and wiping away the dust that has settled on everything.

The house warms up so he removes his coat and vest. He unties the sash from around his waist. Laying it carefully upon the table, he unwraps the velveteen drawstring bag that holds the amazing thing he had lifted; it seems so long ago. As he draws the necklace of Golden Hearts out of its bag and spreads it on the table in the flickering lantern light he is rendered spellbound by its magnificence. Unable to stop staring he sits down enthralled by the luster of the jewels, and the smooth radiance of the gold. Stunned by the way it shimmers and sparkles so brilliantly he picks it up and turning it over and over marvels at the heft and the balance. After a bit he realizes there is something there that he has not before noticed. There are detailed motifs embossed on the back of each heart; intricate and fine. He has never before seen such delicate metallurgical handiwork. Surely he would have noticed something astounding as this. He wonders how it can be so, that in all the times he has previously beheld this item he has not noticed this bit of unworldly artisanship.

He spreads the necklace upside down upon the tabletop, draws his chair in closer, and studies this newly discovered attribute of these Golden Hearts. As he moves the individual hearts into closer proximity it appears that the interwoven designs match up from one heart to the next. He arranges each heart even closer, transfixing them so that the individual patterns link with each other, and form a circle. When the circle of patterns is complete he hears a barely audible click, and before he discerns where the noise has come from, or even if he has actually heard anything, there appears a column of light; a beam shooting up from the circle formed of the hearts. "What the --" before he can even finish his outburst the beam of light coalesces into the shape of a heart. It is as if one of the actual golden hearts has materialized before him and is now slowly spinning in mid-air above the necklace on the table. Diedrik reaches out tentatively to touch the heart that is turning in the air before him, but his finger passes through the apparition. "Unworldly indeed!"

He sits back wondering if he should be frightened, but this thing does not feel threatening at all; it is actually quite nice. He ponders the way these Golden Hearts have always calmed and soothed. He hears a fluttering. He looks around thinking that it may be a moth drawn to the visage as if to a lantern's flame. There is no moth. He realizes that the fluttering is inside him, and that it is matching the pulsing radiance of the mysterious heart floating there before him. As this enchanting quiver vibrates through him he is growing ever more at ease. His thinking slips away and he is happy to let his thoughts go, just as he does whenever he falls asleep. His perspective changes. His eyes, rather than viewing only forward, are now viewing from the sides of his head. It is bird vision. He is aloft on outstretched wings. He is dreaming his favorite dream ... and yet, he is awake. He drifts down and lands within the framework of a windmill's turning sail. The brace that he is perched upon shifts from horizontal to vertical with the turning of the sail. He sidesteps along the board as it tips, moving to the perpendicular board next to it that is now horizontal. He must continually move as each consecutive brace tips up. It takes steady movement and steady concentration to keep himself upright. It is a dizzying effort. When he misses a step he catches his fall with outstretched wings. He notices the fluttering again as his perspective returns to what is familiar. He reaches out with his palm and blocks the beam of light rising from the circle of hearts. The image that has been floating blinks out. He lowers his hand and jumbles the circle of hearts, breaking apart the linked patterns; stopping the magic. Spells. Magics. Enchantments. The dire implications of these words do not describe the delightful sweetness of what he has just experienced.

As he slips the necklace back into its velvet bag and draws the string tight he wonders about the rightful owner. "Could it be a wizard? Or, an enchantress? How could that creepy dockmaster's clerk have outsmarted an adept of the necromantic arts?" That word, necromancy, conjures frightful images in his imagination. What he had just imagined has not been frightening. It has been frolicsome. He opens one of the drawers under his bed and places the velvet bag holding the necklace within the folds of a spare blanket.

He deems it is time for bed. He is warm enough and has a thick quilt so rather than feed the fire he will let it burn down. He blows out the flames in his lanterns and climbs into bed. It is a large soft bed. He is soon asleep, and then dreaming that he is a small blue falcon riding the braces of a windmill's sail round and round.

♡♡♡

Greely DeVoss, having just been served his breakfast, is interrupted by the captain of the cruise ship that has moored in the harbor since yesterday. It had been his duty to inform this Captain that very few of his passengers would be allowed to come ashore. "I am hoping that you can be of assistance," Captain Derek tells him, "I have been told that your company keeps a file of all registered ships. I wish to know the home port of one particular vessel."

"Egad! I do not keep a list in my head of every ship that comes through our port."

Captain Derek does not want to hear excuses, "I am asking if your office keeps a ledger of ships flying the Dutch VOC standard, and if I may have access to this listing."

Greely has begun eating, not giving any sign that he has been listening. This idiot standing here has yet to offer even the smallest coin, thus thoroughly wasting his time and spoiling his breakfast. There is a commotion at the door as a group of VOC soldiers enter. His indulgence is cut short as the commander of the soldiers stops at his table pronouncing, "Greely DeVoss: I declare you hereby under arrest." Before a protest can be uttered soldiers on either side yank him up from his chair, "You will be coming with us." Captain Derek, witnessing the cur being forced away against his will, and noticing that there is still a fair portion of food left on the man's plate, sits down in the vacated seat and proceeds to eat what is there.

Greely is dragged out into the street, where he is finally able to get his feet under him and able to walk on his own, even though it is a quick marching pace, and the soldiers holding his arms are squeezing mercilessly. "You are hurting me," he whines, "You are making a big mistake," he threatens. "I have the power to make your lives miserable," he boasts. "You will regret this," he blusters on and on, even as he is marched into the VOC headquarters. "How dare you treat me like this? I am a decent and upstanding citizen!" He does not stop his threatening diatribe until he is forcefully escorted into the office of his immediate supervisor, Lieutenant Gerardus Hamet.

"Shut up Greely," Gerardus tells him from where he is seated behind his desk. "We have a report that you have been thieving."

"That I have been thieving?" He attempts again to free his arms from the soldiers' enforcing grip. "If I have, it is no more than anyone else doing this same job."

"Careful!" Gerardus stands, "I have been waiting for this day. Waiting for someone bold enough to step forward to press charges. Someone not bullied by your henchman."

"Whoever makes this claim against me is a liar!"

"Gag the bastard!" Gerardus cannot allow this weasel to call the Director, who is standing in the next room, a liar. The gag is tied, yet DeVoss continues his tirade. "Shut him up!" A well flung fist to the belly quiets him by taking his breath away. Holding up a sheath of papers Gerardus continues, "This roster, signed by you, purports that you did oversee the cargo when said misdeed occurred." One of the attending soldiers is now forcing Greely's head close enough to see exactly what is being pointed out to him.

"Ughh ohhyeeuguguhhh," DeVoss attempts to answer. After exchanged nods between the soldiers the gag is temporarily removed. Greely indignantly pronounces, "This man, Voorhaven, is a simpleton. And a wise ass. He failed to be present for his accounting, and then gave us some cockamamie tale to distract us from his smuggling." The gag is reinserted and pulled tight, stopping any further outbursts.

"I tell you again; be wary of who you are calling liars or smugglers." As Christophorus Olmsfeld steps into the office Greely's legs go all rubbery and he is dropped unceremoniously into a hard-backed chair. "Now idiot," Gerardus tells him, "meet your accuser, the man you have been calling a liar. I will allow you to tell our Director what you stole from Nicklas Voorhaven that morning, and then tell him where it is now." He signals to have the gag removed.

"I do not know what you are talking about." The commanding officer steps forward and backhands Greely severely. He squeals, "I do not have it."

The soldier looks to Hamet who nods to leave be for now, then asks, "What is **it** that you do not have?"

Looking back and forth with frightened eyes before at last giving in, "It is a velvet bag ..." When he says no more the soldiers raise him up out of his seat while their commander steps in for another punch, prompting Greely to hurriedly finish, "... filled with gold and jewels."

Gerardus moves from behind his desk. Standing in front of the prisoner flexing his fingers, preparing to strangle this imbecile, he asks in a deeply menacing tone, "Where is it?"

His voice squeaking, "It was contraband, Sir. I was bringing it back with me to register it as such when it was lifted from my coat pocket by a pack of thieving boys."

Hamet's hands come up, but he is able to stop himself before grabbing Greely by the neck. "Two lies in one sentence. You are really aggravating me. The item was not contraband, and you had no intention of registering it as such." Now bending until his face is inches away from Greely's, "Tell me where the necklace is! **Now!**"

DeVoss, bursting into tears, wails, "I do not have it. The pickpockets got it from me. I do not have it. I do not know where it is!" He is a blubbering fool crying hysterically.

Gerardus trades looks with Christophorus, then with a jerk of his head gives the soldiers the signal to take the prisoner out. When they are gone he tells the Director, "We will search his lodgings. We will question his henchman. We will round up all the pickpockets." Wishing he had a strong drink. "I cannot make any guarantees."

"I am certain that you will do your best," Olmsfeld tells him, "Thank you for your prompt attention to this matter."

"My pleasure, Sir."

"Good day."

♡♡♡

Nicklas, having again risen early, has come directly to VOC headquarters, where he has received the paperwork itemizing his cargo and the prices paid. He sits across the desk of a clerk that has presented the documents for him to sign. He is pleased to note that the administrating fees are significantly lower than he has imagined. The sizable balance, registered at the bottom of the last page, is enough for him to consider himself a rich man. He is shaking hands and accepting the clerk's congratulations when Christophorus Olmsfeld sticks his head through the doorway of the cubicle, "A word before you leave?" Nicklas hurries to catch up with the older man who, upon entering his office immediately pours and quaffs a healthy shot of whiskey. As he pours another he offers the same to Nicklas, who would normally turn down a drink so early in the day, but seeing the shaken look of Trinjntje's father accepts, while hinting, by pinching his fingers together, to make it small.

Olmsfeld is in a state; fuming distractedly. Nicklas sips from his glass still standing until the older man sits and motions for him to sit as well. They sit in silence until Olmsfeld shakes himself out of his funk and makes small talk asking, "You have checked your account? Everything is in order?"

"Yes, thank you, Sir."

"Greely DeVoss has admitted to stealing the necklace, but tells of having it consequently stolen from him. Claims a sneak thief nicked it from his coat pocket even before he made it back to his office. So his story goes."

"Oh. Hmmm," Nicklas has difficulty thinking of anything to say, but as the silence grows ever longer asks, "What do you suppose the princess will do?"

"That is what I have been wondering." He stands and goes to the window. Looking out he rambles away, "Her family are royals that no longer rule. They have become shipping magnates with hundreds of frigates traveling the ports of the Indian Ocean. Saarika has operated her family's business in the Far East. She is a consummate business woman that has successfully brokered deals with my company for many years." He moves back to his desk and sits. He is gathering his thoughts, preparing to say more. Nicklas waits. Finally Christophorus faces him squarely, "Tell me, if you will, what your relationship with Trinjntje is?"

"As you know, I was hired to attend to the heavier work involved with the gathering of plants and trees to bring home. We got along well, even became friends. I must say, she is a remarkable woman, unlike others I have known." Then figuring that he had best leave no doubt, "We are not lovers." Looking the older man directly in the eye, "And, I have no desire or hope of ever being her lover."

"Her feelings toward you?"

"The same, as far as I know, but you will have to ask her yourself."

"Thank you." The bell tolls the ten o'clock hour. Standing up and scooting together a bunch of loose papers, "I am late for a meeting. May I ask of you a favor?" Nicklas, already on his feet, nods. "Princess Saarika needs to be told. I would be supremely grateful if you will take care of that bit for me."

"Okay ..." Ugh, "will I find her at your home?" Christophorus nods and they leave the office, setting off in opposite directions.

Nicklas attempts to prepare a statement as he walks through town. He considers stopping for a drink, but determines it better to be done with this assignment he has accepted. A servant lets him in at the gate, and Doortje Olmsfeld greets him at the door. She leads him to the back of the house where Saarika is playing a game of cards with herself. Her face brightens with his arrival. "Have they caught the scoundrel?"

"Yes, but it does no good. What he stole has been stolen from him."

Expecting to witness despair, Nicklas is surprised at her smile as she scoops the cards from the table and shuffles them from hand to hand. "Do you wonder at the importance of this necklace?" He takes the seat across the table from her. She riffles the deck a couple more times, then begins methodically laying out a traditional solitaire spread. "The necklace of Golden Hearts is said to be a gift, aeons ago, from a mythical race of celestials. Do you believe such tales?"

"Do I believe in myths?"

"That intelligent beings, other than humans, have walked this earth; may still be here with us?"

"I have heard myths of Gods and Goddesses."

"Well, there it is." She deals from her deck, laying down and picking up cards as she talks. "The legend of the necklace is told in the murals on the walls of an underground sanctuary that my mother assigned me to visit each year of my childhood. Even though my family is tall, these celestials are portrayed as being even taller. There is one particular mosaic depicting a bronze-haired woman radiating light. She wears a necklace identical in likeness to the necklace of Golden Hearts that has gone missing."

"An underground sanctuary you say? For worship?"

"Yes, before the dominant beliefs of this current age, of one god." She reaches the point in her card game of no more moves and tosses the remaining cards in the midst of all the rest, sweeps them together and begins riffling them again. "Let me tell you something more." She looks across at him, making eye contact, then begins laying the cards out. "Whilst visiting an archive of historical texts in Huaxia I came across a set of pictograms that are similar to the mosaic I have just described. I am led to believe that these celestials may have shared their lives with humanity all over this worldly realm. There was one exceptional series of pictograms detailing three of the tall ones spreading three of the necklaces into a circle." She lays the cards down giving Nicklas her full attention as she finishes, "A beam of light, a column shining into the sky emanated from the circle of Golden Hearts. As the celestials stepped into the circle they each floated upward." She sits back smiling in a broad challenging manner as if she is daring him.

"A portal to another realm? Intriguing, but, emmm ..."

She picks up her cards resuming the game she was playing, "So," she continues, "I have searched, hoping to find other necklaces of Golden Hearts. But, alas, now I have lost the one I had. La."

"I am a bit confused. You do not seem upset as I thought you would be."

She looks to him now, her face encircled by her brightly patterned hijab, her mystifying eyes sparkling, "It does not serve me to be upset because the Golden Hearts seem to be lost. I am trusting that they are not lost. I believe that I shall eventually happen upon them."

Nicklas' intrigue is heightened, "What will you do now?"

"I will not stay here," she answers, while absent-mindedly scrambling the cards, "I have been set on meeting your friend, Trinjntje Olmsfeld, for so long that I am determined to do just that. She awaits our meeting in Utrecht, I will go there tomorrow."

"Oh, will you take a coach, or a barge, or do you plan to ride?"

"Director Olmsfeld has arranged a horse for me to ride. I am to leave from a stable called the Coach House."

"The Koetshuis! That is where my horse is stabled. I would be happy to ride with you." Had he just said that out loud? "What I mean to say," she is grinning at him, "is that I would be honored to escort you m'lady."

She laughs: a beguiling trilling laughter, "Please, do not treat me as someone of higher ranking, and please do not burden me with your chivalry. I would enjoy having you to ride along with me. Perhaps you will be able to acquaint me with the ways of this land. We can compare customs."

"Very well then. Very well indeed." He stands and bows. "I will meet you in the morning at the Koetshuis."

♡♡♡

Captain Derek has again sailed his ship from the Zuiderzee, through the shallow waterway of the IJ, and into Amsterdam harbor. The dock provided for his ship is a distant and seldom-used shambles of rotting timbers. A guard troop stands by as a group of VOC clerks carry out a vetting process before allowing passengers to disembark. Few of the vetted passengers are being allowed off of the ship. Now, the second day here in Amsterdam, while the remaining passengers are subjected to the extreme vetting, the ship's crewmembers are allowed ashore for the purpose of re-equipping stores. The Captain had come ashore early. By asking members of a busy dock crew he had discovered that the offices of the Dutch East Indies Company would not open until later. When passed a coin, one of the stevedores had suggested the name of a VOC man who might be of assistance, and where he could be found taking his morning repast. That suggestion turned out to be of no use when the mongrel had been arrested before providing any information; but all had not been lost, for he had left behind an exceptional plate of food.

He hears the bells tolling ten o'clock as he enters the main headquarters of the VOC. Upon making his request to review the company's ledgers he has been informed by a clerk that the ledgers are not available to the public. Upon his request to see the clerk's supervisor he has been escorted out of the building by two soldiers. He is making his way back toward the docks when, passing an apothecary, he remembers that his supply of elixirs is getting low. He enters and is greeted cheerfully by a large woman. The Dutch are generally bigger around the middle, but this woman is larger around, by far, than any others. She is required to turn herself sideways through the narrow aisles. "What is it that I can get for your ills, Sir?"

"I am needing to replenish my supply of medicinal tobacco," he tells her, "for my breathing," he explains.

"Yes, well here we have your choices; a light Virginian, a bold Carolinian, and something new, this comes from Tennessee. I just adore these new world names." Producing a pipe made from a dried cob she offers, "Care for a sample?"

"No, but I will take a packet of each. I also require tincture of opium. For my cough."

Pointing toward a shelf full of labeled bottles she tells him, "Choose for yourself, Sir, while I wrap up these tobaccos."

There are many different sized bottles; all claiming to have the highest percentage of the active ingredient. He asks, "Can you tell me which of these actually has the highest content, er, which will be most effective on my cough?"

"My husband prepares what is considered to be the best for a cough, Sir."

He picks up a bottle that has a picture on the label that matches the sign over the door, then takes another and sets both on the counter next to the packets of tobacco. He explains, "I have a chronic cough."

"A fine choice, Sir. Will you be needing anything else?"

"Emmm ... something for a bellyache?"

"Well," eyeing him slyly, "we have herbal teas for mild discomfort, but for the extreme topsy-turvy tummy I suggest," lifting a tray of packages from beneath the counter and setting it before him, "Scythian hashish."

"Yes." He smiles approvingly, "That is what I had in mind."

"We have this light gold that comes from Persia. We also have this bhang from India." She sets a small pipe on the counter, then offers, "Go ahead, give each a try."

"Right here? Now?"

"Sure. I have already had my bellyache medicine this morning. I would not want you to go on suffering the discomfort." He smokes a bit of each, and then asks for a generous portion of both. She collects his payment while offering more options, "We have a mixture of dried mushrooms that will benefit your dreams. We also have a root to mix into your tea that will dispel your confusion."

"I do not have dreams, nor am I confused." He takes the bag that she has filled with his purchases and bids her, "Good day."

"Bye Love. See you next time you are in port?"

As he leaves the shop he is thinking that she is the most charming and the most helpful apothecary that he has ever met. He notices the blue sky filled with fluffy clouds. Everyone he passes is kind and friendly; the men handsome and the women beautiful. The bells are ringing, but he loses track of the number of strikes; was it eleven, or twelve? "Oh well, it does not matter. The time is never really important." Walking along the wharf he passes ships being loaded, or off-loaded, by busy dock workers. He admires these hard working men's agility. As he nears the end of the wharf, and his moored ship, he is assaulted by the din of angry voices. It sounds of complaining and discontent.

He walks up the gangway to be confronted by his First Mate, "Sir, where have you been? They are allowing barely any of our passengers to disembark."

"Eh, the hell you say."

"Are you the captain?" Derek turns to a docking clerk, "We have completed our assessment of your passengers. Only a few hold the required paperwork to be allowed into our port."

"The hell you say." Turning to his Mate he asks, "Where is the bloody accountant that sold berths to these people? Have him bring this required paperwork and let us be rid of this lot."

"Captain, Sir." The clerk hands a sheaf of papers over, "This is the paperwork. It shows that your passengers paid for passage to Londontowne."

Turning again to his Mate, "Why then have we stopped here? In Amsterdam?"

The First Mate looks to the docking clerk while shrugging his shoulders helplessly.

The docking clerk is left to explain to the Captain, "There were a few of your passengers set to disembark here. Your manifest lists your next scheduled port as Rotterdam. And, might I add, you have a few passengers who have paid to be let off there."

Captain Derek scans the crowd surrounding him now and then asks again, "Where is that bloody accountant?"

"Our work is finished here." The docking clerk hands over another document and tells the captain, "Here is your departure notice." He makes his way down the gangway, followed by his assistants.

"Bloody hell," remarks Captain Derek as he hands the paper away to anyone who will take it.

There is a commotion on the dock below. A new group of soldiers are leading a prisoner up the gangway. The Captain recognizes the man as the uncivil creep that had been dragged away by soldiers, leaving his breakfast behind. The ship's accountant is with the group. "Where the hell have you been?" Derek demands of the bookkeeper.

"Hunnh! Where the hell have **you** been?"

"We do not have room for another prisoner, er, passenger."

"Yes, we do. The port did allow a few departures during your absence."

Turning to the prisoner Captain Derek asks snidely, "Yer own company's ships not good enough for you?"

Greely DeVoss faintly remembers this man, "Shove off. Leave me be!"

Turning to a steward Derek says, "Show this man to his berth in the hold, where he can be with the other passengers his company has deemed unfit for disembarkation."

"I have paid for a cabin. Show me to my cabin."

The accountant whispers smugly to Derek, "I have exacted an exorbitant amount from this man for the privilege of a cabin."

"The hell you say." The Company soldiers have retreated to the dock, but appear to be remaining until it is certain that their prisoner stays on board. To Greely he says, "You will accept the accommodations that I have recommended for you," then nodding toward the waiting soldiers, "or, you are welcome to take your leave."

Greely, knowing that he has no choice, acquiesces, and says to the steward, "Lead on, then." He scowls menacingly as he passes the grinning accountant, "Thief!"

The gangway is dragged away, the section of gunwale reinserted, dock lines undone, sails raised, and the cruise ship makes its way out of the harbor. In the interim Captain Derek has locked up his medicines in his cabin, but not before a soothing draught of cough syrup. He is back at the helm as they sail out through the IJ, measuring and calling out the depth all the way. He has heard the Dutch call this shallow channel the 'eye', but it has never been explained to him why. Being an Englishman, he looks forward to a day when this IJ, already so shallow, silts up altogether, causing the closure of this port, just as the port of Antwerpen was shut down by the silting of the river Scheldt. A distinct sense of comfort has settled over him and he tells the helmsman, "Let all these Dutch ports silt up. Let Dutch shipping be damned. The English be the rightful masters of the sea!"

"Aye, Sir." Surprised by the Captain's unusual comradery. "Indeed."

Settling In

Yesterday evening Nicklas had informed his landlady that he would be up and leaving early and so would not be needing breakfast, "I will be gone again for a few days, or maybe longer."

"La, you are the easiest tenant I have ever had." He had roused her from her stitching, and she still held her hoop, waving it at him as she teased him some more, "Do you suppose that you will ever actually reside here again, I mean, for longer than a night?"

"Ah, we'll see." Smiling at her daughters peeking out from behind their ma, "I must be off tomorrow, with a new friend, for Utrecht. It is uncertain how long I will be away." Although he is speaking with the mother, he cannot help but notice her daughters, guessing them to be nearing the same age as he. "When I do return, it will not be to my previous vocation of clerking. I am young; I may travel again, or even finish my schooling."

The woman is aware that her girls think this young tenant to be a handsome fellow, as does she, "We will all be looking forward to your return."

Before their mother closes the door both girls tell him, "*tot ziens*," waving sweetly by wiggling their fingers.

He has risen early and upon arriving at the Koetshuis Inn had asked that his and Saarika's horses be saddled. Just moments after seating himself Princess Saarika comes through the door, and he stands as she crosses the room. She is wearing a pale orange abaya; its length accentuating her heighth: she is taller than Nicklas, taller than most people. She sets her shoulder bag on the floor next to his satchel as she takes her seat. The waitress is there quickly, "Our special offering this morning is a stack of pancakes served with a generous helping of ham and eggs."

Saarika defers to Nicklas who answers, "That sounds like a lot to eat; I will have a stroopwafel."

"Stroop waffle?" Saarika asks, "Bring one for me also, with a cup of coffee please."

Nicklas tells the princess, "Stroopwafel is served with coffee."

Saarika laughs, "La, I am learning something new every day." Then, appraising Nicklas' outfit; a russet-colored coat with matching silk braid at the cuffs and lapels, Saarika commends him, "Your riding outfit suits you handsomely."

"Ah, thank you, it is new. I will be traveling on to Antwerpen from Utrecht, to visit my parents, and I want to present myself successfully." He laughs. Their stroopwafels arrive atop their cups of coffee. Nicklas puts his nose down close to the cup and breathes in the aroma of the warming gooey bun.

Saarika watches, then asks, "Why is the pastry served on top of the cup like this?"

"The steaming coffee warms up the caramel in the bun," pointing at the center of the bun while twirling a finger outlining the spiral of sweetness.

"How long until it is ready to eat?"

"Well, let's see," he says as he lifts his stroopwafel, takes a bite out of it, then points out to her the warmed caramel syrup dripping from the center, "it is ready now." She is amused by his clowning. She lifts her own sweet bun delicately, and nibbles a taste, then nibbles a bit more, then smiles her approval. He sips his coffee, then tells her admiringly, "I applaud your language skills. I have difficulty with other languages, yet your command of ours' is beguiling."

She dabs at her mouth with the linen table napkin before explaining, "My family has traded with Dutch merchants for as long as I can remember: mostly coffee." She sips from her cup, then holding it up, "the beans that were ground for this brew may very well have come through my family's warehouses."

"Your family is in Djibouti?" She nods. "Director Olmsfeld mentioned to me that you have been living in Huaxia. Do you speak the Huaxian language as well?"

"Yes. I speak the dialect of the Ming Dynasty. I seem to have a penchant for languages: I also speak Arabic, French, English, Spanish, and Portuguese."

"Remarkable."

"Hmmm, is it so remarkable?" She is interrupted by the hostess telling them that their horses are saddled and ready. Saarika thanks her, then begins again, "I regularly deal with a wide range of people speaking all different languages. You see, my family, upon learning how much Europeans desire porcelain, and having already established a trade network with the Ming dynasty, sent me to purchase, and fill warehouses with porcelain vases, platters, bowls, and, of course, statues. European traders are generally not allowed direct trade with Huaxia, and so are left to deal with us."

"Ah, yes, I remember whilst in the harbor at Formosa, being told that foreigners were not allowed on the mainland."

"European foreigners," she points out. "You may also be wondering why a woman would hold an important position dealing with international trading." He has been wondering why a daughter, instead of a son, is handling the family business. Saarika finishes her bun, licks off her fingers, and then tells him, "I have, as your friend Trinjntje Olmsfeld has, said 'No' to a Prince demanding that I be his wife. A deliberate act of defiance that put my life in danger." She lets that information sink in, "my mother was able to convince my father to send me away rather than having me beheaded." She laughs heartily; a musical laughter that inspires him to laugh along.

"Beheaded?" Laughing some more while wondering if there is any truth to her joking. Then he tells her, "I purchased some porcelain statues while harbored at the port of Formosa. I also convinced Trinjntje to use porcelain vases for transporting the trees she was bringing home."

"There, you see, we have shared business interests even before today." Each has finished their coffee and buns and it is time to be on their way.

Once on their horses they travel steadily. She is fascinated by the many windmills, by the peat bogs, and by the flat terrain that presents such a big sky. She loves seeing the barges in the canal, and gushes at the sturdy horses pulling them along. She asks him questions about everything she sees, and listens patiently to his answers. Hardly a moment passes without conversation. They are well suited traveling companions. They get to Utrecht late in the day and upon his suggestion they choose to stay at the Kikker Gat Public House. They are settling up with Kikkert when Nicklas recognizes Professor Calderon coming through the door. "Hello Professor," he re-introduces himself, "Nicklas Voorhaven; we met at Captain Janszoon's."

"Ah, yes, Nicklas. Greetings." He is shaking hands with Nicklas, but his gaze is focused upon the woman standing beside him."

Nicklas says, "Allow me to introduce my traveling companion," turning to her, "Saarika," she has requested to be introduced by her by name only, leaving off any title, "Paulo Calderon."

Calderon takes her hand, "My pleasure Saarika," taking her hand, "Pardon my inquiring, but is it Princess Saarika?"

She looks questioningly to Nicklas who fills in, "Calderon has served as go-between for the Olmsfelds and their daughter Trinjntje."

Still holding Calderon's hand she says, "Oh, well then I Thank you for all you have done on my behalf."

"My pleasure," he invites them to join him for dinner; warning them that there will be others at the same table. As they are taking their seats Lu-Tang arrives and is introduced.

Hendrik shows up, and seeing new faces says, "Splendid!" as he approaches the table, "We are dining with a crowd." Resting a hand on the back of Saarika's chair while holding out his other he introduces himself, "Henri de Roy," using the French rendering of his name, "It is a pleasure to make your acquaintance."

She introduces herself, "Saarika. Pleased to meet you, Sir." She is intrigued by these three men of clearly different personality types.

Hendrik next whacks Nicklas on the shoulder, "It is good to see you again Nicklas."

In the commotion that Hendrik has stirred up with his arrival no one has noticed that someone else has come in behind him until she speaks up, "Hello everybody." Then, to the unfamiliar guest among them all she asks, "Saarika?" Surprised upon hearing her name, the princess turns in her chair. The bright-eyed woman standing there says, "Hi. It's me; Trinjntje," she is holding out her hand in greeting.

Saarika stands; her eyes wide and sparkling, "I am so very pleased to meet you at last." Reaching out and taking Trinjntje's hand, "I am certain that we will be friends."

"Oh, I hope so." Each of them, looking into the other's eyes, recognizes a kindred spirit.

♡♡♡

On his first morning back at Schoonhoven Landing Diedrik is awakened by a familiar bird call, and glancing out the window sees the bird whose call has awakened him, he is pleased that there is not only one, but a crowd of HooPoo birds in the yard. Sitting up for a better look he laughs at the way they comically bob their heads as they walk. One of them, finding something interesting and calling out *Oop-oop-oop* has all the others of the flock charging toward the sound of the call, sending the first bird on a mad dash to get away. HooPoo birds always make him smile and for a long time has been wanting to add them to his folio. They are here now, but seldom stay long, so he throws back the covers, hops out of bed and hurries over to the table by the window. As he is opening his chest of paints and brushes he hears another excited, *Oop-oop-oop*. He looks up to see that one of them has a beetle in its curved beak. Its crest feathers raise up and down comically as it runs away. The other birds rush after making a lot of noise. As Diedrik pulls out a fresh sheet of paper he hears another *Oop-oop-oop* and looks out to see another HooPoo attempting to get away with a snail in its beak. He un-stoppers his ink, picks a horse-hair brush that tapers to a fine point, and begins sketching. At first there is very little detail, filling the page with quick brushstrokes. The sketches grow in detail as he progresses. He pulls out another page, and opens his tray of colors. Filling his water bowl, picking out another brush, and mixing yellow into brown to match the colors of the birds' feathers, he soon has another page filled with ever more detailed sketches.

While he is sketching he becomes oblivious to all else; totally focused on what he is doing. He has a method of holding his gaze steady and wide to include both the object he is sketching and his sketch in his range of sight, allowing him to paint without having to look up and down, or back and forth. He fills page after page while everything else around him becomes indistinct. When one of the cats walks up the drive all of the HooPoos take off squawking, *Oop-oop-oop. Oop-oop-oop*, and the instant after they are gone Diedrik has sketched the striped cat.

He looks up, blinking to give his eyes a rest. Across the polder he sees Mara with her goats frolicking around her vying for attention. He stands and stretches, then opens the window and hears her singing. Her happy tune carries across the field. He cannot make out what she is singing in her lilting Gaelic, but he likes it. He sits back down and with a fresh sheet begins to paint from his sketches. Mixing brown, red, and yellow he blends shades of russet that match the HooPoos' heads and upper bodies. With these various shades of tan and orange he lays out what will be an illustration of three of the little birds quarreling over a beetle. Later today, or tomorrow, whenever he next sits down, he will fill in the wings. The pattern of the stripes on the wings change as they move. Maybe the flock will return and he will have another opportunity to sketch those patterns some more. As he is imagining another scene: of the startled flock scattering away from the cat he hears someone outside.

"Hey," Audrae says looking in the window, "Whatcha doin'?"

"Nothing," he answers.

"Nothing at all?" Her eyes sparkle, "Do you intend to continue doing nothing?" She giggles, "I would not want to disrupt you from anything as important as nothing."

Diedrik thinks Audrae is a mischievous imp, "I suppose that I could finish up with nothing and do something."

"I found a nest full of eggs."

"Oh good, do you want to show me? That would be something," he stands, then realizing that he is still in his nightshirt, "Oh, but first I had better get dressed."

As soon as he comes out the door she crouches down and challenges him, "Let's race!" Off she goes, running away toward the lake as fast as she can. He is caught off guard, so before he has even started running she already has a good lead. He chases after her. She is fast. Her brothers, busy in the yard at Windweg, drop what they are doing when they see Diedrik chasing after Audrae and follow along. Getting close to the lake she stops and turns with her index finger at her lips shushing the three catching up to her. "Right in here," she tells them as she parts the tall grasses. They all peek through to see a quail hen sitting in a circle of flattened grass.

Audrae pouts, "Ohhh, we cannot even see the eggs."

When the hen discovers the four of them looking in on her she clucks nervously and her top knot quivers. Diedrik tells her with a soothing voice, "Do not be afraid little hen."

"Oh," asks Razs with a grin, "do you think she understands what you are saying?"

Vejz punches his brother, "Everybody around here talks to birds. Mara talks to magpies." Another quail suddenly swoops in close overhead taking up a position next to the little hen. She rises up, and together they ruffle their feathers. It appears as if they are debating whether to run away.

Diedrik tells the two little birds, "It is OK, do not be afraid. We love you." The two exchange some quizzical noises, and then the hen flies off while her mate takes over the chore of keeping their eggs warm.

"I think this little bird wants us to leave," Diedrik tells the others.

"Yeh, I think you are right," Audrae agrees, then using her sweetest voice, tells the little bird, "We love you. We will leave you alone for now. Do not be afraid." She turns to her brothers challengingly.

They grin at each other with big eyes before repeating, "Yep, do not fear little guy, we are leaving now," and then they all back out of the tall grass.

♡♡♡

After dinner, and all the empty plates had been cleared away, Saarika, Trinjntje, and Nicklas had reeled off tales of their recent travels. It had been a humorous commentary that had kept the professors entertained til late. Before bidding them all good night Trinjntje and Saarika had arranged to meet in the morning. Nicklas had walked with Trinjntje back to the cottage serving as her temporary home bringing each other up to date. He had told her that he would not be staying in Utrecht, instead he will make his way to Antwerpen to see his parents. She had told him that she has arranged a meeting with an estate agent in the morning to look at a home available to lease. Nicklas had left Trinjntje listening to the Cathedral's organist, even so late, practicing a joyful hymn. Halfway up the block, in the light of another streetlamp, he had turned to see her, still out front of the cottage, looking up into the night sky.

In the morning Trinjntje awakens to the melodic strains coming from the cathedral's organ, "Geez, there is always someone playing that organ over there." She puts on the long dress with the matching velvet trousers that Calderon had purchased for her. It is a perfect riding outfit, and also very similar to what Saarika wears. She ties a lace scarf over her hair. When she answers the knock at the door, rather than inviting her new friend in, she steps out. Closing the door behind her she says, "Shall we walk?" Holding up a scrap of paper, "I have an address where I am to meet a leasing agent."

"I have done some calculating Trinjntje, and I believe that we may be close to the same age," receiving a nod of agreement, "I have been living on my own for what seems like half my life, whereas, it seems that you have never lived apart from your family, that is, except while away on your voyage."

"Yep. Your calculations are correct. I have never lived by myself, but I like the idea of having my own home." As they walk up the block, the pipes of the organ fade behind them. As they pass the University there are crowds of young scholars hurrying by on their way to lectures. When they reach the canal there is a small café advertising breakfast, "We can get a coffee here."

Remembering yesterday at the Koetshuis Saarika agrees, "Okay. I hope they have those little waffles."

After taking their seats there is a lull as they take in their surroundings, then Trinjntje says, "Now, tell me about this necklace of Golden Hearts," but before she gets a response their cups of hot coffee arrive, each with a stroopwafel on top.

Saarika takes a bite, then says, "I want to learn to bake buns like these."

"You cook?"

"Oh yeah. When I was sent to Huaxia I was not allowed servants or cooks. It was daunting, at first, learning to cook and to clean," she sniffs a slight laugh, then finishes, "to care for myself."

"I spent a lot of time in the kitchen when I was growing up, but was never allowed to do anything. My uncle has been teaching me to cook, but it is all new to me. I want a big kitchen." Unsure of how to broach the subject that has brought them together, but wanting to have it done, she sighs before saying, "About losing the necklace; I wish there was something more that I could have done, or --" she stops when Saarika holds up a hand halting her.

"Please, hear me when I tell you that everything is okay. I have learned to practice the art of stepping back," she reaches her hands out in front of her, "looking at the bigger picture," she widens her arms, " and broadening my perspective." Then pointing a finger at herself, "I like to believe that there is not anything wrong." Now tapping that finger just below her collarbone, "And, I especially like believing that everything is working out."

"Everything is working out," surprised to hear someone else saying what she always likes to say. "That is what I tell people."

"Hmmmmmm," patting a rhythm with her hand at her heart, "I have been noticing other things we have in common."

"La, everybody has a lot in common with everybody else." They both laugh, then Trinjntje asks, "So, the loss of the heirloom will not stop us from being friends?"

"The loss of the heirloom is what has acquainted us so that we can be friends. We will see where this adventure takes us."

Finishing their coffee and buns and thinking of her appointment Trinjntje says, "I better get going. You are welcome to come along."

Saarika agrees to accompany her for the meeting with the estate agent. Walking toward the address on the Weerdsingel, Trinjntje tells her new friend, "I am hoping that this place will not be too big. It is a row house three stories high. It has a yard at the back with a garden wall and a glassed-in growing room."

"A glass growing room? Is that for the winter? How cold does it get here? I am used to warm weather."

When they arrive at the address the estate agent is seated upon the bench outside the home's front doorway. He stands to greet them. He is slimmer than most men his age, and dressed smartly in a grey suit sporting trousers; the latest trend. Before unlocking and allowing them inside he tells them how pleasant it has been sitting here watching all there is to see passing by. He is talkative and points out what is special about this particular home. The main floor has a spacious front room joined to the dining area through an elaborate archway. The kitchen is open and well equipped with counters, cupboards, and drawers. He directs them up the steps to the bedrooms that have built in closets. The third floor has no dividing walls. The long open area has sunlight streaming through the windows of the gables at both ends. Back down the stairs and out through the other door he proudly displays the walled yard and the greenhouse. At a small patio table he lays out the papers he has brought with him to be signed if his potential clients be so inclined. Trinjntje loves the home, but she is caught up trying to remember all she has ever heard her father say about contracts. She ponders overly long. Ending the extended silence, Saarika tells Trinjntje, using a voice loud enough for the man to overhear, "I would like to ask you a question." The leasing agent, catching the hint, suddenly remembers something that requires his attention, and walks off leaving them some privacy.

Once he is out of hearing range Trinjntje whispers, "I have never signed a contract before."

"That answers my question. Do you mind if I read it?"

"Oh, please do. Tell me what you think."

Saarika leans over the table reading what is there, "It looks pretty straightforward, and is not overly binding." Reading some more she comments, "I do not know property values around here, but for this amount, where I have been living, one could live in a palace."

"I did talk with a man at the bank yesterday. He told me the price is fair for this location, and that I have ample funds available to cover the lease."

"Well done. I have another question."

"Well, if you are thinking of staying in Utrecht there is ample room for both of us."

"Okay, that answers that. There is space for more than one signature on this contract. We could share the expense."

The property agent gives them notice by whistling a tune as he comes back up the walk. Trinjntje tells him, "We have decided that we would like to live here. Can we have both of our names on the lease?"

"Oh yes," he responds while dipping the quill, "there are two copies. Each of you sign both copies; then I take one and you keep the other." Trinjntje and Saarika each sign, and each write drafts covering the deposit and first month's rent. He leaves them with a key and another of his cards. When he is gone they look at each other and say, "We need to go shopping."

"Yes, we need to stock our kitchen."

"Where will we begin?" Trinjntje laughs, "This will be fun."

"We need furniture."

"Oh Boy! I just recently helped my uncle move all of his furniture into his new home, so I have some ideas of what I want."

"It is always good to know what you want."

♡♡♡

After climbing up into the cap of Windmidden to see the inner workings of gears and now back on the ground Renaldo asks Diedrik, "Were you serious when you were telling us that you would put us to work scything the flax?"

Diedrik chuckles while answering, "La, no. There is a harvesting crew that travels through the region. They will spend a few days here scything and baling the flax stalks. Then a barge comes along and all the bales of flax are hauled away downriver for processing."

"So the smelly procedure of retting the stalks is not done here?"

Laughing again, "Oh no. Donar likes the Flax, it is easy to grow, and what he earns from the baled flax covers what he pays the harvesting crew. It works out for everybody, without the commotion or the odor."

"Ah well," sighing with mock relief, "that answers one question. We are also wondering," pointing toward the lean-to shed that abuts Windmidden, "what is the machinery inside that shed?"

"It is an invention of my own for making paper. If you like I will show you." As they walk into the shed Diedrik tells him, "Most paper is made from discarded rags: recycled linen." Now waving an arm out toward the fields of tall blue-flowered flax, "Linen is made from flax. Right? Well, Donar challenged me to devise a way of making my own paper directly from the flax." Now inside, "I experimented making paper by hand before coming up with the design for this machinery."

Renaldo, pointing at a long wooden pole coming through the wall asks, "So this shaft is turned by the windmill to drive the gears of your paper making machinery?"

"Yes. I modeled this set-up after my father's re-sawing mill," pointing at a pair of horizontal iron cylinders, "these rollers crush the flax stalks and," pointing to huge pot, "the ground stalks get stirred in this big pot with water and potatoes." Diedrik picks up a wooden mallet, "Donar commissioned a foundry that makes bells to cast this pot," striking the big kettle with his mallet. The entire shed reverberates with the tremendous tone.

When the noise at last dies away Renaldo asks, "Did you say that you make paper with potatoes?"

"Yep, they work like glue to make it hard and shiny." Renaldo follows him out to a series of long open sheds. Diedrik shows him frames that are covered with woven screens. "Donar commissioned a jewelers guild to make the brass wire, and then weave these screens. We lay them down flat and ladle the slurry on top, then squilge the water out and hang 'em to dry."

"Ah, so that is why these sheds have no walls."

"Yep, for a good flow of air. The drying takes a day or two, depending on the weather."

"Will you carry on with this paper making?"

"Indeed I will. I go through a lot of paper."

♡♡♡

Trinjntje and Saarika have been going out each day shopping for all the necessary items to fill their home. Covering the floors with rugs, filling the rooms with furniture, cramming new shelves with new books, spreading blankets and pillows on the new beds and in the window seats, and setting lanterns everywhere for the evenings after the new curtains have been drawn. The kitchen shelves and cupboards are filled with dishes and cookware. Trinjntje has brought home an illustrated cookbook and is determined to master the art of cooking. They have discovered the nearest markets and have filled their larder shelves. Their bedrooms are on the second floor, and the uppermost story is completely open with windows at each end. The sunlight through these windows brightens the open space. They each come up here for their acrobatics or dance practice.

There is the bench outside the front door where they like to sit and watch the canal traffic while greeting whosoever passes by on foot. They also enjoy sitting at the table at the back in the privacy of the walled garden. Flowers line the backyard walkway; pansies, impatiens, and lobelia. Today they are in the greenhouse, having filled a bunch of trays with seed. A little black cat, with white paws and a white breast, walks up the back walk and in through the open door of the greenhouse where the two are finishing up. *Meow.*

"Hello Kitty."

It meows, again while rubbing against their ankles.

Saarika bends down and picks up the little guy calling him, "Mo Nee," pronouncing the second part as a high pitched chirp. She chose this kitten because it is so like a cat that she had before, and has given it the same name.

Finished in the greenhouse, they move to the patio. They unfold the clever little chairs and seat themselves at the outdoor table. These past few days, since moving in, have been a flurry of activity. It is a relief to sit here doing nothing. They enjoy a few moments of quiet before Trinjntje says, "Tell me please, if you will, of the necklace."

Saarika looks up from the kitten, "I suppose that it is only natural that you wish to know." The kitten's contented purring fills the space between them. "My mother's line was the ruling family of our nation. The palace where my parents live was built by her ancestors. Deep beneath the palace is a hidden sanctum. My mother and I were the only two with knowledge of this ancient shrine; or so we believed. The walls of the shrine are adorned with murals telling the ancient legends of winged Celestials bestowing gifts. Two of those gifts remained hidden away there. One of those is the necklace of golden Hearts." She sighs deeply. "When I was young my mother took me into the shrine often. I was assigned to be the guardian of the shrine with the understanding that these marvelous gifts would pass on to be mine." She hears a bird's warbling. Looking up she sees a small yellow bird with dark stripes on its wings. It tips its head, ruffles its feathers, and then warbles some more. "During the time that I was away the secret of the shrine somehow became known, and the necklace removed."

"You mentioned that the Celestials had bestowed two gifts."

"Yes." More of the goldfinches have gathered. The kitten has noticed and is staring up into the tree. "The other is a crown."

Saarika seems to be focused only on the noisy birds in the tree, saying no more of the underground temple or its contents. So Trinjntje tells of a specialist that had traveled on board with them. "He was on a mission to catalogue the species of the Far East. He had taught himself to imitate animal and bird calls. Nicklas and I were able to convince him to teach us some of those calls." She attempts to answer the warble of the yellow birds. They fly away, moving to the arched entry of the garden wall, warbling some more. "Oh, I hope that I have not scared them away. I wish that Nicklas were here; he is always better at this." She tries warbling again. In response one of the birds tweets an extended tirade; during which the garden gate opens and Nicklas walks through from the back alleyway. "Oh Nicklas!" She runs to greet him, "I was just thinking of you."

"Oh, really. It sounded more like you were arguing with the birds." The yellow birds shriek, trill, and twitter as they fly off. "I tried at the front door, but there was no response, so I came around back; and here you are."

She leads him up the walk to the little patio. Saarika and Nicklas exchange greetings, and she explains to him, "I happened to be with Trinjntje on the day she came looking at this place. It is big enough that we decided to both live here."

"Splendid."

"What have you been up to? You are back sooner than we expected."

"I made it to Antwerpen only to discover that my parents are now in Rotterdam. The VOC has assigned my father a post at a currently active port." He looks around the yard while telling them, "So, I traveled to Rotterdam and found them living happily in renewed prosperity. We visited, or rather, I was a captive audience while they told me of my brothers, and of all the wonderfully delightfully enchanting grandchildren." He rolls his eyes. "My accomplishments did not interest them much. My father expects that I will now settle down. My Mother expects that I will now marry; in fact, she made a list of available prospects." He shows an expression of feigned rancor. Trinjntje holds a hand over her mouth to suppress a giggle. "What," he asks, "is so funny?"

She laughs out loud, then changes to an affected sternness, "Perhaps young man, you should be finding yourself a suitable mate."

He looks back crossly, ready to defend himself, and then waves her off with a laugh. "La. Life here seems to suit you. Now, are you going to show me your home? Are you going to offer me something to drink? Any of the socialites my mother would have me marry would have taken care of these pleasantries long ago." He folds his arms across his chest, and looking up at the sky while tapping his toe, releases a deeply offended sigh.

Both Trinjntje and Saarika grab an arm and drag him inside. "Allow us good Sir, to present to you our humble abode; but first, a drink."

While Trinjntje is filling a tankard for him, Saarika gives him her kitten, "Meet the newest addition to our household."

He takes the kitty, rubs behind its ears and under its chin. It is purring. Trinjntje taps his shoulder, and holding out his beer says, “Let us trade.” He takes the mug. She takes the kitty.

Saarika, still wondering at the relationship between these two, asks, “Will you be staying here? In Utrecht?”

I have a room at the Kikker Gat for now,” he sips his beer and smiles his approval. “I stayed up late last night visiting with the professors. When I mentioned that I would be seeing you today, Professor Calderon asked me to relay an invitation for you to meet him at the library this afternoon; says that he has some things that he would like for you to see.”

“He did mention that he intended to dig through his archive of manuscripts and antiquities,” Saarika says, “Hinting that he may have information regarding other Golden Hearts. What time is he expecting us?”

Watching as Trinjntje extracts the cat from her shoulder and hands it over to her friend. It snuggles its nose into the folds of her sleeve. “He told me that he would like us to visit him after the hour of three.” The volume of the cat’s purr increases noticeably now that it is back in Saarika’s embrace.

♡♡♡

Three wagons, adorned all alike with the name of a theatre troupe, stop at Schoonhoven Landing mistakenly thinking that they have reached their destination. The driver of the first wagon calls out to the dock where Diedrik, Renaldo, Razs and Vejz are, asking where to park their wagons for the Market Faire. Two youngsters hop out of the third wagon and immediately began performing cartwheels and back flips. Diedrik calls back, “Keep following this road up the river. You will see a sign directing you to the town of Schoonhoven.” The two acrobats stop, positioned with feet apart and fists at hips.

It is fairly late in the afternoon. The driver asks, “Will we make it there before dark?”

"Not likely." Seeing the man's chagrin, "There is a wide spot not too far ahead that is often used by travelers. You cannot miss it." The man thanks him and signals to his horses to get the wagon moving again. A voice from within the third wagon calls the two disappointed youths back inside.

The Market Faire is two days away. Diedrik, Renaldo, Razs, and Vejz are catching fish out of the river with a plan to have enough smoked salmon fillets to take with them to trade. When the wagons of the theatre troupe are gone they pull in their net and toss the large red fish into a wheelbarrow.

"This is so cool," Razs says, "we have never fished with a net before."

"These fish are so big," Vejz shouts as he picks up another with both hands.

"This is the third barrow-full," Renaldo grabs the handles and starts wheeling it away.

"Yep, we nearly have enough to fill the smoker," Diedrik tells them. He has been taking smoked salmon fillets to Market Faires for a few summers now, but he has never had this much help before.

Mara has taught Annia, Kirin, and Audrae how to clean and fillet the fish. They are soaking the fillets in a salty brine, then tossing them into the wagon to be taken to the smokehouse.

Renaldo wheels the full barrow up as Annia takes the last fish from the other. As he trades barrows he remarks, "Did you see those acrobats?"

"They were kids."

"I could do as well as they did," boasts Audrae.

"Not in your dress," Annia stops her, "maybe we can all show off our acrobatic skills later, after we have cleaned up."

"We all?" Mara asks, "You are all acrobats? I have seen the four kids doing cartwheels and performing flips; have even seen them tossing each other to flip higher. Are you telling me that Ma and Pa are acrobats too?"

Annia smiles and nods, "Yes, it is fun."

Renaldo wheels the empty barrow away. He sees Diedrik rowing away from the dock dropping the net as he goes. Behind him he hears Kirin begin telling Mara how they had become acrobats, "We had a tutor from Greece; a woman. She was brought in to teach us doctoring, but she was also a dancer."

"Doctoring?" Mara asks surprised, "Is one of you a doctor?"

"We all learned doctoring," says Audrae.

"But not all took the exams," Kirin gives her sister a look.

Annia picks up from there, "This woman tutor, the doctoring instructor and dancer, practiced every day. I admired how strong and flexible she was, so I asked her to teach me her training."

Kirin picks up the thread of the story, "So when Ma started doing handstands and cartwheels I started learning and practicing too."

"I was just little," says Audrae, "but it looked fun, so I went along with Ma and Kirin."

Annia says, "The boys did not like being outdone by their sisters, so the instructor's husband, who was also a dancer, began teaching the training regimen to them. Ren did not want to be left out, so we all learned to be acrobats."

The sun is setting when the smokehouse chimneys are opened and the brine-soaked fillets are draped over the rails. Diedrik had started the fire earlier, so there is a fine bed of coals where he sets a blackened pan filled with hickory chips. He closes the doors on the firebox and then looks up," and everyone else looks up with him, as the heavier smoke begins wafting out the top of the chimney. "We will have to tend the fire through the night: not good to let it go out."

"We can help," Razs tells him.

"Yeah," chimes in Vejz.

Diedrik also has a fire in the stove of his outdoor kitchen and grills a couple salmon they have saved for dinner. They enjoy some fresh peas out of Mara's garden with their fish. They have a dessert of raspberries in cream. They are too full to show off their acrobatic skills, so they sit out under the stars and let the fire burn low. "There's a falling star. Did ya see it?"

"Yes." They all answer. There has been quite a number of falling stars tonight.

"There are so many falling stars," Annia says as they all watch the sky.

"It seems like there have been more recently than ever," remarks a sleepy Renaldo.

"I know. You are right. Sitting down by the river at night," Mara tells them, "I have been seeing way more falling stars than usual."

"We have been sleeping up on the stage of Windweg," Razs tells them, "and we have been wondering why there are so many shooting stars; we must have seen fifty last night."

"Will sailors," Audrae asks with sly grin, "who depend on the stars, lose their way if all the stars fall out of the sky?"

"Acchh! Do not be saying such a thing!" Mara chides her while laughing, "Besides, twould not be so. The stars that they steer by are not the falling kind, they will stay where they are forever."

Renaldo stands up, offers a hand to Annia, who also stands, "So if you fellows will be taking care of the smoker fires all night, then we will be off --" he is interrupted as a gigantic blazing sphere streaks across the sky, leaving a fiery trail behind. "Whoa! That was not any ordinary falling star! That was way bigger!"

"Way bigger indeed!" Diedrik shouts, "Whoo!"

"That was huge!" Kirin says, "Whoo-hoo!"

"That was enormous!" marvels Vejz.

"It was a fireball!" raves Audrae.

"Spectabulous!" Mara says without realizing what she is saying.

"Mysteriously huge," muses Annia.

"It looks like it hit the earth," Razs says all excited, "and now there is a big fire."

The spot on the horizon, where the fireball has dropped, is now glowing orange. "Remember Ivan, the Russian tutor, telling us about a crater left by a rock that fell out of the sky?" Vejz reminds his siblings, "He called it a meteoroid."

"Oh yeah, I remember that story," His brother adds, "and the boulder was still there; had a shrine built over it."

"That was only one of his stories," their father adds, "He also claimed that the black stone of Mecca had fallen from the sky."

"Ivan! Yeh. That was his name. I remember him sitting in the garden for, like, **ever** without moving," Audrae laughs, "the birds would perch on his shoulders, or his head!"

"La, his hair and beard," Kirin adds, "looked as if he had let the birds build their nests in there." She laughs and everyone laughs imagining birds nesting in a man's hair.

The glow from where the fireball went down can still be seen, but continues fading, until it is there no more. "It was a long ways off," Renaldo guesses, "Maybe an hundred miles." It is once again their familiar night sky so the Gedimins are off to bed.

Mara remains sitting with Diedrik beneath that starry sky. Diedrik is wondering how he will be able to make a painting of the fireball sweeping across the sky. Mara breaks the silence, "Will you be making a painting of the meteoroid, or whatever it was that we saw?"

He laughs, "I was wondering about that. I have never painted anything that big." He stretches his arms wide, "maybe I could paint it on the side of the barn."

"I have heard Robert describe a landscape, or seascape, or skyscape by saying that there is not a paper large enough to capture a view like this. He paints so he can share the incredible places that he sees."

"That's why I paint. I like to share those moments that make me happy."

"Moments. You and Robert will want to see each other's paintings. He says that he sketches to catch a moment."

"Yeah, it seems like I have to sketch a whole bunch of moments to be able to put them all together as a painting of one moment. I wonder if your Robert will return home with a sketch of the moment a giant fireball flashed across the sky."

The Lullaby

Captain Derek rises from his hammock, while everyone else sleeps, for his nightly inspection. It is one of the Captain's duties that he actually enjoys performing. It is dark here in his cabin, although not totally dark: the light from the stars and the reflection of the starlight off the surface of the water filters in through his windows. He pulls on his boots, buckles the belt that holds his sabre, and then tucks his loaded firearm into that same wide belt. Wrapping his cloak over it all and pulling on his skull cap he is nearly out the door when he decides to have a little nip of brandy. Drinking directly from the bottle is ungentlemanly, so he pours some into his tin cup: just a nip looks so small there at the bottom, better pour in a bit more. There is a lantern that he will carry with him, but most nights it remains shuttered.

He first stops at the helm, greeting the lad stationed there, and then sending the young ensign off to the loo. Out of habit he checks the traverse board, though there are no changes as the ship is anchored, awaiting entry to Rotterdam's harbor. Standing at the wheel surveying the ship, he scans the many passengers sleeping on deck, preferring the open air to the claustrophobically crowded group area below deck. He sees the flash of another shooting star, it seems that recently there have been more than usual. Many of these passengers, already fearful, consider this deluge of falling stars to be an omen. The young ensign returns from his break and resumes his position at the wheel.

Captain Derek remains, only because it is unseemly for a captain to rush off; better to hang around for a chat. The young fellow comments, "Rather ominous, Sir, the number of falling stars--," the night sky flashes bright. A fiery orange flame lights up the entire sky, so that everybody who is awake sees a burning sphere streak across from horizon to horizon. The area where it has disappeared is glowing, as if scorched. "My God! Didja see that Cap'n Sir? It was a ball a' fire!"

"Like nothing I have ever before seen!" Those sleeping on deck begin stirring. Derek pronounces, "They will all be saying that this is an omen."

"An omen, Sir?" the young ensign, raised superstitiously says, "I hope it is a good omen, Sir."

"Good? Bad? Some consider every little thing as an omen." More of those on the deck below them are whispering. The captain dismisses himself from the quarterdeck and walks down amongst the passengers bedded there on the main deck. A mother is rocking a child in her arms and whispering soothing words in a language that he does not understand. A couple of gents share from a bottle to fortify themselves. For a moment Captain Derek actually commiserates with these folks who are so tired from inactivity and dread. The ship has been in queue awaiting entry to the port of Rotterdam for two days. Hopefully it will be assigned a berth tomorrow. If all goes well many of these passengers will disembark.

"Captain?" From the other side of the deck, "A word?"

Derek looks to where the voice is coming from and sees a blanketed figure raising an arm. He makes his way over and bending down close answers, "Yes."

"Begging your pardon, Sir," Derek straightens up upon recognizing the disgraced VOC clerk that had treated him so poorly, "That was a monumental flash. Was it not?"

"Indeed, like a ball a' fire," repeating the young helmsman's turn of phrase.

"Do you not wonder what it is?"

"Will probably never know."

"I have been meaning to ask you about the information that you originally came to me for."

"Oh? Really?"

Not to be put off, Greely DeVoss asks, "Does the ship that you are hoping to find fly the flag of the Netherlands?"

Why have this discussion now? Derek wonders, "Aye. The flag scribed with the trademark symbol of the VOC," inserting a jibe, "leading one to wonder if the company leads the nation. Who rules your land?"

"Spoken like a Brit," Greely sneers before continues, "If the flag is not stolen, and the ship is indeed registered with the VOC, then it will be on file." He remembers years of tedious copying in order for every VOC office to have every one of over twenty thousand ships registered and on file. "You will be able to go into the Company's office at the Port of Rotterdam and they will allow you, beings that you are a ship's Captain, access to their records."

"This is interesting news," Derek says while recalling the dismissal he had received from the VOC in Amsterdam, "So, you are telling me that I will be able to walk in and go through any of the records?"

Greely is surprised at the boorishness of this idiot, but deems it advantageous to remain civil, "There will be certain formalities and nominal fees. If you have a valid complaint regarding the captain of the ship that you seek then someone there will have the duty of assisting you."

The complaint being a piratical act against a ship of the Royal Navy might not be deemed worthy," Captain Derek seems to remember that the Dutch and the English are currently at war over the rights of who controls the Sleeve;

or the Channel as they call it. “Maybe I will have you point out the right person to pay this nominal fee that you mentioned. It may be worth another try.” Then changing the subject, he asks, “Will you be disembarking in Rotterdam?”

“Hah!” Greely scoffs, “I doubt if that will be allowed. I will have to stay on board at least until we reach Calais.” As Captain Derek turns on his heel DeVoss stops him again, “Are you aware Captain, that many more of these passengers would have been allowed off this ship in Amsterdam but for their inability to cover the exorbitant bribes demanded by the port authority’s officials?”

“Is this the voice of experience? Is this how your Company does business in every port?”

“Just saying.”

“Hmm, we shall see what the morrow brings.” He delivers a mock salute as he moves back to his inspection wondering what crime this clerk has committed that has sentenced him to exile.

Greely DeVoss, watching Derek walk away, wonders similarly what act this captain has committed that has sentenced him to the loss of his Captaincy in the Royal Navy.

♡♡♡

Robert is dreaming that he is in his bed at home. He reaches out to Mara, but she is not there. This awakens him to the realization that he is in his hammock aboard the Tulip. The calm stillness bears out the fact that his ship is anchored in the passage that leads into Rotterdam harbor. He is queued for mooring access sometime early tomorrow, and hopefully his business will be finished by midday. Some of the crews of the other ships queued and anchored here around him have been allowed to row to shore for a night of merriment. A few of those sailors can be heard now as they raucously make their way back before ships’ curfews are enforced. Robert rises and checks his anchor lines. The rowdy bunch of sailors are unsteadily climbing the ladder from their rowboat while maintaining the ongoing verses of a ridiculous drinking song. It is a cheerful noise. Another shooting star slices across the sky, followed by three more in quick succession. It is not yet the season for the yearly meteoroid shower.

Deciding on a late night snack, he fills a tankard, breaks off some hardbread, and sits down at the tiller bench. He leans back comfortably and looks up, watching for what is sure to be more falling stars. He loves the familiar night sky full of the constellations that so instantly let him know where he is situated. Before he gets too comfortable he decides that he would like a pickle. As he rises from his seat the sky suddenly glows brighter as a massive glare of fire streams overhead. He watches it disappear over the dark horizon followed by an uproar of voices from the ships surrounding him. There remains a glow on the earth where the flaming orb had made landfall. He imagines that it could not be more than a hundred miles away. He stands dumbfounded for a bit before remembering what he was after. He gets his pickle from the barrel. Biting into its tart bitterness is a puckish pleasure that he calms with a quaff from his mug. The gunwales of the neighboring ships are lined with sailors; their voices echoing mystification and superstition. The glow on the horizon does not immediately fade. Robert decides that this is a once in a lifetime occurrence, and so refills his mug, and settles back down to enjoy this thrill. He falls asleep contemplating how he will sketch and paint a vision of what he has seen this night.

He is awakened by a knock-knock-knock on the hull of his ship. "Captain Robert, are you going to sleep your day away?" Knock. Knock. Knock. Robert rises from his seat at the tiller where he had drifted asleep while watching falling stars and wondering if there would be another meteroid. He walks over to the gunwale where an old friend and business partner awaits in a small boat alongside, "There you are Rob! Halloo. What have you brought for me?"

Robert asks, hoping for some breakfast, "What have you brought for me?" The man in the boat hands up a basket filled with a fresh loaf of bread, a bowl of strawberries, and a jar of milk. "Ah, splendid freshness. It is a pleasure to see you my friend. Did you see the fireball last night?"

"The fireball. The fireball. That is all that anyone is talking about this morning. Sadly, I was already in my bed when the sky lit up. You saw it then?"

Chewing on a bite of soft bread, "Aye, I did. Twas a spectacular sight. I fell asleep watching the glow on the horizon where it landed." He points toward the spot, then asks, "Have you any idea when I will be allowed a mooring?"

"By my count you will be tying your lines to the wharf before midday. I can have a wagon and a couple men awaiting … that is, if you have any cargo for me."

"I have your usual allotment of cold-brewed lager."

Rubbing his hands together greedily, "That is what I was hoping to hear. Brewed from clear mountain spring water. You have kept the casks lashed tight have ya? Not let 'em roll around your hold?"

"Rest assured, they have been lashed tight, and it has been a calm sea for sailing. No shaking of the contents for your patrons."

"Well then, my good Sir, I shall see you on shore later this day."

"*Tot ziens*," waving as his friend rows away, "Thanks for the bonnie breakfast." He has been delivering Norwegian beer to this tavern owner for many years. Having the wagon and men ready for him will allow him to quickly carry off his other transactions, and be out of port early. Life is good.

♡♡♡

Hendrik's upper floor lecture hall overlooks the University's greensward. Looking out the window he sees the sundial below and compares it with the sands remaining in the hourglass he had turned when he began this lecture. He is wrapping up this talk pertaining to the brain and its latticework of nerves, lymph, and fascia by sneaking in a statement reflecting his philosophical proclivities, "This infinite web within the human body that so magnificently processes the insurmountable quantity of sensory input, does not reach conclusions, but merely weighs probabilities." Through the window he sees, walking across the lawn, three faces that he recognizes; Trinjntje, Nicklas, and the princess Saarika. He remembers that Calderon has invited them to a presentation of his research. There is very little sand left in the hourglass. The shadow of the sundial is nearly aligned with the mark of the hour. He strolls to the table that serves as his podium and lays the notes he is holding into his folder, closes it, and pronounces, "Perfecta sunt," *we are complete* Then races out the door, on his way to the library before any of these students has the opportunity to delay him.

This University's library is a scholar's cathedral. Learned men from all of Europe, and beyond, gather here to peruse what Calderon's astute archival objectives have brought together. The architecture itself; the arched pillars, domed ceilings, walls of paned windows, and especially the spectacular stacks themselves, provide an overall homage for the seeker of knowledge. As Hendrik passes through the high vaulted entrance he sees Calderon leading his guests into the library's workroom. A moment later, Hendrik opens that door, sticks his head through, and begs of Calderon, "May I join you?" After receiving an affirmative nod he enters, closes the door quietly behind him, and walks to where all have gathered. For his friend's benefit he performs the gesture of turning a key in the lock of his lips, and then tossing the imaginary key over his shoulder.

The workroom tables have all been pushed from the center of the room leaving a large open space. Calderon unrolls a collection of what appear to be grist bags unsewn to lie flat. As he lays them out on the floor it becomes evident that they are rubbings from what must be a massive stone mural. "I am laying out my original rubbings of this scene, from the floor of the inner sanctum of a Toltec pyramid, so you may be apprised of its size." He continues laying out the sheets side by side, row after row, filling up the entire center area of the room. "As you may well know the pyramids of New Spain are larger than anything built here, and rival the architectural genius of our modern day stonemasons." As the pattern unfolds before their eyes he adds a very interesting bit of information, "I chose to duplicate this image for posterity, because this floor was crafted entirely of gold." He pauses, allowing everybody to visualize the splendor. "The generals and the bishops had the golden plates of this floor ripped up, melted down, and cast into ingots." There is a grim countenance to his tone. As he finishes laying out the last of the sheets bearing the charcoal rubbings it becomes apparent that the central image is bordered with an intricate knot-work pattern. The image at the center is, at first, not as evident.

Saarika recognizes the obscure image, even though the faded charcoal impression is smeared. Calderon hands her a page that has a composite graph of all the rubbings. On it he has outlined the image of a goddess seated at the great harp. She tells him, "It matches the tiled image adorning the underground sanctuary hidden beneath my mother's ancestral palace." Her expression is unintelligible as she asks, "How many sites are there like this in the world?"

Nicklas remembers something she had told him, “Does this resemble the image you found in the Huaxian archives?”

“It does.” She points out, “Here at the top of the harp is the crown encircling the orb. The celestial harpist looks to be wearing a necklace of Golden Hearts.” She waves her hand around the pattern that encircles it all, “The pattern of this outline looks to be an array of connected necklaces, like the one that has been stolen. I was taught that three necklaces are required to form this pattern.” In the unsteady silence Nicklas quickly slides a chair under where she is absentmindedly seating herself.

As Calderon walks back around the room to his work table he tells them, “I have more to show you.”

“Okay,” Saarika tells him, “show us, please.”

Standing at the table, with his back to his guests, speaking quietly, “During my term of duty, in New Spain, I spoke unfavorably too often regarding what I saw as the destruction of an entire culture. Consequently, I was charged with treason and ordered to return home for trial. The Spanish bishops could not agree upon a verdict, so delivered me to Rome; in shackles.” This is a seldom told story. Hendrik has heard it once before and never expected to hear it again. “I stood before a tribunal of cardinals for the consideration of my transgressions. They ultimately sentenced me, rather than excommunication or death, to serve as archivist of the catacombs.” Again, there is silence, allowing all present to ponder the consequences of this sentencing.

Calderon turns and addressing them as a lecturer would a room of historical scholars, “The Roman Empire sent armies of soldiers to conquer, then followed those soldiers with another army; an army of monks, to maintain order amongst the conquered masses. The soldiers’ duty was to bring home the riches of the conquered nations. The monks’ duty was to convince the conquered peoples to comply." He continues, "The wealth of the conquered nations, sent back by the armies of soldiers, was stored in ever larger treasure vaults. The cultural relics of the conquered nations, sent back by the armies of monks, came to the storage vaults of the catacombs, and were left sitting there undocumented for ages. My job was to fill pages with descriptions and rudimentary illustrations before shelving everything away. In my five years underground there were thousands of items cataloged and subsequently dismissed once more."

He begins picking up the sheets of rubbings, carefully stacking, then rolling and tying them again. Speaking, as he works, he continues with the presentation of his method. "My sentence lasted five years. On the day that my term ended I left the catacombs with a few articles, which I had chosen not to catalog, hidden within my robes." He withdraws, from a leathern satchel, a rolled bit of papyrus, something cut off a longer scroll, "here is one of those items," then after unrolling it for all to see tells them, "The scroll that this illustration is cut from was among the articles of tribute coming out of the mountains of the Mughal Empire." All done in gold leaf, it is the radiant image of a male celestial seated at a harp. The mast of his harp is adorned with a crown of golden leaves encircling a golden orb. The strings of his harp appear to quiver as if they have only now been strummed. Bordering the image is an intricate latticework design of hearts, intermingled with the caricatured outlines of frolicking dragons. "I am certain that you all see the similarities in these two artifacts coming from two separate cultures residing on opposite sides of our planet." He places the page on his table next to his rendering from the rubbings. They all gather closer as he points directly at the harp in the center. "There was a harp in another crate from that same tribute that exactly resembles the harp in this illustration. I did not catalog this harp, but I was not able to carry it out with me either. I taught myself to play this instrument and it provided much solace for me in the darkness." Bowing his head he finishes in a softer, reverent tone, "There are qualities of that harp that I am at a loss for words to describe." He spreads his fingers wide and swipes his hand in a circle above the picture. "And now ... I have discovered another harp that I believe is a match." He turns around and says to Saarika, "I invite you to come with me to present what I have found to the keeper of this harp."

"Are you thinking that there is a connection," she asks, "with this harp that you have found and my lost necklace?"

"The evidence that I have presented would support such a theory."

♡♡♡

Diedrik wakes up with rays of sunlight already spreading across the floor. The aroma of hickory smoke reminds him of the smokers filled with salmon filets. Tossing back the sheet, he jumps from his bed, hoping that the fires have not burned too low. Out the door he notices right away that someone else is tending to the fires. He arrives as Kirin straightens up, closes the doors, and brushes off her hands. He greets her, "Good morning."

"Oh, hi. I hope you do not mind my interfering. I watched you do this yesterday, and since I did not see you up and around yet this morning I thought that maybe I should take a look, and well, the fires did have coals left, but had burned low, so I added some more chunks of wood. Maybe you will be wanting to check my work to be sure I have stoked the fires properly." She turns and quickly re-opens the firebox doors that she had just closed.

As Diedrik peers in their shoulders touch setting off something unfamiliar within. He tells her, "You have done it perfectly. Fantastic!" He steps back so that she may close up the smoker again, "Thanks for taking care of this. I slept later than usual."

"Did you stay up late?"

"I did."

There is an awkward moment as Diedrik is wondering what makes Kirin different from her sister. Audrae is so, well, funny and frisky, while Kirin is so, geez, what is it about her? She is turning to go, but he does not want her to go so he says, "I will be brewing some coffee. Would you care to join me?"

"Okay." She smiles. Her eyes sparkle. "You may need to brew a large pot: the others will likely be along soon." Walking back to his house a group of hoopoo birds swoop in and carry on with their delightful antics. "There they are again. Oop oop. Oop oop."

Diedrik gets a fire started, fills the kettle, and is grinding his roasted beans when he notices that Kirin is shuffling through his papers spread out on the table. He wonders what she is thinking.

"Oh, Diedrik, I love these!" She continues riffling through the pages until she comes upon a picture of a kestrel that he has been considering tossing away. "Oh! This is sooo awesome! It looks like the kestrel that we see so often across the way."

"Really? You think so?" He walks over to take another look at what he has determined to be discarded. "See here, where the colors have run. I was actually going to toss it into the fire."

"No!" She hugs it to her breast. "May I have it? Pleeeese?"

"It is a practice. I will be doing it again. I will get it right."

She is looking at the painting astonished by how he has captured the little hunter as it is landing on a branch. "You are crazy. This is perfect. All it needs is a frame." He takes it from her, interested to see if he sees it now as she sees it. She moves close and points to the way he has filled in the underside of the outspread wings.

"La, isn't this cozy! What are you looking at?" They look up to see Audrae peering in through the open window.

Kirin tells her sister, "Come in here. You have got to see Diedrik's new paintings. And, he is brewing coffee." As Audrae disappears from the window Kirin pokes Diedrik playfully in the ribs while stepping away to leave a bit of space between them, "Cozy," she says with a coy smile.

Diedrik opens the door and Audrae rushes in. The two sisters pass his sketches back and forth; oohing and ahhing until he can hardly stand it anymore. "Kirin gets the kestrel. Is there one for me?" She is holding a rendering of a red-winged merel perched atop a plume of grass. Another that he has planned to discard. "I like this."

"The patch of red does not pop out bold enough."

The girls share a perplexed look. Then in unison pronounce, "You are crazy. This is perfect." Audrae finishes with, "It is ready to fly from the page."

Diedrik stands flustered by the overt admiration his paintings are receiving. "I suppose that I can let you have them."

"Yeeesss!" They both exclaim, then ask, "Is our coffee ready?"

♡♡♡

Everybody helps Calderon put his workroom back in order, then leave him on his own. They all agree to meet later at a trendy new public house. Hendrik returns to his own office. Saarika begs off, hoping for some time alone. Nicklas and Trinjntje seat themselves upon a bench near the sundial. The tolling of the hour indicates the ending of another session of lectures. Doors fly open. Young scholars rush out. Nicklas ponders the futility of higher education and whether he really wants to return to school. Trinjntje wonders at the hurried pace, and reconsiders Anna Maria's invitation to attend lectures here. After a few minutes the walkways have cleared again. They sit in silence except for the breeze wafting through the leaves of the trees.

"I have always been amazed by the way some people know so well what they want to do with their lives. I have never been certain of anything in particular." His legs stretch out before him with his boots crossed, one over the other, at the ankles. "What about you?"

"La, I do not know if I will ever do any one thing for the rest of my life." She is quiet for a moment before asking, "What do you make of Calderon?"

"What do I make of the man, or what do I make of his presentation?"

"Either way."

"Lesser men would have been broken by what he has been through." He glances over and meets her gaze, "What he has shown us is intriguing."

"Saarika has mentioned that thing about three necklaces forming a pattern, and has hinted that the loss of her necklace may be the harbinger of the three eventually coming together. Calderon seems to think something akin to what she says."

"Yes, and I do not get the impression that he is a sensationalist. His research is for the sole purpose of expanding his knowledge." Remembering the recent news he asks, "Do you suppose that the Golden Hearts are related in any way to the meteoroid?"

She looks at him in amazement, "Funny that you should ask. I was wondering the same thing, although I do not understand how that could be."

"I know. Right? It must be just coincidental."

"Coincidental that we are thinking along similar lines, or coincidental that a meteoroid has landed as we are learning of a possibly unique occurrence?"

"Yes." He laughs, "I mean, both," then laughs some more.

♡♡♡

Diedrik and the rest of the folks living at Schoonhoven Landing have a few days of excitement planned. They are currently making their way to the market faire in two wagons filled with smoked salmon fillets. Mara and Diedrik ride in the first cart with Renaldo and Annia following in the second, and the four youngsters are taking turns sitting at the back of either wagon with their bare feet hanging loose. This first market faire has them all excited with the prospect of shopping and making new friends. Diedrik has told them that in previous years the smoked salmon has traded quickly, leaving the afternoon and evening open. Mara asks again about their plans for the next few days, "So, you are quite certain that we will be this one night at the fair, and then returning home tomorrow?" He nods, "and then if the Gedimins find no satisfactory horses at this faire you will be leaving early the day after, with Ren, Razs, and Vejz for Utrecht to buy horses." He nods again. She thinks that he is being quieter than usual, "And you know of respectable horse traders, right?" Before he answers Audrae and Vejz, hop off the back of the wagon running to investigate something that has caught their attention. Razs and Kirin, who have been riding on the other wagon jump off to follow their brother and sister. Seeing Diedrik watch them all running off Mara scoots over on the bench, giving him a shove, while taking the reins from his hands, "Run along with the others. I will keep this horse moving."

"Okay." He catches up to the others standing on the trodden path at the river's edge watching a family of ducks swimming away.

"Ohhh..." Says Audrae, then slapping Vejz standing next to her, "You have scared them."

"Not me," giving her a playful shove, "you are the noisy one."

Diedrik catches up, "Hey guys."

Razs has counted the string of ducklings following their mother, "There are fourteen little ones."

"Do they always have that many?" Kirin asks Diedrik.

"Not always," he smiles as a couple more adults swoop in to keep the ducklings in line, "but they usually have about a dozen."

Vejz says, "I wish I could swim like a duck," remembering Shakespeare's character in *The Tempest,* "Trinculo escaped swearing that he swum like a duck."

Diedrik tells them, "There was a fellow that came visiting with Donar's family one time that claimed to be Shakespeare's nephew; he was always spouting lines," laughing, "problem was, he was not much of an actor."

They all turn and race to catch up with the wagons; hopping on and riding for a while until they see a large nest in the branches of an ancient willow and all tear across the marshy expanse for a closer look.

They are all seated back in the wagons when they arrive where the market fair is setting up in a wide meadow. Many have traveled to bring goods for trade. There are rows of booths filling with artisans and crafters. Diedrik shows them that since they are early enough they can back their wagons into the circle that is forming around the booths. Outside the market area is an open space with a stage. A juggler is there entertaining a gathered group of children with her talent. Diedrik is welcomed by old acquaintances who are eager to get some of his famous smoked salmon, and to catch up on what he has been up to. Condolences are expressed at the news of Donar's passing, followed by congratulations at the news of who he has appointed as his heir.

The juggler is followed by a singing duo; a young man with a guitar accompanying a young woman with a clear strong voice. The children around the stage are joined by their older brothers and sisters interested in hearing new songs and meeting new friends. Renaldo and Annia shoo their children away to enjoy the company of others their age. Mara, with a shove, shoos Diedrik after them. The young duo on the stage are joined by someone with a drum, then someone else with another guitar, and a flutist. By evening there is a crowd of musicians onstage, and the area closest to the music is full of dancing and singing. It is a steady back and forth from the stage to the wagons as the younger folk grab a bite to eat and tell of news they have heard and friends that they are meeting. Vejz tells his parents, on one trip back to the wagon, "Everyone is talking about the Meteoroid."

Razs strides up to the wagons, and while layering bread, cheese, tomato slices, and ham announces, "We must bring our instruments next time. We could be up there on stage." Then he takes off again.

Later in the night, when the noise has settled down, most are in their blankets, while a few remain sitting up visiting. Diedrik, laying under his wagon, would like to fall asleep, but there is a crying infant nearby. He wonders how many around him are awake. Mara and Annia are still up and visiting quietly. The baby squalls an extra-long fit of crying. The baby's young mother is attempting to hush the child, but sounds like she is also crying. "This poor child has been fussing for most of the day," muses Annia.

"The child's mother needs a break so that she can settle herself," adds Mara, "are you thinking what I am?"

"That we should talk with the mother," Annia agrees, "to see if she will let us have the child so they both can get some rest?"

"You could sing that lullaby that you sing. About the fern flower."

"The song of Solstice Eve?"

Singing what little she remembers, "When the fern flower flames like the fire in our heart."

"Kupala's Night."

"Yes. Let us go talk to that baby's mother, and you can tell me again of Kupala."

"Kupala is the Goddess of the bath. She is the Spirit of Water." Their voices fade as they walk away.

"Kupala is the Love Goddess," Razs tells Diedrik. Speaking quietly he continues, "On Kupala's Night everyone wears a wreath ... Well, mostly it is girls that wear wreathes. It is the custom that whosoever is asked will answer yes to be a mate for the night."

Diedrik asks in a whisper, "When you say mate, do you mean to lay together?"

Kirin answers, also whispering, "Yes. But only after one is old enough that their parents allow them to go out on Kupala's Night."

They are quiet again when they hear Mara and Annia returning with the squalling baby. "Oh great," moans Audrae. It is a sentiment shared by all of them laying there awake.

As they near the wagon Mara tells Annia, "I will fetch some cream." Annia is rocking the child when Mara returns, "Here you go little darlin', something sweet for ya." The baby quiets, "Ah, ye're a greedy one then, turn loose and I will give ye a bit more now." It is a blessed silence, although there is still the noises of the night, and the soft murmuring of voices across the encampment. "Now Annia, sing your lullaby. Sing this wee child to sleep. Ah, but here is the child's mother. Are ye settled down sweetheart? Come here and sit beside us. Listen while this lullaby soothes our souls."

Annia hums a bit, then coos a bit, then is silent for a bit before singing the first verse.

"On Solstice Eve it is known that we are not meant to be alone," she hums a metre in the same tempo before singing a second line of verse, "Through the forest, with wreath in her hair, strolls a fair damsel to Kupala's Mere." Again, she hums an interlude before singing the chorus, "The fern flower glimmers. The fern flower flares. The fern flower shows us our heart is afire."

Previously, after hearing Annia sing this song at the end of an evening, Diedrik had asked her sons about the fern flower. Vejz had told him, "It refers to a bygone era when some plants and trees had blooms of fire, or sparkings; some even smoldered with an enticing smoke."

Razs had added, "Legend has it that the fern flower still blooms one night of the year; Kupala's Eve. The blooming flames light up pathways through the forest."

Annia is singing the second verse, "On Solstice Eve it is fated that all who seek will be mated," she coos again, matching the lilt of the other lines, "Two young lovers, wearing wreaths on their heads, follow lighted paths through the night." She repeats the chorus the same as before, then continues on with the next verse, "On Solstice Eve it is customary to bathe in Nature's Sanctuary. Ooooo ... These two lovers, for legend's sake, wade hand in hand into the lake." Many who have been listening are already asleep as Annia sings the chorus again. "The fern flower glimmers. The fern flower flares. The fern flower shows us our heart is afire. The fern fire stirs our hearts' golden flare."

Diedrik is roused from his sleepiness imagining that he has heard her singing about golden hearts. Mara, cuddling the babe and its mother, grows attentive at this reference, eager to hear what follows.

"On Solstice Eve legend holds that a wreath of branches becomes gold. Ooooo ... In the sparkling light, the wreath that she wore transformed as betold." Annia sings the chorus again, "The fern flower glimmers. The fern flower flares. The fern flower shows us our heart is afire. The fern fire stirs our hearts' golden flare. Our golden hearts' flare," repeating it on and on until everyone is asleep, "Our golden hearts flare. Our golden hearts. Our golden hearts."

Diedrik dreams of wearing a wreath of Golden Hearts upon his head with the ethereal floating heart hovering above. He feels his own heart becoming warmer, becoming a radiant heat, until he is dreaming that his heart is aflame, and that it is a gentle soothing fire.

Mara has confirmed that what she thought she had remembered hearing is so. Now, she wonders how she will breach the topic with Annia, and when.

♡♡♡

The information that Calderon had presented that afternoon had only been a small part of the discussion around the table where they had all met for dinner. Saarika and Trinjntje walking home afterward, are each pre-occupied in personal thought, while appreciating the comfortable silence between them. It is a pleasant evening along the canal, the commerce of the day is past, families are at home together, and cooking aromas hang in the air. Saarika is wondering about what all Calderon has shown them, and is intrigued by his relative silence through dinner. She is further intrigued regarding this woman that he has recently met; this woman with the harp whom, he reckons, may also have a necklace of Golden Hearts. It is bemusing to think that she may at last meet another necklace holder while her own is missing. She still believes that her necklace will show up, and is filled with anticipation of when that shall be. She also wonders why she continues to keep her crown a secret, surely she could tell Calderon; or Trinjntje.

Upon arriving home, and after lighting lanterns, there is no sign of the kitty. Saarika takes a lantern up the stairs calling out, "Mo Nee. Mo Nee." Upon entering her room she finds books knocked off shelves, vases tipped over, and there on her bed, where her pillow should be is Mo Nee. The kitty is curled up, asleep, inside the circle of her golden crown.

Trinjntje, having followed Saarika, gasps at the majestic opulence of the crown, "Oh Saarika: that is the crown of a queen, your token of royalty!"

"Trinjntje. This crown is not a symbol of my royal status. This crown goes with the necklace of Golden Hearts. This crown and the necklace are of another realm; a realm of immeasurable dimension." She shrugs and smiles mischievously, "A realm that sort of blends with our familiar realm. This crown was gifted to my ancestors along with the necklace, and I am beginning to think that after all these ages the harp that this crown is meant for has been discovered. We're going to be witnesses to a miracle." She picks up the sleeping kitten; it wakes only enough to purr. With her other hand she picks up the crown and hands it to Trinjntje.

Taking it gently and carefully, awed by the magnificence; diamonds are sprinkled like dew amidst a circle of golden leaves. She asks, "Is this the crown that sits atop the harp in Calderon's drawings?"

"I believe so. I have been taught that there is an orb meant to sit within this crown atop the celestial harp. My necklace of Golden Hearts is one of three necklaces that are to be joined. Each necklace has a token; this crown accompanies my necklace, the orb accompanies another, and the harp must be with the third."

"Oh, then when your necklace shows up, and if this harp that Calderon has found is what he thinks it to be, then there will be another necklace? Oh! Maybe the woman with the harp already knows where the third necklace and the orb are!"

"That is an exciting prospect." These secrets, that Saarika has imagined to be the edicts of ages past, are difficult to share, and yet also freeing something loose within her. She holds the kitten up and rubs her nose to its nose asking, "Did you dream remarkable dreams my little friend?" Then to Trinjntje, "The gift from this crown is dreaming. Perhaps dreaming is the gateway into the other realm. Or ... perhaps the three necklaces form a gateway between the realms."

Trinjntje is feeling a tingling through her fingers from holding the crown. For some crazy reason she puts the crown on her head. Everything is the same, except she is dreaming. It is a familiar dream. It is so like being awake, but there is no narration going on in her mind, and time is inconsequential. She has a distinct knowing that everything is okay.

Saarika knows what is happening, "You are dreaming a nice dream. Right?"

"I am," Trinjntje removes the crown and hands it back, "I better not wear it too long, or I will not let it go."

Saarika makes no move to accept the crown from Trinjntje. "It will let you go."

Trinjntje places the crown back on her head, and knows she is dreaming. Something occurs that reminds her of Uncle Cornelius, and then she is walking through the door of his home. There he stands at his table filled with astronomical data. He has set up an observatory and is keeping daily charts of the positions of the planets and their moons. He keeps records of the night sky. He has tracked the trajectory of this most recent meteoroid and is calculating where it has landed.

He has Trinjntje look through his telescope set on Jupiter and its' many moons. Then she is in space. She is looking at the giant planet from one of its circling moons. She looks back at the sun; smaller now that she is farther away. She turns outward again with a desire to know how far it all goes. She realizes that the cosmos is vast and wishes to see more. A cosmic wind picks her up and carries her along; toward infinity.

♡♡♡

Everybody had arrived home from the market fair with all sorts of goodies: clothes, kitchen utensils, dishes, candles, and books. There had been good music, acrobatics, and the theatre troupe. They are all excited to go to the next market fair in a couple weeks. A postal rider had been awaiting their return, bringing separate posts for Diedrik and Mara from Professor Calderon. Mara finished reading first, and then had told everybody, "The professors that visited a while back are coming to visit again; the day after tomorrow." Then bemusedly, "Paulo Calderon expresses the notion that I may be able to help him with some of his research. La, what research could that be?"

Diedrik then told them what had been in his post, "He is begging a place for six, possibly seven, people to sleep the night after next." Knowing how eager the Gedimins are to have their new horses he tells Renaldo, "I think that will still allow us enough time to visit the horse traders that I have in mind and still make it back for Professor Calderon's visit." The postal rider had been hired to deliver these posts, and then to bring back the replies. Diedrik signaled for the man to follow, "Come with me and have a pint and a bite to eat while I write my reply."

Renaldo had caught up with him and asked, "Are you certain about not changing our plans?"

"Indeed, I am. In my return post I will tell Calderon that we have prior plans, but that we intend to be back here late on the same day that they will be arriving. I will let him know that if they arrive before us to make themselves at home. They will be sleeping in Windmidden, or on the lawn, or in the barn with their horses. I must get my note written and not keep this rider waiting." It is pleasing to think of a crowd of guests at Schoonhoven Landing again. Donar's spirit will be overjoyed. The postal rider was sent off with replies to Calderon from both Mara and Diedrik welcoming him and his friends.

The next day has Renaldo, Razs, Vejz and Diedrik on the road to Utrecht early, intending to bring home some light horses. It is a pleasant morning that has them appreciating everything as they ride along. They are glad that there is such a clear sky today. They like how the sun warms the ground and how the cooler air blowing in from the sea is making its way up the river. As they ride past some tall wildflowers they are pleased again, to see hummingbirds amongst the blooms buzzing about like bees. One whirrs past Vejz so close that he flinches, bringing out a laugh, "That was close!"

Diedrik is playing his counting game in his thoughts, but instead of counting birds he is counting all that he appreciates. He is glad to be riding today with Ren, Razs, and Vejz. He is delighted that all the arrangements that they have made have not been altered because of the guests arriving tomorrow. On their return they hope to be leading these heavy horses they are riding behind newly purchased light horses. Diedrik smiles at the memory of his first impression of the Gedimins with their travel wagon. He had wondered if they were a family of full-time wanderers. Diedrik appreciates wandering. He likes pretending that he is a wanderer. It is a favorite sensation of his, to be moving steadily along while everything changes. He enjoys pretending that nature moves past him, instead of him moving through nature.

The first horse lot they stop at, midway to Utrecht, is very ostentatious. The White barns are new and larger than other horse barns. The pastures are vast. The straight fences are kept remarkably white. There are many wonderful horses here; including many Arabians. A salesman, wearing a very modern suit of clothes, rides out offering assistance, "This is your lucky day, you have come to the right spot, we have what you are looking for, and if we don't have it, we can get it." Looking up and down at the four horses these prospective customers have ridden in on, he says in a confidential tone, "I fear that I will not be able to offer much for the horses that you are riding."

Renaldo holds up his hand stopping the man, "We are not trading today. We are looking buy three, maybe more, light horses for riding; not farm work, or pulling wagons. We already have fine horses for doing the chores." He points toward the herd of Arabians and tells the man, "I like the looks of those."

"Well, I tell you what, we have the original documents of registry for every one of those beautiful horses." He stops talking to let that information sink in, leading Diedrik to think that he is placing a high value on his stock.

They have the man cut out a stallion and a couple of mares. Renaldo is considering starting his own herd if he finds the right horses. He bargains with the man with little satisfaction, the prices remain high. He tells him, "We will keep looking. Perhaps we will be back tomorrow."

The next horse lot is on the outskirts of Utrecht, and there are many people looking to buy here. Walking along the fences scouting for horses that suit them, and noticing that there are two haggard-looking men showing horses to lackluster buyers, has Razs, thinking out loud, "It'll be midnight before either of those guys will have a chance to talk to us." Everyone looks at him. He stretches out his arms in an exaggerated shrug and asks them all, "Well?" They all laugh. "How about we get something to eat?"

Later, having arrived at the Kikker Gat, and after settling their horses in the barn, they are sitting at a table in the dining room with pints of beer, munching from a plate of thin potato slices that have been fried to a crisp. Professor Calderon comes through the front door and immediately walks over to their table, "Diedrik. Hello my good man. How is it with you? I received your post, it is good to see you." They shake hands, and Diedrik re-introduces the professor to the Gedimins. Hendrik and Lu-Tang arrive shortly thereafter and two tables are pushed together for family style dining.

After dinner, while Renaldo shows Calderon a list of books, Hendrik scoots his chair over closer to where Diedrik sits and asks, "Do you remember the Bi-noculars that I carried with me on our last expedition?"

"Your field glasses? Right?"

"Indeed." Now, raising his eyebrows and squeezing his cheeks in an impish smile he says secretively, "After discovering that the craftsmen who had put together that pair are now producing a more powerful pair of scopes I had to have them. And now that I do, let me tell you, they are sooo much better than the others!"

Diedrik remembers the clarity presented before his eyes when he had looked through Hendrik's field glasses. "I cannot imagine what can be better, but I suppose that the applied science continues to improve."

"Being the artist of nature that you are," Anna Maria must have told Hendrik of Diedrik's hobby, "you will be able to bring your subject closer."

Diedrik is thinking that there may be enough time in the morning to stop at the scientific instruments shop that sells these paired scopes. He could ride home with his own binoculars.

Revelation

As a wee child Mara had envied the boys for the trousers they wore. Asking her Ma for a pair of her own, "Shush!" Her Ma had scolded, "Ye'll wear a gown like a proper lass." When she was old enough to ride a horse she again envied the boys as they hopped on and off so easily. When she complained about her bare legs being rubbed by the horse's hair, "Throw a blanket over the horse's rump when you take it for a romp," chortled her Ma, who did not ride herself. In a rebellious moment Mara purloined a pair of her brother's sturdy woolen pants. After cinching the waist and rolling the length into cuffs at the ankles she wore them for her daily ride. At the sight of her daughter wearing trousers her Ma expressed astonishment, "What are ye wearing? Ye will not be leaving this house dressed like a boy!"

"I call these my rompers," she told her Ma, "I will wear them whenever I go for a romp on my horse." Out the door she went, a'riding her horse to go. Since that defiant adolescent moment she has sewn many pairs of rompers from a womanly-shaped pattern of her own design.

Annia, Kirin, and Audrae, wanting their own rompers, had chosen a bolt of cloth while attending the market faire: enough for each of them to have a pair. Using Mara's pattern, each allowing for their own individual sizes, they have cut the pieces and now are busy sewing. Renaldo, Razs, Vejz, and Diedrik have left early this morning for a couple of days, intending to return home with horses for them all to ride. So, it is the anticipation of their new horses that has them sitting here in Mara's front room busily sewing away.

When a bird's chirping is heard, Kirin tells them, "That is the call of the *roodborstje*."

"*Roodborstje*," Mara imitates the pronunciation, "That is a robin-red-breast."

When another bird twitters away with a variety of different sounds Kirin tells them, "I think that is a *boerenzwaluw*."

"*Boerenzwaluw*," Mara repeats, "Aye, a barn-swallow will make all sorts of sounds." They are all learning from Diedrik.

Annia finishes up a seam and folds the material, "This is heavy cloth. My fingers are stiff from pushing the needle. I am going to take a break." She puts it all away in her sewing basket. "I shall walk home and get dinner started." To the girls she says, "Do not be much longer," and to Mara, "You are welcome to share our meal."

"I would like that. Thank you," laying her own sewing aside, "I will see to my chores, and then be down. I will bring a bottle of wine." When they are gone and Mara steps out the door on her way to the barn, she looks up to the moon that has been out all afternoon, determining that it will set in the middle of the night. She keeps track of how long Robert has been away by checking on the moon. This voyage has lasted nearly as long as he had predicted, and so she is expecting him home any day; perhaps tomorrow. She is always excited to have him return, especially excited to hear if he has followed the map found in the drawer left by the fleeing monks. She takes care of her chores in the barn; these simple everyday tasks that she appreciates so much. As she exits the barn she pauses in the dappled shade of the wavering leaves. Her heart is full as she looks out across this land, her new home; so peaceful, so serene. Her thoughts turn again to Annia's lullaby, with its mention of golden hearts. She has been wondering about the possibility of another necklace and wanting to ask Annia. They have been together all day and yet she has not figured out how to broach the subject. She promises herself that she will ask Annia this night, after dinner, about the Golden Hearts mentioned at the end of the final chorus of the lullaby.

She walks the length of the polder, from her home near the river's bank, down the gentle slope past the middle windmill, to the far end: Windweg. The three mills stand in a row, aligned with the prevailing wind; the wind-way. As she nears the Gedimins' home she is, as always, taken by the eccentricity of the architecture. The house had begun very similar to the house she lives in, but has been regularly added on to, so that there is a sprawling mass of roofs, and a variety of architectural styles. It possesses a distinct charm far from its original design. It is a scene that she loves walking into: the house set near the shore of the lake, with the windmill standing tall, and the windblown waves in the grass. Annia is cooking dinner at the outdoor stove while Kirin and Audrae set plates and silverware on the patio table. "Tis a pleasant evening to eat outside," she says setting the wine she has brought with her on the table.

Annia, looking over, laughs, "La, you said a bottle of wine, but that is a jug," then she tells her daughters, "Pour us each a glass please. This," referring to what she is cooking, "is almost ready."

Through the meal Kirin and Audrae talk of Diedrik, "He has given us brushes and ink and challenged us to sketch."

"He has stacks of paper, and says to use as much as we want."

When they are all finished eating and the dishes taken away the girls bring out their sketches for Mara to see. Audrae, despondently, shows her work, "Diedrik says that it does not matter how it looks at first; to keep practicing. Hmh! I am not seeing any improvement."

"Robert says the same thing. He keeps practicing until he gets it." Holding up the sketch for appraisal Mara is impressed, "Audrae, I like this. I think it is very good. Robert will want to see these. He will often sketch something many times over before ever being satisfied."

Kirin asks, "What sort of things does he like to sketch?"

"La, he sees extraordinary things as he wanders the sea and likes to sketch the most remarkable sights, and then paint them for me hoping that I will be as amazed as he by what he sees. His paintings are of seaside villages, creatures of the sea, and the mountainous crags of the fjords. He paints the giant storm swells, and then the smooth waters of quiet coves. He has made a number of sketches of two ships a' war blasting their cannons at one another, and is attempting to paint the scene in full color." Thinking of the map he planned to follow into the hills above Vik, "Occasionally, he is able to leave his ship anchored, and he will walk, or hike, inland. He has climbed many mountains, and followed many rivers. I like his paintings of nature. He used to bring home pictures of the cities, but no matter what city, they all look the same."

"Are his paintings true to life?"

"Oh, yes. He has trained his talent with steady practice."

"I wish I had more talent."

"Everyone has talent," Mara tells her, "at least, that is what Robert tells me. He believes that everyone has talent, and that everyone is an artist. And, he says everything we do, everything anyone does, is an artistic expression."

"Oh, I like that!" chimes in Annia.

"I am particularly interested in the sketches he will be bringing home with him from this trip."

"Why is that? Has he gone somewhere he has not been before?"

"Well, on the day that we sailed from Éire, some monks that were also losing their home, their friary, left us with an assortment of artifacts: maps, paintings, books. Old things, very old. Ancestral. Robert has made copies of those maps, and hopes to follow them to a mountaintop tower."

"How very interesting," Annia says, than asks, "Is there something particular he is hoping to find there?"

"Oh, well, perhaps some family history. Maybe something old, something like that old lullaby you sing; the one that you like to finish the night with; the song you sang while holding that young girl's baby the other night."

Surprised by what seems a sudden change in the subject of the conversation, Annia says, "I learned that ancestral lullaby from my mother."

"Before hearing your song I had never heard of Kupala. Do you worship Kupala?"

It is a moment before Annia answers, "Our ancestors worshipped many Gods and Goddesses, as did all the clans of the mountains." She sips her wine, looks up at the rafters, then back across the table to Mara, "We have been taught that even the Romans worshipped a court of eternal beings before they became worshippers of the One."

"I learned the songs and lessons of my ancestors," offers Mara, "who also worshipped many Gods and Goddesses; that is, until as you say, the Romans brought their doctrine of the One."

"Did your mother ..." Audrae asks with bright eyes and a quirky smile, "teach you what her mother's mother and her mothers' mothers' mother taught her?" She is giggling even before she is done asking her silly question.

Giggling back, Mara answers while nodding emphatically, "La. Yes. She did." She pours wine into her glass. "My Ma sang songs of Brigid. But, back to your lullaby," she breathes deep, gathering her wits, "In the later chorus of your Kupala lullaby there is mention of Golden Hearts. One of the ancestral paintings that I mentioned is of a Goddess wearing a necklace of Golden Hearts. Do the tales taught to you by your mother tell of these Golden Hearts? And what of them?"

Annia and her daughters exchange glances. The concept, her mother had taught her, was to introduce the idea of the Golden Hearts by singing the lullaby at gatherings so that anyone familiar with them would be enticed to step forward. Could this be happening now? "The tales match the lullaby; that Kupala replaced the young woman's wreath of evergreen branches with a necklace of Golden Hearts, and bequeathed the young man a golden orb. It is said that this necklace has a jewel set in each heart, and that the orb of gold transforms into a clear blue crystalline ball." She pauses, unsure of how much she wants to divulge. "Legend tells that when three of these necklaces of golden hearts are connected something amazing will occur."

The silence lasts for longer than a moment. When at last Mara speaks she is looking directly into Annia's eyes, "Likewise," her voice is very deep and very quiet, compelling the others to lean in closer, "I learned a similar tale: that our Brigid gifted a necklace of Golden Hearts to a favored lass. Furthermore, the lass received, as a wedding gift, a golden harp crafted by the *Tuatha Dé Danann.*" She scans the faces of the others, making eye contact with each of them, "I have dreamed the same as your legend, that there are three such necklaces, identical in nature, and that a day will come when the three of them will be joined in a circle."

"Are there many on your isle who dream of these Golden Hearts?" Annia asks, "Or who even know of them?"

Mara has the strange sensation that she is remembering this moment as it happens, "On the isle of Éire the legend of the Golden Hearts is known only among those who pass the necklace down from generation to generation," nodding her head, and seeing the comprehension in the others' eyes, "I know the legend because I have inherited a necklace of Golden Hearts, and also the harp, though it is not of gold." She waits.

Annia, staring back into the depths of Mara's eyes, wants to speak, but as in dreaming, cannot find her voice. She breathes deeply until something loosens and her voice returns; then she is able to tell Mara, "I have also inherited a necklace of Golden Hearts."

Both women have been taught to imagine this moment. Both women realize spontaneously that they each know one another's thoughts. A sudden wind gusts through the patio, lifting the tablecloth and rattling the plates. Everyone reaches quickly to keep wine glasses from tipping over. The wind is gone as suddenly as it had arrived; and now they raise their glasses saluting the moment.

♡♡♡

After days queued for entrance into the port of Rotterdam the announcement that there is available mooring at last arrives. Captain Derek sails into his ship's allotted berth immediately greeted by a complement of VOC clerks, backed up by a squadron of VOC soldiers. The deck has filled with passengers hoping to disembark. It is an anxious crowd. The gangway is opened. A loading ramp is settled into position. The chief envoy of the VOC delegation comes on board and tells Captain Derek, "We have advance notice of your ship's arrival, and so we are aware of the nature of your passengers," handing over an official document, a list of names, "you will note that only those with family here or previous business relations will be allowed ashore." A translator, among the exiled, reports what has been declared to all his fellow passengers, causing an immediate uproar from the crowd. The clerk stomps his foot, "Captain! Quiet this rabble!" The soldiers move closer.

Captain Derek casts the translator a flinty look. The man turns, shouts, and waves his arms attempting to silence the concerned mob. When the uproar settles to a murmur the Captain hands over the list to the translator who calls out the names of those to be allowed ashore. There are only a few, leading the crowd to become riotous again. As the chief envoy turns to go the Captain checks him, "Sir. Please. What does your company require for more of these people to disembark?"

"These people ..." he begins, and the rabble stills a bit, "... Outcasts from their own countries, will not be allowed to disembark. We will not grant rabble-rousers or criminals access to our city." His words are translated; setting off a greater uproar than before. The clerk straightens up defiantly. The soldiers behind him unsheathe their swords. "Captain Derek! Silence this mob!"

"You Imbecile. You expect me to silence them after the vilifying words you have spoken of them?"

"As Captain, it is your duty!" The noise of the agitated crowd increases in volume.

"Bloody Hell." In a fit, Derek draws the firearm from his waistband and fires it into the air. In the moment of quiet that follows he surreptitiously hands the man a purse of guldens. He begins telling the man loud enough for the translator to hear, "You have a mistaken evaluation of these people," as his words are translated the crowd quiets down a bit, "these are good people. They do not, any one of them, fit your mistaken description. I beg of you to reconsider." The noise behind him raises as soon as he stops, so before it can crescendo again he rushes on, "I am certain that your company will stand to profit if overland transport can be arranged."

The clerk scowls while wondering if anyone had seen the purse handed him, and if he will have to share this bribe. If there is a profit to be made then it is his duty to make it happen. He glances behind him at the soldiers, then facing the crowd he raises an arm for quiet. "I can think of one possibility: a canal barge. I am making no promises." He gives Captain Derek an indecipherable expression, then turns, and down the ramp he goes.

"Well done Cap'n Sir," says the first mate, slapping Derek on the shoulder, "I'ud never've thought ya had it in ya."

Captain Derek is not sure if this is praise or just another insult, but is relieved. He tells the man, "I am leaving you in charge for a while." Down the ramp he goes, thinking that since DeVoss' suggestion of a bribe had worked, he may as well follow up on the man's other suggestion for obtaining information regarding the Tulip and her captain.

At the VOC office he waits in line for an available clerk. Behind a counter lined with clerks, there are more clerks; a brigade of clerks, seated at desks, busily scribing away. When he gets his turn Derek states his business, "I seek the whereabouts of a single masted sloop that flies your nation's flag; a ship called the Tulip."

"Are you the Captain of the English ship that is overloaded with passengers?"

"I am."

With a snide expression the clerk asks, "Are you imagining that the Captain of the Tulip will agree to transport some of your cargo?"

Checking his anger, Derek explains, "I have been informed that your office keeps records of all ships flying your company's flag."

As the clerk shuffles through a basket of papers he tells the Captain, "We will not have to dig into our records." Now holding up the sheet he had been looking for, "The Captain of the Tulip was in this office less than an hour ago to pay his docking fees." Now waving the sheet of paper tantalizingly, "But, we are not allowed to share this information." He is toying with the Captain. Snickering. English folk receive little respect in this part of the world.

Captain Derek is irked by this man's disrespect, but his excitement is greater, "What must I pay to acquire this information?"

The man laughs, "I can hardly charge you for information you can glean for yourself. The Tulip is currently moored here. If you take a stroll down the wharfside you will find the ship you seek." Turning his attention out to the waiting line, "Next."

Derek follows the clerk's advice and walks along the wharf that is lined with hawkers. He passes offers for a pint, offers for a smoke, and offers for a bowl of stew. When he comes within sight of the Tulip he admires her sleek lines. He cannot help but appreciate the life of this Captain/Merchant that dares the sea alone. Getting closer he sees the man that he plans to take into custody rolling barrels of beer tenderly across planks slung from his ship's gunwales to a parked wagon. There are two other men helping him. They seem to be laughing and having fun. Derek walks on, each step bringing him closer to the Tulip. It becomes clear that the captain of the Tulip is enjoying the company of these two young men helping him with the barrels of beer.

Robert, between one barrel and the next notices the man walking up the dock toward him, concluding by the man's cocked hat, tails, and saber, that he is a ship's captain. There is something familiar about this captain; and then, though he had only seen the man through a scope, he remembers who it is.

Captain Derek stops at the wagon. Robert and the two men helping him, after tipping up another barrel, straightens up, and brushes off his hands, then smiling to the captain standing there says, "Good day to you Sir." Neither captain salutes the other.

Without a word of introduction, "Are you the captain of this ship?" The Englishman asks.

This brings a smile to Robert's face. He raises his eyebrows and grins at the two young fellas in the wagon with him. Turning back to the Brit, and feigning a solemn air, he answers, "Yes. I am."

"I am hereby taking you into custody for the sinking of the Naval Frigate HMS Cooper."

Robert asks incredulously, "Ha! You are arresting me?"

"Yes. I am," pulling a sheaf of papers from within his cloak, "You are hereby under arrest."

The two young men are looking at Robert with wondering eyes. He smiles and pats his palm downward in a settling gesture letting them know that there is nothing to worry about. He looks back to the Englishman asking, "By what authority do you arrest me?

The Irishman has him there; being no longer an officer of the Royal Navy. Yet if he can bring this scoundrel to an English court then he will satisfy the penalty charged against him. "I represent the justice of the Royal Navy. Do you deny the charges?"

Telling the tale for the sake of these two lads here in the wagon with him, "I have to admit that a while back, I was followed by a pesky vessel that had attempted twice to cut off my route." Thinking back on the incident, "I was forced, for my own safety, and that of my beloved who by happenstance was sailing with me, to take evasive action."

Again, he shares a playful grin with the two young men. "But ... Who would ever think that a vessel this size," sweeping his arm to indicate his ship, "could sink a frigate of the Royal Navy?"

They are all sharing a good laugh, except of course, Captain Derek who has drawn the flintlock from his waistband, "You will come with me!"

"Wait. Wait, wait, wait, wait," says one of the young fellows in the wagon to Captain Derek, "Are you the captain of the ship of outcasts that has arrived in port this day?"

"Downcasts, not outcasts."

"Whatever," he slaps his partner on the back, then asks further, "and is that the gun that fired a shot earlier."

Throwing his chest out proudly, "Yes."

"Well ... it looks to me Sir, like maybe you forgot to reload it." He and his buddy snort and laugh.

Derek looks at his firearm sideways, "Bloody Hell!" He shoves it back in his waistband, and then directly grabs the hilt of his sabre, but before he has it fully unsheathed he notices a dramatic change in the countenance of these two young men, who are no longer laughing. He slams the sabre back into its scabbard, he curses himself for this ill-thought plan, "Damn me!" Turning on his heel he makes his way around the wagon and back up the pier. In frustration he stops, turns, and shakes a fist." Which brings on another bout of laughter from the two young men, who are looking forward to telling this tale many times for the benefit of their drinking cronies awaiting them back at the pub.

After finishing with the kegs of beer, and then when the rest of his business in the harbor is complete Robert slips the Tulip from her mooring. When he is out away from the dock he looks back with his scope. Espying the English passenger vessel he focuses in to see a milling crowd on the deck, and people being herded down the gangway and gathering in a crowd on the wharf, surrounded by soldiers. He shifts his scope to the helm where the captain stands in position. A big sloppy-looking oaf bumps the captain, then shoves him out of the way. It does not appear that the captain gives the oaf any sort of reprimand, and this gives pause to wonder at such a humiliating fate. "Hmmmm," ponders Robert, "does he have no respect for himself?" *Tis a sad fate indeed to deem oneself unworthy.*

He shifts and re-sets his sail, now picking up speed. When he takes a last look the English Captain has his spyglass pointed this direction. Robert raises his own scope for a closer look, and for a moment they stare across the water at each spying the other. Captain Derek lowers his scope, removes his cocked hat with a flourish and performs an extravagant bow: concession, or admiration? So, Robert returns a smart salute to the Englishman, while wondering if they will ever meet again.

♡♡♡

Annia's marveling at Mara's revelation is a feeling like no other. She is blissfully enchanted. Has she experienced this moment before? Looking into her daughters' eyes she has the impression that they are thinking the same thoughts that she is thinking, that they have intuited a familiarity with Mara since first meeting her. As if awakening Annia jumps up, "I will get my necklace," hurrying inside, "I will be right back."

"Did you know this would happen?" Audrae asks Mara as soon as her mother leaves.

"I was almost certain. What about you?"

The two sisters look at each other, then Kirin answers hesitantly, "I may have dreamed this happening."

Audrae raises her eyebrows, "It feels like I might be dreaming now." Their laughter breaks the tension.

Amidst the laughter Annia returns, carrying her chest, "Let us walk up to your place so we can compare the two." As they begin their walk she asks, "Mara?"

"Mm hmmm."

"There is another item that accompanies the necklace," indicating the box she is carrying.

"Eh? Is it the orb that you mentioned in your legend of Kupala?"

"It is. I believe it may be intended to fit atop your harp."

"You may be right. Hmmm, when we get to the house I will show you the old painting of the angel at the harp."

They walk in silence beneath the multi-hued sky of the sunset. Their attention is drawn upward at the approach of a siege of cranes. The huge flock flies in from the river and the magnificent birds land in the field of tall flax, until there is an unnatural congregation of the majestic birds settling in for the night.

"Wow. They are beautiful!" Kirin whispers, "Would that Diedrik were here to sketch this scene."

"We can sketch them," Audrae says, drawing with her toe in the soft dirt of the wagon path, "here is the curve of the neck, then the wing, and there are the legs." It is a simple three-line drawing that cannot be mistaken for any other bird. Kirin joins in, and they move ahead up the path drawing crane after crane in the soft earth of the wagon path, laughing at each other's struggle to maintain balance. Annia and Mara watch them hopping along and giggling. Audrae calls ahead asking, "Having Cranes coming for a visit is good luck: Right Ma?

"La, tis so."

Then their attention is drawn by the noisy squawking from a passel of stellar jays perched upon the rail of Windmidden's stage. These large jay birds are a deep shade of blue, nearly indigo in the light of the setting sun. Their crests rise and fall as they call out, squawking intermittently back and forth amongst themselves. "These noisy jays," Mara tells Audrae, "are also a sign of good luck."

"They are as big as ravens," Kirin adds. "I remember Grandma telling us that birds bring messages from heaven." They laugh some more, and wonder what sort of message these graceful cranes and these raucous blue jays may have brought with them.

They arrive at Mara's and once inside she tells them, "Have a seat," while she retrieves her heirloom from the drawer of her wardrobe.

Looking around this house and the framed paintings adorning the walls, Annia is reminded of Mara's mate, "Will Robert be home soon?"

Setting the carved wooden box that holds her necklace on the table she answers, "I've a feeling that he'll be home tomorrow, and I cannot wait to tell him of this." As she places her hands to lift the box's lid Annia does the same with her's. The opened boxes reveal velveteen pouches of similar color; deep rich purple. The girls gather closer, looking back and forth in amazement as their mother and Mara each loosen the drawstrings and withdraw their precious necklaces. It is immediately evident, as the two are laid side by side that they are perfectly, unmistakably, remarkably identical. A gust blows through an open window across the room and out another. A billowing curtain brushes the strings of the great harp and for a moment the room is filled with the presence of all who, before them, have cherished these Golden Hearts. Another gust. Another brush across the harp strings and the four of them are jolted awake, although they have not been asleep. Each quivers now with goose bumps.

Annia withdraws the golden saucer and places it on the table, and then sets the golden orb within. The familiar glow radiates as the globe clears and becomes crystalline. She spreads her necklace around it and invites Mara to do the same. Mara moves the other necklace around the orb, and then rushes to bring out the ancient portrait, pointing out the position of what appears to be the orb at the top of the harp's mast, "I wonder," then, moving over to her harp, asks the girls, "Bring a chair please," and telling Annia, "Let's see if there is a space designed to hold your shining orb." The girls bring two chairs, one apiece for Mara and Annia to stand on, situating them one to either side of the harp. Their examination reveals that there is indeed a rounded hollow sculpted into the top of the harp's column. Annia lifts the joined saucer and orb, and is not really surprised that they fit perfectly into the hollow space; and *Ohhh*, the harp comes alight and from within its glow there sounds a melody: the tones from the strings like bells: deeply resonating bells.

♡♡♡

Captain Derek is thinking mutinously. Is it mutinous for a captain to consider abandoning his own ship? It would mean abandoning his life. Would that be so bad? He busies himself with the charts and the instruments, while seething inside. He is angry at himself, angry at this port, angry at his disrespectable crew, and angry at his employers who have over cumbered him with these homeless castaways. He paces the deck in his dark mood. He considers his outs: it would be easiest to slip ashore alone, or he could depart in the ship-to-shore craft, but he would need help handling the stubby little pinnace. He catches motion from ahead on the foredeck. It is someone waving. He notes that it is the scoundrel DeVoss attempting to get his attention; probably intending on pressing for a favor. He can wait. He turns and walks to the upside-down lifeboat. Peeking underneath he sees the oars, mast, and keel board. He is in the midst of imagining getting it into the water in the dark of night when he is interrupted, "Captain Sir," It is the man that has been translating indefatigably through all the negotiating with the VOC, "May I have a word?" This may be along the same line of thought currently being considered by the captain, so he nods. "There are some amongst us who are wondering how seaworthy this small boat is." Captain Derek, having been wondering the same, nods again. "The decision of these officials of this *Vereenigde Oost Indische Compagnie* may entail leaving some, who wish most to disembark here, onboard this ship," spoken in the Dutch language, to an Englishman; a second language to both men. The captain is surprised to realize that he has, for the first time ever, heard the official title of the Dutch East Indies Company pronounced in full, rather than merely by its anagramme. The discussion is cut off by the return of those company officials. Derek nods, and then moves toward the gathering.

The top man of this VOC council explains that they have procured one canal barge that will port thirty passengers, give or take a few, to the border, via a network of canals. The proposed fee, per passenger, is extravagant. Those eager passengers that have been sanctioned to depart rush to be first in line. A table is set up at mid-deck. The translator moves to facilitate the proceedings. No one leaves the ship without first having paid for the privilege of riding a flat bottomed barge through the lowlands.

Derek, back to considering his own departure, knows that the lifeboat is not designed for canal travel, nor does he wish to take the tiny craft out into the Nord Zee. He needs a chart of the river. Perhaps that cur, Greely DeVoss, would know how to get such a map. He looks, and there is the man now, leaning on the forward gunwale, gazing out across this bay, this river, or what-ever; this crazy shallow port of the lowlands. Captain Derek dismisses himself from the helm; dismisses himself from these administrative proceedings; and sets about taking the first step of his plan that will dismiss him from this current life as he knows it. Rather than crossing the open deck to speak with DeVoss, he slips below decks, and while making his way forward he is inventorying what he will want to grab in the dark of his mid-night inspection. He comes back up on the top deck through a seldom used hatch, surprising all nearby. Especially pleased that where he has popped up is right next to where Greely is standing and asks, "What is it?"

"What is it?" Repeated back dumbfoundedly.

"Oh," complacently, "It appeared to me that you were attempting to attract my attention a while ago."

"Yes, oh yes," shaking inside at having to deal with this pinhead, "I was only hoping to know if you have been able to find the information that I had directed you to: the ship and its Captain."

"I found the man." Captain Derek does not wish to tell of the confrontation, "Now I am wanting something else. A map," lowering his voice to a whisper, "a river chart."

"I noticed you over there looking at the rescue boat. Do you have a plan?"

Not wanting to tell this stranger too much, and not having a full plan yet, he skips answering, "Can you get a chart?"

Greely turns his gaze outward again. He asks himself why he should help. He turns back to the uneasy captain. "I will need to get ashore. I will need the darkness of night in order to steal into the VOC office. It would be an act of thievery, so I will need to escape with those you will be sending on the little sloop."

With the plan coming together in his mind now, Captain Derek tells him, "You will need to help getting the boat over the side, sometime after midnight. Once in the water, you will be dropped off at the nearest dock," nodding toward the spot, "and then the boat will be rowed toward the outer moorings," nodding again in the intended direction, "where you will be picked up with the navigational chart you have promised to procure."

"Are you making this up as you go?"

Derek ignores the quip and drops down the hatch, letting the lid fall above him with a loud THWACK. Traveling back below decks he is feeling emboldened by the audacity of this undertaking. He comes on to the helm through a gang way, like the one he had just been through at the other end of the ship, a little out of breath from the hurrying. Once above deck and looking down at the table of clerks he is nonplussed by the tedium of these greedy bureaucrats. His feelings are mirrored all around him; sleepy sailors at their posts, sleepy advocaats shuffling papers, and sleepy passengers under the late afternoon sun. He closes his eyes, nodding off while standing sleepily at attention.

"We have completed our work here, Sir."

Startled awake, and embarrassed to be caught sleeping on his feet, "Very well," he says as he scans the scene around him while assaying the state of affairs that has evolved in however long he has been sleeping. The head magister stands before him. Behind him stands the rest of the crew of clerks; hats on their heads, folded chairs and table already carried off. Captain Derek, wanting to leave a good impression, reaches into a tiny pocket on the front of his vest, pulling out a sizable gold coin, and bowing upon presenting it to the magistrate, "Thank you very much for working with me on this. Thank you very much." Hoping like hell that this will be enough to show his appreciation. The man's look of astonishment and the smile he shows to his cohorts are encouraging indications that he has made some new friends. He may need more friends before this night is over.

The contingent of clerks leaves the ship and quite a number of passengers leave with them. The soldiers remain on the dock. Derek scans the deck. There are still a lot of people aboard this ship. "Captain, Sir." It is the same man, the translator, "We did not finish our discussion."

"Walk with me." Once they are away from listening ears the captain tells the man, "This night, instead of my usual inspection, I and one other will be leaving in the life boat." He lets that news sink in. "I am willing to take with me as many of you as will fit."

"Oh, splendid Sir."

"Be ready to go. Be silent. Remember, only as many as will fit."

Later in the night Captain Derek rises from his sleeping bed for his nightly inspection; his last nightly inspection of this particular ship. Tonight he lights his lantern, and sitting at his desk, writes a letter of resignation, leaving all his captain's duties to the first mate. He leaves the note out where it will be easily seen. He has his few belongings already stowed in a bag. He has another satchel of maps and navigational tools. He strolls out onto the deck and up to the helm. The helmsman, having nothing to do while in port, is fast asleep: all the better. He makes his way aft, where the little getaway ship sits upside down on the deck. A small crowd awaits him, among them is Greely DeVoss, who he puts to work helping connect the lines that lift the boat upright and over the gunwale. They all toss in their belongings, then carefully drop it down to the water's surface. Climbing over the gunwale and descending one by one; there is a family with two youngsters, a roly-poly fellow who refuses to leave without his tuba, and a self-important looking man accompanied by a very beautiful younger woman.

As they push away from the ship Derek swabs the oarlocks with purloined lard, then assigns the tuba player and the children's father to man the oars. The keel board is dropped through its slot and by the time the mast is tilted up they are close enough to the dock for Greely to jump ashore. As he races off Derek wonders if he will ever see the man again. He stands at the bow, for the moon has set, leaving sparse light for navigating. They ease quietly past the many docks where moored ships are tied off. A few have lanterns lit at gangways. There are some that have crews working through the night; loading, or unloading, by lantern light.

The round fellow is consistently splashing his oar, so Derek delivers a quick demonstration of proper rowing technique. It helps some, but the noise grates on his anxious nerves. Nearing the last of the docks there is no sign of DeVoss, but there is no light to tell for sure. Again, Derek wonders if the man can be counted on. Rather than hoping that these oarsmen can bring the boat in the captain takes to the tiller and steers them closer. The pinnace bumps gently against the dock. Derek is wondering if he should tie off and wait, or let DeVoss be damned, when he hears the slapping of flat-heeled boots getting nearer. Greely jumps aboard and hands Derek a map case. The oarsmen get back to work. Greely also holds a strongbox, which he pats while whispering, "We will let the VOC fund this endeavor." He has stolen from his former employer, rationalizing that he has taken what he deserves.

They stow the oars, raise the sails, and begin sounding the depth as the captain, at the tiller, guides them out of the harbor. They slide past the queue of ships awaiting their turns for moorings. Once into the river's current they tack between two frigates. Captain Derek is not planning on sailing far in the darkness, but instead is hoping to drop anchor until there is enough daylight to inspect the maps stolen from the harbormaster's office. In the shadowy darkness he imagines seeing a shape ahead of them. He is shifting the tiller and readying to adjust the foresail to take them around whatever lies there before them in the dark, when a lantern is lit, illuminating the deck of the ship that is anchored there in the river, also awaiting the daylight. Holding the lantern is the captain of the Tulip shouting, "Ahoy!"

Captain Derek, opening and holding up his own lantern so he can be seen, shouts back, "Ahoy!"

"Ahh, we meet again Captain," Roberts calls across the water. "A pleasant night for sailing. It is a bit shallow here. That is why I chose to anchor. I suggest you do the same, that is, unless you have someone in pursuit. If you are determined to sail on in the dark you will want to follow Sirius, and continue taking soundings."

Derek answers back, "If it is all the same to you, we will drop anchor here."

"Ye'll not be waving that firearm at me again I hope."

"Hah! Ye'll not be lobbing flames?"

"A truce."

"Agreed." They each shutter their lanterns and the night returns to darkness.

♡♡♡

Diedrik wakes early, dresses, and is down the stairs and into the Kikker Gat kitchen where Rhetta is busy with the day's bread. A pan of sticky buns already sits on the counter cooling. She hands him a cup of coffee and tells him, "Have a seat here and tell us how it goes with you."

Kikkert, leaning in the open doorway between the front and the back of the public house agrees, "Yes, tell us what you are doing with yourself."

"Well, I have returned to where I was living before, only now it is officially my home."

"And how are the three windmills?"

"All good."

"And you have a sizable polder?" Kikkert asking now, "Rhetta believes that your land called you back."

"It does feel like I belong there. The polder has a crop of flax, just as it has these many past years."

"You are continuing on as before then?"

"With the flax? Yes."

Rhetta wags a finger at him, "The land will thank you and bless you."

"Well, it is the easiest thing to do." It is pleasant sitting here in the warm kitchen with his old friends. "I am also considering adding a loading crane to the stone wharf, and re-building a warehouse on the foundation of the original. We might as well take advantage of the river traffic. I think it would be better than sub-dividing the polder."

Kikkert smiles and nods encouragingly, "It is good to have a plan. You will enjoy bringing it all about." Hearing someone else coming down the stairs in a rush, he turns to see Calderon, "You are early Sir."

"Yes, well, my traveling partners will be here soon, but I am on my way to the library first."

"What is so important that it cannot wait?"

"Diedrik's friend, Renaldo came with a list of books that he has asked me to procure. Mostly textbooks for tutoring." Now on his way out the door, "I have many of them available at hand, and told him that I could have them here before he is ready to leave this morning." As he is passing through the front door he waves, "Bye. I shall be returning soon."

"If he has time to get to his library and back, then I have time to visit the lens grinder's shop." Diedrik sets his empty cup down and follows Calderon out the front door, "Bye. I shall be returning soon." He enjoys walking the morning streets of the city. It is nice to visit, but he is grateful that he does not live here. Everyone seems so intent on getting where they are going. The Lens Grinder has a shop that is not far from the Kikker Gat. Luckily, the man is an early riser and is already at his work. From his work bench he tells Diedrik to look around a bit, that he will be with him soon. The shop is filled with marvels: magnifying glasses, spyglasses, eyeglasses, microscopes, telescopes, and twin-scopes.

Diedrik is admiring the twin-scopes when the shop keeper comes out from his workroom. "Are you interested in a set of field glasses? Bi-oculars is what we are calling them now."

Pointing at a set that is smaller than the others, "May I have a look through those?"

"A good choice Sir. These are our most popular model. They have nearly the same power as larger models, but are much easier to carry." Diedrik looks through the lenses out the front windows of the shop and is immediately startled by the closeness of a person passing by. The man behind the counter laughs, "You will get used to that. You will also learn to hold them steady, for not only do they magnify what you are looking at, they also magnify the unsteadiness of your hands."

Admiring the high quality workmanship, "This is a work of art."

"Thank You."

"I will be wanting the case also." A stiffened leather shell that has been contoured specifically to match the shape of these twin scopes is on the same shelf behind the counter. As he pays for this new toy he is appreciating that he has the means to afford extravagance. "Thank you Sir."

He walks back to the Kikker Gat in high anticipation. He wants to look at everything through his new scopes. He imagines that this leathern case holding the bi-oculars must resemble the purses he has seen many carrying. He has always scoffed at the notion of carrying a purse, yet here he is carrying one. He takes the alley that runs between the Kikker Gat's kitchen and stableyard. Hearing horses behind him, he steps aside while turning to view who it may be. He recognizes Nicklas Voorhaven, whom he had met once before at the home of Captain Janszoon. Riding with him are two women; beautiful, smartly dressed women. All are riding good horses: very good horses. The stable man, the fellow that has taken Diedrik's prior position, comes out of the barn greeting these early morning patrons.

Nicklas dismounts and walks over, "Diedrik, my good man," reaching out with a hearty handshake, "We had not expected to see you til this evening."

"Ah, yes. Right. You must be Professor Calderon's traveling companions."

"Are you here to escort us?"

"La, no. I am traveling with friends; seeking horses." Diedrik catches a better look at the two women traveling with Nicklas as they walk over.

"Allow me to introduce you to my friends. You may remember briefly meeting Trinjntje."

"Trin?" Taking her hand in his and tipping his head, "I am pleased to be properly introduced."

"Hoi," She smiles winsomely, and holding his hand a little longer adds coyly, "Last time we met, I was wearing my vagabond disguise."

"Mm-Hmm." Perhaps one day he will hear the full story. For now he turns to the taller woman.

Nicklas introduces her, "Saarika."

She reaches out and firmly shakes his hand. "I am pleased to meet you Diedrik. The professors speak favorably of you. I congratulate you on your recent good fortune."

Taller than most. Beautiful. Intriguing. Diedrik, caught at a loss for words, is relieved when another horse comes into the alleyway. It is Calderon.

He rides up and dismounts. "Good Day! I see you have all met. Good. Good." He removes a pack from his back, and handing it to Diedrik asks, "Will you see that Renaldo gets these books please?" The other two professors come out carrying satchels. The stableman leads two more saddled horses out of the barn. Turning to the others Calderon asks, "Will any of you be needing anything? Breakfast? Coffee? Or shall we be on our way?" They all answer no and climb back on their horses and away they go.

"See you all later." As Diedrik waves he is struck by an unwelcome thought: wondering what all these new friends would think of him were they to know that he has been a thief, and that he stills holds on to something stolen. Renaldo, Razs, and Vejz come out carrying their satchels. They are ready to get going. They briefly inspect the books Calderon has brought them, and are pleased to have this wealth of new knowledge to digest.

Renaldo had been lucky enough to speak last night with a man that runs a stable of Arabians. The stable is not far away, and three young mares are ready for inspection when they arrive. Evidently the price has already been agreed upon. The entire transaction occurs quickly and easily. Everything is settled over glasses of cold coffee.

Conversation turns to the meteoroid. The horse trader tells them, "There are many people, after hearing the tales, who are traveling to the sight of the meteoroid's landing. It is said to have gouged a tremendous furrow."

"Have you been told of the location? Is it far?" Razs asks excitedly.

"To the South; in France. Some two hundred miles."

They leave with the Gedimins riding their new horses: the heavy horses following behind on a lead. They are all thrilled. Diedrik agrees to stay with the heavy horses while the others race. He takes this opportunity to pull his new bi-oculars from the case he still carries over his shoulder. Peering through the lenses is difficult at first, because of his horse's gait, but he gets used to the motion as he brings things up closer. He follows a bird flying overhead. He is fascinated by the leaves at the top of a tree quivering with the breeze. He is thrilled by the natural rippling occurring over the surface of the water. Following the flight of a duck he notices something floating way out there. It is a log, and there is a sleeping grebe perched there. It awakens and looks directly into the lenses. He is startled by the detail he is able to make out from the distance. It occurs to him that everything appears flatter, less dimensional. Does this trick of bringing things closer squish the intervening spaces together? As in dreaming his thoughts have stopped, until he is aroused by the return of his three companions.

"Just as we thought," they chide him. Without realizing, he has come to a stop while his attention has been so totally focused in this new way of perceiving the world. He lowers these twin scopes that have transfixed him with a wider field than he is used to, and upon seeing the smiling faces of his companions, breaks out in laughter. They laugh with him as they turn back to the direction of home.

Arrival

Mara awakens and opens her eyes to the familiar sight of the rafters above her bed. She feels perfectly warm and all tingly inside; she has been dreaming wonderfully. She closes her eyes remembering the way the evening had unfolded; from comparing the necklaces, up to the moment she sat down at her royal harp. She recalls the way she had reached out her fingers toward the strings, and then the voices of the strings singing at her lightest touch. She recollects her own voice singing a traditional ballad; only now that she is awake, she does not remember ever knowing the song.

Annia, upon awakening from pleasurable dreaming, opens her eyes to the sight of the rafters above the bed; very similar to the rafters in her own home: remembering that she and her girls have stayed the night at Mara's. She closes her eyes for a moment before the prattle of reasoning begins. She invites the memories of the previous evening, recalling the moment she had set the orb in the hollow at the top of the harp, and the glowing that immediately followed. She recollects the beautiful *euphōnia* that flowed from the strings as Mara played; music like she had never felt before. There had been an instant when, instead of Mara, there had been a golden haired celestial plucking tones from the harp's strings. Those tones had quavered through her body, had quavered through the house, had set her entire world to quavering.

Mara slips out of bed quietly and picks up her folded clothes to dress in the other room, not wanting to wake the others. Annia hears her get up and follows. They slip on their clogs and head out to the barn. Mara milks the cow while Annia milks the goat. They feed the chickens and collect the eggs. Because the men are gone, they will be taking care of all the chores, and so continue on to the next barn. On the way Mara tells Annia, "My Ma and Da told me that the Golden Hearts are about dreaming and memory. Nearly every morning growing up one of them would be waiting by my bed for me to awaken, then immediately have me describe my dreams."

"Oh? My folks did the same with me. Ren and I have done it with our kids." At the Windmidden barn they feed Diedrik's chickens and leave the eggs in a bowl on his kitchen table. Strolling on down to Windweg, basking in the freshness of the summer morning, Annia says, "So, I have never before met someone learning as I learned growing up about dreaming."

"So, we share the understanding that dreaming and waking coincide?" Repeating an oft-repeated adage, "Happy dreaming assures happy waking."

"La, and *vice versā*; happy awake: happy asleep." After finishing in the Windweg barn, and walking back up across the polder, Annia says, "I am imagining that we may discover a third necklace."

"Well, there will be visitors here today, and Professor Calderon hinted at something without providing any particulars."

Arriving back at Mara's they find Kirin and Audrae in the kitchen warming the kettle. Audrae, holding a jar of sweetened powdered cocoa asks, "May I?"

"Certainly you may." Mara scans the great room of her home. The orb is wrapped in its silken bag and on the table next to the necklaces in their own velvet bags. "We will have to put our treasures away. I will need to sweep and clean. A crown -- Er," laughing at her slip-up, then correcting herself, "a crowd will be arriving later."

"Oh, yeah!" Kirin says excitedly, "Da and Razs and Vejz will get home with our new horses."

Her mother adds, "Besides our men and Diedrik, Mara is expecting company," turning to her new-found sister, "how many?"

"The professor's last post advised me to expect six, or possibly seven. And if my Robert returns, there'll be another. I will need to prepare plenty to eat."

Audrae spouts, "We'll help."

"Okay, you can start now," teasing, "slice this loaf while I dish up cheese curds for each of us."

While slicing the bread Audrae asks Mara, "Have you worn your necklace often?"

Mara dreamily remembers, "Each year on the first day of spring, Brigid's day, my Grandma would wear the necklace and play the harp. I was still a child when she put the necklace around my neck and allowed my first touch of the harp's strings. It was if the harp played itself. Each year on the Eve of Imbolc I would wear the necklace and sit at the harp, then ma, and then Grandma. The whole clan would awaken the next morning remembering marvelous dreams."

Annia nods, "Twas the same for me, except twas the first day of summer each year."

Kirin remembers wearing the necklace for the first time and asks Mara, "Did your family all have the same dream?"

"I always imagined so," remembering those days fondly, "there are none of my family left at home, but I still dream with them."

Annia remarks, "It is wonderful that in our dreams everybody we have ever known, even those that have passed from this life, still dream with us."

♡♡♡

Morning arrives with the sun barely peeking through the lavender-pink wisps of cloud above the horizon. Captain Derek, anxious and uncomfortable, has not slept. His passengers begin stirring. This pinnace is too small for so many to spread out comfortably. He sits up. Looking over to the Irishman's sloop he sees nothing moving. He opens the box of food that he has squirrelled away, and suddenly everybody in the boat is awake and hungry. He divvies out equal portions. They share from a jug of light ale to wash their breakfast down. He goes through the papers that DeVoss has stolen, and finds a chart of the river that is full of scribbled notations. Getting his compass out and comparing his direction with the rising sun he turns the map to its proper orientation. Noting the many channels to this river he is pleased that there is inscribed a dotted line marking the proper passageway. Fortunately, he will not have to sail far before the channels are one and there will be less chance of straying off course. The wind is blowing favorably with little chop. It should be smooth sailing.

Robert had fallen asleep staring up at the stars. He is still there, stretched out on the bench sleeping. He is dreaming as a golden-colored eagle looking down through his eagle eyes at himself sprawled across the tiller bench: a young eagle, not long away from hunting with his parents, up before full daylight on an empty belly. Then he sees what he has been hoping for; a fish surfacing from beneath one of the two unmoving boats. He folds his wings and dives headfirst; at the last moment flipping and grabbing the fish in his talons. The fish fights. It is big; nearly outweighing the fledgling eagle. He is too close to the ship to spread his wings properly, so he struggles to turn. When he finally breaks free from the pull of the water the shore looks too far away to carry this burden. In desperation he drops onto the nearest thing available, which is one of the anchored boats. Releasing hold of his catch, he stands back while the fish flips and flops all over the exposed deck.

The commotion wakes Robert. He finds himself staring at what a moment ago he had been dreaming. The young eagle is looking his way, startled and now afraid that this larger beast may steal its meal. It screeches a warning to stay away. Robert tells it, "Do not worry little friend." He unsheathes his knife while rising up, and with a quick cut separates the fish's head from its body. Tossing the head to the bird Robert tells it, "Do not fly away yet, for I'll be givin' ye some more." The bird snatches the fish head and backs away before tearing into it.

Robert does not want the eagle to think it has lost its meal, so he waits a bit as the eagle, busy with the fish's head, watches trepidiciously. Knowing the eaglet will be wanting more, Robert, with knife still in hand, makes a slight move toward the fish. The eagle whistles a warning and spreads its golden speckled wings. With swift precision Robert grabs the fish, slices the belly, scoops out the innards, and tosses the glob to the bird. The eagle pounces on the fish guts. Robert watches while peeling off the skin and filleting the meat from the bones. The tail and skeleton go over the gunwale. As the eagle is finishing up the entrails Robert tosses one of the fillets over and asks, "Will this be enough?" In answer the bird grabs the fillet and hops atop Robert's tarpaulin covered cargo to begin its meal in earnest.

Now Robert looks around him. All aboard the vessel anchored next to his are staring open mouthed at what has just transpired. He laughs at the expressions on their faces. "Greetings fellow voyagers. How does the wind blow for ya? I hope that you slept well."

Captain Derek, who had spoken in his own language to this man yesterday, does not understand the language Robert is using today, so asks DeVoss, "Is he speaking Dutch?"

"Barely."

"Well then, I leave it up to you to talk with him."

Greely DeVoss calls over to Robert, "Do birds often bring you fish to gut for them?"

"Hah!" Robert would not have thought that such a pinched faced man as this would have a sense of humor, "It happens all the time ya know," he says while laughing heartily.

Captain Derek gives the command, "Pull in those anchors." He does not wish to while away the morning listening to others' small talk.

Greely tips his head sideways, with a nod toward Derek, and asks Robert, "What is it between you two?"

"My people are at war with his."

Captain Derek is busy raising the sails, disappointed that the mast and sails are so short and muttering to himself, "This ship could stand a taller mast, and a deeper keel, but alas it will have to do." As the little ship moves away he turns to the Irish lout with a sloppy salute and sneers, "Faretheewell."

Robert had not heard what the captain had said, and sees no reason to return such a sloppy tribute. The Englishman's half-hearted gesture felt more like a dismissal. His hatred of the invading armies, and his anger of being forced off his land are momentarily stirred up within. He does not want to feel this way or think these thoughts. Luckily he is distracted by the little golden eagle flying off with what is left of the fillet, leaving the second fillet untouched. So he starts a fire in his stove and sets a pan to warming. Pouring a bit of oil into the pan reminds him of the barrel they had set alight under the English captain's ship; a memory that has him laughing out loud. He cuts a potato into bits and adds them to the now sizzling oil and sprinkles salt on top. He keeps a hand on the skillet, shaking it and flipping the potato bits so they do not stick. When all is heated through and nicely browned, he lays the fish fillet over the top of the mound to warm and leaves the fire to burn itself out.

He looks up the river noticing that the lifeboat, with its odd assortment of passengers, is out of sight. He imagines that he will catch up and pass it before the day is half over; his Tulip is fast. He is grateful not to be among the unfortunate souls aboard that little open boat. While digging in to his breakfast, he thinks ahead, expecting to make it home before the evening meal. "I wonder who all will be there."

♡♡♡

Paulo Calderon is pleased that he had not kept his friends waiting with his impromptu foray of the library's shelves, and pleased that they were ready to go at the appointed time. He is further pleased that they have maintained a steady riding clip and have arrived at captain Janszoon's as early in the day as he had hoped. Cornelius emerges from the barn to greet his guests. Trinjntje embraces her uncle and introduces him to Saarika. The horses are drinking thirstily from a stone cistern just outside the barn. Nicklas comments, regarding the cistern, "This is new Cornelius. Very nice. Does is fill itself automatically as you planned?"

"Yes it does, that is, whenever the mill is turning." He waves his arm to his beloved windmill.

"But, where is the canal that brings the water from over there to over here?"

"Ah," winking, and taking great pleasure in the telling, "The water comes through pipes buried in the ground. It is another of Phillip Haumann's engineering feats." Turning to the crowd, "I have prepared stalls with food and water for each of your horses, and I have also prepared a luncheon for us. Ta. We can eat while your horses rest." After the horses are fed and left to cool down Cornelius leads them to his garden gate telling them, "We will go through this back way so that you may all see how glorious Trin's garden is growing."

A wide array of flowers are blooming. Young trees and shrubs are thriving. Rows of peas and beans and corn bear the promise of fresh veggies in the weeks ahead. Walkways are clear. Trinjntje rushes to the greenhouse where a mass of foliage is evident through the windowpanes, Saarika follows. Janszoon calls after them, "Do not be too long, our lunch is ready, and we have yet a ways to ride this afternoon."

Nicklas asks, "Will you be riding with us?"

Janszoon answers, "Indeed I will be riding with you."

"Splendid!"

"Yes, Phillip has told me of the crowd living at Schoonhoven Landing. I am particularly interested to meet the Irish sailor."

Calderon tells him, "Your Irish sailor may not be back yet from his latest expedition."

"Ah, well, another time then. Mostly, I am pleased to have you all here, and I am so looking forward to riding with you." In the kitchen, besides various wines to choose from, there is also a small keg of beer. He invites all to serve themselves. He leaves them to fill their glasses and moves into the dining area where he begins lifting the cloths that are covering the food. There is a board filled with sliced breads, cheeses, and meats, jars of pickles and relish, and bowls of salads, and a cake. "Dig in." He has arranged all the chairs on one side of the long table so that all will be seated looking out the windows at the scene of the turning windmill. "Now, where are those women?" He makes his way out to gather his niece.

After filling his plate Hendrik takes a seat, and while shaking out his serviette comments, "I love this house." Everybody is admiring the house, seated here at the first of two tables in the great room. The other table, a worktable, is covered with books, maps, graphs, and the Captain's assorted mechanical instruments for determining the positions of the stars. Beyond that is a central hearth with sleeping quarters on the other side. Hendrik directs everyone's attention to a pair of statues that are positioned before the windows, "I do not remember those being there when we last visited."

Nicklas, still busy filling his plate with his back to the wall of windows, looks to see what Hendrik has seen and is surprised, "Oh! Those are part of the cargo that I brought home." He turns all the way around to admire the decorative porcelain statues. "I was unaware of the Captain having acquired these." Shaking his head in wonder as he takes his seat, "I was able to purchase these at a discount. Twenty sets of these had been crated up and hauled to the docks, then left behind for some unknown reason. I felt very lucky to have been there at the opportune moment."

Janszoon comes in from the kitchen with Trinjntje and Saarika. Playing his role as host he inquires, "I hope I have prepared suitably," and is met with a chorus of appreciation.

Nicklas catches Saarika's attention and tips his head in the direction of the statues. Upon seeing them she declares, "My family holds an exclusive contract with the guild that produces these statues!" She turns back to Nicklas with astonishment in her eyes, "How remarkable it is that they have found their way here."

Captain Janszoon, as host, is the last in line to fill his plate. Upon hearing this discourse regarding his statues he looks questioningly to Nicklas who explains, "Surely you remember telling me that Saarika's family has traded in the Orient since long before any of the Europeans arrived. She has served as director of her family's business in Huaxia for the past ten years."

"So, the two of you have met previously?"

She answers, “No. I was stationed on the mainland.”

“Ah, where Europeans are not allowed.”

“We had shipped this lot,” extending an arm to include the statues, “to Formosa harbor where, for some forgotten reason, they were left sitting on the dock. I was very pleased that an interested party came along,” turning to Nicklas, “did you get all twenty?”

“I did, twenty matching pairs,” then saying, “I have yet to learn the identity of these two characters.”

She defers, “I believe we have someone here at our table who may be able to tell us who they are.”

Lu-Tang speaks up, “These statues represent Bodhisattvas, described by the Doctrine of the Elders as enlightened beings who walk this earth with us humans.” Scooting back his chair and standing up, he walks around the table and over to the windows where the statues are displayed on pedestals. He stops before a statue of a woman riding on an ocean wave and carrying a bottle. She has intricately painted features and is smiling beatifically. She wears a long windswept gown. Her hair is piled thick on her head. “This will be Quanyin.” Walking over to the other statue, this one a laughing man holding a jug and standing atop a wave, also painted with great detail, “This will be Jenrezig.” Now spreading his arms wide to include both figures, “Both represent the bodhisattva of compassion and mercy; man and woman, mother and father, brother and sister.”

“It looks like they are standing on waves,” Hendrik asks, “do they walk on water?”

Saarika adds what she knows, “In the stories that I have been told these two always arrive from across the water; a lake, a river, or a sea. They bring water with them; thus her bottle, and his jug. I love these because they are each so happy.”

They are quiet for a moment before Calderon tells them, "I like the idea of enlightened beings walking this earth and accompanying us. I like that they are depicted as male and female, for I believe that the Spirit within us all is neither one nor the other, but both."

"Ah," says Hendrik, "that matches what I have heard Anna-Maria say regarding our Spirit Self."

They are all standing now and as they begin gathering up and putting everything away Nicklas tells Cornelius, "I am very pleased to see these statues here."

"Indeed! You have an eye for this sort of thing. I think that you should set out on another voyage and see what sort of interesting finds you will bring home."

"My voyage turned out very profitable for me, but I am not sure if I want to go sailing again anytime soon. Ah, but who knows what lies ahead?"

"Well said." With the table cleared, "Shall we ride?"

♡♡♡

As Diedrik, Renaldo, Razs, and Vejz get close to the Haumann sawmill they are surprised that they are not hearing the noisy racket of the big saw blades dropping. Eventually they do hear the quieter sound of the smaller re-saw blades; the finer toothed saws dropping in shorter strokes is at first a tick-tick-ticking, and even as they get closer the sound of the smaller mill's shaft turning and dropping the saw blades is still not nearly so overwhelming a noise as what they have come to expect when visiting Phillip Haumann. Renaldo and his sons are grateful that it is not necessary to plug their ears. As they ride into the Haumann yard the noise stops altogether. As they dismount Phillip greets them, "Halloo. What a surprise it is to see you. Are these new horses?" The Gedimins all nod with big smiles. "They are beautiful." He slaps Renaldo on the shoulder, "Well chosen," he adds as he walks around the mares, patting flanks, and smoothing necks. He asks, "Can I coax you to come inside?" Raising his eyebrows tantalizingly, "I have a keg of *KikkerBier*."

"Maybe, but first I have something I want you to see," Diedrik unslings the case holding his new field glasses, "Or rather, something for you to see through."

Phillip takes the bi-oculars carefully and raising them to his eyes focuses toward the tall grasses across the mill pond, "We have been watching a family of herons. Miniature herons."

Diedrik's ma comes out, hugs her son, and then asks, "What have ya got there?"

Her husband hands the twin scopes to her, "Have a look for yourself. It is like being up close."

She looks at the family of little herons and gasps, "Oh! Remarkable!" Turning to her son, "I suppose that now your paintings will show even more detail."

"I have been using a scope for a long while Ma, but these will provide me a wider range."

Gazing through the field glasses she asks, "Are we correctly calling these herons? They are so little."

"You may call them whatever you like. Nearly anything with a long neck gets called a heron. I might classify this family as bitterns. They are so itty bitty."

Phillip interrupts the word play in a surprised tone, "There is Captain Robert's Tulip!" He is pointing toward the far side of the river. Taking back the scopes, he looks out across the wide expanse of water. "His ship sits low in the water, he must be bringing home granite blocks. Usually when he is carrying a load of blocks he is bringing them here," he watches the Tulip as it sails along, "but Robert does not intend stopping here today."

Vejz, whose turn it is with the bi-oculars, asks, "How does he sail so fast when the river's current is flowing the other way?"

"Well I do know that ships steer away from where the current flows strongest," Phillip answers, "and that ships' captains have a knack for keeping the wind in their sails."

Razs has a turn now, "Robert has his spyglass trained this way. Oh, now he is waving!" They all wave across the water. "I wonder, if we were to leave now on our horses, would we get home before he does."

They all look to one another. There is excitement evident in the boys' eyes. Renaldo, with the same excitement flashing in his eyes, turns to Diedrik who laughs, "Go ahead you three. Race the sailor. I will follow with your other horses." The three hop astride their new steeds and gallop out of the yard.

"I will need to follow them before long. We are expecting guests."

"Oh," Beatris bemoans, "You have just been to the city and you haven't any news to pass along?"

"Everyone is talking of the meteoroid. It seems that crowds are converging upon the site where it hit the earth."

"Are you thinking of traveling there yourself?"

"Well, offhandedly we were discussing the best route, and wondering how long it would take."

"Oh geez," Phillip says, "When I was your age one would have been thought crazy to travel so far from home." Shaking his head and kicking the dirt. "There were armies fighting each other everywhere. The thieving soldiers harassed travelers. It was best to stay home. I hear that this meteoroid landed some two hundred miles away."

"Yes, that is what we heard. Were we to ride we would need to get our horses across the river."

"You will need to carry a lot of supplies."

"Or maybe you can convince Robert to sail the bunch of you to Calais," Beatris adds with a wink, "then take a barge from there."

"Aye," Phillip agrees with his wife, "That may be your best plan."

"Hmmm. I am not sure if I want to be gone from home for so long. I imagine it would take a month, or more, to get there and back."

Phillip puts an arm around Beatris, squeezes her close, and with a smile says, "If we were younger, we'd be off to see the thing."

"La, no, we would not. Your father is having a joke." She puts her arm around Phillip's waist, "I would like to see Calais again. Such a beautiful place." The couple had splurged a few years ago; leaving the sons in charge of business while they went on a *vacation*.

Diedrik smiles at this sight of his parents embracing starry-eyed. He gathers the leads of Gedimins' horses, hops astride his own, and as he bids them *vaarwel*, tells them, "I may have to come back, and stay longer, to make a study of your itty bitterns." And off he goes.

It is pleasant to be riding along the familiar river track. He notices another ship sailing the river. As it tacks his way and he gets a closer look he notices that it is a ship full of people. It is not big enough to carry much cargo anyway. It is different from most boats that he sees sailing the river. He considers scoping it to see what sort of folks are sailing upriver, but has already learned that to view through his new glasses it is best to stop. He does not want to stop, and neither do the horses. They know that they are getting close to home and their own barn.

♡♡♡

Annia and her daughters have gone home, leaving Mara on her own. Because guests will be arriving she is checking the readiness of Windhoek, her own personal windmill. She comes here nearly every day, so she knows it is swept clean, yet she brings her broom anyway. Professor Calderon's letter, explaining that he has something to show her, has her vaguely wondering what that can possibly be. Her thoughts return also to the drawer of antiquities left in her keeping by the fleeing monks. She is eagerly anticipating Robert's return and hearing the tale of what, if anything, he has discovered by following the map. In her distraction, as she opens Windhoek's door and is stepping over the sill, her ankles are brushed softly, and there below her peripheral zone she sees faeries. Instantly she focuses, and looking fully down sees instead, a stone marten taking advantage of the open door to facilitate its escape. "How did you get in here my dear?" The silver sheen of the marten's undercoat must have been what sparked her impression of faeries.

Before closing the door she hears two voices speaking her name, "Mara." Her intense dreaming of last night has her imagining aroused; her King and Queen that she visits in her dreams are here. She bows her head and curtsies, though they wear no sign of royalty. She feels the brushing on her ankles again. A faery mother leads her three children in. The King and Queen hold out their hands to the faeries who rush to them for a moment of cuddling. A breeze closes the door behind her, and in the moment's distraction; there is the marten leading three fuzzy babies to a corner. Dreaming of faeries, especially daydreaming of kind-hearted faeries moving in, betokens goodness, light-heartedness, and fun.

Mara shakes out the blankets that cover the beds. She checks inside the chest that holds extra pillows and blankets; all is good. On the table there is a full lantern and matches. She climbs the stairs. Everything is much the same; two beds, a chest filled with blankets and pillows, a lantern on the table: all in readiness. She leaves her broom here and walks up the steps and through the door onto the stage where the windmill's direction is adjusted. She loves to walk the full circuit of this boardwalk. There is a decidedly comforting view from wherever she stops. She sits herself down in the chair she keeps for watching the river. She particularly likes this spot where she is able to see whatever is moving up or down the river. There is lightness in her heart.

At the other end of the Polder as Annia enters her bedroom she sees, outside the windows, the animals that partner with her in dreaming: a lynx and an owl. Seeing them reminds her of the rift between the realms following yesterday's dreaming. As soon as she has acknowledged the dream creatures their visage is gone; leaving her with déjà vu. She opens the drawer where she keeps her treasures and there is the book her grandparents had given her after she had first dreamed of the lynx and the owl.

It had been a dream; a dream of visiting her ancestors, the Husarz. After relaying the dream to her parents she had been sent to relay it again to her grandparents who had given her this book of pictures. There are pictures of the winged soldiers; the stuff of legend. There are pictures of these same winged persons enjoying everyday life; feasting, entertaining, and playing. In all of the illustrations these humans with wings are accompanied by the beautiful orange eyed and tufted-eared lynxes and owls: the companions to her mystical ancestors. Her grandparents had told her that legends are the tales of past dreaming.

Annia is flipping through the pages of legend when Kirin and Audrae come in behind her, "Ma? You have been so long, we thought that you must be napping."

"La, has it been so long?" She sits down on the edge of her bed and pats the mattress to both sides of her inviting the girls to sit with her, "Let us look at these pictures again."

As she flips the pages Audrae asks, "Was the lynx so much larger in the past?"

"Evidently so."

Kirin asks, "Are their eyes really orange?"

"Mm-hmm."

"Are these folk angels?"

"Legend has it that a race of these winged humans lived with us in this realm for an age. Some believe that Kupala was a member of this legendary race."

"What became of them?"

"Ah, have you not dreamed of them?"

"Oh, yeah, well ..."

"I can only guess that they have receded from this, our everyday realm, into their own."

They are silent until Kirin states, "Both realms are the same; at least that is how it seems."

"So, they are still here, but we do not see them unless we dream them. Right?" Audrae asks.

"To explain another realm in the words of this realm defies logic. Best to let it be." Annia wraps up her picture book and puts it away in the drawer with the orb and the necklace. "Your father and brothers should be arriving soon. Shall we go up by the river to greet them?"

Mara is enjoying the warmth of the afternoon. She periodically scans the upriver track for the arrival of Calderon and his crew, and then she scans the other direction: checking downriver for the Tulip, and the track for Renaldo and his sons. She hears the voices of Annia and the girls. When they come into view she calls out, "Up here." They look up and wave, then enter the windmill and she hears them climbing the stairs. As they come out onto the stage with her she apologizes, "I have only this one chair." She is going to add that she has not seen anything yet when she notices something coming up the river, "Oh, look. What is that?" They all look toward where she is pointing. Soon it becomes apparent that it is a ship. Mara stands, leans over the rail attempting a closer look, and then bursts out, "It is the Tulip! My man returns!" Down the steps she flies even though it will be some while before the ship arrives at the wharf.

"Oh look," Audrae shouts, but they have all seen Renaldo, Razs, and Vejz riding speedily along the way. "Are they racing Robert's ship?"

"Where is Diedrik? And the other horses?" Kirin wonders.

"They will all be here soon," Annia shouts as she races down the steps following Mara.

♡♡♡

After Captain Derek had sailed off in his lifeboat full of refugees Robert had eaten and then pulled up his own anchors and raised his sails. After being on his way for a while he notices the young eagle circling overhead and keeping up with him. They are both enjoying glorious sailing. The wind is cooperating splendidly as he tacks the Tulip back and forth, seldom having to cross the river's main channel where the current runs strongest. Midmorning has the golden speckled eagle screeching above. Robert turns in the direction of the bird's whistling tone and watches it dive and capture a fish easily. Instead of taking its meal toward shore and an abandoned tree, it brings the fish to the Tulip. Releasing its catch on deck it steps back eyeing Robert who makes no move, only wanting to maintain his speedy passage homeward. The fish's flipping and flopping moves it across the deck. The eagle jumps on it again and with the strength of its wings hops it back within closer proximity to the man-being that had so efficiently prepared its meal earlier in the day. Robert laughs, "Oh, I see how ye are. Ye are a young one; used to having your parents ready your food, eh?" From his seat at the tiller he is able to reach out with a toe and nudge the fish back toward the anxious raptor.

The eagle cocks its head, ruffles its feathers, and sucks in a questioning sound, *Eeeeeekh?* Stirring Robert to laughter again.

"La, surely yer parents trusted ye to know what to do with yer catch my little friend, else ye would still be in their nest."

Eeeeeekh? It grabs the fish, which is no longer flopping so energetically, and hops it even closer to Robert, and then backs away while giving Robert a stern look with its eagle eyes.

Robert, laughing some more, gives the fish a good kick this time, sending it across the deck. The bird hops onto its prey and carries it to the top of the cargo where it had eaten before. Releasing the fish it steps back allowing Robert one last chance.

Robert laughs and shoos the creature with a backhanded wave, "Have at it my little friend. I have food of my own to eat." The eagle hops onto the fish and tears into it greedily. When it has eaten enough it preens itself and eventually falls asleep.

Even with the fine wind and smooth water Robert does not catch up with the short English ship as early in the day as he has expected, "So, this English captain does indeed know how to sail," but eventually he does pass the pinnace. Captain Derek acknowledges his slower pace by lifting his hands with palms up and then pointing disdainfully at the short mast and sails. The other passengers of the lifeboat wave and smile: except for the pinched faced one, who probably never smiles? Robert cordially returns their waves as he passes by.

As he nears the Haumann mill he is surprised not to be assaulted by the roar of machinery. His course has him sailing on the far side of the river. He looks through his spyglass to see Phillip with a crowd. They are handing something around; something that they bring up to their faces. He waves, and then looking some more, he recognizes Renaldo Gedimin with his two sons. Phillip's wife Beatris is there, and another man. Could that be the son that he has not seen much of these past few years? There are extra horses. He watches Ren and his sons mount up and ride out of the yard. "Ah hah! Methinks this be a race. My pace today is too fast for your horses." He laughs some more. "What an excellent day this is turning out to be!"

Schoonhoven Landing comes into sight and there is Mara on the wharf to greet him. He proceeds with a wide tack that turns the Tulip all the way around. He lowers his sails and allows the river's current to bring him in. He tosses the aft line to his sweet gal there awaiting him, and then races forward, picks up the bow line, hops over the edge and onto the dock. As he stands from tying the line she is there in his arms. After a bit, they lean back to take a look at whatever changes these past weeks may have brought to the other. "You look mighty full of yourself," Robert tells her as they pull each other closer and kiss.

"I am eager to hear news of your voyage, but ..." she loves looking into his sparkling eyes, "... But I must first tell you my news." By the look of her Robert determines that this must be especially good news. He nods encouragedly. "I discovered only yesterday that our neighbor, Annia has a necklace of Golden Hearts: and I have told her of mine."

Robert looks over to the shoreline where Annia, Kirin, and Audrae are greeting home the men of the family as they come riding in on beautiful horses. "Well then," he says, "This is a momentous occasion. She will be as interested as you to hear the tale of what I came upon by following the map."

"What did you find?"

"I found a tower that has been built around a rock that fell from the sky." He looks up to see the Gedimin family looking this way. "Let us tell our tales later."

"Aye. We have neighbors to greet." She kisses him again, and then releases herself from their embrace. Offering her elbow, "La, lead on then, Captain."

"Indeed." Ah, she is a beguiling woman.

The greetings are a bit stiff at first, but it is Razs who warms things up while shaking hands with Robert, "Will you teach me to sail? Or, at least explain to me how you make your ship go upriver so easily?"

"Of course I will," now Robert is laughing. He reaches out to pat the neck of the horse standing nearest, "These are some fine looking horses you have here."

"We picked them out this morning. We met an honest horse trader whose specialty is Arabians."

"Well, I believe that you have a good eye for horseflesh Sir."

Vejz interrupts, "There is another ship coming up the river," everyone looks where he is pointing, "And it is a cute little boat."

Robert tells them, "It is a pinnace; a ship to shore vessel from off a frigate. A lifeboat." He lowers his voice and tells Mara, "It is the English Captain."

Astonished, she asks, "Of the ship that went down in flames?"

"The same," grinning at his friends, "someday we will have to tell you that tale."

Annia asks, "Has Mara told you that we are expecting guests. We will be joined this evening by a company of professors."

Slapping her forehead Mara bemoans, "Ach, there is so much to tell ya!" Tugging on Robert's arm, "We are having visitors and they will be staying the night," leaning away with big eyes made bigger by raised brows, "I expect they will be arriving soon. Oh," she remembers, while he laughs, "and we have a landlord living in the *Windmidden* home."

"I think that cute little lifeboat is coming in to the dock," Vejz tells them all.

They all watch as Captain Derek uses the same maneuver as Captain Robert; tacking in a circle and drifting in on the current. Robert tells everyone, "Wait here," as he marches back out onto the wharf. Even though he had told them to wait, everyone is following him. He arrives as the little craft glides in, "Ahoy," and is tossed the bowline with little room to spare as he hurriedly ties the knot that will keep this second sloop from bumping into his. The English captain has tied off the aft line and now approaches. Robert folds his arms across his chest, wearing a stern expression, "Hmmmm. We meet again."

"On behalf of my passengers," the unkempt Captain pronounces, "we petition thee to allow docking for this night." Robert, looking back to shore, now realizes that everyone else has followed and are standing here on the dock with him. They are all looking at the forlorn folks sitting upon the hard benches of this little craft.

Renaldo answers before anyone else, "We have room for them," and then offhandedly finishes, "some may have to sleep in the barn."

Captain Derek sighs deeply. Greely DeVoss speaks up, "This English Captain does not speak our language, and neither of us speak the language of these folks. We will have to figure out how to tell them that they are welcome here for the night."

Renaldo calls out in his own language. The passengers answer back. Understanding each other, they are able to discuss the situation. Kirin is telling Robert and Mara what is being said, "These people have escaped an invading army.

They had hoped that they would be able to return home from the port of Amsterdam, but were not allowed to disembark, and were not let off in Rotterdam either. These two have helped them escape."

Razs finishes, "Now Ma and Pa have invited them to come ashore."

"Very well," DeVoss acknowledges, then turning to Derek, "did you catch all that?"

Captain Derek opens his coat pointing out for Robert no flintlock, nor even a sword, "To be sure that you know I am of civil intention, Captain," then releasing his coat's lapels, and standing at full attention he delivers a proper salute, "Sir."

"Well then," Robert waves generously toward his home, "You are all our welcome guests."

Captain Derek and Greely DeVoss stand back and watch while the other passengers disembark. The first out of the boat and onto the dock are the two youngsters that have been leaning eagerly against the gunwale. Next to be offered a hand is their mother, and then their father. The four of them are led to shore by the Gedimin offspring. As the pretty young woman, traveling with the older man steps up on the bench both Annia and Mara recognize that she is pregnant and rush forward offering steady hands. The older gent is left to step over the gunwale on his own. The last is the round fellow with his tuba. Renaldo leads him away, following the others. Robert allows Greely DeVoss to pass while holding back Captain Derek, "Who is this other fellow traveling with you?"

Captain Derek sighs deeply before answering, "This man, being a former clerk for the accursed VOC, has been of aid to me in this endeavor," then lowering his voice, "I do not entirely trust him."

Robert tells him, "Well then, how 'bout I trust him as much as I trust you," and they shake hands on this cryptic bargain of fealty.

♡♡♡

As Diedrik approaches Schoonhoven Landing he sees a group of riders coming from the other direction. Even without his new field glasses he recognizes that it is the professors and friends. He is pleasantly surprised to see that Captain Janszoon rides with them. He also notes that behind Robert's ship tied at the wharf is tied the other smaller sailing craft that he had seen earlier. "Oh my," he thinks, "We certainly have a crowd. Donar will be so very pleased."

"What took you so long?" Vejz teases him, as he and his brother meet Diedrik and retrieve the leads of their horses from him.

Ignoring the jibe he asks, "Were you able to keep up with Robert's sailing?"

"Alas, no," Razs answers, "but our new horses loved the pace."

Gesturing toward the dock and the extra ship Diedrik comments, "It appears that we have even more guests than planned." Then pointing them toward the crowd approaching from the other direction, "The crowd we are expecting is also arriving."

"Wow. We will have a party," Razs tells him, "everyone is up on the lawn."

"The Windhoek yard?"

"Yes. I suppose because it is the closest."

"Donar always enjoyed having his family and guests gather there around him of an evening." As the others ride up he calls out heartily, "Halloo! I am pleased to see you all looking so well after your long ride." They pause there on the track and he explains, "It appears that our Captain Robert, who has been away, has returned this day, and has brought an extra shipload of guests with him: but have no worries there are beds enough for everybody."

Riding into the yard now, with the Utrecht crowd following close behind, Diedrik recognizes Captain Robert awaiting them in the drive, a man whom he remembers as a business partner of his father's, but whom he has not seen for quite some time. He scans the yard of familiar and unfamiliar faces seated there. Among the unfamiliar sits a man whose presence sparks a memory that has his heart suddenly feeling like it has stopped, for that man is the very clerk that he had lifted the golden hearts necklace off. "What is he doing here?" he mutters under his breath while unconsciously pulling in the reins, bringing his horse so suddenly to a halt that all behind him are caught off guard, and are bumping nose to rump all the way back.

Robert, who has positioned himself to greet these new arrivals, is surprised when they all stop short of where he stands. He strides forward, reaching out to shake hands, "Hello Diedrik. It has been some years since we last met."

With noisy jibes being shouted from behind, Diedrik is distracted. He turns to his friends calling out, "Everything is OK. My apologies. I --," he begins to say something more, but is afraid that he will be thought a fool, "I am a fool," he tells them. He reaches down to shake Robert's hand, "Welcome home, Sir. I have been looking forward to your return."

"Aye. Likewise, indeed." Robert looks down the line of eager faces who now have their horses lined up properly again. "Another ship has followed me home. We have offered its passengers our hospitality. I sincerely regret if the presence of these unexpected guests will impose upon these, your intended guests."

"I know for certain that there are beds enough for everyone. It is common to have a crowd this size gathered here. The old man loved having lots of company." He dare not look in the direction of the despicable clerk. "There is room for this new bunch at Windmidden."

"Splendid."

The line of horses begins moving again, but after only a few steps Saarika, surprised to recognize the captain of the ship she sailed on from London, and then startled as she recognizes Greely DeVoss, in her consternation repeats Diedrik's impulsive yanking on the reins while muttering, "What is that horrible man doing here?"

All those behind her, after getting their horses moving, to be caught off guard once again by another sudden halt, and each bumping into the horse that is immediately in front of them in line, cry out, "What now?!"

Greely DeVoss looks up at the commotion, and into the piercing eyes of a woman he recognizes, *oh damn*, ruing the day that he met this princess, whose arrival had brought about the ending of his illustrious career.

Saarika gathers her composure. Now is not the time to be discontented. Turning her gaze forward and pressing her heels gently into her horse's flanks she gets moving. Those behind her encourage their horses forward, albeit apprehensively.

Nicklas leaves plenty of room between his horse and the horse in front of him, but when he recognizes the thieving clerk he, as the others before him, involuntarily yanks on his reins, bringing his confused mount to a sudden stop. "What is he doing here?" Trinjntje's horse, behind him, is able to side step allowing her to wonder what has them continually stopping. Nicklas nearly jumps off to throttle the man, but his better nature prevails, and instead he turns his horse forward and rushing to get moving digs his heels into his horse's flanks, unfortunately a bit too vigorously, bringing the beast up on its hind legs. He reaches down patting the horse on the neck, "I am so very sorry," and telling it soothingly as it settles with all four hooves on the ground, "you did not deserve that. You may kick me back when I have dismounted," and then rides to catch up with the others.

Trinjntje asks her uncle, whose horse has stopped sideways next to her, "What is going on?"

Cornelius scans the crowd as he turns his horse. He notices, amongst the crowd seated there on the lawn, two questionable looking characters, "I am not sure, but we will certainly find out soon enough." Before he has his horse moving again the ginger bearded fellow that has greeted them all introduces himself. Janszoon does likewise and delivers a proper salute, which Robert returns: Captain to Captain.

Liberation

Diedrik's thoughts are reeling with the implications of the presence of that smarmy VOC fellow. He dismounts clumsily upon reaching his barn, and while swinging the doors open he expels all the air from his lungs in an effort to calm himself. He pauses with his head down to quiet his thoughts, not wanting this moment to be tarnished by a mistake of his past, then turns to his guests, "There is feed inside, and stalls enough for all your horses, unless you wish to turn them out to pasture," indicating the field of grass beyond.

The barn is strangely silent as all dismount and begin caring for their horses. Lu-Tang is sensing an edginess from his horse that has come on suddenly, and he is noticing that this same agitation seems to be the prevailing mood among his fellow riders. He says, to no one in particular, "I will choose a stall for this mare. Something has her disturbed."

"Yes," concurs Hendrik, "mine too. She has been steady all day, but now is discernably distraught. Please," now addressing Diedrik, "have you a brush that I may use to give her a calming rubdown?"

"What can it be then," muses Calderon, "that has our horses in a flurry? Has a snake crossed our path?"

"A snake indeed!" Saarika pronounces with a huff as she lifts the saddle and blanket from her mount and then places it over the rail next to where Diedrik has placed his. The others of the group stop what they are doing and look to her for an explanation. She turns, and noting that she has everyone's attention, tells them, "There is a man among the crowd on the lawn whom I dealt with when I first came to Amsterdam. He is a conniving cheat with a nasty temperament!" Facing Nicklas she pronounces, "The clerk that stole from you is here!"

Nicklas confirms what she has said, "Yes. I noticed and I was barely able to keep myself from rushing over there, and oh, I cannot say what I may have done, but strangulation is what first comes to mind."

Captain Janszoon, with raised eyebrows comments, "I thought that I recognized a clerk of the VOC port authority! Now you are saying that he is the man that you believe stole from you?"

"I doubt very much that he is still employed by the Company," concludes Nicklas, "not after Trinjntje's father finished with him. Besides, the scoundrel claims that the necklace had been stolen from him by a sneak thief, a pickpocket."

Diedrik, beginning to understand the nature of what is unfolding, feels cold rivulets of sweat running uncomfortably down his ribs.

Trinjntje, who has her horse's bridle undone, but still resting over the horse's neck, having stopped in the middle of what she is doing, disbelievingly asks, "Are you saying that the man who stole the necklace is here?"

Diedrik experiences a flash of comprehension as the pieces fall into place. One of these people is the rightful owner of the necklace stolen by the clerk; the clerk whose pocket he had consequently picked. He feels happy that now he can return the necklace of Golden Hearts to its true owner, yet frightened at the prospect of disclosing his deed. Terribly frightened. Not wanting to, but knowing that he must, he summons his courage to ask, "This necklace?" His voice quavering, his face a ghostly shade of pale, "Is it an array of Golden Hearts set with jewels?"

All stop what they are doing, and look toward the one person of the group who would not know what they are speaking of. Lu-Tang is remembering the tale that Diedrik had told in confidence, of his previous short-lived career, and calls to mind his own speculating upon what could have been lifted from another's pocket that would so alter the young man's course of destiny. Now, noting Diedrik's ashen countenance, takes his young friend's arm and leads him to a bench near the wide doorway. Once seated he says consolingly, "Easy now. Everything is OK. You are amongst friends."

In a stupor, Diedrik looks around at the assembled crowd gathered in a circle before him. He wants to talk, but his voice is caught in his throat. Trinjntje, not sure what has Diedrik looking so stricken, sits down next to him and takes one of his hands in hers' consolingly. He is afraid to look at her; afraid to look at any of them. He blinks and feels tears run down his cheeks. Hendrik hurriedly steps forward handing over a clean kerchief. After what seems like an eternity of wiping away his tears his ability to speak returns and he blurts out, "I know where the necklace is."

"How do you know of the necklace?" Saarika asks.

"I too recognized the VOC villain," taking a breath to steel himself, and then continuing quickly before his voice fails him again, "for I am the thief that picked the necklace from his pocket." There. He has said it. His ordeal will now be over. He no longer has to hide his guilt. Abruptly he stands, "I will get it now." Off he runs toward his house, leaving Trinjntje and Lu-Tang staring wordlessly at the empty space between them.

Hendrik, before anybody has a chance to say anything, raises a hand and while flourishing his fingers, as would a stage magician before a dumbfounded crowd, exclaims, "I daresay, no one has expected this!" Saarika collapses cross-legged onto the hay-strewn floor. Nicklas and Cornelius exchange bemused expressions of fascination. Calderon, stroking his beard, contemplates the nature of a Universe that is able to orchestrate such circumstances into being.

Diedrik reappears before anyone else has spoken a word and rushes forward, stopping before Nicklas holding out the velour sash that holds the necklace within its folds. Nicklas shakes his head and says, "Not me."

So Diedrik turns to Trinjntje who is still seated on the bench, who also shakes her head, "Not me either." She tips her head toward Saarika, who is rising to her feet.

Diedrik turns and steps to Saarika holding the object out for her to take. He holds his head bowed in shame. Saarika does not at first take it from him. The atmosphere inside the barn crackles with anticipation. Diedrik squeezes his eyes shut, and then to his surprise, his vantage point shifts so that he is watching the scene from above it all, as if he is up in the loft. Saarika reaches out at last, placing her hands on his upper arms and gripping firmly until he lifts his head and looks up into her eyes. He is distracted at that moment with déjà vu and, not surprisingly, with an overwhelming sense of release. Letting go of his arms, she takes the velvet sash and unfolds it enough for a glimpse of the spectacular Golden Hearts within. She passes the article to Calderon without removing her intent gaze upon Diedrik, then stepping forward and embracing him fully she pulls him tightly against her and raising up to her full height lifts him off his feet, and swings him round and round as a parent would a child. "Thank-You. Thank-You. Thank-You." She sets him back onto his feet, takes his face in her hands, and with her own face close enough for him to discern the individual sparkling stars in the sky of her eyes, tells him, "You, my dear man are the link that has made it possible for all of us to be here. It is your doing that has congregated us together. You, Dearest, are part of something greater than us all. You, Diedrik, are special ... Very special indeed!" She tilts his head and places a loving kiss centered just between his brows. Her tenderness has him feeling lighter than he has ever felt before. So much that he has held inside has been released. He is free.

♡♡♡

Captain Derek, all of his passengers being cared for by these kind-hearted Windmillers, is suddenly without responsibility. He has been told by his host to feel at home, and to keep his tankard full. He and his little band of refugees have eaten from the food spread out on the table, and drank from the keg there in its cradle. Oddly enough, all the windmillers are nowhere in sight. So he refills his mug and walks down by the river where he finds a bench to sit upon while contemplating his fate. The river chart, confiscated by DeVoss in his late night prance through the offices of his former employer, shows an easy passage that anyone could sail, but Derek is a sea captain, not a riverboat captain. It is a foolhardy thing he has done; this giving up everything, throwing away everything. But then again, he had nothing to throw away. It would have been foolhardy to stay, "I wish that I did not believe myself to be such a fool."

Greely DeVoss has slipped away, feeling out of place, and not knowing where all the folks who live here have gone. He finds himself at the river's edge and sits down on the same bench as Captain Derek, holding his mug out for a toast to their accomplishment. They each know very little of the other's language, making conversation an effort. Neither man is in the mood, nor cares for the other enough to make that effort just now. So they sit here unspeaking. Greely grows steadily more irritated by the constant noise of the birds cawing, twittering, quacking, honking, screeching, hooting, whistling, cooing, and singing. He wonders peevishly if there is anyone, besides poets, who actually considers the sounds that birds make to be anything like singing. He wallows in his pettiness. He does not want to be petty; so let them call it singing, the fools. His pettiness holds his thoughts of the princess at bay. Besides the princess, there is that wise ass Voorhaven; the very scoundrel that had been attempting to smuggle the necklace of Golden Hearts into Amsterdam. Now his heart skips a beat as he considers facing either of them again. He has treated both of them disdainfully. He does not wish to be reminded of how he has treated others. He has lived believing that there are no decent people in this world, thus giving himself permission to treat others indecently. He does not want to be a vile person, but it is a vile world. Right now he has the opportunity to change, for he is a homeless man traveling with others who are homeless. He can start fresh. What will he do?

After Greely has taken his seat, and after they have agreed wordlessly to abstain from any attempt at conversation, Captain Derek returns to his thoughts. What was he thinking about? He was wondering what he is doing piloting this disgusting pinnace up an unknown river. Has he ever done what he wanted to do? As a boy he had dreamed of going to Paris. As a boy he had dreamed of riding horses. As a boy he had enjoyed the company of others while attending school at Cambridge, but then he had gone on to the naval academy at Portsmouth, and then still very young, he had been stationed, through family connections, as an officer aboard ship. He has never been effective as an officer, nor has he ever enjoyed being a captain. He has never felt welcomed into the brotherhood of sailors. Will he ever fit in? Floundering in self-pity he gives way to his weariness. His chin sinks to his chest. He sleeps and his unwelcome thoughts become his unwelcome dreams.

Greely DeVoss notices Captain Derek's chin sinking to his chest, and waits a bit to be certain that the man is sleeping. He determines that now is an opportunity for him to be gone. He steals his way down the wharf and slips into the little English ship that is not a ship, sailed by a captain that is no longer a captain. The strongbox that he had grabbed when he had stolen the maps is stowed away in a compartment under a bench. He wrangles it out, and it takes some wrangling for it is a tight fit. He opens it up. He would like to take it all, but surely someone would come after him if he did that, so he will only take a share. He takes his coin purse from the pocket of his waistcoat and fills it with guldens. Then he digs through his satchel and comes up with a leathern drawstring bag, which he fills with more guldens. This is enough, but there is still so much left in the box: so he fills a sock with coins and ties it with a knot. That'll do. He closes the lid of the box, but because it is so difficult to get back into the compartment beneath the bench, he leaves it laying out in the open. He latches his satchel, then gripping its handles he jumps up onto the bench and leaps from the boat to the dock. He is almost skipping like a boy up to the shore where he tips his hat to the sleeping Captain Derek, "Thanks for getting me out, fool." He takes the path that leads on up the river. He almost looks back, but catches himself: there is no looking back.

Captain Derek is awake for a bit before all the thoughts he had been thinking begin again. He checks down the bench noticing that his criminal cohort is no longer seated there, although his mug is. His very next thought, nay, more of a realization, is that DeVoss has gone. He lifts his own mug, happy to see that there is some left, and he finishes it off. He then stands and makes his way down to the dock and as he comes alongside the little ship that is not really a ship he spies the purloined strongbox sitting out from its hiding place. He steps over and onto the bench, jumps down, and opens the box to see that some has been taken, but most remains. "Hmmmm. A clever ploy. Take plenty while leaving plenty." Now, no longer thinking of himself as a captain, he brings his coin purse from a pouch at his belt and fills it with guldens. He then withdraws from an inner pocket of his coat an embroidered drawstring bag, normally used for carrying his smoking paraphernalia, and he fills it with more guldens. Lastly, he opens his duffel and stuffs handfuls of coins into deep hidden compartments. Snapping his duffel closed, and slamming the lid of the box down, he leaps up onto the bench and over to the dock. He speedily makes his way from the wharf to the shore and follows the river trail north. He suffers only a slight qualm at leaving behind the responsibility of his passengers. He suffers no qualms whatsoever regarding leaving behind the life he has lived.

♡♡♡

The Gedimin family, having gone ahead of Diedrik and the Utrecht crowd, are leading their horses down the drive toward home. Renaldo asks Annia, "So, how did you discover that Mara has a necklace of Golden Hearts?"

"As I think back on yesterday my memories are like dreaming." That does not answer his question. She can tell by the way he is smiling at her. So, she begins again, "The other night at the market fair Mara had intentionally kept herself awake through the lullaby. Hearing the line referring to our golden hearts left her pondering, and eventually to ask, just as I was always taught it would happen." The children are all riding the horses, leaving Renaldo and Annia on their own, "First she asked me about Kupala and the story in the lullaby. She compared it to a story she had learned as a girl. Then she asked about the wreath of golden hearts, and if we believe that the golden hearts had ever been, or if they still may be. She told us that where she comes from, only those families with the golden hearts know the tale. Since she knows the tale, she was basically revealing to us that she has some Golden Hearts of her own. So I told her that I have some, and then went to get my necklace to show her."

The children have returned, excitedly circling their parents on their new horses. Then after a bit Kirin asks Renaldo if he is hearing the full story of Mara's revelation. He answers, "Yes, she has reached the part where she went to get her own necklace."

Kirin adds to what her Ma has been telling her Pa, "We compared the two necklaces side by side and they are the same."

Now Vejz wants to know, "Does Mara also have a golden orb?"

"No," Audrae answers, "but you might be able to guess what she does have that goes with her necklace."

"Her harp." Razs says it in the same instant that the light flashes in his memory, "She plays her small harp, but I have never seen her play the large harp."

"Brilliant!" Annia tells him, "There is a hollow at the top of her harp's column that matches the shape of our orb in its dish."

Now Audrae is telling the story, "Ma stood on a chair and when she set the orb in that spot at the top of the harp's post it all hummed and glowed."

"The strings played a melody that sounded like bells," Kirin finishes.

Renaldo is thinking out loud, "Do you suppose ..."

"What?"

"On his last visit, I noticed that Professor Calderon spent a lot of time examining Mara's harp."

"Are you supposing," questions Vejz, "That the harp is why he is here again?"

"Well, he is a scholar. He is well-traveled and has done tremendous research."

Arriving at their barn Razs offers, "We will have a lot to carry back with us, so I will tether a fresh horse to the cart. Let's take our instruments. We can dance and sing."

"Woo! Hoo!" Annia does a little dance. "But first, I will help put these new horses in the barn. It is my turn to get to know them." Taking her husband's elbow and smiling into his eyes, "Come my dear, tell me about these fine horses you have brought home for us to ride."

♡♡♡

While preparing more food to take outside Robert asks Mara, "So, how did you discover that Annia has a necklace of golden hearts?"

"Have you heard the lullaby that she sings so sweetly?"

"If I have, I was possibly asleep while she was singing."

"She sings a lullaby that is a fable from olden times. I have stayed awake after all others have been lulled into sleeping. In the fable there are ferns with blossoms of fire, lovers wearing wreaths on their heads, and there is a gift bestowed; a gift of Golden Hearts."

"She sings for anyone to hear of the Golden Hearts?"

"The bit about the Golden Hearts comes at the end, after most are sleeping. It is a tradition of her family. It is a snare intended to catch the attention of anyone familiar with the reference."

"La, a subtle hint. How sublime."

Mara is enjoying telling this story as they are preparing for their guests, "It took me a full day, and a few glasses of wine, to gather up the courage to broach the subject with her." She stops what she is doing. He stops and their eyes meet across the room, "Annia is so wonderful, and Kirin and Audrae are darlings. It all turned out to be easy; and we had fun. Oh la, we had fun. We compared the necklaces. She has a golden ball," holding her hands out to show him the size, "that sends them to dreaming, same as the harp. That little ball fits into the shallow hollow at the top of the harp's column and made it all light up! The strings hurummed like celestial bells."

"Wow!"

"And Rob, for a while there, my parents and grandparents and all their parents and grandparents, everybody who has ever cherished the Golden Hearts for a lifetime and strummed their fingers across the strings of the golden harp were here with us. It lit a flame in my heart Robert."

Remembering the tale that he wants to share with her of the two that had visited with him at the high mountain tower, and remembering that there is to be three of the necklaces, "Are you imagining that the third necklace of Golden Hearts is close by?"

"Oh. Yes, it must be. Come 'ere and give me another hug. I am so glad that you are home!"

♡♡♡

Hendrik is teasingly pointing out to Diedrik the chains that attach his coin purse and wallet to his belt. Diedrik almost enlightens the professor that the chains are no deterrent for a master dipper. Instead, he tries to explain his remorse, "I do not know what came over me. Luckily I learned my lesson. It is these Golden Hearts that made me stop."

"Well, I say that what you were doing did not suit your nature." Now Hendrik straightens himself, and presenting his professional demeanor pronounces wisdomatically, "Many of us pass through unexplainable phases on our path through this *Mysterium* that we call life. Those who are willing to acknowledge that they have made mistakes find consolation knowing that they have learned what they do not want; thus allowing them to move toward what they do want."

"Hmmm. I will consider that."

"I am also led to ponder on what Anna Maria would say."

"Oh, I would so love to have her visit here again."

"She might tell you that it is Universal Forces that have drawn you in to their master plan of returning the Golden Hearts to the rightful owner."

Calderon, who has been listening in, now joins the conservation, "Your Universal Forces theory sounds plausible to me, Sir."

Captain Janszoon rises from the crate that he has been sitting on, "Well, since I am a part of all this, may I have a closer look at these Golden Hearts? And perhaps a little background, *s'il vous plaît*, regarding these hearts."

Saarika hands over the necklace, wrapped again within the folds of Diedrik's sash, "This necklace of Golden Hearts has been passed along through a sisterhood of priestesses since before history has been written; or so I have been told." She looks around as she wonders what next to say. "I am no priestess, but I am the next in line. My wayward brother's proposal, the villainous clerk's thievery, and Diedrik's brief foray is why we are all here today."

"My brief foray," Diedrik snorts.

Calderon, looking out through the open doors as the Gedimin family passes by with their horse and cart says, "Let us not keep our hosts waiting. It shall be fascinating, shall it not, to see how the circumstances of this day, this adventure, continue to play out?"

Diedrik agrees, then tells them, "I will follow shortly, for there is food and drink that I have set aside to add to what the others have prepared." He takes his wheelbarrow and walks out of the barn. Lu-Tang follows and helps him load beer, wine, sliced meats, and a box of fruits.

Lu-Tang fills in for Diedrik, "Through years of research relating to ancient histories, Calderon has determined that where there is one necklace of Golden Hearts there will eventually be two more."

"Is he of the notion that there are more Golden Hearts here?"

"He is. He has made this trek for the purpose of presenting the results of his extensive research. I am certain that you will be fascinated by what he is prepared to show us."

A large brightly colored long-tailed bird flies overhead. It is like no other bird Diedrik has ever seen. He abruptly sets the wheelbarrow down, taking his gaze away for a mere moment, but when he looks back he sees a familiar dark blue crane. "Whoa? What happened?"

"Eh?" Lu-Tang follows the direction of Diedrik's gaze. "Has something appeared suddenly different than the way it had appeared before?"

"Indeed."

♡♡♡

The young Estonian family that has sailed here with Captain Derek has been walking the polder investigating these tremendous windmills. When they return to where the rest of the displaced of their homeland sit they find the young pregnant woman sleeping, while her father paces. The gentleman with the tuba raises his full mug and smiles. They ask, "Where are all the Windmillers?"

The older gentleman asks, "Where is our Captain?"

The tuba fellow remarks, "I say not to worry. Since the moment that my troupe was rounded up as instigators against the new rulers I have been mistreated, crowded onto a ship bound for who knows where, denied the right of liberty, and led to participating in a clandestine escape." He raises his glass to the others and drinks heartily before continuing, "I sit here more comfortably than I have for quite some time, and I am feeling in my heart that everything will work out for us after all."

The woman that had been sleeping sits up and asks, "Is everything okay?"

The children's father, whose family's home has been burned because of his position as a community servant sighs, "It is this feeling that we are leaves blowing in the wind that is disheartening. I look forward to when we will at last come to ground again."

The melancholy mood of uncertainty is dispersed by the arrival of the Gedimins. The Estonians are all pleased that these who know their language are back. Renaldo formally introduces himself, "Renaldumus Gedimin, at your service," then takes his wife's hand, allowing her to introduce herself.

She curtsies and pronounces, "Annia Gedimin," and then turns to her sons and daughters who have lined up by age.

"Razs," bowing handsomely.

"Kirin," curtsying respectfully.

"Vejz," bowing less formally.

"Audrae," delivered boldly.

Before the introductions continue Mara and Robert emerge from their home, both bringing more food to the table. Robert sets a steaming pot on a pad, then turns and waves his guests to come on over. Mara sets a platter of sliced meat on the table, tugs at her husband's sleeve, and they both return inside for more.

The professors and their traveling companions arrive and whatever introductions left to be made are performed as the milling crowd assembles around the tables, and everyone who has not already eaten fills their plates and mugs. It is a beautiful evening for a picnic. The Gedimins all take part in translating so that the little ship's passengers are included in the social banter.

Amidst the revelry Diedrik notes the arrival of one more guest; a woman who has frequented many of Donar's gatherings in the past. He rushes forward as she dismounts her horse, "Anna Maria," he bows down on one knee and reaches for her hand that he may place a kiss upon her fingers, "I am so very happy to see you."

"Oh, stop," she raises him up, and throwing her arms around him and embracing him tightly. "Diedrik," scanning the gathering, "this is magnificent! Donar would be so pleased that you are entertaining so many!" She hugs him tight again, and kisses his cheeks, as a mother or a sister would.

Hendrik is there to greet her next. Releasing Diedrik, she extends a hand for the professor to kiss, and explains, "I returned home yesterday, and upon finding you missing from your lecture hall was informed by one of your assistants that you have traveled here, to Schoonhoven Landing. It has been so long since I have been here that I decided I must join you." She reaches out and takes Diedrik's hand and squeezes it tightly, "Besides, I have wanted to see what this fine young man is up to."

"You rode here, from Utrecht, on your own?" Hendrik asks her in a flabbergasted tone.

"La, how cavalier of me. Right?" The sparkle in her eyes, the quickness of her smile, and the ease of her nature reminds the two men why they love her so as they follow her into the barn. While she stables her horse she tells them, "I have been away on a silent retreat, so this gathering will be the perfect antidote for my days of silence." When her horse has been put away she takes them each and leads them by the arm back outside to the gathered crowd, "Let us join the fun. I am famished."

♡♡♡

Saarika is sitting on the ground with her back leaning against a tree; her hands folded in her lap, her legs crossed comfortably at the ankles, and her eyes closed. She has been sitting like this long enough for others to imagine that she is sleeping, but she is not sleeping; she has been focusing upon calming her mood. Coming from the barn she had hardly been able to focus her thoughts and her heart had been pounding. She has been seated here long enough that the rhythm of her heartbeat has returned closer to its natural pulse. She is thinking back on the events of the day, even before arriving here at Schoonhoven Landing. As she recollects their first stop and the Captain's statues she wonders about what had been said about these angels that walk this earth. Are they born knowing that they are angels? Or, are they born as all humans are born, forgetting all other lives and all other realms, so that they may experience the fullness of being human? She is attempting to imagine how it feels to be an eternal being coming to this human realm in order to experience the sweetness of mortality. Do they come here as a challenge to see if they are able to discover their eternality within the span of a human lifetime?

Trinjntje sits herself down next to the pensive princess, carefully, so as not to spill the two full pint glasses she has brought with her. She shakes her head in an attempt to get her hair out of her eyes as she searches the crowd for the evil man whose presence had stirred up such discomfort among her companions. Not finding him, her sights fall upon the latest arrival, Anna Maria van Shooman, who seems so at home here. The woman is a celebrity, yet she has ridden here on her own, and acts like a relative to Diedrik. Now Trinjntje is sipping from one of the glasses that she is holding, and then saying out loud, "I came over here with an extra glass of beer in case anyone would be interested, but it seems that I will have to drink both glasses of beer myself." She looks up into the branches of the tree and sees a robin eyeing her. "Hello Robin. Care for a beer?"

Saarika opens her eyes laughing, "La, you are such a dope!" As she is reaching for the extra glass of beer she invites Diedrik who is passing by, "Join us," she points to a spot between her and Trinjntje, indicating for him to sit.

He sits down rather timorously, wondering how this exchange can be handled: will he be witty, will he be ashamedly regretful, and will he be himself? Not sure of what to say he follows the first rule of small talk, "It is a beautiful day."

Both women smile, then Saarika says, "Tell me about being a sneak-thief. Is it exciting?

He looks back and forth, from one set of sparkling eyes to the other. Both women appear to be genuinely interested in what he has to tell them. "Ehh," he clears his throat, "Umm ... well ..."

Trinjntje punches his upper arm, "Tell us! What did you think when you discovered you had lifted the necklace of Golden Hearts?"

"It scared the hell out of me!" Oh, now they are laughing, and his nervous spell is broken, "I was dumfounded. I thought I had stolen crown jewels. I had no idea what to do. I wanted to give it back. I knew someone would be searching for it. I ran. I packed my bags and I left Amsterdam."

Trinjntje does a quick calculation in her head, then gleefully tells him, "So, you must have been running away from Amsterdam on the same day that I was running away from Amsterdam."

"Coincidentally amusing," ruminates Saarika, then back to her questions, "Had you ever before picked anything nearly so amazing?"

"It was my second day of picking pockets," he blurts out in his defense, "purses and wallets, nothing more." For a moment they are all wondering; Saarika wonders if the necklace chooses its path, Trinjntje wonders what set this decent fellow up to thievery, Diedrik wonders if he can turn the conversation to something else. He tells Saarika, "I liked having the necklace. I hid it inside the sash, to wear beneath my coat and it felt good to have it there next to me. I would get it out and marvel at its magnificence. I discovered that by linking the pattern on the back of the hearts there is a," what else can he call it, "a magic."

"La, more than you have yet imagined," while thinking that she does not remember there being patterns on the backs of the hearts.

♡♡♡

The two children from the lifeboat have asked Audrae and Vejz to walk with them down to the river. "We have not seen our English captain, nor his sneaky-eyed cohort for a while," the oldest tells them.

"We think that they are gone. They have stolen away," adds his younger sister.

Audrae asks, "Why are you traveling on that lifeboat anyway?"

At first, neither answers, but then the boy blurts, "Because we are refugees."

"Our Ma and Pa do not want us to say that."

Vejz asks them, "Why did you have to leave home?"

"Soldiers made us go with them to a ship that took us to Kopenhagen."

"Then we were made to go on another ship that we snuck off of in the middle of the night for this little boat."

"Whoa," Razs wheezes, "Why did soldiers do that? Did you break the law?"

"Pa says that there is a new ruler."

"The soldiers called Pa bad names, and told Ma to shut-up"

"We left our home, but it was our choice," Vejz tells them, "our Da worked for the king, but when the king agreed to let his people vote they voted in new leaders who appointed someone else to do Da's job."

"We were not forced to leave, but we did not want to stay either," Audrae adds as they are walking out on the dock.

"Oh, so you are refugees too?" the girl asks.

"Reefoogeez?" Vejz asks, "That is the second time I have heard you say that word."

"It means that you do not have a home," she explains.

"We have a home. It is on wheels," Audrae informs them, "that is how we traveled here."

Vejz adds some details, "We came over the mountains, and then we followed this river. Now we are living here."

"Will you ever see your home again?"

"This is our home now," Audrae answers.

"Do you like your new home?" both ask.

"For now," the other two answer back, "but there are no mountains."

"I know! Right?"

♡♡♡

Razs remembers to ask Robert, "Did you see the giant fireball streak across the sky?"

"I did see a mighty ball o' fire, and I was wondering, as large as it was, if maybe you folks here were seeing it same as I was."

"Yes. We did see it, and we have heard more news of it today."

"Well, tell me lad what ye have heard."

"That it is a giant-sized boulder as big as a hill, and that it gouged a ditch across the land until it stopped at the base of a mountain, and that it burned all surrounding it to ash."

Renaldo, smiling at his son's exaggerating, adds more, "We hear that it is still hot."

"How far away is this now?"

Diedrik answers, "My Da has told me that it is about two hundred miles away."

"The sons of the horse trader," Razs starts in again, "told me that people are traveling from all over to see the site, and that there is an encampment with so many people that it is a little city," he is holding his arms wide to show everybody listening how big this event has grown.

Robert blurts out, "A star-seed!" not realizing that he has spoken out loud. Upon seeing the vexed expressions showing on the faces of those listening, he adds sheepishly, "It is something that I heard whilst on my last voyage." In the back of his thoughts he is pondering that this seems similar to the rock in the mountaintop tower he had visited. His thoughts drift further to the star-folk that had visited him, still uncertain whether or not he had dreamed them.

He is startled out of his reverie when Captain Janszoon speaks up, as if he too is thinking out loud, "A starseed, eh? So the stars in the sky, like the plants of the earth in the proper season, set loose a horde of seeds across the galaxy?" He drops his jaw comically for emphasis, "As an astronomer I realize that the stars in our sky are very far away," now laughing, "and now, you say, that they send out seeds the size of boulders! That is a phenomenal proposition. I like your idea! I like it very much indeed! It may be a feasible explanation for why there are so many stars in the heavens."

Robert is as bewildered as Cornelius; that a glimmer of sparkling light in the night sky would send out a seed the size of a boulder. He is surprised by the direction of this discussion and adds to what this Dutch captain has said, "There are so many stars. The night sky is awash with them, and they form a pattern that can be followed from anywhere in the sea, or anywhere on the earth." They nod agreeably toward one another. He decides that now is as good a time as ever to tell his story, or at least a part of his story. "During my stay-over in Norway I visited a mountain tower that is indicated on an old map," he tips his head, "actually, there were two old maps."

Now he beckons Mara, who has just been telling Professor Calderon of the drawer, to come closer, "After following the first of the ancient maps, a familiar route, I left my ship at anchor in the port of Vik determined to follow the second map into the hills," smiling now, "which rise up immediately from wherever one stands in Norway." Sensing that a story is being told, others discontinue their conversations giving Robert their full attention. He is a good story teller, and upon noting that he has the crowd's attention carries on, "I showed my map to the old man whose grandson runs the boarding house where I was staying. This old fellow, a centenarian, was familiar with the trail from his youth. The trail that I wanted to follow, he told me, had been buried beneath a landslide almost a lifetime ago." Following his directions had me breaking my way through thick brush until reaching the wall of rock and rubble and debris which was where the landslide, *skritha* is what they called it, had covered the trail."

He takes a break to quaff a bit of brew, then whilst setting his mug down he scans his crowd of listeners, enjoying his role of storyteller. "I made my way up that wall of boulders," spreading his arms, "and believe me when I tell you that it was a massive feat of endurance. When I reached the top of the scree I was able to see before me where the vast hillside had collapsed," waving a hand before him, "probably during the rainiest of rainy seasons," nodding to include everybody in the understanding. "Continuing to follow where I assumed my trail to be led me along a stream that meandered across a wide expanse of meadowland." He has thought out how he would be telling this tale to Mara, and now that he is telling it to this crowd he is wondering how much to tell. "It was a wonderful sunny day for traversing a montane meadow, and though it seemed to be a relatively flat path I was steadily climbing," raising an arm to signify the increasing altitude. "The stream led me into a gorge between two sawtooth ridges. By late afternoon my trail became very steep indeed," shaking his head, "but I continued following the stream, which was now a series of deep pools and waterfalls. My path looked to be well used and cleared by the hooves of the enormous, yet fleet-footed animals living there," again spreading his arms wide, "Norwegians call them *Alce*." He considers telling of the huge herd he had seen, but does not wish to distract from the point of his narrative. "That steep trail led me to a mountain lake of beautiful stillness that reflected perfectly the bowl of rock cliffs surrounding it. Ya know, that trail I climbed was the only way leading in to that marvelous place. It was truly heavenly. I sat down next to the rivulet that is the outlet from the lake, and was also the very stream I had been following all day. I had reached the headwater. I looked around me in wonder at the magnificence of the scene created by nature. And then, to my surprise, I beheld an amazing structure." It is a perfect time to pause, allowing his listeners to curiously engage in surmising what this wonder may be. "A stone structure, assembled by master stonemasons to appear as if formed naturally from the cliff it is assembled against. A tower, nearly as tall as these windmills, encircled by a roofed double wall. So masterful was the masonry that the slates of all the roofs were still in place. High up on the tower there are arched windows that let in the light. The circling walls emerge from the cliff, yet the passage leading between those walls goes in and through the solid rock to make a full circle." He decides to leave out the part where the sound of his voice brought light into the darkness of this circling passageway.

"I have made sketches of what I beheld, and perhaps later I can bring them out for all to see." Then turning to Razs, who had asked him of the fireball, "I have also attempted to sketch the flight of the meteoroid as it streaked across the night sky."

"Did you go inside the tower?" Trinjntje asks, "Surely you went inside?"

"Well, my dear, it was late in the day. I needed to gather wood for a fire before darkness set in."

"Ohhh," she was hoping to hear more.

He smiles as he looks around the group; all had been eagerly anticipating a further description. "La, even though I did not go into the tower that day," he smiles smugly, "I followed the pathway leading through the tall arched entryway first light next morning." All eyes watching him are expectantly wide, "This was when I discovered that the ring wall had the walkway leading in both directions, but I saved that for later, and continued through into a small courtyard, which was surprisingly clear of overgrowth, in fact, everything was surprisingly tidy," he shakes his head bewilderingly. "Before me rose the tall entry arch leading into the inner chamber," everybody follows his gaze as he looks up with one arm held high, "above that grand archway rose the tower, like I said before, as tall as these windmills, and beyond that the rocky cliff ascended even higher."

"Was it not frightening to be there alone," asks Kirin, "inside those ruins?"

"La, my dear, I am used to being alone," beginning to wonder how much he will tell, "Besides, the tower was clearly old, but not in ruin." He smiles reassuringly before continuing, "I went in carrying a lit torch, but once inside realized that there was enough sunlight streaming in through those windows high above that it was unnecessary." He pauses a moment, as he has been throughout this telling, to allow Renaldo to translate to the boat passengers the gist of his tale. "I stood within a large circular room with a large rock, a boulder, positioned in the center," raising a finger signifying for all to take note of this fact.

"The walls were adorned with murals made of colored tiles, the foremost being a surprisingly well preserved depiction of an angelically beautiful woman sitting at a golden harp." He sees recognition in Mara's eyes, but also notes Calderon exchanging expressions of recognition with others of his party. "Though I did not need the torch I still held it and the flame seemed to set the scene all aglow," now reaching out with wriggling fingers, "and in the flickering of the torch's flame I imagined the celestial beauty's fingers caressing the harp's strings," everybody gasps, "so lifelike was it that I believed to have heard the resonance of those strings, as if they had been plucked in that very instant." He looks around at the faces of the crowd all held in rapt attention to his tale.

"But what about the starseed?" Vejz challenges, "Have you forgotten why you were telling us this story?"

Robert laughs, "Oh, well, my apologies young Sir. The great grandad whose directions I was following is the one who called it the starseed shrine."

"What does that mean?"

"Remember I told of the rock in the center of the tower? The ancient text that came with the maps, and translated by the old man, describes that rock as a meteoroid, calling it a starseed."

"Was it incredible?"

"Well, it was not as large as a mountain," holding his hands wide, "about so big it was, and dull and scarred; a rock, no more. I have made sketches of it all."

Professor Calderon wants to see Robert's sketches so that he may compare them with the sketches and the stories he has brought with him. Looking around he wonders who all will be included in this further conversation. Mara had just told him of the monk's drawer full of antiquities. That must be where the maps Robert had followed came from.

Saarika is remembering the tiled mural in the hidden temple of her home, and even surprised to remember that ensconced in the floor before the mural was a large unremarkable boulder.

Mara is anxious to examine Robert's drawings and compare them with the drawings of the drawer left by the fleeing priests. When Professor Calderon had begun telling her why he had come to see her, he had started by telling her that he had once been a priest, so she had told him of the drawer left by the priests, but before she told him very much about the drawer's contents their conversation had been interrupted by Robert's tale.

Lu-Tang is recalling the site of a shrine shown to him by nomads of the northern wastes. Robert's narration could be describing what he had seen there; a mural portraying a Goddess seated at a harp, and a boulder worshipped as a gift from heaven.

Annia has a portentious stirring within her breast. She takes Renaldo's hand and gives it a thrilling squeeze.

Hendrik is remembering Calderon's painting fashioned from the rubbings of the Toltec pyramid. Now, amidst this mention of meteoroids, there is the notion of a new meteoroid having so recently fallen to the earth. Scanning the gathered crowd and wondering how many of them are aware of the Golden Hearts, and how many of them will be attending Calderon's presentation. Noticing that Kirin has just finished a lengthy discourse with the Estonians he asks her, "Have they heard the news of this most recent meteoroid?"

Her eyes light up and she turns and asks them. After a bit she tells him, "They all saw the flaming thing as it flew across the sky, and even thought it portentious to their own circumstances. Beyond that they only speak of returning to their homes."

"Is that their purpose for sailing up this river?" Captain Janszoon asks, "To get them closer to home? Where is their captain?"

"Their captain has not been seen for a while," Audrae tells them, "him and his mate may have left these folks behind."

"Hmph!" Scoffs Janszoon, "As I supposed. They are scoundrels. Tell these folks please, my dear girl, not to despair. We will do all we can for them." He turns on his heel and makes for the dock to ascertain what is to be done. In his head he is already calculating whether he is willing to sail these folks upriver, and how long the voyage would keep him from his own home.

Robert catches up to Cornelius, "Are you supposing that the English captain has cut and run?"

"It is uncommon for a captain to leave his ship behind," now looking to Robert for confirmation, "but if I have ascertained this situation correctly, this man has left one ship and crew already."

"Aye. The wretched soul has lost his bearings."

"Indeed. I can tell you Sir, with certainty, that his partner lacks any modicum of integrity." As they pass the riverside bench each notices the empty beer mugs left behind. Janszoon tells Robert, "Men of unscrupulous nature are what have provided the reasoning for many to disdain the Company that employed my services these many years." Robert keeps his own thoughts regarding the Company to himself as they make their way out to where the English pinnace is docked. "Eh? What have we here?" Cornelius leaps easily from the dock into the lifeboat and lifts the lid of the strongbox which bears the VOC emblem. Turning his body to allow Robert to view the coinage, "What make you of this?"

Directing Cornelius' attention to the map case, also bearing the VOC emblem, "Looks as if someone has visited the port office of *your* Company."

"It is not *My Company,*" Cornelius scowls until he notices by Robert's mischievous grin that he is being teased. "Ha! You have caught me. While still employed I developed a habit of defending the company I worked for, even though I never fully agreed with many of its practices." He picks up and opens the map case to reveal the river charts. "These will make passage upriver easier." Handing the case and its contents to Robert he asks, "Have you sailed this river?"

"Only a short ways beyond this landing." Surveying the river chart, "I will agree with you that this will facilitate passage," then pointing to the upper reaches of the river shown on the map, "especially once one has reached where it narrows. Are you considering sailing these folks?"

"I am weighing the options."

"Well, Captain Sir, if you do not choose to take the helm, then I suppose that honor would be left to me."

"But you have only now returned home ... Nay, I will take them up this river. I am in need of adventure." Now sweeping his gaze over this little vessel; even though it is an English ship, it is clearly Dutch craftsmanship. "It is a fine little sloop, although it should have a taller mast. Perhaps after sailing these folks as close to home as possible I could sail it back to keep as my own. That is, if I could be so inclined as to abide what may be considered an act of piracy."

"The piracy is a foregone act. Besides, stealing from the Brits is not considered piracy, but rather a public spirited achievement. You will retain your innocence."

"What are your thoughts relating to this stolen coffer that has been left behind?"

Peering into the open strongbox, "Hmmm," running his fingers through his beard while pondering the ethical solution, and then holding up his right hand with fingers spread wide, he begins counting, tugging the index finger, "First off, the money is already stolen." Now tugging on the middle finger, "Secondly, you will have need of funds." Tugging on third finger, "Upon disembarking, your passengers will still have far to go and may require financial support for the continuance of their homeward journey." Tugging on the pinky finger while rolling his eyes up in contemplation before displaying a wide grin, "Have more fun!" Lastly, with hand open, palm up, and all fingers splayed wide, "Or play the righteous fool and make way forthright to return this ship and its passengers and the stolen loot back to wherever you may assume they belong: which may turn out to be an unsurmountable, and even thankless, task!"

These remarks have them laughing. Both men's eyes sparkle with delight. Cornelius slaps Robert's open hand with his own open hand, then grabs hold and tugs himself back onto the dock. Shaking hands with this new friend he proclaims, "Great minds think alike! Eh?"

They are both still laughing as Renaldo and all seven of the Estonians make their way toward them on the dock. "These folks are very interested to discuss with either of you the possibility of stewarding them in this boat up this river as far as possible."

Captain Janszoon answers, "We have already made a decision. I will sail them as far as this ship will go. I am," finishing with a bow, "At your service."

The Golden Hearts

Anna Maria had ridden here on a whim; she likes to regularly practice allowing herself to follow her impulsive thoughts. She had been surprised this morning when told that Professor Hendrik would not be delivering a lecture, and bewildered when told of his destination, for in all of her visits to Donar van Eyck's Schoonhoven Landing she had never encountered her professor of medicine. Now here she is again at last after nearly a year, and Diedrik, who had been Donar's molenaar, has inherited the estate. She is pleased to see that Diedrik is carrying on Donar's heritage. He has graciously introduced her to all present in true gentlemanly fashion. The couple from Ireland who are inhabiting the home that had been Donar's personal residence are a delightful pair. She finds it very interesting that the family from Poland place such importance on their children's learning, and that their daughters are as well educated as their sons. She is saddened by the circumstances of the homeless Estonians; especially saddened that the invading armies that have cast them out are Swedish, for she has long corresponded with Christina, Queen of Sweden. She consoles herself that it is the men of Christina's council who are making the decisions to send the invading armies. She is enjoying hearing from Diedrik of his progress on the bird folio and admiring his new field glasses. When Hendrik sits down beside her she asks, "What brings you to Schoonhoven Landing Professor Regius?"

"Paulo Calderon is on a research mission, pursuing the pieces of an historical puzzle. I came along for the ride." She raises her eyebrows expecting more, "We were here not long ago, tagging along with Lu-Tang on his windmill tour."

"Oh, right. I remember now."

"Paulo discovered something here that piqued his interest, and now has come back with some of his research materials. His plan is to make a presentation, but with the crowd of this other ship here he is having to bide his time."

"What is the nature of this research?"

Hendrik raises his eyebrows, smiling impishly and wobbling his head, "To divulge that information would be to steal his thunder. I daresay, you will have to wait along with everybody else." He then whispers secretively, "The story told by Captain Robert holds an unexpected clue regarding what Calderon has come looking to find."

She turns to Diedrik, "Do you know what Professor Calderon is up to?"

"Ehmmmm, no ... Well, a little bit. Actually, I may know even less than you." She laughs, thinking that they are deliberately keeping something from her. Diedrik changes the subject, "We saw the meteoroid from here, and it was truly amazing. Did either of you see it?"

Hendrik shakes his head, while Anna Maria nods, "I saw it. As a matter of fact, I was fairly near to where it landed. Close enough to hear it. I was awakened by its roaring, at first thinking that a most powerful wind must be blowing, then stunned that outside my window the sky seemed to be ablaze, bright with yellow and orange." She laughed some more and touching Hendrik's arm confided, "My first thought was that it was the end of the world."

"La, the end of the world, indeed," He laughs.

♡♡♡

When Paulo Calderon had finally been able to broach the subject of this visit with Mara he had begun with, "I believe that we share something in common."

"Oh?"

"Yes, during my years as an archivist for the church of Rome --" She had interrupted him.

"The church of Rome, hmmph, thieves. I know that your church practiced stealing away any reminders of our ancestors' worship."

"Really?!" Pained that she referred to him as a priest, but more interested to know, "How are you aware of this?" She relayed to him the circumstances of the fleeing monks and their drawer full of antiquities, but before she had the opportunity to show him the drawer and its contents, and while he was wondering why those items had never been forwarded to Rome, Robert had begun telling his tale of following the maps that they had found in the drawer.

Now that Captain Robert has finished his tale and gone with Captain Janszoon to the wharf, followed by the Estonians, Calderon begins again, telling Mara, "I have found, and brought with me for you to see, evidence similar to what Robert has described."

"Why? I mean, how did you know what he would find?"

"Oh, dear me," he is not prepared for her questions, "I did not know what he would find, but it is a fascinating coincidence that what I have brought to show you corresponds with what he has discovered. What I have brought to show you is about your harp."

"What of my harp?"

"I have seen one like it before." Her eyebrows go up and her jaw drops a bit, "I served a term in the catacombs beneath the city of Rome. There are uncounted artifacts gathered there; artifacts similar to what you describe in your drawer. Articles gathered from wherever the Romans have conquered." He stops because she seems distracted, she is searching the crowd and does not seem interested in what he is telling her.

She is interested, though, and noticing that he has stopped talking she turns back and tells him, "Wait a moment please." She is searching for Annia, waving her over to join them, then turning back to him smiling, "I am not the only person that will be interested in what you have to say." When Annia is standing there with them Mara tells her, "Professor Calderon is telling me that he has seen a harp like mine before."

"Really," Annia's eyes light up, she turns to Paulo and asks, "where?"

He is thinking that all this is very peculiar, "Amongst the plunder of the ages in the catacombs of Rome there is an identical harp." Annia and Mara share an excited look that the Professor cannot fathom. A bit disconcerted, yet trusting, he continues, "I am unsure how long this instrument has been hidden away in the darkness, yet it gleams as if new. All of its strings are attached and tuned properly." While wondering if he should bring out his portfolio he tells them, "I have brought with me a picture that I drew of the harp."

Both women ask in unison, "Did you pluck the strings of the harp?"

"Y-Y-Yes." They watch him expectantly. Unprepared to be interrogated in this manner he stammers, "I taught myself to play, and soothed myself in the darkness."

Again, both Mara and Annia beseech him, "And?"

"And," he answers apprehensively, "I dreamed," seeing both women nodding he is encouraged to tell more, "The tones from the harp's strings transported me into dreaming; pleasant dreaming, amazing dreaming." Both women's eyes expand even brighter as he explains more, "Serving penance in the underground sends most people into an inner darkness: a madness of the soul. Yet, I escaped that fate through the tenderness flowing from those strings through my fingers and into my heart. I became someone different: the man I am today." Never before has he made this confession.

Feeling the gentle touch of someone beside him, he turns. It is Trinjntje and she holds his portfolio asking, "Are you ready to show your pictures?" Princess Saarika is there also.

"Yes, I believe so. Thank-you." They move to the table and clear away a spot large enough to display what he has brought with him. He opens his folio and shows them his painting of the harp he had found hidden away in the catacombs. Others begin gathering closer. He tells of the rubbings made from inside the Toltec temple in New Spain, and presents to them his rendition of the scene, specifically pointing out the harp for them. He explains, "The Toltec people believe dreaming to be as real as waking. Their pyramids were cathedrals for dreaming. I am under the impression that these beliefs are held by other civilizations. Here," picking up the next item in his portfolio, "let me show you something else." He shows them the piece from the Mughal scroll with its depiction of a Celestial seated at a harp; the scene similar in all ways to the others.

Annia takes a look and says, "These look like what Robert described," and to Mara, "it is also similar to the painting that you've shown us from the monk's drawer."

"Wait here," Mara tells them, "I shall get it." Off she goes. Normally in such moments of excitement her thoughts would be all a jumble, yet now her thoughts are clear, her mood eager.

She returns with the painting of the Goddess playing the harp. They compare the beautifully colored composition with the others and note the many similarities. Saarika tells them, "There is another scene the same as this in an underground temple of my parent's estate."

Mara is more than surprised to hear this from the princess and asks, "Was there also a harp?"

"There is a crown," pointing to the ornamentation shown at the top of Calderon's depiction of the Toltec Goddess, then pointing to the same adornment at top of the harp in the painting Mara has shown them.

The air sizzles around them. Annia points to the necklace worn by the harpist in both illustrations and asks the princess, "Is there also a necklace of Golden Hearts?"

"A necklace of Golden Hearts?" Saarika smiles teasingly, "Yes, there is a necklace of Golden Hearts." Both Mara's and Annia's mouths drop wide in astonishment. Saarika's eyebrows raise and her smile widens as she tells them, "The necklace was lost for a while," she is so amazed that this is happening, "but it has been found," tapping her pocket, "I have it with me."

Robert, Renaldo, and Janszoon, having shown the Estonians to their beds, arrive at this moment of revelation and seeing all that is spread out on the table ask, "What have we here?"

Annia and Mara, speaking as one, tell their husbands, "We have just now been told that the third necklace is here!"

♡♡♡

Anna Maria pipes up from where she has been watching from the edge of the crowd, "I would like to see these necklaces. I would like to know what this is all about."

Annia says, "Mine is at home."

Mara says, "Well, let's go get it, but first I'll get mine."

Everybody sets off down the drive with Mara, Annia, and Saarika leading. Calderon continues presenting the details of his research for the benefit of all who are unfamiliar with the subject. "Evidence of Celestial harpists matching what

Robert found in the mountaintop tower exists in various locations, amidst diverse cultures, around our world. The legends telling of the harp, and its complimentary components, credit them as gifts from Celestials."

"When you say Celestials," Anna Maria interrupts, "are you referring to angels?"

"Yes, other-worldly creatures of hope and guidance; otherwise referred to as Angels, Gods, Goddesses, Deities."

Diedrik asks, "Do you mean like the divine creatures of myths and legends?"

"Yes. Let it be clear though, that in all the descriptions that I have borne witness to, these Celestials are benevolent. They are loving and kind-hearted."

Cornelius asks, "What is the significance of three necklaces? Why three?"

"The patterns on the floors of the shrines all match a three-pointed design that would be created were three of the necklaces connected together in a circle."

"Okay, so what happens when the three necklaces are connected together?" Nicklas wonders, "Will the world transform? Will a passage open leading to the Celestial's realm? Will the harpist visit us?"

"From my research," Calderon answers, "I have not deduced a clear answer regarding what will occur. I can only speculate. It would seem, evidenced by the murals and paintings, that the Celestial harpist will appear; which leads one to imagine that a passage between the realms will have been opened."

Kirin tells them, "Ma was taught to seek two more necklaces, implying that something wonderful will occur when the three connect. Her ma, my grandma drew a pattern of how she imagined three joined necklaces would appear, and made a quilt of the design."

"Oh, I would like to see that," Robert says, "Mara has only recently told me of discovering in dreaming that there are two more necklaces."

"In dreaming," Audrae asks him, "were you dreaming when you hiked up the mountain? Was your tower a dream tower?"

"La, I may have been dreaming, twould make the memory no less real."

♡♡♡

Arriving at Windweg, Annia hurries inside for her necklace. As she retrieves it and the orb she hears a voice calling her name, "*Deviannia*," and wonders if it is her ma. She is prompted to also take the quilt that her ma had sewn; the quilt with the pattern of what she had imagined three necklaces clasped together would be like. The pattern had come in dreaming. As a younger woman Annia had spread the quilt and sat in the circle willing herself to dream the pattern.

"Ma?" Kirin calls to her, "everybody is waiting. The sun is going down."

"Oh, have I been overlong? I have only been here a moment." By the look on her daughter's face she gets the impression that she must have been here longer than a moment. "I have the quilt."

"Pa has cleared and swept a spot. Everybody has gathered and spread fresh grass. The quilt will be perfect. Come on. Everybody is excited!"

And so the quilt is spread over the layer of sweet grasses that have been gathered and spread out. Annia brings out her necklace and arranges it to match the pattern of the quilted template. Mara follows, and then Saarika. In the fading light of the dusk everyone looks on in silent expectation. The faceted jewels sparkle in what little sunlight remains. The sparkling is not the glowing they had all believed would ensue, nor any imagined or hoped for magical appearance of Celestials. The three women kneeling there reach out and hook the clasps together, but still nothing happens. They rock back on their heels, and then stand, awaiting a revelation. The rest of the group stand in a perfect circle around the centerpiece in awe of the magnificence of so much gold, so many jewels, and the perfect symmetry of the joined necklaces. There is no breeze, nor birdsong, nor insect hum, nor even the frog's chirrup. An owl flies silently overhead. The dusk turns to darkness, stars appear.

Mara, thinking out loud, asks Saarika, "Have you your crown?"

"I do."

"Perhaps we should assemble your crown and Annia's orb upon the mast of my harp." Everybody overwhelmingly agrees. The necklaces are unclasped from each other and put away, each in its individual bag. The quilt is folded.

As the entourage begins the walk back across the polder Audrae breaks the silence, "We took this same walk last night. Ma carrying her necklace and orb to compare with Mara's necklace and harp."

"Was it only last night?" Kirin asks, "La, it seems so long ago."

As they walk along Robert reaches around and hugging Mara tells her, "I must confess my dear, as I stood there just now, scanning the circle of disappointed faces I nearly burst out laughing."

She punches him playfully, "It is funny. All of us not knowing what to expect, but expecting something at least! Then nothing, La, it is funny." The somber mood is broken: everyone laughs.

Calderon theorizes, "It does seem reasonable to me that the assembled harp will spark the connection of the necklaces." Many of the others are not so sure that anything special is going to happen, but nobody wants to be the first to voice any pessimism.

Trinjntje walks at the back of the crowd with Audrae, "I am told that you are a family of acrobats."

"Yep."

"Show me something."

"In my dress?"

"It is dark. Nobody will see your underwear." Audrae is still unconvinced. "Okay, I'll go first." Trinjntje performs a cartwheel, followed by a backflip. Audrae, not to be outdone, repeats the same moves, then adds a spinning flip. "Wonderful!" Trinjntje claps her hand, and then performs three flips in succession. They continue showing off, and falling further behind the rest of the crowd.

When everybody else arrives at Windhoek they all agree to a short break. Lanterns are lit. Glasses refilled. Anticipation restored. Calderon is standing outside looking up at the stars with Captain Janszoon when Trinjntje and Audrae catch up. Noticing their tussled hair he asks, "What have you two been up to."

"Being girls."

"Having fun."

♡♡♡

Everybody agrees that they want to do this outdoors, and besides there is not enough room inside for so large a crowd as this. So Mara's harp is moved out to the patio with Robert supervising the young fellows that have rushed to help. Anna Maria is astonished by the size and beauty of the instrument, "It is a Grand Empress of a Harp." On the walk just now Calderon had retold the story of the harp in the catacombs for the benefit of those who had not already heard. Turning to him now, after seeing this one, "You say that the harp that remains underground is identical to this magnificent instrument?" He nods. "Oh, it must be rescued and brought out of the dark into the light of day."

"Indeed," Cornelius agrees, "I would be willing to engage in such a rescue mission. Twould be a fantastic adventure."

As everybody is gathering closer Saarika walks among them showing off the golden crown and allowing everybody to hold and touch this treasure. "I have always loved it so; the delicacy of the leaves with the diamonds sprinkled upon them like droplets of fresh morning dew."

Annia follows with her orb and its dish, "It is not solid," tapping on little globe with her fingernail, "Its glowing is triggered when it is set in its saucer, but it was even brighter than usual when we set it atop the harp last night."

Diedrik surprises himself, impatiently urging them, "Let's see. Set it all together. Please." Everybody anxiously agrees.

Two chairs have been brought out and set on either side of the harp. Annia steps up on one and Saarika steps up on the other. Anna Maria, standing next to Diedrik, tells him in a whisper, "I hope that you are sketching this scene in your mind." He nods his agreement without taking his eyes away as the crown and the orb are lifted up.

Kirin, next to Diedrik on the other side whispers, "Now watch, the orb will be snatched from Ma's hand."

But first, it is the crown that is snatched from Saarika's hands. It settles on top of the harp's mast with a startling clap: everybody exclaims, *Oh!*

The orb and saucer float from Annia's hand and by unseen forces centers itself within the crown of golden leaves. There is an extended moment of supreme anticipation, long enough for everyone to steal a glance of all the others. They are startled again by a loud clap accompanied with a sparkling burst. A collective gasp erupts all around. The brilliant flash cools to an ethereal glow. All stand in awe; this is a most assuredly uncommon thing to behold. The harp's strings are glowing, and humming with the resonance of the light radiating throughout the entire body of the harp. The light reaching out is felt tangibly; a caress that raises goosebumps, even though the air is warm. Diedrik realizes that Anna Maria and Kirin have each grasped ahold of his arms. Razs, Vejz, and Audrae who had sat down in front of him now appear to be hovering an inch or two above the grass. He looks around the circle at everybody else. Trinjntje is holding on to Calderon with both hands, their faces radiantly enthralled. Lu-Tang, Hendrik, Janszoon, and Nicklas stand shoulder to shoulder bathed in luminescence. Annia has stepped down from her chair and is snuggling within Renaldo's arm wrapping around her shoulders. Mara is leaning back against Robert, his arms circling her waist, both immersed in the radiant brilliance.

Saarika, after stepping down from the chair is the only one moving. She is closer to the harp than any of the others, and entirely immersed within the harp's aura. Seating herself at the harp's stool she asks Mara, "May I?" Receiving an encouraging nod, she bows her head and whispers a prayer. Then reaching forward, and tentatively plucking one string, she is taken aback as the wavering tone ripples through the air, through the circle of friends, and on outward, calling to all living things. Sound and light emerges and engulfs them all, feeling like a breeze in their hair, a caress upon their faces, a bubbling forth of pleasure. When at last she plays some more the melody from the harp's strings shifts them all into dreaming.

Nicklas feels the change in his perspective, feeling his senses perceiving the resonating frequencies all around him.

Vejz spontaneously lifts himself to a handstand and walks with ease around the circle with his feet up in the air.

Hendrik pulls a little flute from an inner pocket and adds an impromptu melody to Saarika's joyous hymn. Everybody is swaying, then dancing. Beyond the circle of light and sound a host of woodland creatures gathers; predator and prey side by side. Feathered, furred, and scaled all together swinging and swaying to the celestial harmony.

When Saarika finishes her song and removes her hands from the strings the resonating sound continues and carries on out into the night. She jumps up and yodels, "Aiyeyeyeyeyeeeee!" She spins round in a circle and when she stops proclaims jubilantly, "The harp is set, now let us connect the necklaces again."

By the light of the Harp the quilt is spread and the three necklaces placed and clasped as before. They all crowd again in a tight circle around these combined Golden Hearts. But alas, nothing more happens. Mara takes a seat upon the harp's bench and allows her spirit to guide her fingers to the strings. The tune she plays has them all feeling light-hearted. Meanwhile, nothing is happening there upon the quilt where the Golden Hearts remain spread out in all their magnificent glory.

♡♡♡

Everyone is wondering what will happen next. In the interlude Mara playfully asks Calderon, "What does your research suggest we do now?"

He smiles, and shaking his head says, "I had expected that by now we would have been visited by a Celestial," laughing, "I suppose that I will have to continue searching for more information."

Diedrik tells them, "I have a suggestion," remembering the illusory heart that appeared after sliding the hearts together, "Turn the hearts over and align the patterns that are etched on the back."

"What patterns?" Annia asks, wondering what Diedrik knows of the hearts.

"Is this what you mentioned earlier?" Saarika asks him. All three kneel down on the quilt while disputing his claim that there are patterns engraved on the back of the hearts. None of them are remembering those lattice-like patterns, yet upon turning the hearts over, discover that they are strangely familiar. "Oooo, these lines, yes: so intricate, so delicate."

Diedrik instructs them further, "You may have to push them closer together for the patterns to match up." Mara and Annia both give him astonished looks, still wondering how Diedrik knows of these Golden Hearts.

Saarika explains, "Remember I told you my necklace had been lost?" They nod, she continues, "Diedrik, led by Circumstance, was in the right place at the right time to find it, and has been graciously holding it for me." She winks, for Diedrik's benefit alone, then begins pushing the Golden Hearts of her necklace closer together, with an eye to matching the lines of the elaborate patterns. Mara and Annia do the same, and as the hearts of their necklaces come closer together the delicate lines begin to shine from a source within.

"This is something that I have never been told of, nor imagined," Annia says while continuing to nudge the hearts closer together. Then there is a burst of sparkling light jolting the three of them, rocking them back on their heels, and nearly tipping them over. They gasp, "Look what we have done!" as they stand up and back away from the circle of Golden Hearts that is now floating up from the quilt.

At about waist height, the circle of Golden Hearts begins spinning, slowly at first, but then gaining momentum, faster and faster, until it appears more like a golden disc. They all watch as this spinning disc of hearts tilts itself upright, and begins turning on its axis. The pace of the spinning and turning golden disc quickens, until it is whirling fast enough to appear as a sphere; a sparkling sphere glimmering with flashes of color. There are the ruby reds, emerald greens, and crystalline blues; sparkling, flashing, erupting. There is a sheen, a golden glimmer like an outer shell, and as the sphere gyrates faster the colors blend and the light within becomes brighter orange and yellow as if afire. The three women step back a bit further; everyone steps back as it keeps getting bigger and bigger and bigger: until it is encompassing the harp. An inner prompting that everybody feels has them reaching out to whomever is next to them to clasp hands. They become a circle of spellbound souls surrounding the harp. Likewise, beyond this circle of humans the circle of creatures embrace one another.

Another inner urge has each of them stepping sideways, all in the same direction. The circle of humanity, along with the circle of all other creatures, turn evenly around the radiant centerpiece in perfect coordination. Just as the whirling of the sphere of Golden Hearts had accelerated, now these outer circles of watchers accelerates. They are moving faster than their legs can carry them; faster than could be imagined. As the circle of Golden Hearts has become a sphere of blurred colors, so too these outer circles of humanity and wildlife become blurred multi-hued rings spinning round and round as the earth beneath them drops away.

All sense of individuality is gone: as one they have become a new entity, a new star in the sky, shooting away from the blue and green planet of its birth. Greetings flow in from the vastness; they are welcomed by the multitudes of stars. Each and every star, like them, is a congregation of entities gathered as one. All the stars are a galaxy of one. All the galaxies a Universe of one.

Eventually the awareness of dreaming brings back individuality, and they find themselves awakening on an unfamiliar hilltop, looking out across a vast plain. They look up at a familiar star-filled sky, where a shooting star is followed by another, and another until they understand that they have been transported to the night of the most recent meteoroid's collision with the earth. There is a roaring that Anna Maria remembers hearing before, "That is the sound of the meteoroid." The hilltop where they stand, the valley below them: the entire countryside is suddenly lit up as bright as day. With blinding brilliance a fiery ball appears and careens into the farmland of the valley below. Its momentum carries it the length of the valley, digging a massive trench. The fields are set ablaze. Where it stops there is a newly formed mound of earth that burns. The fires spread. A wave of heat blows up and over them at the top of this hill, so far away. They watch as lightning bolts explode up from the earth all around that bright orange center. More lightning strikes, an explosion of lightning from out of the earth forms dark heavy thunderheads that begin dumping rain, extinguishing the flames, until eventually the sky is clear and the stars appear.

Music is coming from the harp; a gentle lilting tune. They are awakening on the lawn, the three necklaces spread on the quilt are no longer emitting light, yet there is light, even though it must be the middle of the night. All eyes are drawn to the light of a golden-colored Celestial sitting at the harp; her fingers thrilling the tones from its strings. She is a glorious creature, wearing a coat of feathers. The song that she sings, heard in their thoughts, begs of them to take their necklaces of Golden Hearts to the meteoroid they have been shown during their bout of communal dreaming. Upon receiving her request everybody is determined to make it so. Her visage fades, though her love remains as a flame within; the heart's gentle flame.

♡♡♡

Diedrik wakes up the following morning feeling light-heartened. Not only is the burden he has been hiding gone, but the unfolding of events that had followed his disclosure revealed wonders beyond his imagination. Only now, after last night's dreaming, it seems that nothing is beyond his imagination. The morning sunshine through the windows reminds him that he has animals waiting to be fed. He hops out of bed, then remembering that he has a guest sleeping in the other room, tiptoes quietly to the kitchen, gets a fire started and sets a kettle to warm. Slipping into his clogs he steps outside into the fresh morning dew. He lets the scenes of yesterday play across his imagination. There are so many remarkable scenes that he even considers making an account of yesterday with a combined series of illustrations; a graphic telling of the story.

As he enters the barn his horse snorts a greeting. He answers back, "*Goedendag Paard*". He scoops a mixture of oats, corn, and barley into a flat wooden tub and sets it on the shelf next to the manger in the horse's stall. While the horse is munching away on its grains Diedrik leans on the stall's gate talking to his four-legged friend, "I tell you what big guy, and I am certain that you will agree, yesterday was an amazing day." Then he remembers that Nicklas had chosen to sleep in the barn, and now wonders if he should not be quieter. None of his guests' horses are waiting in the barn this morning; perhaps a large meadow of fresh grass is better than what they are used to.

He feeds the chickens, collects the few eggs, and then tosses carrots, parsnips, and cabbages into the hog pen. He laughs at the picture in his mind as he remembers when Kirin had ridden on the hog's back: she had never ridden a pig before, and was surprised at how docile it is. He remembers Kirin yesterday explaining to him about her mother's orb, and the dreams it inspires. He stops in his tracks as he remembers the dream they had all dreamed together. It was not quite like dreaming, but he has no other way to describe what had occurred after the golden hearts had connected and spun into an ever larger glowing orb. He remembers loving everyone, beginning with their dancing to the harp music, and continuing on through the night's adventure. He remembers the feather covered Celestial playing the harp. She was truly divine. He remembers Kirin asking him if he is loving himself, and answering without hesitation, "Yes. Yes, I do. I love myself." He begins walking again. It is nice to love one's self, and easy to love others.

"Good day to you Diedrik."

"Ah, Kirin, I was just now thinking of you." He catches himself thinking of her often these days. "Will you join me for a cup of coffee?"

"I was hoping that you would ask. I would like that very much. Is Anna Maria awake yet? She is an uncommon woman. I recognize her likeness from the etchings hanging on your wall"

"Yes, her self-portraits." Arriving at the door to the house, "We shall see if she has risen yet," tipping his head and waving her through first. He sets the eggs on the counter, then lifts the steaming kettle from the heat, thankful that it had not yet reached a full boil. Kirin sits herself down at the table while he pours roasted beans into the grinder. As he is turning the great crank that spins the burred grinding stones he hears a stirring from the other room, and looking up greets his houseguest, "*Goedendag* Anna Maria."

Kirin stands and curtsies, "Good day to you Anna Maria."

"Hi," she smiles and stepping into the kitchen pauses next to Diedrik busy at the task of grinding, "That smells delicious. Will you brew enough for me to have some too please?"

"Coffee instead of tea?"

"Mm-hmmmm."

"I am grinding enough to brew a full pot."

"Splendid," She moves to the table and takes a seat next to Kirin. She has a hair brush with her and as she begins untangling her tresses remarks offhandedly, "La, my hair must look a fright."

"Oh, I will brush your hair for you," Kirin jumps up, "May I?"

"I would like that very much. Thank you." Diedrik is lining a funnel with filter paper and thinking how different women are. He would never suggest brushing another man's hair. He perches the funnel atop the coffee pot, measures the proper amount of ground beans, and then slowly pours the heated water through his makeshift sieve. "I remember that the best coffee was served while you were working at the Kikker Gat." He looks up to acknowledge Anna Maria's compliment, and for an instant the two women glow, as everyone had glowed last night.

"I am thinking that the two of you, one brushing the other's hair, would be a very nice scene for a painting."

"Hmmm, you may be right. Everyday scenes are trendy these days in the art world."

"Are you imagining how you will capture the light coming through these windows?"

He carries three cups to the table, "I was wondering how to capture the glow." He returns with a cream pitcher and a sugar bowl. "Earlier I was wondering if I will be able to accurately capture the scenes of yesterday." Now he pours the brewed coffee into the cups, returns the pot to the edge of the fire, and takes his seat at the table across from his charming guests. "Share with us, please Anna Maria, your thoughts regarding what transpired yesterday." He sips his coffee.

She closes her eyes for a moment. When she opens her eyes again she asks, "Where does one begin?" She sips her coffee, then answers, "Robert's tale of the tower, and then hearing that there are other similar sites, has me wondering if these are Dream shrines."

"Dream shrines?" asks Kirin.

"Yes, allow me to explain. In my pursuit to better understand biblical writings I have taught myself the original languages of the accounts. After the news had spread, amongst the community of letters, that I have learned the ancient Greek and Hebrew I was deluged with scrolls and copies of venerable tracts in hopes of translation. One tablet in particular that held my attention is a very old journal, written in Greek, describing the rituals and subsequent dreaming engaged during periodic visits to a dream shrine."

"So, people went to a shrine intending to dream?"

"From what I gather, yes. There may have been many dream shrines in the Grecian lands of old." Sharing her knowledge with others delights her, "I gathered from this ancient journal that one would spend a few days fasting, cleansing, and quietly contemplating what one hoped to dream of. There would follow consultations with a priest or priestess of the shrine to determine the nature of one's request. There were dreams for healing, dreams for understanding, dreams for righting wrongs, and even dreams to visit with celestial guides."

"Do you suppose," queries Diedrik, "that with the coming of this latest meteoroid that there will be a new dream shrine?"

They all sit silently for a bit before Anna Maria continues, "That is my thinking, although I inherently know that one need not attend a shrine for dreaming, just as one need not attend a cathedral for praying." She has spoken while stirring a bit more cream into her coffee. She sets the spoon in the saucer. "I am still left bewildered by our communal dreaming. That we all dreamed as one, has me thinking that the mechanism of the combined hearts transcends all current *technologia.*

Diedrik muses, "Most people are wary of modern *technologia*, wary of anything based upon newly discovered scientific phenomenon."

"I have never heard my mother refer to her necklace of Golden Hearts as scientific, only that it is older than anything else. Are you imagining the golden hearts, along with the harp, the orb, and the crown, to have been created by the scientists of a civilization advanced beyond the scholars and scientists of today?"

"If that were so, what happened to this advanced civilization?" Diedrik asks, figuring that there is really no way of knowing.

"Hah!" A memory pops into Kirin's thoughts and she tells them, "We had a tutor, who came from Russia that taught us exceptionally curious doctrines. He claimed that civilization, as it stands now, has risen and fallen numerous times."

Anna Maria is intrigued, "That reasoning would explain the Golden Hearts coming from another time," then asks, "But how to reason if they have come from another realm?"

"In our shared dreaming we crossed the expanse of time and location back to the where and the when of the meteoroid's arrival. Could we have just as easily crossed realms?" They all contemplate this. "What will happen when the three necklaces are taken to the meteoroid as the Angel requested?"

"We'll see when we get there."

♡♡♡

Nicklas awakens, at first uncertain of where he is, then opening his eyes, beholds the vast upper chamber of this loft where he has slept, and dreamed so vibrantly, in the hay. The barn is silent; all of their horses have found their way to the pasture. He rises and picks up his boots, steps down the ladder and heads out. He likes the feeling of the grass on his bare feet, so he leaves his boots there by the door. He decides to walk down to the lake. He nearly steps on a little green snake, sending it slithering away through the grass. Nicklas is startled, but unafraid, and as he stops the slender green and gold snake stops too: each taking a long look at the other, each holding very still. "Hello friend. Were you dreaming with us last night?" Stepping wide around the snake, "There now, enjoy your day." The snake blinks, turns its head, and is instantly gone. Following the cart path down across the polder Nicklas realizes how empty his thoughts are this morning. He likes this empty-headedness.

As he passes the third windmill and its collection of sheds, its barn, and its remarkably eccentric home he hears a voice from behind, "Where are you going so early in the day Nicklas?"

He turns to the young woman who has caught up with him, "Good Morning Audrae. I am on my way to the lake." He smiles, remembering how much he likes this frisky young lady. "You are welcome to join me."

"I can take you out in our boat. I am very good at the oars."

"It will be an odd reversal for a boy to allow a girl the effort, but Okay."

Audrae surprises him by taking his hand, and tugging eagerly, "Let's go!"

When they get to the boat she has him take the seat in the stern, then sets the oars in their locks and pushes the boat out into the water. Once afloat she jumps in, the wet hem of her frock dripping onto the slats lining the bottom of the craft. Nicklas enjoys watching the concentration on her face as she manipulates the oars in opposition, spinning the boat around, then rowing rhythmically without splashing. He is fascinated by the coordination of her movements, and pleasantly surprised by how quickly they are moving along the shoreline. He is lulled by the motion of the boat, the gentle swooshing of the oars, and the warming of his face in the sunshine. He feels no breeze, yet looking up notices the clouds drifting by at a cross direction, creating a pleasant meandering sensation. "Audrae," he asks, "were we all dreaming the same dream?"

"I believe so." She tosses her head in an effort to stop her hair from falling across her cheeks, "Have you shared dreaming before?"

It seems that she is teasing him. "I have dreamed of others," now teasing her, "how am to know if others were dreaming of me?"

Audrae likes this handsome fellow and is considering that he may not be so very much older than she. He is watching her closely as she asks, "Did your parents not teach you of dreaming? I learned of dreaming before learning anything else." She likes the color of his eyes. "I have a different question."

"Yes?"

She is still rowing steadily, "How is it that Mam, Mara, and Saarika all ended up here?" She turns her head to be sure of her bearings.

Nicklas shrugs while smiling back at her. "I do not have an answer to your question. How will it be when they take their necklaces to the meteoroid?" He follows her gaze up toward a bird that is circling overhead

She follows his line of sight, "I think that is the little eagle that followed Captain Robert home." They have shifted from gazing up, and now are looking into each other's eyes again. "Will you be going with us to the meteoroid?"

"Of course. The Lady invited us all."

Arriving at the shore he signals for her to remain seated as he jumps out and pulls the boat up onto the beach. She lays the oars inside the boat and then when she stands and turns Nicklas is awaiting with the gentlemanly gesture of an extended hand to assist her stepping out of the boat. This is something new for Audrae, and brings a warming blush to her cheeks. She accepts his proffered assistance, and as her feet touch the cool sand she plays at curtsying, "Thank you Sir."

"Sir," he scoffs jokingly. He does not immediately let her hand go, nor does she let go of his. "Do you suppose everyone is making plans for the trip to the meteoroid?"

Her eyes light up, "Let's go find out." Dropping his hand and charging off, "I'll race ya!"

♡♡♡

Hendrik awakens, and upon opening his eyes, while realizing that he is not in his own bed, memories flood his imagination. Rolling over he sees, across this windmill's upper room, Saarika in the other bed still sleeping. He slips back the cover, and deciding to be daring, heads up the stairs that hug the rounded wall of this cavernous windmill. At the top of the steps he opens the door out into the fresh morning atmosphere and is bedazzled by the radiance of the sunshine on the clouds, the leaves of the trees, and even sparkling off the surfaces of the river, the canal, and the lake. His heart is uplifted joyfully by the full array of the magnificent panorama before him. He is surprised as he realizes, standing at the stage's rail high above the ground, that he feels no anxiety, no vertigo, and no fear. He is so delighted that without hesitation he places the back of his left hand on his hip and his right index finger at the top center of his skull, then begins playfully spinning round, like a marionette. While dancing his little jig he does not notice the door opening.

"Good Morning Professor."

Startled and embarrassed he stops his silly dance and bows, "Indeed, a good morning it is Saarika," noticing that she is not wearing her headscarf he quickly looks away, "Oh dear."

"What?"

"Is it not unfortunate for a woman of your stature to be seen with her head uncovered?"

"I thank you for your deference toward what you imagine to be my stature." She had awakened, risen and gone up the stairs before thinking to cover her head, or her feet. Now here she stands bare-headed and bare-footed before a man, also bare-headed and bare-footed. Under the circumstances she does not feel uncomfortable, nor does she want Hendrik to feel uncomfortable. She reaches out and with her fingers at his chin, turns his face upward, "Let's be easy about this, shall we?" His eyelids flutter at first, but then he visibly calms, and looks admiringly up into her face, "There, much better."

He is of an average height for a man, yet the top of his head reaches scarcely above her shoulders. She is slim, and tall, and her hair, unseen before now, is a thick mass of long braids. His voice is caught momentarily in his throat. He gathers his wits and offers his elbow, "Shall we walk?" She accepts. As they stroll around the windmill he feels that he is more graceful in her presence. "I daresay that I will see this world forever differently after yesterday. Upon returning home I must begin my preparations for the journey to the meteoroid."

"Yes, a journey to the meteoroid," she muses, then remembering his profession, "Will you be giving a lecture explaining for others the surprising details of our experience?"

"Oh ho, I do not know for sure if I will. Before delivering a lecture the subject will first have to pass the process of the four philosophers' rules."

"The four rules?"

"Yes; Tally, Consider, Sort, and Perceive." It is a process he has lectured on frequently. "The goal of the process is to prove the details of what is perceived. My credibility would be questioned were I to deliver a lecture regarding a subject that cannot pass the four rules."

"Who determines whether a subject passes these rules?"

"It is a general consensus of thought. There is considerable correspondence carried on between the thinking minds of this age; the astronomers, philosophers, chemists, physicists, and," with an off-handed wave, "well, anyone with a forward thinking mental aptitude."

"Hmmm. Let's see." They have walked to the side of the windmill that faces the lake where there is a bench and they agree to sit. "Firstly, my necklace of Golden Hearts awaiting me here. Secondly, the joining of my crown with Annia's orb atop Mara's harp. Thirdly, the three-pointed circle formed by the connected hearts. Fourthly, the dreaming that we all shared. What is so difficult to comprehend?" While she talks her hands are continually moving. Hendrik is admiring those beautiful hands with their long fingers unadorned by rings, her delicate wrists wearing no bracelets, her slender arms unblemished by tattoos. "The spectacularity of the event," she begins swirling her hands, then stretches out her arms, "Is really beyond conceivability. Perhaps we will be keeping the tale to ourselves."

"Or, we can leave the telling to Paulo."

"How will he describe where we were in that vast emptiness? Or even explain that we were somewhere else? Like dreaming: the scenes changed so suddenly. Standing on the hillside watching an enormous fireball streak across the sky," her arms wave, "Whoooosh! It was so fast!"

Hendrik is bobbing his head up and down listening as she describes what he too had witnessed. "We jumped to another time and to another place. And then we returned to an angel playing eloquently and bidding us on a quest." He is smiling impishly, there are gleams in his eyes. "La, were I to deliver such a lecture it is certain that the general consensus arrived upon by my students would be --"

"That you have gone completely bonkers!" They both laugh.

♡♡♡

Upon awakening, perceiving that she is not in her own bed, Trinjntje holds her eyes closed, momentarily thrilled by the uncertainty of where exactly she has slept. Before determining her location she allows her awareness to recall her most recent dreaming, and to the events of last night. The scenes of her memories take shape in her imagination. Just before waking she had been dreaming of walking with Paulo, a dream actualized from their positions on the bed. She had been so bold as to lie down next to him and he had consented. Then she remembers floating amongst the stars. Her dreaming in the vast emptiness between the pinpoints of light had been similar to when she had worn Saarika's crown. This dreaming induced by the spinning of the hearts, this shared dreaming: oh, what a wonder!

Now she opens her eyes to the vast area inside this windmill where they have slept. She recollects pleasantly that this structure has a name, Windmidden. She raises herself up to lean on one elbow. She feels a pleasurable buzz to be here alone with Paulo. His breathing is so calm as to be barely perceptible.

He opens his eyes, "Good Morning Trin." She likes that he has used her nickname. He lifts himself up and leans on one elbow facing her, "What astounds you the most about yesterday?" Her blinking eyelashes wiggle a few strands of hair hanging across her forehead. Without thinking, he reaches over and brushes aside the unruly bit of hair, bringing a tender smile to her face, and lighting up her eyes. It is an intimate moment for two unused to intimacy.

"Hmmmmm, everything about yesterday is so very astonishing." She emphasizes what she has said with a little shake of her head, loosening the wayward strands of hair to fall again across her brightening eyes. She sits up and crosses her legs beneath her, still facing him, "I was amazed that Robert's sketches and the painting from out of that old drawer held so many similarities to your pictures." She tips her head back and shakes her hair into order. "It was remarkable to finally see the necklace of Golden Hearts again, and startling to see all three identical necklaces." She places her hands, palms up, in her lap and closes her eyes. "Then with the harp's heavenly music that had us all so alive and free!" She breathes in deeply, her exhale is a sigh. "I was most perplexed at first when the spinning hearts sent us all into the dream together, for I have never shared dreaming." She opens her eyes again and leans forward, "But you asked what I loved the most. It was the storm that followed the meteoroid's plummet. The lightning, flashing up from the fiery stone, forming those dark clouds that poured down enough rain to put out all the fires! That was awesome!" Animated now, she jumps off the bed and hops over to curl up in the windowsill with her arms wrapped around her legs. "And then, awakening on the lawn with an actual feathered being playing the harp and whispering in our minds to take the necklaces to the meteoroid. Ah, she was a beautiful creature."

Calderon sits up and leans himself against the headboard. He extends his legs and crosses them at the ankles. He laces together his hands leaving the index fingers straight and tucked under his chin. He closes his eyes and appears to have fallen back into slumber. Trinjntje watches and waits silently until he lifts his head, opens his eyes, and tells her, "I was hoping for a visit from Celestials, and so was most inspired by that creature at the harp. I am looking forward to this excursion of delivering the necklaces to the meteoroid, and perhaps seeing, and even visiting with more of these angelic dream-beings."

"I have been visited by creatures such as her before; only smaller." This gets his attention. "Oh yes, they live with us here, appearing as recognizably everyday creatures. Perhaps one will show itself to you now that your mind is opened to their presence." Opening the window casings, breathing in the morning air, and raising an arm with her fingers extended a small yellow bird lands there and twitters a greeting. "Hello dear," she says to the little creature while bringing it closer and whispering something more. Caressing the bird's feathers has it responding by pressing itself into her palm with a sound coming from within its tiny frame that is remarkably like a cat's purring. "Our little friend here has a desire for you to see her as she sees herself, which is different from this recognizable everyday creature." Tossing the bird toward him, he watches as it transforms, so that what lands upon his belly is a tiny imp that immediately digs long fingers into his ribs. His ticklish reaction has him sweeping his arms down across his torso, but the imp is no longer there to be swept away. Instead it is circling on its gossamer wings around his head and pulling at his hair. As he tips his head back to look up his loose hair falls away. The creature, after buzzing in a circle, darts in and touches a finger to the tip of his nose sending a thrilling spark rushing through his body and escaping out his fingers and toes. He explodes into laughter.

Trinjntje is once again holding a bright yellow goldfinch. Her laughter is a melody as she releases her little friend back out into the open air. Turning back to the man on the bed, "There you are Sir. We see what we want to see."

They hear Saarika and Hendrik descend the stairs from the room above where they have slept, "There is a crowd gathering at the wharf," Saarika tells them, "it looks as if the ship of castaways is preparing to depart."

They continue down the stairs without stopping; Hendrik waves, "*Tot ziens.*"

Trinjntje jumps from the windowsill, "Wait. We will come with you."

Sailing

Cornelius Janszoon has slept comfortably in Mara and Robert's extra room. He hears them stirring and then hears them going out the door. Sitting up he is able to see them through the windowpanes walking to the barn. As he is thinking how pleasant it is here memories of yesterday pop up to surprise him, "Has all this really happened?" Holding his hands up for scrutiny while asking himself, "Could I still be dreaming?" Remembering the sense of waking on the hilltop vantage and witnessing the meteoroid crash down, then remembering the sense of waking on the lawn to the Celestial harpist, and now waking here with the morning sunlight streaming through the windows has him pinching himself to determine that he is really awake. After laying his head back down upon the pillow he is pleased with how circumstances have developed; he is more than pleased. He had come along with Trin and the professors as a distraction; a distraction that has become an adventure. Remembering that he has agreed to sail the lifeboat of castaways up the river, and remembering that Lu-Tang has asked to accompany him on this cruise up the river and back pleases him immensely. He is pleased to be able to aid this little group of homeless folks, and pleased that upon his return they will all be embarking upon another excursion; the meteoroid journey requested of them by the Celestial harpist.

Remembering with delight the scene that had unfolded in the barn upon their arrival, when the young van Haumann,

Diedrik, had surprised them all with the necklace of Golden Hearts. He likes that young fellow and considering the circumstances, a country boy in the city on his own encountering all sorts of new temptations, it is no wonder that he fell into a wayward trap. It is evidence of his good nature that he got himself away from all that. Even more profound are the circumstances that put the necklace of Golden Hearts in his hands. This thought calls to mind again all that had occurred after the pieces of the harp had been put together and the three necklaces assembled. The memory of shared dreaming has awakened pathways in his memory to other dreaming experiences, reminding him that he has long considered that dreaming might be as real as waking, and now he finds himself amongst others who have believed this for all their lives. He had told those he will be taking upriver to be ready early, so he puts aside dallying, gets himself out of bed, and dresses for his day.

Mara and Robert return from their chores and while preparing breakfast tell Janszoon, "It is a good thing you are doing for these people Captain."

"Ah, thank you, but I must confess," grinning, "I am doing this for myself."

Selfishness is not necessarily the sin some believe it to be.

♡♡♡

Lu-Tang is familiar with being conscious while dreaming, but dreaming shared with others is an all new experience. The dreaming with the invitation for them all to bring the necklaces to the meteoroid had thrilled his inner core. On his last visit here he had enjoyed sleeping up on the windmill so much that he has slept the night up on the stage of Windweg. The boys, Razs and Vejz have slept up here with him. Yesterday, while Captain Janszoon and Captain Robert had been inspecting the little English ship he and the boys had asked the two captains questions about sailing. He had finally told Janszoon, "I would like to learn the skill of sailing. Perhaps, if there is room in this little boat, I could sail with you."

Captain Janszoon had replied, "Well, I am in need of a Mate. We plan to sail early so that we can take advantage of the morning breeze blowing in from the *NoordZee*."

"I will join you then."

Now, in the crisp morning air high above everything else, Lu-Tang is rolling up his blanket and preparing in his mind for this next great adventure. Razs, waking up, asks, "Are you really going to sail with Captain Janszoon and the refugees?" Lu-Tang nods affirmatively. "What about your companions? What about your lectures?"

"My companions, as well as my students, are familiar with my idiosyncrasies." He finishes tying his rolled blanket and stands to leave.

Before the professor can bid a farewell, Razs is up, "I will come with you to the river." He slaps his brother's foot, "Come on Bro," he tells Vejz as he rushes to follow Lu-Tang.

Vejz, awakening from the slap, "What? Where are you going so fast?" Tossing his blanket back he jumps up. There is a moment of vertigo as he remembers where he is, then he rushes through the door and down the steps after the others.

The boys and Lu-Tang meet up with their parents who are also on their way to see the refugees off. Audrae and Nicklas catch up from behind. Passing Windmidden they are joined by the guests who have traveled from Utrecht, along with Kirin, Diedrik, and Anna Maria. Reaching the river they find a crowd assembled on the dock. Captain Janszoon welcomes them all, "We are ready to set sail." He assists his passengers aboard and tells Lu-Tang, "It is the mate's duty to free the ship's lines from where they are tied at the dock."

"Aye Sir." Lu-Tang eagerly executes his first chore as a sailor. He is the last to hop over the gunwale. Janszoon leaves him holding the tiller while raising the sails. These passengers are already aware of the importance of keeping themselves below the swinging boom. The wind catches and the little ship is already away as all aboard turn to wave good-bye to the kind-hearted windmillers.

♡♡♡

The crowd of folks left on the wharf turn and head toward shore. Hendrik suggests to his friends, "We ought to be on our way too."

Calderon half-heartedly agrees, "I suppose so."

Mara teases, "I hope that your research here has proven to be worthwhile."

This has him smiling, "Oh, indeed!"

Anna Maria tells the professors, "I will ride with you."

"That will be splendid."

Nicklas tells them, "Cornelius has asked me to take care of his horses while he is away. I will be riding his stallion and staying at his place."

"Will you have us lead your stable horse and return it with ours?"

"Thank you, yes please. The stable will be glad to have their horse, and I will not be owing them extra."

On the riverbank Saarika draws Diedrik aside, "I like it here. I slept well in your windmill. May I stay?"

"Yes. Yes, indeed you may."

"Thank you." She calls out to her friends, "Will you also lead my horse back to its stable? Diedrik has invited me to stay."

Trinjntje almost says that she wants to stay too, but then changes her mind, thinking that Saarika, Annia, and Mara may be wanting to compare whatever similarities they all share. "We will take your horse then. Post me if you decide to come home."

Before leaving, Calderon tells his hosts, "We will be making plans to return in a fortnight when Captain Janszoon has returned." Looking around and noting he has everyone's attention, "We shall keep each other posted as we make ready for our visit to the meteoroid."

As his friends ride off toward Utrecht, Nicklas, on Janszoon's stallion, rides the other direction.

♡♡♡

When their guests are gone Mara asks playfully, "La, now what will we do?"

Diedrik tells them, "I am behind on my molenaar duties. The wind has long since changed directions."

"I'll help," Kirin says, then to Saarika, "You may enjoy coming along as we turn the windmills to properly catch the wind."

"Turn the windmill?"

"Only the top of the windmill: the cap," Audrae tells her.

Robert says, "While you take care of that I have a ship to unload."

Renaldo says, "I'll help. How about it boys?"

"Sure."

♡♡♡

Nicklas is riding along the river path, his heart light and thoughts easy. Cornelius' stallion is spirited, yet well-mannered. He is impressed at the difference he feels, compared to the stable horses that he has been riding since returning the horse he had borrowed from Janszoon. He stops when his attention is drawn away by an infant's laughter. Looking toward the sound he sees a young woman bathing a child in the river. She is lifting the baby up out of the water, and then dropping it back down with a splash; the baby laughs again, and again, and again. The child's laughter has Nicklas laughing.

It takes only gentle pressure with his heels and the horse is moving again, already knowing his intention. He comes to a grist mill that sits next to where the canal meets the river. He waves to the miller who has stepped to the doorway. After crossing the bridge over the canal's lock he turns and takes the wagon path that follows the canal. He looks over to see that the miller is still watching him, and has been joined by his woman. They all wave again. Nicklas realizes that they are most likely admiring the magnificent horse that he is riding.

The road he is on and the canal beside it stretch straight out before him as far as he can see. There is no one else. He is speculating that he does not remember ever riding a horse quite like this one, so he asks the stallion, "Do you like to run?" It exhales a short whinny while lifting its head just a bit. The quickening pace has Nicklas bouncing uncomfortably on the saddle at first, but the gait steadily lengthens and smooths out. Now they are moving faster than Nicklas has ever ridden before. He wonders if he should be frightened at such a speed, but there is nothing frightening about this. Nothing at all frightening. This horse is magnificent! This is exhilarating! He rides crouched low. He watches ahead, and after a while notices his crossroad, amazed that he has already come this far, and reluctantly sits up. The stallion slows even before Nicklas has made any change in the pressure on the reins. "Oh, you are a fine smart horse. I love this. I love **you**." He runs the palm of his hand along the horse's neck.

The road they have come to is the road that leads to Janszoon's estate. The stallion, knowing the way home, quickens the pace and soon they are flying smoothly along again. Nicklas barely notices the passing landscape as he is lulled into a reverie by the steady rhythm of the horse's masterful gait. He is stunned when he catches sight of the familiar windmill, thinking that it must be another, for how could they have already arrived. The stallion slows its pace and they ride into the drive of the Captain's estate. Dismounting at the water tank, the horse drinks while its saddle is removed. Cornelius' man comes to greet them. Nicklas tells him, "Captain Janszoon has taken an unplanned river voyage. He expects to be gone a fortnight, and has asked me to take care of the horses."

"La, he rides the horses plenty, and nearly every day harnesses and drives his team."

"Right, and that is what I intend to take care of for him."

"He ought to hire himself a stable hand. Twould allow him more leisure."

"I believe," Nicklas tells the man in a confidential tone, "That it is the excess of leisure that has our Captain jumping at the opportunity of sailing up the river."

♡♡♡

Calderon, Hendrik, Trinjntje, and Anna Maria have ridden home at a steady pace, intending to arrive while there is still daylight. They have eaten very little all day, and so agree to stop in at the pub next door to the stable. Being close to the University it is an upscale public house, catering to an educated crowd, and offering an admirable cuisine. A wine steward visits, and then the waiter.

They sit silently during the interlude until Trinjntje says, "I have been thinking --"

"Really," Hendrik, sitting across the table from her, interrupts, "I daresay we have all been thinking, for barely a word has been spoken amongst us since leaving Schoonhoven Landing." She kicks him playfully under the table. His eyebrows go up. His eyes widen, and through his laughter, "I beg your pardon, my dear lady. Carry on, please."

"I have been thinking of our involvement in this whole affair and wondering will anyone believe the telling of what we have witnessed?"

"I have already determined that I will not be lecturing about this experience," Hendrik tells them.

"There are two, maybe three that I correspond with regularly that I am considering sharing the tale with," Anna Maria confesses, "but only with the direct command that the account not be re-posted." Looking to Calderon, "And you Professor? Will you be writing a dissertation for publishing?"

With a smile he answers, "I daresay, were this story to be published, it would be presented by booksellers under their novel category of fiction." This comment draws light laughter all around the table, for who reads these made-up tales that grow ever more popular these days? "I will continue gathering notes, but as for publishing my results, I believe that would lead to the questioning of my credibility."

"Hmmm, well I have no credibility to be questioned," Trinjntje announces, "Nor do I have correspondents." She wonders if they think her simple.

"You lucky girl," Anna Maria proclaims. "You are free. Your life is easy."

"La, yes. Free and easy. Hmmmm." She has not thought of her life that way. The steward brings their wine. "So, we have a couple weeks to prepare." She will be living alone. "Perhaps I shall attend a lecture."

"Oh yes do," Anna Maria responds, "You can sit with me behind my little screen."

The waiter brings their plates. They dig in hungrily. After a bit Calderon, speaking quietly tells Trinjntje, "You are welcome to visit the library."

♡♡♡

Robert, with the help of Renaldo, Razs, and Vejz installs his grandfather's mast-crane. "Grandad seldom sailed into ports rigged with wharves and loading cranes. Ofttimes traders brought their cargo alongside his anchored ship on rafts, and between swells a quick snatch of a cargo net worked much better than attempting to hand contraband piece by piece over the gunwales." Robert now shows them long leather straps, "I got these from the quarry men." Each strap has iron rings attached to the ends. "Now, while I get my fingers under this first block and lift it up a bit, could I get one of you to slide a couple of these straps underneath?"

Razs slides two straps under the block, "Like that?"

"Perfect. This will be the first block to be moved. Now, the other straps will go under a block over here for our counter-weight." A hook from a line through the pulley on the crane's boom is attached to the rings of the first block, and a hook from the line through the counter weight pulley is attached to the rings of the other block. Then Robert instructs Renaldo to pull steadily on one rope while he pulls evenly on the other. The weight of the blocks sets off a frightening creaking through the overhead beams, but soon the stones are sliding out of position and eventually swinging free. "Okay, now hold steady Ren while I raise this one up." When the stone to be off-loaded is high enough they swing the crane's boom until the heavy block is hanging over a chalk mark on the dock. Robert lowers it slowly down allowing Razs and Vejz to situate it on the mark. When is settled into place, Renaldo lets the counter-weight down until both ropes are slack. They all shout, "Hurray!"

Robert hops over to the dock and lifts the stone while the boys pull the straps out from under, then while dusting off his hands says, "That is one in place; only ninety-nine more."

♡♡♡

The fortnight passes quickly by. In Utrecht the professors make arrangements for their leaves of absence. Trinjntje hires an agent to watch her property. Anna Maria sets her household in order. They all organize what they will take along with them. From Schoonhoven Landing Robert visits Phillip Haumann and orders a mast to be turned and a keel to be built for Captain Janszoon's pinnace. Renaldo, Razs, and Vejz continue helping Robert stack the blocks and install the boom of the dock's new crane. Diedrik makes a trip to Utrecht for supplies, and while there places an order for new sails to match the height of the new mast. Razs, Kirin, Vejz, and Audrae study their new texts. Meanwhile, Nicklas spends his days with Janszoon's horses, even buys a horse for himself. Posts are sent back and forth discussing the details of their trip. Decisions are made as to their route. Saarika, Annia, and Mara all discover what Diedrik had told of: connecting the engraved designs on the backs of the hearts of their individual necklaces to produce the floating illusory heart. There is an underlying mood of eager anticipation. The days fly by quicker than anyone could have imagined.

♡♡♡

Cornelius Janszoon, sitting leisurely at the tiller in the early morning sunlight, expects to arrive back at Schoonhoven Landing by midday. Lu-Tang sits equally at ease occasionally sipping from a bottle of cold tea. Both are silently contemplating the completion if this journey while anticipating the next. Their voyage has been successful, and they are returning a few days earlier than expected. Their passengers, weary from travel, weary from homelessness, and weary from uncertainty, had expressed considerable relief upon reaching their final disembarkation. Cornelius and Lu-Tang have enjoyed each other's company immensely; sharing tales of their travels, exchanging philosophical perspectives, and allowing one another quiet moments of introspection.

Cornelius notices a speckled gold and tan bird flying up the river and wonders if it is a hawk or an eagle. Now overhead, the bird with its wings splayed, makes a wide circle. He determines by the shape of the bird's tail that it is an eagle. Now he remembers a similar eagle that he had seen at Schoonhoven Landing and asks Lu-Tang, who is also watching the little eagle, "Do you suppose that is Captain Robert's familiar?"

"If so, will he fly ahead of us now to announce our arrival?" They continue watching the bird's downriver flight as it disappears ahead of them.

Lu-Tang has grown accustomed to sailing. The distance that they have traveled in these past days would have taken so much longer afoot, and the captivating sights he has beheld would have been fewer and less frequent. The perpetual motion provided by the wind in the sails is a mystifyingly marvelous sensation. The brisk rate keeps him ever attentive, for there is always something new, yet Captain Janszoon has oft repeated, "This craft would be swifter had it a taller mast and matching sail, along with a deeper keel." Lu-Tang has difficulty imagining sailing faster, but has the urge to discover the thrill for himself.

Earlier than he had expected, Cornelius espies what is most assuredly Schoonhoven Landing, yet there is a difference. He withdraws his spyglass and with it extended to its full length he twists it into focus. He recognizes Captain Robert's ship, the Tulip, moored there. The wharf is different though. There is a loading crane that he knows was not there before. "Magnificent!" Handing the scope to Lu-Tang he says, "Here, take a look. There is an addition."

Lu-Tang is able to make out the details of the addition to the wharf. "It is of well-laid stone; a robust tower, and a stout boom." Lowering the glass and looking to Janszoon, "Who would have imagined that this could have been constructed in the time we have been away?"

Accepting his spyglass and raising it to take another look Cornelius answers, "The Irish Captain's ingenuity is impressive."

Drawing closer now, the sails are trimmed as they guide their ship toward the stone wharf, and then with only the tiller biting into the river's current they slip gently alongside. Lu-Tang hops over with the bow line, Cornelius has the aft. Straightening up they congratulate each other for a job well done. They turn to inspect the handiwork of this addition to the pier. There are tools strewn about; evidently it is still a work in progress. There is a ladder against the tiered wall of the crane's tower. It is not as large as seaport cranes, yet will easily handle the cargo of the smaller ships traveling this river. Noticing the boom attached to the Tulip's mast Cornelius exclaims, "Ha, a smuggler's mast-crane. There is the means for such a rapid construction."

"Smugglers," a voice behind them says, "Not only smugglers, the mast crane is a handy item on any smaller vessel."

"Robert!" Cornelius and Lu-Tang greet their friend, "Congratulations on this fine addition to your quay."

"Thank you Sirs. It is indeed a satisfying accomplishment." They all shake hands while slapping one another heartily on the shoulders. "You are both looking well. I am assuming that your voyage has been a success. You are home sooner than we expected."

"Yes Sir," Lu-Tang announces, "all has gone well indeed."

Cornelius, standing hatless, coatless, and bare footed is noting that here he stands with two other men dressed as casually as he, "This is all very good."

"So, tell me," Robert asks, "How far up this river have you sailed?"

Cornelius withdraws from his pocket a tattered map he has made for himself and points out for Robert, "We sailed up the Rijn and then the River Main, following in reverse the route taken by Renaldo and his family. The River Main is navigable as far as a township called Bamberg where there is a community of expatriated Estonians, Latvians, and Poles. The funds left with this ship were sufficient, not only enough to establish dwellings for all the passengers, but also to maintain their well-being until they are able to return home." Now waving toward what lies beneath the tarps, "On our return downriver I have scouted trading opportunities and have even acquired supplies for our next venture."

"Splendid," slapping his hands together and then wringing them greedily. "I have some news you may appreciate," Robert tells him excitedly, "we have a new mast and a permanent keel for your pinnace. It'll be a proper sailing ship."

"Oh, that is splendid; indeed! Is your new crane ready for such a project?"

"Oh yes, we have worked hard to make it so."

Mara joins them, "Greetings, and welcome back. I assume all has gone well." Both nod. "While you have been away we have seen a great number of folks pass by on their way to visit the meteoroid."

Lu-Tang laughs, and withdraws a printed article from his pocket, "here is an account that includes an engraved illustration of the Meteoroid."

Cornelius adds, "We have heard the meteoroid discussed *ad nauseum* in public houses. La, there is even a new popular song with a line about," in a sing-song voice, "the 'firestone that has spilled from a bowl of stars'." After his laughter subsides he asks evenly, "Do we have a plan for our own pilgrimage to the site?"

"Oh yes." Robert answers enthusiastically, "We have agreed to sail."

"Mmmm-mm."

"Downriver to the Nord Zee and into the Channel."

"Calais?"

"We may spend a night in the harbor at Calais before sailing on for the Baie de la Somme and the port of La Crotoy."

"I like it." Nodding his head, "And you are planning to take both these ships?"

"We are, that is if you are still planning to go along with us."

"Hell, yeah! It will be a great adventure!" He punches Lu-Tang, then continues telling them, "We have been looking forward to seeing for ourselves what all the commotion of this meteoroid is about."

Lu-Tang asks, "Will you be able to mount a new keel and a new mast before we are ready to sail?"

Both Captains answer, "Oh yes, indeed," each being familiar with the process.

Mara finishes, "Diedrik is going to Utrecht tomorrow to bring the professors, Trinjntje, and Anna Maria." Now she winks, "He is also bringing back with him new sailcloths sewn to fit your taller mast!"

"Whoo-Hoo!"

♡♡♡

During his last few days at Janszoon's estate Nicklas has made arrangements with a young neighbor fellow to take care of the feeding and exercising of the stable's horses. He has been to Amsterdam sorting out what little affairs of his needed sorting, and leaving his landlady scratching her head again over another of his one-night stays. He has maintained correspondences with the professors and Trinjntje to verify the date they have set to meet at Schoonhoven Landing. He has chosen to arrive at Schoonhoven Landing a day ahead of all the others. He is riding his own gelding, a three year old Arabian, and is leading the Captain's stallion. He has been following the river and when the landing comes into view he notices the crane, "Whoa, look at that!" He then notices two ships at the dock; recognizing the smaller ship being the pinnace that Janszoon had sailed, "Home sooner than expected." Hurrying his steed a bit now he notices a group of folks there on the dock, "There is a busy lot," urging his horse a bit more, "let us see what they are up to."

On the embankment above the wall of pilings at the river's edge, watching it all, sits Princess Saarika. She turns at the sound of his arrival and jumps up to greet him, "Nicklas, my friend," she rushes forward, "it is so good to see you again." She lays a hand on his horse's neck, giving it a smoothing, "What a beautiful ride you have Sir!"

"Sir," he scoffs, "Indeed he is a wonderful beast," he tells her as he dismounts, "Being around Cornelius's stable of fine horses has inspired in me the need for a fine horse of my own."

"He is splendid," she turns fully to him now, "and you are looking very fine yourself. Give me a hug." She surprises him as she wraps her arms around him in a firm embrace.

It is a very familial-like embrace, something he is unused to. He squeezes back tentatively, "Living here seems to suit you."

Cornelius has rushed from the dock. He pulls Nicklas away from Saarika, shaking hands vigorously and reaching around to slap the younger man's back, "Look at you! Look at this fine horse you are riding! It is good to see you again my friend."

"Likewise, Sir. Have you been here long?"

"We arrived yesterday. Lu-Tang has gone with Diedrik to Utrecht." Turning with a sweeping gesture toward the wharf,

"Everyone else is helping with the refitting of my ship." Now waving for Nicklas to follow, "c'mon." Saarika, already holding his horse's reins, lifts her chin encouraging him to go on.

Everyone who lives here is on the dock and they all greet him with smiles, welcoming him like family. Mara is there with a horse harnessed to a line that runs through the new crane's pulley blocks. "We have just now set this little ship back in the water with its new keel in place," she says as the crane lifts a beam that has two wide straps hanging from it.

Renaldo strides over, "Welcome Sir. Are you here to help with our shipbuilding?"

"Eh? Shipbuilding?"

"We cannot have this one slowing us down," Robert fills in smiling a silly grin.

"Yes," Cornelius explains, "We have determined to take both ships on this meteoroid expedition. A new keel has been set, and now we are ready for the new mast."

"Remarkable!" Nicklas is astounded. "Will it be ready to sail tomorrow?"

"We shall be ready to sail before the day is done."

A line from the crane is attached to the smaller ship's mast. The pegs that hold it are driven out and the mast is lifted away, then carried ashore by all of them together. They pick up the new taller mast and carry it out on the dock. It is lifted and set into place with the new crane. By evening the new mast is set and the little pinnace can now be called a proper sloop.

"All we need now are the new sails."

♡♡♡

Lu-Tang, before settling down as an Easterner living in this Western society, has played the role of wanderer, watcher, listener, and vagabond. His restless spirit consistently urges him to walk on. It is an unfathomable complacency that has held him here in the lowlands for this long. Now, he has made the decision to once again move on. He has come to Utrecht with Diedrik, and upon his arrival has resigned his position at the University, finalized his lease with Boomkikker, discarded his few unnecessary belongings, and is now prepared to return with his friends to Schoonhoven Landing for their planned voyage to the site of the meteoroid.

He sits in the main room of the Kikker Gat. The dining room and the kitchen are brightened by the daylight shining in through the large casements of latticed windows at the front and back of the space. In the kitchen Rhetta and Kikkert laugh while Diedrik, they are still calling him Dirk, turns the handle on the wheel of their new high-capacity coffee mill. He listens as Kikkert is bragging about the hourglass grinding stones, "that make quick work of a full hopper of roasted beans."

Rhetta finishes, "One hopper in the morning provides enough grounds for fresh coffee all day." Her hand rests on Diedrik's shoulder as she talks. She is truly fond of this young man. "We are getting coffee beans that have been shipped from Afrika."

"Saarika tells me that coffee was first brewed there," Diedrik says as the last of the beans drain through the hopper. "Her legends say that coffee was discovered by goats."

"Ha! Goats," laughs Kikkert.

"The goatherd," Diedrik continues, "noticed his goats dancing merrily after eating coffee berries and decided to try some himself."

Lu-Tang's attention is drawn to the front entry as Trinjntje and Anna Maria come through, each carrying a travel satchel. He hears Calderon and Hendrik's footsteps coming down the stairs. The gathering crowd all greet each other. "Everyone here?" Diedrik calls out from the kitchen, "The wagon is in the back alley ready to go."

Anna Maria greets Lu-Tang, "Welcome back, Sir. I hope all went well on your river voyage. Has Captain Janszoon made you into a sailor?"

Lu-Tang shrugs, "Our voyage went better than expected, and I have gained a knowledge of sailing; but will not yet call myself a sailor."

Trinjntje asks him, "Are you ready for this next voyage?"

"I am, and you?"

"La, I am sooo ready!" Not only ready for this trek to the meteoroid, but she has retained the services of an agent to watch her home indefinitely should she choose to continue on after their intended rendezvous.

After completing their goodbyes to Kikkert and Rhetta they make their way out to where Diedrik's cart awaits them. The new sailcloth nearly takes up all the room in the back. Diedrik tells them, "Two of you can ride up front with me on the bench, and for those of you riding in the back, well, these sails will soften the ride." Trinjntje and Anna Maria sit up front on either side of Diedrik, while Hendrik, Calderon, and Lu-Tang climb up on top of the folded sailcloth and sit with their legs dangling over. "Yee-ah," he encourages his horses. Then for all, "Here we go!"

♡♡♡

With the work finished on Captain Janszoon's ship, everyone is left with little to do while they await Diedrik's return. Cornelius asks Razs and Vejz, sitting next to him on the strand, "What have you fellows been doing to keep yourselves busy?"

Razs answers, "We have been helping Robert build his crane."

"And we have been carving," Vejz adds.

Robert pulls a rune stone out of his pocket and tosses it over to Cornelius. "There is a clan, near the port where I trade in Norway that chisels runes into stones. These runestones are great for trading, especially when they are fitted inside a like-shaped wooden box."

Saarika withdraws a small wooden egg from a pocket, "Here is one I have carved." She hands it to Cornelius.

"You carve?" He asks, then upon seeing her reaction, "Pardon me. I was doltishly assuming carving to be a man's diversion." They are all amused by his embarrassment. The wooden egg has a barely perceptible seam, and by holding the two halves gingerly between his fingers, he pulls them apart, revealing the stone inside that has an odd symbol carved on it.

She tells him, "It is the rune of tranquility."

He presses the two halves together, then pulls them apart again. "This is masterful workmanship!"

"I thank you, Sir." She accepts the smooth wooden egg back. As she slips it into her pocket she tells him, "It is of no finer quality than the wooden cases carved by any of the others." She gestures gracefully with her arm to include all present.

Annia asks, "Are you a carver Cornelius?"

"Oh yes, indeed. Sailors carry a knife with them always." He reaches into his pocket and pulls out his ebony handled folding knife for all to see. "There is always something aboard ship in need of replacement; pegs, mallets, hatches, handles, ladder rungs, spindles, buckets, batons, and oh, the list goes on and on, right Robert?"

"Indeed," he laughs.

Kirin stands, the first to notice Diedrik's wagon coming up the riverway, "Here they are!"

"Hello dear friends," chimes Hendrik as he hops down, "We have arrived with Captain Janszoon's new sails."

Diedrik maneuvers the wagon around, then backs it down the riverbank to where the dock meets the levee. "There," he says as he sets the break and jumps down, "The sailmaker tells me that by grabbing this corner," he lifts a corner of the sailcloth and starts walking away, "the mainsail will unfold naturally." As the layers unfold others rush forward to grab hold so that it is not dragged on the ground.

When the unfolded cloth is stretched out Saarika shouts giddily, "It is like a Huaxian Dragon!"

"What?" They are all perplexed.

Except for Lu-Tang who laughs, "La, it is so. In Huaxia there is a tradition for groups of people to parade the streets under a long serpentine cloth resembling the length of a dragon."

"All we are missing," Saarika tells them, "is a majestic papier maché dragon's head at the front of it all."

The sail-brandishing cortege reaches the smaller ship and together Robert and Cornelius tie the loops attaching it to the mast. Standing there on the dock, Audrae asks Lu-Tang, "Are there dragons where you come from?"

"Legend says that there used to be dragons. Some believe that they still exist."

Cornelius adds, "Everywhere I have ever traveled has tales of dragons."

"Indeed," Professor Calderon announces, "Literature from all corners of the world show that dragons once lived upon this earth, and flew these skies."

The mainsail is attached and everyone hurries to bring the foresail. When it is ready Robert claps Cornelius on the shoulder, "Well Captain, shall we test your new sloop?"

"Verily, I say, we must." The mooring lines are loosed and as the ship drifts into the current the sails are raised. Wind immediately billows into them and away they go. "There is a difference," said appraisingly, "let us turn full into the wind," then excitedly, "hold on!"

With the ship listing dramatically Robert nods his approval, "I do believe your keel will keep us steady." They both whoop with joy as they race away across the vast river.

♡♡♡

"This day has finally arrived," Trinjntje says as she joins the expectant crowd on the quay. Each is carrying a travel case and a sack of food. Casks of water, wine, and beer have already been stowed securely aboard.

Philip and Beatris van Haumann are there to see them off. "Ha, there is quite a number of you," he attempts to count heads, "Is everyone prepared to spend the next three days sailing?" Phillip has agreed, along with a nephew, to watch over the animals and the windmills while the inhabitants of Schoonhoven Landing are away on this escapade.

"That is three days under favorable conditions Sir," Captain Janszoon points out with a grin, and then to tease the others, "We could be out a week or more."

Robert takes up the jest, "Aye, we might be lost at sea, or worse yet, raided by the bloody English in **'their'** channel." This brings laughter from some, wariness to others.

"Oh?" Anna Maria joining in with a bit of her own levity, "We have been led to believe these ships, and their captains, to be seaworthy."

Mara punches Robert playfully, "Let us have no more talk of trouble, even in jest." She looks around at all who are gathered there, "Ah, a fine looking bunch we have here. Let us board and be on our way."

It is an easy day of sailing down the vast River Rijn. It grows ever more expansive as they get nearer to the sea. The balmy autumn weather suits them well. They anchor in the evening near the same spot Robert and the English captain had stopped, just upriver of the channel leading into the Port of Rotterdam. The plan is to navigate through the crowded shipping lane tomorrow, as early in the day as the tide will allow.

♡♡♡

They set out soon as the tide has turned, sailing easily until they reach the bottleneck of ships awaiting to enter the port. Weaving between ocean going frigates requires intense concentration from Robert and Cornelius. They reach a point where they are held up behind a squadron of VOC battle-ready frigates slated for patrolling the Channel. When the two smaller vessels are finally allowed to pass it is after mid-day. Sailing out into the open waters of the North Sea fills many of the travelers with the foreboding that only the first time at sea inspires. Encountering the larger swells gives them a sense of their diminutive presence here. They remain close to the coast off the port side, but off starboard is a vastness that many of them are unprepared for. The captains, after the slow advance so far today, allow the wind to fill their sails, compelling everyone to set aside hats and to tighten scarves so as not to lose them in the gale of their passage. As both ships lean auspiciously each captain directs passengers away from the lee. They huddle together against the hulls: it is exhilarating and breathtaking as the ships skip across the breakers.

The afternoon passes quickly and the sun is setting as they follow port-bound fishing boats into the harbor of Calais. With the slower pace and calmer waters everyone settles down and relaxes after realizing how tense they have been holding themselves throughout the past few exhilarating hours. They drop anchors at the edge of a slew of fishing boats. Not bothering with the stove, for no one wants tea or coffee, they all fill glasses with beer or wine. It is not long before their tired bodies are drifting off to sleep. The night is filled with the sounds of night birds scavenging, lines snapping against spars, waves lapping at hulls; and faraway, the yipping of foxes in the hills surrounding the harbor.

They are awakened in the morning by the patter of fisherfolk methodically returning to their daily tasks. There is a chilling mist that has some of them curling up tighter within their blankets. The early risers have gathered around the warmth of Robert's cookstove and sip hot cups of coffee that have been garnished from a packet of chocolate powder that Anna Maria has brought along. "I slept surprisingly well," she says.

"Aye, me too," Mara tells her while offering a bottle of cream, "would you care to add a bit of this with your mocha?"

"Oh, yes, thank-you."

Robert, who likes his coffee black, passes her the sealed jar of sugar, "Here you go, you will probably want to add something else to hide the actual flavor of what you are drinking."

"Ah," she accepts the sugar, "you are a purist then? Eh Captain?" She smiles sweetly.

"A purist?" His eyes twinkle with humor, "More like a simpleton."

"I will accept a bit of cream in my cup," Renaldo joins them, "but I will pass on the sweetening, thanks." He sips and them smacks his lips, "Ah, tasty." Looking out at the rising mist he asks, "So we will not have so far to sail today, eh Captain?"

"Not nearly as far as yesterday."

Captain Janszoon, awake now, but still rolled in his blanket pipes in from over the gunwales, "Once we are out of the harbor we should be able to see Britannia across the way. That is ... after this fog lifts."

♡♡♡

Anchors are weighed, sails unfurled, and the two ships join the line of fishing boats leaving Calais Harbor. Diedrik has his bi-oculars out and is sharing them so all can take a closer look at the long white line of cliffs across the way. The narrow passage is filled with ships of all sizes, including frigates of the Royal Navy, battle ready merchant ships of the VOC, fishing boats scattered along the coastlines, and all sizes of ships ferrying cargo between the island and the continent. Hendrik, viewing the expanse through the lenses of his own set of twin scopes, pronounces didactically, "So, it is this narrowest portion of the passage connecting our NoordZee to the Atlantic," lowering his field glasses, "what we call the sleeve," now grimacing, "the English are claiming as their own channel. Ha!"

"Do all the fish swimming here belong to the English then?" Trinjntje teases.

A cracking sound, like a burst of faraway thunder is heard followed by more. "Oh! There are ships over there firing upon one another!"

"Let me see. Please." Vejz begs. The field glasses are passed around for everyone to get a look at the faraway frigates blasting at each other with cannon. Soon there are ships a fire and smoke billowing. Neither Cornelius nor Robert are willing to slow and watch this spectacle play out. From experience each knows it is best to gain a wide breadth from such as this.

Following the coast sets them on a course due south. They pass rocky outcrops and long cliffs separated by sandy beaches and a smattering of small bays, coves, and inlets. Captain Janszoon, more familiar with this coastline, leads the way. It is still early in the afternoon when he signals that he is turning inland toward their destination; *Le Baie de la Somme.* They sail into the shallow bay where the River Somme empties into the sea. In Calais there had been, besides the fishing boats, a large port for merchant vessels. There is no dedicated merchant port here, only the fishing village of La Crotoy. The town's population grows during the warm season with the influx of nobility, and the nouveau riche, seeking reprieve from the grandiosity of their existence. A pier stretches out into the bay from a sandy beach fronting a fairly new structure built to resemble a castle, or more appropriately, a monarch's country estate. This is where they intend to stay.

All but the two captains disembark and make their way up the pier toward the lavish *auberge*. Robert and Cornelius steer toward where other craft are anchored. Razs and Vejz turn over a beached skiff and with the oars stored beneath row out to retrieve the captains. The rest of the company follow a boarded walkway that leads them across the sand to a flight of stairs at the breaker wall. A stone walkway leads them on across a well-trimmed lawn up to a wide stairway giving them access to the spacious portico fronting this prodigious retreat. The over-sized front doors are opened and the concierge steps out to greet them and proceeds to assign rooms. Porters lead them up either of the wide stairways that border the enormous lobby that is fronting an equally spacious, and well accoutered dining area.

It will still be a while before dinner is served so Razs, Kirin, Vejz, and Audrae walk the beach to the fishermen's wharf. It is a busy place and they have to be careful to stay out of the way. A crane lifts a net full of squiggling fish out of the belly of a moored boat then swings it over to a waiting cart. "Wow! That is cool," Vejz proclaims. "It is exactly like Robert's crane."

"*Bonjour*!" Says one of the men who is part of the crew managing the crane. He, like all of the workers, is wearing oversized pants that are slick and shiny, like nothing these young folk have seen anyone wearing before. Everything around them is like nothing they have seen before; the slick stone wharf, the colorful fishing boats, and the smell. The odor of fish is overwhelming. As the man in the shiny pants finishes coiling a rope he says to them again, "*Bonjour les jeunes*."

"Bonjour," says Diedrik who has come up behind the others.

The man laughs. He is unused to having guests of the fancy resort visit his wharf. He asks them, "*Qu'est-ce qui t'améne?*"

Again it is Diedrik who answers, "*Le météore.*"

"*Le météorite,*" His eyes get big as he waves them closer while reaching into an inner pocket, "*Le météorite.*" His tone expresses awe. He unfolds the page of newsprint that he has withdrawn from his pocket and holding it out tells them again, "*Le météorite.*" He is showing them an engraving, centered amidst the printed words, that shows a crowd gathered around a large egg-shaped object. Many are holding the palms of their hands against the egg. Now the fisherman points at his chest, then pantomimes for them, his arm stretched out palm forward, the same as the people in the picture. His head is tipped back with his eyes closed, as he sighs deeply and visibly relaxes.

Behind him, one of his mates picks up a tiny fish that has escaped the net and tosses it, hitting the man in the back of the head snapping him out of his reverie. It does not seem to bother him that his mates are all laughing. He laughs too as he folds up his picture, puts it back into his pocket, and returns to his duties.

Walking back to the resort Razs comments, "He makes it look as if it is a wonderful thing to touch the meteoroid."

"May-tay-oh-reet," Vejz mimics the fisherman's pronunciation.

Audrae tells them excitedly, "I am going to touch the may-tay-oh-reet."

♡♡♡

The wait staff have pushed enough tables together in a row to accommodate the large group. The tables are set with fine porcelain from the Far East. Wine is presented in crystal decanters and poured into matching thin-stemmed goblets. Dish after dish is set upon the long table to be passed around. Afterward there is cake, pie, and pudding offered for dessert. It is late when everyone is finished. After three days of sailing this delicious meal is marvelous. Everyone is stuffed. The waiters and waitresses clearing the table have recognized that these folks are not like the usual hoity-toity guests that they are used to serving here and so offer conversation.

A young woman, with curls escaping from beneath her cap asks them if they are on their way to see the meteoroid. When told that they are she stops what she is doing, brings her hands together at her heart, tips her head back with eyes closed, and sighs deeply before telling them emphatically, "You will love, love, love it. It is the most remarkable thing ever to behold!" Noticing an older waitress eyeing her darkly she quickly returns to her tasks.

A young fellow with sparse whiskers repeats the motion of bringing his hands to his heart while telling dreamy-eyed, "It is heavenly. Most heavenly."

The *Maî-tre d'hô·tel*, who has also been to see the meteoroid, explains that there is a nicely fitted barge that will take them up the River Somme, and then from Amiens there are coaches to the site of the meteoroid's landing. He finishes, as the others before him, with his hands at his heart, "*Magnifique! Très Magnifique!*"

♡♡♡

Morning finds them all gathered in the Dining Hall again, sipping coffee and snacking on biscuits. Coaches arrive that carry them to the end of the bay and up the river to a barge landing. The barge that is awaiting them has rows of benches enough, and more, for all of them to sit. A chestnut Breton with flaxen mane and tail is harnessed to the barge. Cornelius, admiring the animal says to whoever is listening, "What a beautiful beast. It must stand at sixteen hands, if not more."

When they are all seated the bargeman whistles to the black and white dog seated in the towpath next to the great big horse. The dog jumps up at the sound and begins trotting up the path. The horse follows and the barge is on its way. This River Somme, much narrower than the Rijn they are used to, has farmsteads with acres of tilled fields stretching away beyond the tall grasses lining the riverbanks. The day passes uneventfully. The hard benches lead many of them to hop ashore and walk to alleviate the stiffness in their backsides. This river boat ride will take two days. Their stopover for the night is a miniaturized version of the previous night's extravagant lodgings. The second day has them traveling into a more populated area with farms and hamlets closer together. Upon their arrival at Amiens they disembark and are pointed in the direction of this night's lodging. Their walk takes them past a cathedral that is said to be the tallest anywhere. Situated at a crossroads the city has become a crowded hub for the masses making their way to and from the site of the meteoroid.

After settling in to the rooms of the manor house where they will spend this night they split into smaller groups and venture out into the revelry going on in celebration of the meteoroid's arrival. Dancing crowds have gathered around lively musicians. Stages have been set up where acrobats with slim figures perform tumbling acts between the productions provided by itinerant troupes of actors. Stalls have been set up along every street and alleyway for fleecers to pass off their un-credentialed products. Halls have been rented out by speakers woefully denouncing the coming of meteoroids and pronouncing the arrival of more fireballs bringing the end of all that is so dear. Handbills decrying these circumstances litter the ground.

"I do hope that this circus atmosphere does not extend to the actual site of the meteoroid," Nicklas comments to Cornelius as they make their way along a crowded thoroughfare.

"I look forward to seeing this impromptu city of tents."

Arrival

There are coaches transporting inquisitive sightseers from Amiens, but because of the congestion, taking a coach is no faster than walking. There is a steady stream of foot traffic even so early in the day. The roadway is lined with food vendor's tables advertising hot breakfast sandwiches and souvenir cups filled with steaming coffee; later they will be offering dinner sandwiches and stronger fare to fill the garishly painted cups. There are also booths selling mementos: vials of scorched earth, etchings of the meteoroid's impact, scarves and caps woven with blazing orbs, billiard balls repainted flaming orange, plates commemorating the event, and meteoroid inspired jewelry. Shortly past the outskirts of Amiens the roadway dwindles to a cart-path, then branches off on a newly trodden byway leading to the site of the meteoroid. Farther along the landholders have routed the course to follow property lines rather than allow the multitude to traipse across their cultivated fields. This massive crowd of eager wayfarers move along quietly, yet happily.

Walking amidst a collected mass of humanity of such proportions would normally be a daunting experience, but the pervading cheerfulness has everybody treating each other politely. "Have you ever seen so many people all in one place?" Trinjntje asks Lu-Tang as they walk along.

"I have," he tells her, "Amongst the Black Rock Mountains of Karakorum there is a Holy Mountain: the

Crystal Mountain. Pilgrims, thousands and thousands of pilgrims, visit every summer intent upon traversing the pathway that circles the Holy Mountain; pilgrims of many faiths. Everywhere around the mountain there are monasteries with colorful rounded spires, shrines with prayer flags fluttering in the winds, lakes as large as seas, and hot springs where the wayfarers gather to soak in the healing waters. Whilst visiting the Crystal Mountain during its season of pilgrimages one is always surrounded by a throng of others; eats amidst a multitude, and sleeps amongst however many will fit into a wide spot along the path. The difficult passage around the mountain is congested with others, everyday people, following the same path; going both directions around the mountain. There may have been as many people all around the holy mountain as there are here today."

"So maybe," Trinjntje muses humorously, "We are pilgrims and this is a holy pathway that we tread upon toward a holy destination."

♡♡♡

Diedrik, looking in front of him, sees people as far as he can see, then turning behind him sees the same, "We are like rows of ants going back and forth from the anthill."

"I know. Right?" Nicklas responds, "It is almost like looking down from a bell tower, at the crowds filling the streets and plazas below."

"Everybody here seems happier than the people in city crowds."

"Indeed," Nicklas agrees, "I am happy; happy to be here, happy to have become involved in the circumstances that led us here. Ya know, I often find myself wondering why I have been included or, how do I say it, why I have been drawn in as a participant with you and all the others."

"La, me and all the others?" Diedrik shakes his head, "It was foolishness that led to my involvement."

"Whatever, foolishness or circumstance, either way here we are," Nicklas tells his new friend with a companionable slap on the back, "You want to know what else I wonder? Has this happened before? Was there once upon a time long ago another group like us carrying three necklaces of Golden Hearts to a new meteoroid?"

"You mean, after dreaming together of a Celestial Harpist?"

♡♡♡

Paulo Calderon wonders about the astronomical significance of this meteoroid. He is walking alongside Cornelius Janszoon, so mentions, "I noticed when visiting your home the presence of a telescope positioned to monitor the sky."

"Yes," Cornelius answers, "Following the stars is a captain's duty, which I carry on out of personal interest. Familiarity with the night sky is the key to navigation."

"You are acquainted then with the current theories regarding the orbital pathways of the planets?"

"Indeed, I have studied what Kepler and Galileo have to say, that the planets, rather than travelling round the sun in a circle instead take a more oblong path."

"Do your years of notations support their claims?"

"Indeed they do. As a point of fact, I was very pleased to read the published accounts of what I, and other ships captains, have deduced in our everyday tracking of planetary orbits."

"I am very impressed Captain Janszoon that you are able to calculate as accurately as the leading scientific minds of current times." The Captain scoffs, and for a moment his pleasant countenance turns sardonic, surprising Paulo and prompting him to ask, "Have I misspoken?"

Janszoon replies rather pedantically, "There are tens of thousands of ships traveling the high seas, and upon each of those ships is a Captain, or his First Mate, keeping track and making notations of the stars and planets in the night sky. I reckon that there are more than a few that have deduced the elliptical orbits of the planets around the sun."

"Are you telling me that what is being proclaimed as the most modern astronomical datum is actually old news?" The Captain's wry sideways glance tells him that his assumption is correct. "Well then, elucidate for me Sir, if you will, based upon your years of astrographical analysis, the nature of this meteoroid."

"The nature of this meteoroid," Cornelius repeats, and then laughs, "It is astonishing, as I compare my notes over time, how precise are the movements of all the planets as they orbit the sun: so precise that one is able to calculate in advance a planet's location. One who is familiar with the grand design recognizes a perfect order to the cosmos."

Calderon interrupts, "I love the idea of there being a perfect order."

"This meteoroid," Cornelius resumes, while extending an arm, indicating the direction they are headed, "is a bit of **chaos** crashing through the established order."

Calderon bursts into laughter and it is a bit before he is able to gather his wits and explain, "Forgive me Captain," he says while attempting to suppress his laughter, "You have used the very words spoken by the lead cardinal presiding over the tribunal of my inquisition, "Brother Paulo," mimicking the cardinal's voice, "You are the harbinger of **chaos** into this Order." Paulo laughs some more and Cornelius laughs along with him.

Hendrik, who has been walking beside these two asks, after laughing along, "Have either of you a hypothesis as to the origin of this *'Chaos that has crashed through the Order'*?"

"Well," Janszoon begins, "at first I speculated that it may be just another falling star; but disregarded that quite early on as purely fantastical as there is little known evidence regarding the size of the stars. Then I thought that perhaps it can be explained by something as colossal as one of the other planets of our galaxy veering off its course." His raised eyebrows indicate his pessimism toward this notion. "I have further speculated, because of my witnessing of a volcano on an island of the Jayakartan archipelago spewing hot molten rock, that a volcano on one of those other planets," waving his arm upward, "having similar violent eruptions may have spewed a fireball in our direction."

"Hmmmm," Hendrik asks rhetorically, "like a cannonball shot across the abyss of space."

Calderon continues with the rhetoric, "Directed at our planet, or landing here by pure happenstance?"

"If not happenstance, then how came it to be here? Are you presupposing that some force may have drawn this rock to our planet? That would indeed be a thing of *gravitas.* Hmmmmm." Cornelius carries on, "If so, then our discussion returns to speculating as to the possibility of whether this be an occurrence of chaos, or a continuance of order. Something drawn into our familiar order from another, unfamiliar, order."

"Are we discussing Astronomy," Hendrik laughs, "or Philosophy?"

♡♡♡

Mara, Annia, and Saarika, walking together as the path rising before them is getting steeper, have each been wearing their necklace of golden hearts, out of sight beneath their clothing, since the day they left home. It is longer than any of them has ever worn these articles of personal reverence. "You know ..." Saarika tells her two companions, who she now thinks of as sisters, "Diedrik told me that at first he wore this necklace in a sash beneath his coat for safe keeping, then he continued to keep it near him for its remarkable soothingness." The roadway, looking ahead, is clearly getting steeper. "After wearing it steadily these past few days I am feeling the remarkable soothingness he speaks of: and more. I like it."

"Aye, I like it too," Mara agrees.

"As a girl," Annia speaks up, "I only saw this necklace of Golden Hearts worn one special day each year. After it became my responsibility I was bold enough to occasionally put it around my neck, and then I did not want to take it off. Now I wish that I had worn it longer and more often. I wish I had let others wear it." She places a hand above her heart feeling the necklace there. "It is soothing and more, I am also feeling a sisterhood, a brotherhood; oh I do not know what words to say that describe the way I feel toward others. Everyone is my family. There is love wherever I look."

"La., yes!" Mara declares and then laughs, "You say that you do not know what words to use, but you have described perfectly the way I feel." The path they walk upon steepens even more. "There is something else," the climb has her breathing heavier than usual, "I am remembering," spoken breathily, "as a young woman, about the age of your Kirin and Audrae, my Ma would have me sit still out away from home, somewhere alone, wearing this necklace of Golden Hearts round my neck and," She breathes deep, "so that I would have visitors." Her voice changes to a volume barely above a whisper, "All sorts of creatures would sit down with me; rabbits, foxes, birds, grasshoppers, deer, bees ... and they would each show me their other nature: and because I wore the necklace of Golden Hearts I witnessed who they see themselves to be." She takes another deep breath, then sighs before continuing, "All the familiar creatures wanted me to know that their other natures are the rarely seen creatures of the mysterious fables told by the old folks round the fire." Nearly to the top of the incline she finishes, "And when I came home I would sneak a look into my Ma's mirror; wondering if I had another nature, and if the mirror would reveal it to me."

Coming over the rise, at the top of the hill they have climbed, puts them at the very spot where they had stood in their shared dreaming. They recognize this spot even though it had been nighttime when they had been here before. The plain stretching out below is the same, though filled with a massive milling crowd of people. They sit down with many others of the throng, who have stopped to rest after climbing the hill, dumbfounded at the sight. The scorched furrow carved by the fireball has had enough time for grasses to grow and is green again; the bright green of new shoots. The meteoroid, had pushed the earth before it, and created a sizable amphitheater where it had come to rest. The center of the semi-circle of mounded earth is thick with a dark mass of humanity. The number of people swarming there is incomprehensible. Radiating outward from that center, amidst the roiling convolution of the gathered thousands, stand row upon row of temporary structures, interspersed with passageways wide enough for horses and carts. It is an overwhelming sight indeed: a city of tents resembling a massive army's encampment.

It is Audrae who pronounces what everyone else is thinking, "It will take forever to get through all those people!"

♡♡♡

Having made their way down the slope and now approaching the first avenue of tents they are greeted by one of many people wearing sashes identifying themselves as members of *La Société de la Météorite Moderne.* These volunteers are providing printed flyers and asking for donations to support their continued organizational objectives. Their flyer includes a map of the sight, outlines their plan of building a shrine, and offers a message of hope for the well-being of all human-kind. The young man that is handing out these flyers suggests, "You may wish to check out the message boards we have situated around the site where visitors post their personal experiences." Moving on with the flow of the gathering they come upon one of the message-boards and stop to read what others have written, hoping to discover what the mystique of the meteoroid offers.

A post written with superb calligraphy catches Annia's attention, "*To touch the stone is to discover Love.* Ah, I would be willing to discover love."

Standing next to her, Renaldo points out a note written in a bold scrawl, "Angels Walk amongst us."

Razs reads from a small note pinned low on the board, "*I come away from the meteoroid knowing that I can be and do and have whatever I desire,"* then says, "I have always known that," to his parents, "It is what you have always taught us."

Audrae and Vejz point to a note that has them laughing, "YIPPEE! YAHOO! HOORAY!"

Kirin reading through the variety of impressions posted there says, "All these notes are about feeling good, being happy, and loving. No wonder there are so many people coming here. Look at this one, *dreaming is supposed to be fun."*

♡♡♡

Interspersed throughout the tent city there are covered tea shops, ale stands, and open-air kitchens. Saarika has them stop at a booth that is being run by folks resembling her in heighth and color and serving her style of flatbread. She greets them in her native tongue, and they share a lively exchange while she ladles from a bowl they have set out for her onto a piece of the flatbread, rolls it up, and then hands it to Diedrik, "This is what I grew up eating. I want you to try it, I think you will like it." She continues talking and laughing with the folks of the booth while filling and handing another rolled up flatbread to Trinjntje, "These people come from the mountains not far from where I grew up."

"Mmmmmm," both tell her, "This is delicious."

She laughs and hands a roll-up to Calderon, "They are telling me that they have traveled here from where they are now living on the southern coast, near the town of Niçard."

Calderon, with a mouthful of food, "In the Duchy of Savoy, on the coast, a part of the world that I would love to visit."

Trinjntje says, "Maybe after visiting Paris we can travel there for the winter."

While filling a flatbread for herself Saarika tells them, "They also tell me that we need to make our way to the meteoroid now, or we will be in line until after midnight." Before she takes the first bite of her roll-up she is distracted by a very small child, barely old enough to walk, tugging at her abaya, and reaching up to be held. Saarika laughs musically while handing her roll to Diedrik, and then lifting the child up and spinning round and round; both squealing delightedly.

♡♡♡

Coming upon a large awning with tables and chairs beneath it Nicklas suggests, "Let's sit for we have done enough walking. Let us take a break and watch the people going by."

Cornelius agrees and turning to Robert and Mara, "Care to join us?" They choose a table. Pints of beer are delivered, and then a plate of sizzling bite-sized sausages along with a board of bread and cheese. "The same as what we would be served if we were in a city pub." From their seats they have a splendid view of the steady stream of humanity flowing past. "There are all classes represented in this gathering."

"And all ages," Mara notes.

"And from many cultures," Robert points out the differing outfits worn by passersby.

"And those seeking miracles," Nicklas nods toward a cripple hobbling past on crutches, "Twould be nice for that man's belief to match his desire."

"Aye," Robert says, then noticing Hendrik and Anna Maria passing by, calls for them to come have a seat, but the two are intent to move on, "Perhaps we should not sit here for too long either."

♡♡♡

"I think I recognize that man," Hendrik tells Anna Maria, directing her attention toward a fellow carrying on an animated discussion with a Jesuit, "I believe it is the self-proclaimed mystic Jean de Labadie."

"I am familiar with his writings," she tells him, "he was a Jesuit, but is now with the Reformed Church."

"His ideas may be even too radical for them," Hendrik jeers, "If I am correct he advocates the doing away with all churchly rites in favor of a solely personal experience."

Looking askance at him, "I have heard similar ideas from you, Sir," with dubiously raised eyebrows, "even after the decree banning you from lecturing your philosophical edicts." They join the crowd that is listening in on the discourse between the two men; a crowd comprised of many who are returning from their own personal experience with the meteoroid.

The Jesuit is agreeing with something Labadie has said, "Yes, I do believe that as I was touching the meteoroid I did indeed feel," patting his heart, "what you are referring to as Spirit within, and it felt of being born anew."

"Now that you are familiar with that feeling you will seek it evermore." Those in the crowd listening in who are returning from the meteoroid agree heartedly, and to them Labadie turns to say, "You will not be satisfied until you discover for yourself how to feel this way for a bit of every day. I believe that we have all been blessed with this ability even before we have made our pilgrimage to this meteoroid."

Anna Maria tells Hendrik, "I like that, and perhaps I shall look further into what this man has written."

♡♡♡

The Gedimin family stops to watch a busy crew of engineers. There are architects making notations on large blueprints laid out on spacious tables. There is a band of surveyors calling out measurements. Another group, stonemasons, calculate how the architect's plans can be matched to the surveyor's valuations. Members of *La Société de la Météorite Moderne* have cordoned off the area where the men are working. Renaldo asks one of them, "Will something permanent be built here?"

"*La Société de la Météorite Moderne* has commissioned a shrine to be built that will eventually cover this modern oracle so that its wonder may be enjoyed for all time. Young King Louis has visited *la Météorite* and requested that his godfather appropriate such funds as required to aid in this remarkable project of our *Société*." Very proud of this accomplishment, and very proud of her own individual contribution here, the woman directs them to move on, "*Continuez à Avancer, S'il vous plait.*"

"So," Razs ponders, "do you suppose that someday there will be a permanent settlement here? Will it be called Meteoroid Valley?"

"Or, how about," Kirin says in jest, "Fire Rock City."

"Maybe," Vejz joins in, "Star Seed Gardens."

"I think it should be called something dreamy; like Paradise, or Celestia," Audrae adds.

"I like that," Annia smiles, "Celestia. A city for Celestials."

"Are you supposing," Renaldo asks, "That Celestials will visit?"

♡♡♡

A clamoring flock of over-sized birds circling overhead draws the attention of everyone in this massive crowd and soon has all eyes turned skyward. These birds have not flown overland; they are descending from beyond the highest elevations of the dark azure sky far above. First seen as mere specks, then dropping closer taking on the appearance of birds, a very large flock of birds, a multitude of birds. The combined chorus of this flock is creating a comical clamor of clatter that has everybody smiling. As these birds drop closer it is becoming evident how large they are; very large, extremely large; larger than any other bird. They have brightly colored feathers with a variety of patterns; no two alike. They form a circling host encompassing the entire vista of this wide valley. There are more and more of them. The crowd watches from below in hushed amazement. Something remarkable is happening; something nobody has expected. These amazing avian creatures begin landing at the edges of the crowd and beyond, except for three, which move in and hover near the meteoroid. As they descend the people directly beneath press quickly back in an attempt to clear a landing area. This close it becomes apparent that these are not birds, nor any familiar creature, yet it is clearly evident that there is nothing to fear, in fact the opposite is what folks are feeling: they sense a supreme beneficence, a kindly nature, even a delightful humor. The crowd of humanity is pleased that these guests have arrived. These charming avian-type creatures stand half again as tall as a grown human, and though rather than arms they have wings, they resemble humans, which has many wondering if these could be angels, yet would the denizens of heaven be different from us in so many ways? So odd looking? These three Aviants, standing at the meteoroid, scan the crowd as the rest of the flock continues coming to ground and mingling there on the outskirts of the amassed congregation. More are arriving. The already huge crowd grows exponentially in number.

Upon folding their wings these sweetly smiling creatures emerge somewhat less bird-like. Their appearance inspires a bit of hilarity, their bodies are covered in feathers, but it is the wild cluster of plumage upon their skulls that makes them appear so loony. Their arms are wings, but long feathers at the tips articulate, yes like fingers; fingers that never seem still, as if a current of energy constantly flows through them. And yes, the feathered legs end in leathery ankles extending to long-taloned toes. Lengthy tail feathers extend behind, bobbing up and down in sequence with the jouncing of the head. They have rather bulbous eyes that are changing: changing color, changing focus, changing size; but in the most delightful manner. These laughter-filled eyes are situated on the sides of the head, separated by a nose shaped similar to a beak: a nose that also forms into a mouth, with barely a chin. It is an altogether silly looking face. It is a face that invites laughter; not derisive laughter, no, more the laughter of infants, the laughter of youth, the laughter of freedom. These Aviantory creatures, although they do make those unique bird-like calls, do not speak audibly with voices, but they do speak; their words are expressed, and heard, from within: joking, teasing, and shifting the entire mood of the gathering toward a humorous bliss.

One of the three that has landed near the meteoroid, adorned with orange, brown, and red feathers, scans the assemblage, turning its entire self, unaware that the folks behind it have to rush to be clear of its sweeping tail feathers.

It stops when it has sighted and lined up with Saarika, then proceeds marching decorously toward her. The crowd parts, making way before it. Standing before her now, Saarika locks eyes with the speckled eyes of this being and the two of them communicate silently. Silently, yet all present know what is being said. "*Greetings Princess*," is what is heard in their thoughts; oscillating in a widening pattern so that everybody is sharing what is transmitted. Then it lifts its head and calls out a celebratory salute, "YaaaaaaaaAAk." Each person present receives the inner prompting to repeat the call, and as one the crowd of humanity calls out, "YaaaaaaaaAAk," which is then repeated by all the Aviants, "YaaaaaaaaAAk." The earthly crowd is beginning to think that this feels like dreaming. It is a fun dreaming that allows them to know that they are imagining their dreaming: that they are imagining themselves to be who they are and what they want to be, and a general sigh of relief is exhaled as everybody allows themselves to imagine freely. This brightly orange colored Aviant has stopped and with a distinguished air is bowing to Saarika, then is standing upright, and gracefully extending a wing in the direction of the meteoroid as an invitation for her to lead the way. The sea of humanity parts, allowing her and her winged guide easy passage. She is beckoning, then encouraging her friends that are with her; Diedrik, Lu-Tang, Hendrik and Anna Maria, to come along with her.

Another winged emissary has strode out and made its way from the meteoroid toward Annia and her family. Having appeared mostly white from below, now with wings folded, appears to be wearing a cloak of blue; bright indigo blue. Its breast flashes pearly white. The creature's eyes radiate cheerful ease. Silently, yet heard by all it says, "*Greetings Princess.*" Annia kneels and bows her head. This Aviant's scalp feathers go up and down twirling in all directions; it is laughing, and its laughter is transmitted; felt and heard by everybody. Soon they are all laughing: the entire gathering is laughing gaily. This amazing creature reaches a wing out to Annia, and with its feather fingers gently lifts her chin until its eyes meet hers. Her happiness, her freedom, her inner joy, all ripple outward touching everybody. All together each person remembers imagining this happiness; and now they are allowing themselves to feel free and happy. The indigo feathered Aviant raises its head and crows, "Ha-Ha-Ha-Hoooooo! Ha-Ha-Ha-Hoooooo!"

Everybody, not only those nearby, but everybody, mimics the call, "Ha-Ha-Ha-Hoooooo! Ha-Ha-Ha-Hoooooo! Ha-Ha-Ha-Hoooooo!" The laughter that follows is a massive wave rolling over the plain. A wing is extended toward the meteoroid inviting Annia and her family to proceed forward. The crowd opens up a pathway for them to follow.

"It's funny looking," Vejz whispers.

"I know, right?" Audrae giggles.

"The feathers on its head look like it just got out of bed," Kirin laughs.

This creature, hearing them, responds by turning and spinning its big eyes comically. Razs says, "It is because of his silliness that he looks so silly."

"*It's fun to be silly.*" Silliness and laughter abound.

The third of the Aviants that had landed there close to the meteoroid, plumed in green and gold, has made its way through the crowd and as it bows to Mara intones, as the other two have, "*Greetings Princess,*" Its hooded eyelids close down secretively, "*We have met before.*"

She remembers, during one of those revelatory moments when her mother had left her sitting alone with the necklace of Golden Hearts around her neck, this creature had visited, "My Ma told me that you were an angel."

"And did she tell you that you are also an angel?"

"Yes. She told me that we are angels visiting this earthly realm for the fun of it."

The Aviant's laughter lifts it up from the ground, and spinning there above them it calls excitedly, "Yezz-yezz-Yezzy! Yezz-yezz-Yezzy!" It's wide spread wings sends a breeze of remembrance over all.

Everybody present gasps, then shouts, "Yezz-yezz-Yezzy! Yezz-yezz-Yezzy!" The wave of remembering that we are here for fun radiates like ripples out across the gathering.

Settling with its feet back upon the ground, its emerald green feathers shining golden in the sun, the chuckling Aviant extends a wing toward the meteoroid indicating for Mara to lead on. She grabs Robert's hand and tugs him along while waving for Janszoon, Nicklas, Trinjntje and Calderon to come along. They make their way through the opening created as the crowd moves aside.

Trinjntje points out for her companions what is occurring beyond the outskirts of the assembled throng. More of the birdlike Celestials are arriving and the gathering flock is spreading up onto the hillsides surrounding this vast plain. "There must be as many of them as there are of us."

"It is as if they are arriving at an appointed time for a special event," Cornelius speculates.

"The crowd," Nicklas calculates, "has doubled."

"This is remarkable. Delightful. Fun!" Shouts Calderon.

"They glow," Trinjntje pronounces what everyone is noticing. The assembled congregation of these avian beings does indeed have a sheen; a colorful shifting sheen. And they are a noisy bunch: their excited murmuring heightens the excitement of everyone present. The sweet mood of anticipation bubbles up in each and every heart.

♡♡♡

The ushers of *La Société de la Météorite Moderne* are clearing the area around the meteoroid in anticipation of the three

Aviants marching forward. Upon their arrival Mara, Annia, and Saarika, along with their families and friends are stationed near the boulder. Seeing it up close they all wonder what can be so special about this inglorious-looking object: that is, until they feel its warmth. In close proximity they begin to feel the steadily radiating ambience. There is the feeling of satisfied joy, yet there is also an eagerness: an anticipation of wonder. They remember feeling this way before; they are re-experiencing how they felt while dreaming together on the night the three necklaces had clicked themselves together.

The three Aviant escorts situate themselves equidistantly around the rock with the three necklace bearers positioned before them; all facing the meteoroid. They lift and spread their wings touching tip to tip forming a circle. Throughout the assemblage arms and wings raise up and reach out, spontaneously matching the gesture, linking all members of the crowd. Saarika, Mara, and Annia lower their head cloths, and release their hair. Saarika's bronze mane shines red and orange in the sunlight. Annia's smooth line of tresses, reaching to her waist, glimmers with dark purple and deeper blue. Mara's golden waves shine with highlights of copper and red. Following an unspoken directive each of them unclasps their necklaces of Golden Hearts from around their necks, which upon being freed, jump from their hands to form a circle that hovers over this large egg-shaped stone. A hush falls over the crowd as the circle formed of necklaces begins to slowly spin round. Arms and wings are lowered as the golden glimmering ring floats high enough for all, even to the very outskirts, to behold.

The meteoroid is glowing brighter and brighter, and there is a rumbling birthing, "Brrmm-rrmm. Brrmm-rrmm. Brrmm-rrmm." The deep tones resonate through the ground, pulsing rhythmically from deep below the surface, and are felt through the feet, up through the legs, the belly, and in betwixt the ribs. It is the heartbeat of the earth matching with and welcoming the pulse of all present. Could anything be more grandiose?

The purled filigree of golden thread that has held the Golden Hearts together for aeons untwines and now the disassembled hearts are dancing individually. It is a merry dance of hopping and twirling: each Golden Heart an entity expressing the freedom it has long imagined. The vast flock of Aviants roars a welcome to the Golden Hearts. This is what they have come for. The Golden Hearts respond. Streams of light shine out from within each of them. The facets of each Heart's jewel disperse these streams of light. The many-colored beams are shining out in all directions; a feast for the eyes to behold. The celebrating Hearts inspire everybody to celebrate. The celebrating Aviants mingling with the celebrating Humans is the happiest party ever.

Eventually these Golden Hearts have reformed into a flattened circle hovering over the meteoroid. A circle with all the jewels aiming toward the center creating the appearance of a flattened disc; a stage. All the colored light streams meet there in a burst of twinkling light, pulling light up from the meteoroid, then like a pot bubbling over, the twinklings float up and up in a beam, an ever-widening beam of light; multi-hued light shining up, up, and up into the farthest reaches of the sky. The partying legion quietens and is again watching enthralled for what may come next. The circle of Golden Hearts is an opening, a channel, a sleeve that the force rising up from the meteoroid passes through: beaming itself higher and higher into the midday sky. The ray of light becomes a pillar extending beyond the atmosphere, into the eternity of the heavens. Everybody is watching, watching, watching; silently awaiting what will assuredly follow.

Wondering what this shaft of light might be, Calderon, thinking out loud asks, "Can it be forming a connection to another realm?"

"An entrance to whatever lies beyond?" Lu-Tang muses.

"Possibly a passage into the unknown," speculates Hendrik.

"Probably a passage," Cornelius invokes.

"A passage for what?" Trinjntje begs.

"Whatever." Whispers Audrae, "I am so excited!"

The Aviant escorts, matching her whisper, advise in their unspoken way, "The festivities have only just begun."

This melodic whispering from the triad of Aviants nearest the meteoroid can be heard as a message for all, "Only just begun." The message passes outward inviting all present, "Only just begun." Inviting, teasing, building anticipation, "Only just begun," until the message has reached even those dearhearts standing at the outskirts. A bout of laughter arises from the Aviant flock when the message of more to come is whispered.

Vejz asks, "What will happen next?"

"Look," his brother tells him, "follow the beam of light."

There is barely perceptible movement within the iridescent shaft of light shining up through the ring of Golden Hearts and up into the heavens. There appears a multitude of little flitterings: flickering prisms scattering the light into spangles of color.

"Are they dragonflies?" Saarika asks her escort.

The creature tips its head in an appropriately bird-like manner, "*Is that what you are imagining?*"

"Possibly butterflies?" Trinjntje speculates.

As the cloud of tiny critters drop closer Kirin shouts in surprise, "They have arms and legs. Oh! And hands and feet. And faces. They are," she gasps, "Faeries."

"Fae?" Diedrik asks in amazed wonder as these charming sprites pass through the ring of Golden Hearts and begin landing upon the meteoroid. These faeries are sweet. They look around approvingly; smiling, happy, bright-eyed, pointy-eared, and with translucent skin revealing the soft bones and organs within. As the surface of the meteoroid becomes overcrowded they begin to fly off into and over the crowd: living lights on shining wings. More and more drop through and fly out over the gathering. Bits of sparkle, drifting from their wings, float down upon the cheeks of upturned faces; tiny whiffs of kisses, sparklings of love and laughter. As the swarm increases, the buzzing of wings is mixed with the delicate pitch of infectious laughter. The Aviants raise themselves up above the ground and welcome this batch of sprites with bits of their own sparkle flung from the long curving fingers at the tips of their wings. Children in the crowd began holding up their hands for the little imps to land, cooing and giggling, wanting to share the fun they bring with them into this realm.

"They are garden sprites," Trinjntje claims, "This meadow will be filled with wildflowers."

"Aye," Mara agrees, "And besides the buds, blossoms, and blooms there'll be grasses with graceful plumes."

"Ah look," says Razs breathlessly, "Something different now." A bit larger than the sprites, about a hand's breadth in size, without wings, and dressed in outfits of fur; some sleek, some fuzzy, and some fluffy. Dropping down from above on gossamer threads, upon reaching the meteoroid, they gleefully slide down and immediately scurry off. "Minkin," he pronounces as this new horde rushes out, yipping and yahooing, between the ankles of the crowd. He reaches down and one of the little characters jumps into his hand, scurries up his sleeve and down into his shirt where it sets to tickling him.

"Elves?" asks Renaldo.

"Leprechauns," laughs Robert.

"Pixies," Trinjntje giggles, "garden dwellers full of mischief!"

"Brownies," Annia tells them laughing, "To help us with our chores."

"To keep the forest tidy," Calderon concurs, standing very still as he watches the scurrying bodies flash by below. Normally humans will cringe at beasties this size, yet as he looks around he sees everybody reaching down to pick up and hold one of these critters, welcoming them into this world. He laughs along with them all at the nimble antics displayed by these little ones. Trinjntje catches his eye and he knows from her look that, just as the little bird had shown him its true nature, these delightful creatures represent the nature of all the small furry creatures abiding in gardens and forests. These Minkin are comfortable with the humans and the Aviants, as they are picked up and tickled, then kissed and handed over to others.

Two have scurried up Lu-Tang's pant leg, past his waist and out through his collar, "Oh my gracious," they seat themselves on his shoulders and tug at his ears, "Oh my gracious," they fly in a circle around his head inciting him to laughter, "Oh my gracious!"

Trinjntje, directing her friends' attention back to the shaft of light, "Look what is arriving now. These creatures are getting bigger!"

"Is that a cat? A lynx with wings?" Cornelius asks astonished, "With an owl riding on its back?" As soon as the cat lands on the meteoroid it spreads its wings and flies off. The owl touches the stone, and then flies after the cat. "That Lynx has wings!"

"That owl has fur!" Lu-Tang spouts, "And paws with claws! Oooh!"

Audrae can't help but tell him, "It is an owly-cat." They laugh. Everybody is laughing as the happy creatures darting by overhead playfully yip and howl. A continuous host of furred and feathered beasts arrive on outstretched wings; ever larger, yet all friendly and enjoying themselves as they mix into the crowd that is growing thick with all these new attendees. The crowd is doubling again.

All manner of mythical creatures are arriving and scurrying off into the expanding crowd. There are winged cats and dogs resembling familiar household pets. There are also larger cats; lions and tigers strolling unmenacingly. And there are wolves, with furry wings, frolicking playfully. It is something new for many present to realize that all creatures of all realms want to be with us. There are no distinctions of predator or prey in this dreaming. There are larger beasts; elephants, whales, and dragons stationing themselves further out where there is still some open space available.

After watching the larger animals, including the dragons, circle overhead, Audrae is disappointed when they land so far away and she is not tall enough to see over the heads of everybody surrounding her. So she hops up off the ground, hoping to catch a quick glimpse of more, and is pleasantly surprised when she remains floating above where she had been standing. "Oh, now I can see them!" She sees elephants with wings and dragons that are even larger than the elephants. But some of the dragons are not so large; they are all different sizes, and they really do breathe fire, but the flames are harmless. "I see them breathing fire that does not burn."

Transfixed by Audrae's floating, Trinjntje jumps, "Oh!" Seeing the different colored dragons breathing different colored flames she announces, "I want to breathe fire." She drops back to the ground, inhales deeply, and then exhales a cute little flare that licks at Calderon's hair, but instead of burning, he is tickled and bursts into laughter with flickering flames bouncing off his tongue. The fun of breathing harmless fire sweeps the gathering, and has everybody jumping up and laughing flames. It is a new method of tickling one another. The assembled mass of humans, Aviants, and mythical creatures becomes enlivened with frivolity; as dreaming is meant to be.

Everybody takes advantage of their new-found lightness of being. As each one of them hops up and floats for a bit they are able to see, as Audrae has seen, the full expanse of the assemblage. They all share the realization that they are dreaming; that their everyday waking has comingled with their everyday dreaming. They are becoming aware that living is supposed to be fun and easy. In this delight-filled moment of infinity the earth begins a melodic quavering. A tone hums beneath their feet. Another tone harmonizes. As more tones are felt a cadence develops. Every member of this audience feels the plucking of their heart-strings as they realize '*We are the tones of Infinity*'. The rhythm lifts each and every one into the weightlessness of blissful dreaming. They begin settling in with the rich sounds of the music, and look back to the meteoroid, back to the stage above the meteoroid created by the spinning circle of Golden Hearts.

♡♡♡

The pillar of bright shining iridescence beaming up from the meteoroid and through the circle of Golden Hearts is expanding outward. As more and more become encompassed within the ever-widening circle of light the tones of the amorphous melody shift. Rather than the deep reverberating tolling, the air now crackles with a celestial rhapsody. Appearing there at the center is the Imperial Harpist strumming the strings of her magnificent Harp. Flowing forth from the harp are waves of extraordinarily beautiful tones. A calm silence settles over the gathering.

Many are moved to bow down in abeyance. Others settle comfortably upon the ground feeling the harpist's refreshing stream of music flowing through their bodies.

Her appearance resembles the Aviants, in that she has wings, but she is different in that her face more resembles humans: she is Angelic. Extending from the tips of her wings are the same long articulating finger-feathers plucking extraordinarily at the strings of her magnificent harp. She wears a crown of Golden Hearts furbished with jewels. A Golden Orb floats above her. She is the Queen – the Empress – the Goddess of the ancient shrines. Mara recognizes her from the painting that she found in the monk's drawer. Robert recognizes her from the tiled mural of the mountain tower. Saarika recognizes her from scene in the underground temple. Calderon recognizes her from the golden mural of the Toltec pyramid. Annia recognizes her from paintings of her ancestors. In fact, everybody present recognizes her from somewhere in memory, knowing that she is the personification of love and happiness. Her smiling countenance radiates love and happiness. Her music broadcasts love and happiness. A collective sigh rises from the gathered crowd, *Ahh, Love.*

The tune she is playing crescendos and bursts, reverberating into an encompassing blanket of soothing comfort. As the final notes she has played continue humming she rises, spreads her wings, and stands to her full height on long slender legs; her wing feathers appear as a robe of brightest white. Her eyes, her magnificent crystalline eyes, view all before her and all around her, near and far. She turns round and round until all present have beheld her beauty. She continues turning, casting blessings that match the newly identified hope that has always lain there within each heart. She turns and turns until her form is a whirling spiral. The Golden Orb spins above her head. The crown of

Golden Hearts floats up from where it has been resting on her cranium to encircle the Golden Orb hovering there. Her spinning form becomes a luminescent oval; an egg shaped aura. The colors of light within transform. A ray of brilliance shines through the center and up into the Golden Orb within the Golden Crown. These same circumstances are replicated throughout the entire crowd. Each entity, whether human or otherwise, is a glowing egg of soft luminescence. Threads of brilliance twine upward from each. There is an interval of silence.

The interim provides space enough for thoughts to begin taking form within the cognizance of dreaming. "I hope that I will always feel this way," Saarika thinks to herself.

"This is more remarkable than anything," Mara whispers to herself.

Annia, focusing upon the lengthened spinning ovoid of the harpist, wishes for another song.

Diedrik envisions the Celestial's ovoid shape duplicated as a tall domed shrine over the meteoroid.

Hendrik, examining the entire crowd of luminous eggs, remembers this vision as if he has seen it before, "We are beings of light."

Robert does not want this to be over yet.

Renaldo considers reaching above him to feel for the shining thread that he sees floating up from everybody around him, but his arms feel asleep; his entire body is immobile.

The Aviants, which are creatures of the same celestial realm as this harpist, behold the Humans relating to what is so very familiar in their own realm. The humans, scanning the crowd, notice that Celestials and Humans appear alike: as luminescent eggs. We are all creatures of light.

♡♡♡

Before anyone's first thought gains enough momentum to become a dialogue, there is an epochal snap. The spinning aura of the harpist has transformed into a different colored aura. Is it a different Celestial? The harpist, having initially appeared as a golden female, is now appearing as a bronze male creature. And yet, all feel that it is the same spirit here before them. These wonders continue to broaden the possibilities available to the imagination.

This now bronze feathered Celestial scans the crowd while turning a full circle. Its piercing eyes create a stirring deep within the belly as its gaze is met individually by everyone present and watching. Spreading its wings reveals a lighter underside of orangish feathers; orange tinged with pink. One extended wing swats the harp's strings producing a discordant blast. It laughs, "Ah-Ha-Hooooo." Raising its wings and sweeping them dramatically he encourages all to join in, "Ah-Ha-Hooooo. Ah-Ha-Hooooo!" He spanks the harp strings again, laughs, and then slaps them again and again. This behavior heightens the stirrings that everybody is feeling in their belly, inciting laughter; belly laughter, freeing laughter, hilarity. This bronze fellow now jumps and flips in the air before landing again upon its feet. Instantly every single being in the gathered congregation jumps and flips in the air: a feat that few would ever have imagined themselves accomplishing. "Ah-Ha-Hooooo. Ah-Ha-Hooooo! Hoo-hoo-hoo-hoo-hooooo!" Mirth. Bliss.

Now this silly Celestial leans a shoulder to the harp and reaches forward to the strings with one long wing-finger about to play. The crowd waits. Teasing now, he stands straight again. The red Bronze Crown floats up from his head and encircles the red Bronze Orb. With a mischievous grin, he steps away from the Imperial Harp, while pointing a finger toward a particular string, and then wiggling that long pointer producing the same note as if he has plucked the string. As the tone resounds he twirls his long feather-finger and the tone wavers. He repeats this with another tone, and another. More and more folks in the watching crowd are feeling the wavering at that tender area between their hips and waist: they are being tickled. Spasmodic giggling ensues. Waves of giggles ripple outward, over the crowd, and across the plain. Everybody, young and old, human and celestial is giggling breathlessly. Fortunately the harpist stops tickling before anybody pees their pants. He presents another comical expression, then calls again, "Ah-Ha-Hooooo!" then flips in the air again. As before every individual of the crowd is prompted to shout, "Ah-Ha-Hooooo," and flip themselves. To participate in such dreaming is profound.

Consequently, each person discovers, as they look to their friends and neighbors, a peculiarly stunning situation. Men are now women; and women men. Husbands and wives have traded gender. Sisters are now brothers, and vice versa. Yet, the surprise is not so great as would be expected: it turns out that being male or female is not so different. The Aviants, and the mystical creatures are unsurprised, for the distinction is unknown to their nature. The giggling subsides as all involved swipe their hands down along the new angles of their bodies. After the initial response of ease, thoughts begin, and folks respond to one another.

Kirin and Audrae say to their brothers, "You are both very pretty."

"And you are both quite handsome," they answer back.

Mara asks Robert, "Will we trade chores?"

"Ach, no. Stay home while you do the sailing!?"

The lady that Hendrik has become smiles to the gentleman that Anna Maria is, "Now you will be the lecturer while I listen from behind the screen."

Nicklas, Cornelius, and Diedrik look to one another in astonishment. Saarika laughs a deep booming laugh.

Annia and Renaldo hold a hand to one another's face; this has happened before in dreaming, but it is still remarkable.

Once again, the pause is not enough for more than one thought before attention is drawn back to the center as the delighted bronze feathered Celestial begins sending out his happy music from the strings of the harp; dashing away all thought, lightening all focus, and prompting everybody to dance. It is a dance of innocence, and of naiveté. Any ill-willed thought that has ever been expressed toward one's self is pardoned. Freedom reigns.

This red, orange, and bronze Celestial steps away from the harp, but the music continues. He is waving his wings and fluttering his feather-fingers in a pantomime of plucking the harp's strings. The music crescendos, sounding more like an hundred harps. He turns himself around on the stage of light, where it hovers over the meteoroid, and then takes a theatrical bow, down on one knee, humbling himself before all. He lifts his head, his mouth grinning mischievously, his eyes sparkling, and the crest of feathers on his pate rising and falling. With a smooth fluid motion, standing to his full height with one wing remaining low while the other wing is raised high, he turns his gaze upward. His pose has all eyes looking up to behold what is above.

♡♡♡

Above the harpist the Orb and the Crown, once golden and then bronze, are now Crystalline Blue. The ray of light that has been shining up from the meteoroid through the circle of Golden Hearts, now shines through Hearts of Blue Crystal. This light is separated and multiplied by the facets of the now Crystal Blue Orb, and then partitioned again through the facets of the Crystal Blue Crown. Without anybody having noticed a transformation occurring, the harpist's feathers are now indigo on top and azure beneath. Her feathers are crystal, and as the partitioned light from the

Crown and the Orb strike these crystalline feathers they flash beams of radiant blue outward. As she turns everybody is touched by the multi-faceted beams of this blue radiance. With that touch of the crystalline blue light a bit of blue crystal is felt within each breast; to remain and be felt there forever. It is a welcome gift, a blessing, a second heart; A Blue Crystal Heart.

The harpist returns to her instrument; now a Crystal Blue Harp. The music she plays is stirring wonderful memories. It is the waves rolling to the shore and back. It is the soft rain of a warm summer evening. It is the cold crispness of a clear mountain spring. It is a welcome breeze. It matches the rising and falling of ocean swells. It is a baby's laughter. It is the surprise of first love. It is the beginning of spring. It is the pleasant moment before awakening. It is the easy flight of a bird. It is the first grasp of a newly born babe. It is frolicking all day without fatigue. It is moving swiftly and easily across a vastly beautiful world. It is the expansive view from a mountaintop. It is swimming with dolphins. It is a happy family together on a wonderful day. It is walking bare-footed through warm grass. It is standing beside a waterfall. It is the bright colors of autumn's leaves. It is fog resting on a mountaintop. It is a blossoming tree. It matches the warmth inside of knowing that everything is okay.

Recognizing that she will eventually awaken, Trinjntje places her hand at the top of her breast where she feels the presence of the Blue Crystal that has beamed into her. She knows that this blue crystal heart will remain in her waking. She is looking forward to living with this dream crystal.

Mara feels the presence of the blue heart as an eternal gift of trust. Next to her Robert has closed his eyes and is imagining this new blue vibration attracting all he desires.

Lu-Tang, with a palm resting high on his breast over the Blue Crystal there, wants to share this feeling with all the world.

Saarika, feeling the Blue Crystal as she breathes, knows her life has turned.

Paulo, holding a hand at the base of his neck reverently, accepts that he has found what he has always sought.

Deviannia feels her breath pass through this blue presence and welcomes this new spark of life into her world. Renaldo clearly understands that all is as it is meant to be. Razs imagines a bright future. Vejz senses this blue heart as liquid love. Audrae is thinking that this is the most fun ever, and that it is only the beginning.

Nicklas understands, as the warm blue in his breast tells him, that he will be happy for the rest of his life; for eternity.

Hendrik, feeling more hopeful than ever before, accepts that he is, and has ever been, following the perfect path.

Anna Maria, standing amongst these friends, amidst this crowd feels assured that all abiding here in this world, in these realms are born of love and light.

Cornelius loves this color, this blue has always been his favorite.

Diedrik, imagining that he is feeling a pulse from the Blue Crystal, believes in the goodness of the totality of himself, indeed the goodness of all that is. Next to him Kirin feels light hearted in the knowing that she has found true love.

Everybody in the entire crowd of humans and celestials, feeling this new presence as a part of who they have now become is appreciating this moment.

The harpist finishes, and as before, her music carries on. She brings feather tips to her face and then releases a cloud of kisses that float out to all. She is a dream angel bestowing blessings. She floats up and fades. The shaft of light dims. All of the celestial beings of the crowd dissipate, except for the original three here at the meteoroid, holding the necklaces of Blue Crystal Hearts to Mara, Annia, and Saarika. These Aviants bow reverently to the ladies and then they are, like all the others of their realm, off and away.

There is silence. It takes a bit before thoughts begin and then, looking about at everything that has once again returned to familiarity, folks begin speaking to one another in tones of awe and wonder. "Look," Vejz says pointing up, "The sun is where it was before all this happened."

"Indeed!" Captain Janszoon pronounces, "Our notion of time has been displaced."

Stretching and yawning Diedrik, still feeling frisky, asks, "Was that just a long nap?"

"Ach!" Kirin punches him playfully, "How can you say that?" He pokes her back, as he would a sister, or a sweetheart.

"I wish that I could have seen myself in a mirror," Razs says.

"Perhaps next time you are dreaming," Annia tells him, "you will see your reflection."

Anna Maria says, "I shall cherish the memory of this day for the rest of my life."

"I daresay," says Hendrik, with his hand still resting where his collar bones meet senses the presence of a blue glow, "The rest of my life shall be nothing at all similar to what my life has been thus far."

"Ah," Robert claps him on the shoulder, "And that be a good thing, right?"

Mara is approached by a well-suited member of *La Société de la Météorite Moderne* and asked politely, "Please dear lady, tell us how the three of you came by these necklaces."

"It is a long story. For another time," she answers. Then turning to Audrae, standing closest, "While we are so near perhaps we should lay our hands upon the meteoroid."

The meteoroid is still warm, and as they all take turns they feel the calm serenity that they have been told about. The *Société* gentleman informs them, after touching it himself, "The sense of peacefulness has not changed," now laying a hand high on his breast, "except that I am carrying that very peacefulness here with me for always."

♡♡♡

Epilogue

When accounts of what occurred that day are compared, amongst those who had been in attendance, there is very little difference; most agree upon the particulars of the experience. Upon returning to their homes participants discover the happiness and abundance they have always desired, for they now choose to believe anything to be possible.

From Amiens, part of the Schoonhoven group sets off for Paris; Saarika wants to see more of the world, Trinjntje and Calderon want to be together, Nicklas will visit his brothers and all his nieces and nephews, while Hendrik and Anna Maria are looking forward to the intellectual stimulation of the great city.

The rest ride the barge back to La Crotoy. From there Captain Janszoon, with Lu-Tang, Razs and Vejz set off across the channel to London, where Lu-Tang plans to live for a while. From there the Captain intends to tutor the boys in the art of sailing.

Robert sails the Tulip accompanied by Mara, Diedrik, Renaldo, Annia, Kirin, and Audrae for Schoonhoven Landing; home. Saarika has sent her necklace with Diedrik, to be stored away with her crown, and near the other artifacts. He marvels that he has the necklace again, although no longer golden, and he is eager to see if the crown of golden leaves will have also been transformed to crystalline. Likewise, Annia wonders if she will discover her golden Orb transformed. And Mara too, wonders the same of her great harp. Their nostalgia for the passing of the Golden Hearts is barely noticeable in light of their excitement toward these Blue Crystal Hearts.

♡♡♡

In the years that follow there is indeed a magnificent shrine built over the meteoroid. Occasionally, visitors to the shrine will report dreamy occurrences, but never anything remarkable as the Dream of the Harpist; the name given the yearly celebration of that momentous occasion. *La Société de la Météorite Moderne*, after the establishment of the holiday and completion of the shrine disbanded.

Many of those who had been in attendance that day, those of the Blue Crystal, return to the shrine often. It is said that these folks live charmed lives, and that their children grow up differently; always happy. They are known as The Children of the Blue Crystal and they are born into this world knowing that they create what they are living.

About the Author

Jerry D Cook lives in Southeastern Washington State with his wife and their cats. His hobbies include gardening, camping and hiking. He likes riding his motorcycle, or driving his old Jeep into the hills around home. The Golden Hearts is his first venture at writing and publishing.

www.ingramcontent.com/pod-product-compliance
Lightning Source LLC
Chambersburg PA
CBHW020741100426
42735CB00037B/154
* 9 7 8 0 9 9 9 7 1 8 0 1 8 *